INSIGHT GUIDES

aRIZONa & THE GRAND CANYON

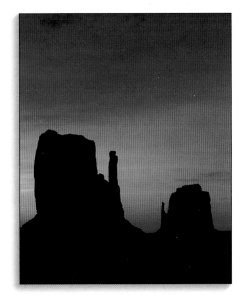

Discovery CHANNEL

APA PUBLICATIONS
Part of the Langenscheidt Publishing Group

INSIGHT GUIDE
arizona & the Grand Canyon

ABOUT THIS BOOK

Editorial

Editor
John Gattuso
Editorial Director
Brian Bell

Distribution

UK & Ireland
GeoCenter International Ltd
The Viables Centre, Harrow Way
Basingstoke, Hants RG22 4BJ
Fax: (44) 1256 817988

United States
Langenscheidt Publishers, Inc.
46-35 54th Road, Maspeth, NY 11378
Fax: (1) 718 784 0640

Canada
Thomas Allen & Son Ltd
390 Steelcase Road East
Markham, Ontario L3R 1G2
Fax: (1) 905 475 6747

Australia
Universal Press
1 Waterloo Road
Macquarie Park, NSW 2113
Fax: (61) 2 9888 9074

New Zealand
Hema Maps New Zealand Ltd (HNZ)
Unit D, 24 Ra ORA Drive
East Tamaki, Auckland
Fax: (64) 9 273 6479

Worldwide
**Apa Publications GmbH & Co.
Verlag KG (Singapore branch)**
38 Joo Koon Road, Singapore 628990
Tel: (65) 6865 1600. Fax: (65) 6861 6438

Printing

Insight Print Services (Pte) Ltd
38 Joo Koon Road, Singapore 628990
Tel: (65) 6865 1600. Fax: (65) 6861 6438

©2003 Apa Publications GmbH & Co.
Verlag KG (Singapore branch)
All Rights Reserved

First Edition 2002
Reprinted 2003

CONTACTING THE EDITORS
We would appreciate it if readers
would alert us to errors or out-
dated information by writing to:
**Insight Guides, P.O. Box 7910,
London SE1 1WE, England.
Fax: (44) 20 7403 0290.
insight@apaguide.co.uk**

www.insightguides.com

This guidebook combines the interests and enthusiasms of two of the world's best-known information providers: Insight Guides, whose titles have set the standard for visual travel guides since 1970, and Discovery Channel, the world's premier source of nonfiction television programming.

The editors of Insight Guides provide practical advice and general understanding about a destination's history, culture, institutions and people. Discovery Channel and its website, www.discovery.com, help millions of viewers explore their world from the comfort of their own home and encourage them to explore it firsthand.

Insight Guide: Arizona & the Grand Canyon is structured to convey an understanding of the state and its people as well as to guide readers through its attractions:

◆ The **Features** section, indicated by a yellow bar at the top of each page, covers the natural and cultural history of the state.

◆ The **Places** section, indicated by a blue bar, is a complete guide to all the sights and areas worth visiting. Places of special interest are coordinated by number with the maps.

◆ The **Travel Tips** listings section, with an orange bar, provides detailed information on travel, hotels, shops, restaurants and more. An easy-to-find contents list for Travel Tips is printed on the back flap.

The contributors

This book was produced by **John Gattuso** of Stone Creek Publications in Milford, New Jersey. He is a

ABOVE: Arizona cowboys flee from Apache raiders in Frederic Remington's 1889 painting *A Dash for the Timber.*

veteran of more than a dozen Insight Guides and editor of the Discovery Travel Adventures, a series of illustrated guidebooks for travelers with special interests such as bird-watching, scuba diving, African safaris and astronomy.

Gattuso's first recruit was writer **Nicky Leach**, who divides her time between Flagstaff, Arizona, and Santa Fe, New Mexico. A frequent contributor to the Insight Guides and project editor of *Discovery Travel Adventures: Wild West* and *Whale Watching*, Leach covers a host of Arizona topics, from geology and archaeology to ghost towns and cultural history, then leads readers into every corner of the state, from the saguaro-studded Sonoran Desert to the lonely expanses of the Arizona Strip. The award-winning author of several guides to Southwest parks, she is a founding member of guidebookwriters.com, an online travel writers resource, and writes for *Sunset* and *New Mexico* magazines.

Arizona writer **Rose Houk** covers familiar territory – the Grand Canyon, where she worked as a park ranger before embarking on a writing career, and Flagstaff, her home for some 13 years. She contributes to *Arizona Highways* and has written many books on the Southwest, including one on Arizona mountains.

Nora Burba Trulsson has lived in Arizona long enough to see golf courses outnumber dude ranches. She writes about both in "The Arizona Cowboy" and "Golfer's Paradise." She is a contributor to *Sunset* and *Phoenix* magazines and co-author of *Living Home*, a book on sustainable architecture.

Santa Fe writer **Richard Mahler** guides readers to "Arizona's West Coast," a stretch of the Colorado River on the state's western border. Mahler is a columnist for the *Albuquerque Journal* and a prolific author.

With more than 30 years' experience as an editor and writer at newspapers in the New York area, **Edward A. Jardim** knows how to transform a complex story into a concise narrative. Here he condenses four centuries of history into an engaging chronicle. He is also a major contributor to *Insight Guide: Museums and Galleries of New York*.

The book was indexed by **Elizabeth Cook** and the cartography editor was **Zoë Goodwin**.

Map Legend

The main places of interest in the Places section are coordinated by number with a full-color map (e.g. ❶), and a symbol at the top of every right-hand page tells you where to find the map.

CONTENTS

Inside front cover:
Arizona
Inside back cover:
Arizona's national parks and
monuments

A river guide muscles
through a stretch of
whitewater on the
Colorado River in the
Grand Canyon.

Travel Tips

Information panels

Places

THE GRAND CANYON STATE

The Grand Canyon, one of the world's great natural treasures, is just the first of Arizona's many wonders

Visiting the Grand Canyon in 1903, Theodore Roosevelt delivered a speech that would become a classic summation of conservation principles. "Leave it as it is," he declared. "You cannot improve on it. The ages have been at work on it, and man can only mar it. What you can do is keep it for your children, your children's children, and for all who come after you, as the one great sight which every American… should see."

Five years later, he declared the Grand Canyon a national monument to prevent it from being "improved upon" by human hands. And though a clutch of hotels and parking lots now stand on the rims, and the Colorado River has been restrained by dams, the canyon remains an emblem of the grandeur of the American West, its protection a watershed in the history of environmental stewardship.

Even more wondrous is that the Grand Canyon is just one of Arizona's many natural treasures. From the sandstone monoliths of Monument Valley and the soaring walls of Canyon de Chelly to the trees-turned-to-stone of the Petrified Forest and the giant saguaros of the Sonoran Desert, the state is a catalog of wonder.

The human imprint is just as fascinating and, despite the proliferation of strip malls, tract housing and other modern developments, surprisingly ancient. The mesa-top villages of the Hopi include the oldest continuously inhabited town in the United States (since AD 1150), and their culture is filled with echoes of the long-vanished Sinagua and Ancestral Puebloans, or Anasazi, whose ruins are strewn throughout the northern canyons.

The Navajo and Apache, both descendants of Athabascan nomads who migrated into the Southwest six centuries ago, integrate traditional values into their modern lives, as do the descendants of the Spanish and Mexican immigrants who settled the missions and ranchos of the south. Cowboys still ride the range in remote corners of the state, and a few lone prospectors scratch a living from played-out mines. Even Phoenix, the country's sixth-largest city and a prime example of the New West, sits atop an ancient Hohokam settlement, whose elaborate irrigation system, once used to water fields of maize and melon, now serves corporate towers and shopping malls.

Travelers with a taste for creature comforts will find no lack of plush resorts and trendy restaurants, and enough golf courses to keep them swinging for years. But those who venture beyond the usual tourist trails will discover that Arizona, like its best-known feature, is a place of uncommon depth. Seeing the big picture can be overwhelming at first. Only by descending beneath the rim, exploring the state layer by layer, is its true nature revealed. ❑

PRECEDING PAGES: horseback riding in Paria Canyon–Vermilion Cliffs Wilderness; mountain biker in red-rock country; a stretch of calm water on the Colorado River. **LEFT:** the mineral-laden waters of the Little Colorado flow into the Grand Canyon.

Decisive Dates

Prehistoric Cultures

circa 10000 BC: Paleo-Indians enter the region, hunting big game such as woolly mammoth and giant ground sloth with stone-tipped spears.

AD 1: Earliest evidence of pottery. Living in pithouses, people of the Cochise culture sustain themselves by hunting, gathering and farming.

50: Hohokam begin building irrigation canals near present-day Phoenix.

1064: Sunset Crater erupts. Sinagua farmers later return to the region attracted by increased rainfall

and moisture-retaining properties of ash-covered soil. Construction of Wupatki Pueblo begins.

1250: Ancestral Puebloans, or Anasazi, begin construction of Betatakin and Keet Seel in Tsegi Canyon, now part of Navajo National Monument.

1250–1450: Settlements throughout the Southwest are abandoned due possibly to drought, disease or overuse of resources.

1250–1450: Athabascans migrate from the north, and later diverge into Navajo and Apache tribes.

European Arrivals

1540: Coronado expedition extends Spanish domain to the Southwest in futile search for reputed cities of gold.

1582: Antonio de Espejo finds near present-day Prescott some of the silver and copper deposits that would yield immense riches three centuries later.

1598: Juan de Oñate crosses Arizona and establishes first European settlement in the Southwest, near Santa Fe, New Mexico.

1680: A sudden rebellion by Pueblo Indians costs the lives of more than 400 settlers in Arizona and New Mexico.

1687: Father Eusebio Francisco Kino begins the wide-ranging efforts that make this "Padre on Horseback" and founder of Tumacacori and San Xavier del Bac settlements the most celebrated of the Spanish missionaries.

1751: Pima Revolt leads to establishment of a presidio at Tubac – which was moved to Tucson in 1776 – to protect missionaries and settlers from Indian attack.

1805: A Spanish military expedition into Canyon de Chelly results in the massacre of 115 Navajo, virtually all of them women, children and old men.

1821: Mexico wins independence from Spain, thereby ruling Arizona.

American Takeover

1848: The United States, victorious in war with Mexico, takes over most of Arizona.

1854: The remaining southern strip of Arizona is part of land acquired from Mexico for $10 million in the Gadsden Purchase.

1858: Discovery of gold nuggets in a prospector's pan on the Gila River gives rise to Gila City, first of many Arizona mining boomtowns.

1859: The first of Arizona's Indian reservations is established at Gila River. The greatest of all will be the Navajo Nation, covering nearly 16 million acres (7 million hectares), the largest reservation in the United States.

1863: President Abraham Lincoln signs a statute recognizing Arizona as a territory separate from New Mexico.

1869: Civil War veteran Major John Wesley Powell leads a pathfinding three-boat expedition down the Colorado River through the Grand Canyon.

1877: Arizona enters the era of transcontinental railroading with erection of a bridge over the Colorado River at Yuma for the Southern Pacific. Three years later, the line's arrival in Tucson sets off a grand celebration.

1881: Wyatt Earp, two of his brothers and Doc Holliday survive shootout at the O.K. Corral in Tombstone that becomes a Western legend.

1884: Two mining companies, Phelps Dodge and Copper Queen, tap into a rich vein in Bisbee, one of many deposits that will produce vast fortunes and make Arizona famous as one of the world's greatest sources of copper.
1885: University of Arizona established at Tucson.
1886: Surrender of Apache warrior Geronimo marks end of Indian resistance.
1889: Phoenix becomes Arizona's state capital.

Modern Times

1911: Dedication of Roosevelt Dam is first step in a federal irrigation project in the Salt River Valley that spurs development of the region.

1941: The nation's entry into World War II makes Arizona a busy location for defense purposes, stimulating population growth and transforming the state's socioeconomic character.
1960: Sun City, a new community near Phoenix equipped with golf course and shopping center for "active" senior citizens, puts five model homes on display on January 1 and is besieged by thousands of prospective buyers.
1963: Arizona's claim to a major portion of water from the Colorado River is upheld by the United States Supreme Court.
1968: Congress approves the Central Arizona Project, a large-scale effort to deliver water to the

1912: Arizona becomes the 48th state in the Union.
1917: About 1,200 striking copper miners and their supporters are removed from Bisbee by train and deposited in a desert hundreds of miles away as labor-management conflict intensifies.
1919: Grand Canyon National Park established.
1937: Frank Lloyd Wright, consultant on the spectacular Arizona Biltmore Hotel in Phoenix, establishes a home and studio, Taliesin West, near Scottsdale, where he works until his death in 1959.

PRECEDING PAGES: Copper Queen smelter, Bisbee, 1898.
LEFT: Hopi priest, around 1910.
ABOVE: Thomas Moran's impression of the Grand Canyon, *Chasm of the Colorado*, 1873–74.

state's most populous region.
1983: Governor Bruce Babbitt calls out the National Guard after strikers shut down the Phelps Dodge mine in Morenci. The company eventually sells part of the mine and closes other operations in Ajo and Douglas.
1990: London Bridge rises again, this time at remote Lake Havasu in western Arizona. The improbable British import, rebuilt stone by stone, makes the reservoir area the most popular tourist attraction after the Grand Canyon.
2000: United States Census reports Arizona's population has reached 5.1 million, an increase of 40 percent in 10 years; the state is second only to Nevada as the fastest-growing in the nation. ❏

NATIVE HERITAGE

*Archaeologists studying Arizona's prehistoric people find evidence of complex
societies engaged in an ever-shifting network of cultural exchange and conflict*

People have lived in Arizona for at least 11,000 years, perhaps longer. In southern Arizona are remnants of hunting camps, cave shelters, bones of extinct megafauna, and stone tools from paleo and archaic times, as well as Hohokam pithouses, great houses atop platform mounds, and 1,000-year-old irrigation systems. To the north, colorful sandstone canyons and high-desert knolls are the settings for pithouses, multistory cliff dwellings, and granaries that blend so seamlessly with their settings that they seem more like natural outcroppings than man-made structures.

In between, atop and below central Arizona's Mogollon Rim and along the Colorado River, are the remnants of the Mogollon, Salado and Hakataya cultures, influenced by the powerful Pueblo and Desert cultures yet different enough to keep everyone guessing about who they were, where they came from, and where they went. Far from being monocultural, prehistoric Arizona was a melting pot of highly adapted cultures interacting with each other through trade, marriage, warfare, and overlapping territorial boundaries.

This fact was lost on early 20th-century archaeologists. Impressed by the beautifully built pueblos discovered at Mesa Verde in Colorado and Chaco Canyon in New Mexico, they came to believe that a single, evolving culture migrating through different environments was responsible for the ruins of the Southwest. They spent time among the Hopi and other contemporary pueblo tribes and used them as a basis for understanding prehistoric pueblo people, forgetting that modern pueblos have undergone a great deal of cultural change over the past 400 years.

By the late 1940s, the single-culture model was out of favor, and the prehistoric picture in the Southwest was looking far more complex. It remains so today, as archaeologists continue to identify distinct and shared traits among the Southwest's cultures.

Ancient hunters

The earliest people in Arizona were paleo-hunters at the end of the last Ice Age, when the climate was cooler and big game lumbered

across grasslands and forests in what are deserts today. These ancient hunters trapped mammoths and other prey in marshy areas or drove them off cliffs, making their kills using percussion-flaked Clovis arrowheads attached to spears. They butchered their prey on the spot, leaving behind tools and bones that have been uncovered at the Murray Springs Clovis Site in the San Pedro River Valley and in the recesses of Ventana Cave on the Tohono O'odham Indian Reservation, both in southern Arizona.

The big-game bonanza didn't last. Eventually, overhunting and a drier climate doomed the woolly mammoth, ground sloth and other large mammals to extinction.

LEFT: White House Ruins, in Canyon de Chelly, was inhabited by Ancient Puebloans from AD 1040 to 1275. **RIGHT:** potsherds at Homolovi Ruins, a 14th-century pueblo at the edge of the Painted Desert.

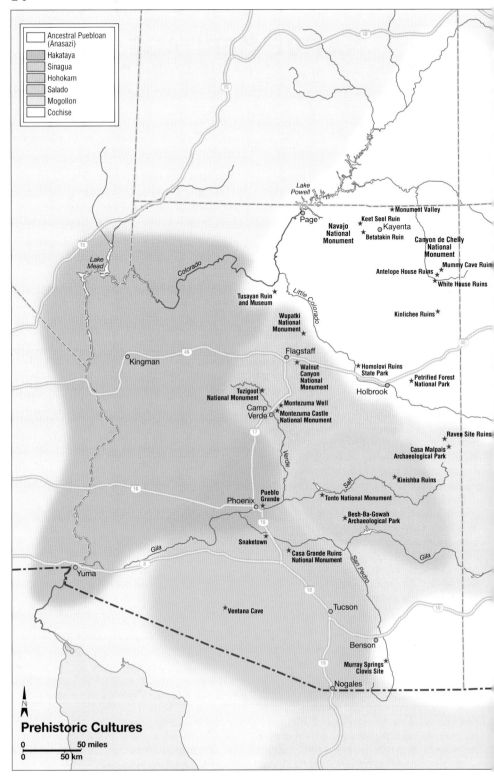

Prehistoric Cultures

Legend:
- Ancestral Puebloan (Anasazi)
- Hakataya
- Sinagua
- Hohokam
- Salado
- Mogollon
- Cochise

0 ___ 50 miles
0 ___ 50 km

N

With the loss of their main prey, paleo-hunters were forced into a different lifestyle. The Southwestern Archaic period (8,500 BC–AD 300) was a widespread hunting-gathering adaptation to the changing climate. The Archaic people were autonomous groups with defined territories. They moved around seasonally, taking advantage of a wide range of wild plants and small game, which they killed using spear-throwers known as atlatls. Artifacts from this period include chipped stone tools and debris and occasionally sleeping circles and cleared areas.

In southwestern Arizona, the San Dieguito I period of the Archaic is represented in the Barry Goldwater Bombing Range (north of Cabeza Prieta National Wildlife Refuge), which preserves evidence of mortar holes in rocks, where stone and wooden pestles were used to grind seeds and bean pods into flour. In northern Arizona, split-twig willow figurines, thought to be hunting fetishes, were secreted in caves high above the Grand Canyon.

Cochise culture

In southeastern Arizona, University of Arizona archaeologist Emily Haury dubbed people of this Archaic period the Cochise culture and divided them into three phases: Sulphur Springs, Chiricahua and San Pedro. As the culture advanced technologically, such artifacts as stemmed points, storage pits and heavy millstones indicate that farming became an influential factor in the subsistence of the culture. Irrigated and dry farming of squash and teosinte, a Mexican grass that later developed into corn, produced reliable food supplies and resulted in permanent settlements.

About 2,000 years ago, the introduction of pottery from Mexico offered desert dwellers a new and important technology, allowing for storage of water and dried food. By the final San Pedro phase, Cochise people were living in small pithouses. It is believed that the San Pedro phase of the Cochise culture evolved into Mogollon tradition of the central highlands.

The Mogollon

The Mogollon people lived in the mountains along the Arizona–New Mexico border and

---

RIGHT: archaic pictographs adorn a stone wall deep within the Grand Canyon. Evidence of human habitation in the canyon stretches back more than 10,000 years.

south into Mexico from 100 BC to the AD 1400s. Considered the least complex of the three main cultures that came to dominate the prehistoric Southwest, the Mogollon were farming and making pottery earlier than any other group in the region. Perhaps it was merely their isolation in rugged mountains that prevented the mobility and exchange of ideas that allowed other cultures to advance.

Sometime between AD 900 and 1100, the Mogollon culture merged with that of the Ancestral Puebloans (formerly known as the Anasazi) to the north and ceased to exist as a separate entity. The Mogollon began constructing

multistory pueblos but continued to favor rectangular kivas (ceremonial chambers), such as the great kiva found at Casa Malpais in Springerville, Arizona, built in AD 1277. In New Mexico, around the same time, they built the unusual Gila Cliff Dwellings beneath canyon overhangs.

Their basic red pottery also evolved into beautiful black-on-white vessels, perfected by a branch of the culture living on the Mimbres River of New Mexico. It featured human-like figures, lizards, birds and scenes that depict trade in tropical birds. It is believed that the merged Pueblo and Mogollon culture contributed to the cultural background of the Hopi, Zuni and Acoma pueblos and the Tarahumara Indians of Mexico.

The Hohokam

In the Sonoran Desert, around 300 BC, Archaic people were evolving into the Hohokam, a Pima word for "all used up," proposed by archaeologist Jesse Fewkes in 1910, while he was excavating the Hohokam "great house" of Casa Grande, south of Phoenix. Like other archaeologists of his day, Fewkes made no cultural distinction between the Hohokam and the Pueblo people to the north, believing that the same culture had built all the ruins.

All that changed in the late 1920s, when Harold Gladwin, a Wall Street financier and archaeology enthusiast, financed the excavation

of sites in the Sonoran Desert. The breakthrough for Gladwin and his research organization, the Gila Pueblo Foundation, came in 1935, during the huge Snaketown dig. Project archaeologist Emil Haury and his team used new dating techniques and comparisons of building styles, pottery, and burial practices to establish the Hohokam as a distinct prehistoric culture. In the 1930s, and during a second major excavation of Snaketown in the 1960s, Haury refined the Hohokam cultural sequence, consisting of four main phases: Pioneer (300 BC–AD 550), Colonial (AD 550–900), Sedentary (AD 900–1100) and Classic (AD 1100–1450).

Hohokam dwellings were single-story oval or rectangular huts built over shallow pits using a framework of poles, brush and reeds, covered with caliche mud. They included entryways, living areas with basin-shaped firepits, and storage space for single families. An outdoor shade structure, or ramada, protected residents from the sun. More than 60 pithouses were uncovered at Snaketown, a site in use for almost the whole of the Hohokam period. Pithouse dwellings have been found in Organ Pipe Cactus National Monument and as far north as Montezuma Well in the Verde Valley.

The Hohokam specialized in making a distinctive red-on-buff micaceous pottery, coiled on an anvil support and smoothed with a wooden paddle. Large storage jars, flat-bottomed dishes, jars with narrow openings, and legged containers such as incense burners were covered with geometric designs, curved motifs, and animal or human figures.

The Hohokam also invented a process for etching shell imported from the Gulf of California, using fermented cactus juice and wax to create lizard, toad and other motifs; they traded these prized artworks for red argillite and other resources. Macaw feathers, pyrite mirrors and copper bells, probably used in rituals, were imported from tribes in Mexico and distributed throughout the Southwest.

More than 200 Mesoamerican-style ball courts have been found at Hohokam sites. Introduced in the 700s (Casa Grande has the earliest known ball court) and aligned to the cardinal directions, ball courts were probably used for games that involved keeping a heavy rubber ball in play without using hands or feet. Ball games provided an opportunity to interact with neighboring villages, arrange marriages, exchange goods, and mediate disputes, but they probably also had a symbolic aspect: the movements of the ball and players reenacted the annual passage of the sun, moon and planets around the heavens and ensured cosmological harmony.

The importance of astronomy to desert farmers may also account for the introduction of multistory adobe structures atop platform mounds during the final Classic period. The four-story Casa Grande building, the only great house to survive, is 35 feet (11 meters) high and contains 11 rooms. The existence of window alignments has suggested that such structures may have been inhabited by ritual specialists who tracked the movements of celestial bodies and predicted rainfall, the desert's most precious commodity, during times of increased drought.

Platform mounds like the one at Casa Grande have been linked to the Hohokam's sophisticated canal irrigation system and may have played a part in regulating water use along the Gila and Salt Rivers. More than 85 miles (135 km) of irrigation canals have been mapped at Casa Grande, with many more lying beneath the freeways, buildings and modern

ANCIENT ARTISTS

The Hohokam traded for seashells from the Pacific Coast, which they etched with fermented saguaro juice, strung into bracelets and necklaces, or decorated with a mosaic of semiprecious stones.

descendants of the Hohokam who had reverted to a simpler life of hunting and gathering.

The Puebloans

It's not hard to understand the appeal of the Pueblo people's dramatic stone villages for 19th-century archaeologists, who perhaps interpreted the move from simple pithouses to high-rise "apartments" as an orderly progression in the rise of civilization. But, like the Hohokam and Mogollon, the Pueblo people started out as

canals of Phoenix. These canals were undoubtedly the key to supporting the estimated 24,000 people who eventually concentrated in the Salt-Gila River Basin in the early 1300s – a remarkable population for such an arid region. It may have been the collapse of this irrigation system, perhaps during a major flood, that spelled the end for the Hohokam. When the Spanish arrived in the 1500s, they encountered Akimel O'odham (Pima, or Water People) and Tohono O'odham (Papago, or Desert People), probable

LEFT: a Tohono O'odham woman, a descendant of the ancient Hohokam, photographed about 1907.
ABOVE: Casa Grande, a Hohokam settlement, in Phoenix.

hunter-gatherers during the long Archaic period and gradually evolved into farmers.

Around the start of the Christian era, ancestors of the Puebloans were living in scattered pithouse villages and making baskets, which led cowboy archaeologist Richard Wetherill to name them Basketmakers. By the Pueblo I period, between AD 700 and 900, people living in small hamlets of multistory dwellings had incorporated earlier pithouses as underground ceremonial chambers, known as kivas. They were now hunting with bows and arrows and farming more extensively. During the Pueblo II (AD 900–1100) and Pueblo III phases (AD 1100–1300), larger towns appeared and, in the 1200s, the cliff dwellings that spark our fascination today.

Pueblo civilization seems to have benefited from coalescence and the exchange of goods and ideas. Each community began to have its specialties and to reach new heights of invention, building more sophisticated structures, creating beautiful baskets, weaving fine cotton cloth, firing distinctive pottery, and refining tools. Centralized towns could stockpile and share food with surrounding villages during times of shortage and demand tribute and manual labor in return. This may have led to the rise of the Chaco Canyon site in New Mexico, which may have functioned as a kind of redistribution center, carefully orchestrated by "priests" whose understanding of astronomy allowed them to predict favorable planting and harvesting times.

At the height of Pueblo civilization, the fertile bottomlands of the Colorado, Little Colorado, San Juan and Virgin Rivers quickly filled up with farmers. The Tsegi Canyon-Marsh Pass area near Monument Valley, on today's Navajo reservation, was occupied for centuries by Kayenta Anasazi people, a western branch of the Pueblo culture. The Kayenta were less celebrated for their architecture than the Chacoans or Mesa Verdeans to the east and north but were

THE ABANDONMENT

They built great cities of stone, became successful traders, and reached heights of aesthetic brilliance. Then, between AD 1300 and 1450, the major cultures of prehistoric Arizona simply disappeared. What happened?

The straw that broke the camel's back seems to have been a severe drought between AD 1276 and 1299. Crop failures would have been a disaster for civilizations that had risen to power during times of plenty, specialization of labor, and adequate leisure time to create trade goods. Now it was every man for himself. The hilltop pueblo of Tuzigoot shows clear signs of battening down the hatches. The cliff dwellings at Navajo National Monument hide in plain sight in their alcoves. Add to this the environmental havoc caused by overuse of resources, the subsequent social breakdown, and you get the picture. Time to move on.

Where did they go? Clan by clan, the Ancestral Puebloans migrated to the Hopi Mesas and the 19 pueblos strung along the Rio Grande. The Hohokam probably never left. When the Spanish arrived in the mid-1500s, the O'odham claimed to know nothing of their predecessors, yet lived in houses that resembled 1,000-year-old Hohokam dwellings. A coincidence? Archaeologists doubt it. The old way of life was simply, as the O'odham say, *hohokam*, "all used up."

distinguished by their resourcefulness, adaptability during hard times, and fine polychrome pottery. In the mid-1200s, increasing drought and shrinking resources forced families to engineer the impressive Betatakin and Keet Seel sites of Navajo National Monument. Nearby Canyon de Chelly and Monument Valley also contain Kayenta Anasazi ruins, while the Arizona Strip, on the border with Utah, was the domain of the Virgin River Anasazi. Perhaps an offshoot of the Kayenta, the Virgin River people built pueblos and grew corn, a skill they taught the incoming Southern Paiute, who claim links to these early Puebloans today.

Museum of Northern Arizona, the Sinagua straddled the frontier between Anasazi, Hohokam and Mogollon territories, apparently absorbing aspects of each culture. They began as pithouse dwellers near Sunset Crater around AD 500, but were forced to flee south to the Verde Valley following the 1065 eruption of the volcano. While in the Verde Valley, contacts with the Hohokam and other tribes exposed the Sinagua to new ideas and influences. The large Tuzigoot Pueblo, built on a defensible knoll above the Verde River in AD 1000, is Sinaguan, as are nearby Montezuma Castle and the multistory cliff dwellings

The Sinagua

The Sinagua ("without water" in Spanish) were dry-land farmers living in the Flagstaff area of northern Arizona a thousand years ago. They built the lovely but lonely pueblos of Wupatki National Monument between the San Francisco Peaks and the Painted Desert and cliff dwellings at Walnut Canyon that look surprisingly like those constructed by the Mogollon above the Gila River in New Mexico. First investigated by Harold Colton, founder of the

LEFT: lightning pierces the sky above Lomaki Ruin at Wupatki National Monument north of Flagstaff.
ABOVE: Sinagua ruins are tucked into Walnut Canyon.

around Sedona's picturesque red-rock country.

When Sunset Crater Volcano stopped erupting, a prehistoric land rush seems to have occurred in northern Arizona, attracting the Sinagua and other tribes eager to take advantage of the fertile volcanic soil and increased rainfall. This combination of cultures may have been responsible for development of Wupatki Pueblo, near Flagstaff, which contains Chaco-style masonry and overscaled public architecture. The pueblo also has a Hohokam-style ball court, the northernmost ball court in North America and the only one lined with masonry. Also noticeable is the loosely mortared, blocky style of Kayenta Anasazi construction in the many small outlying pueblos and field houses scattered between the main pueblo and the Little Colorado River. Ceremonial burials of high-status leaders and the presence of Mexican macaws and other imported items suggest that Wupatki may have functioned as an important trade and ritual center following the abandonment of the Chaco Canyon pueblos. By AD 1250, after just a century of use, the Sinagua had abandoned Wupatki and Walnut Canyon, and probably resettled on the Hopi Mesas to the east and at Zuni and other pueblos along the Rio Grande in New Mexico, where their descendants still live.

Prehistoric puzzles

Similarly enigmatic in their origins and disappearance is the Salado ("salty" in Spanish), a name given the tribe by Padre Eusebio Kino when he discovered its people living along the Salt River in the late 1600s. Known for their beautiful cotton cloth and polychrome pottery, the Salado originated in Pueblo territory, along the Little Colorado River, and settled in the Salt River Basin, picking up Mogollon traits along the way. Filling a niche between the Mogollon to the east and the Hohokam to the west, the Salado seem to have influenced the Hohokam during the Classic period, from about AD 1300 to 1450. They built the multistory cliff dwelling

of Tonto National Monument and the large pueblo of Besh-ba-Gowah in the city of Globe, which has yielded large quantities of pottery.

The Sinagua and the Salado weren't the only tribes that didn't quite fit the emerging picture of prehistoric cultures. In the late 1940s, new research and dating techniques revealed many local deviations in cultural traits, especially in the area where the Colorado Plateau meets the Colorado River valley and adjacent low deserts.

This group of cultures, dubbed the Hakataya, after a Yuman word for the Colorado River, included the Cohonina, south of the Grand Canyon; the Cerbat, who lived along the Colorado River where it emerges from the Grand Canyon; the Prescott, living in the verdant areas of west-central Arizona; and the Laquish of the lower Colorado River. Modern descendants include the Hualapai and Havasupai of the western Grand Canyon, the Yavapai of west-central Arizona, and the Quechan, Chemuevi, and Mojave desert people of the lower Colorado River.

Athabascan immigrants

The cultural picture was complicated further by the arrival of Athabascan hunter-gatherers from western Canada about AD 1400. The Athabascans later diverged into two distinct groups – the Navajo, who settled in the plateau country of northern Arizona, and the Apache, who roamed southern Arizona and New Mexico.

The Navajo were deeply influenced by their Pueblo neighbors, taking up corn farming, weaving and various aspects of Pueblo religion, and later by the Spanish, from whom they adopted sheepherding and silversmithing. The Apache, on the other hand, remained hunter-gatherers and broke up into wide-ranging bands. The Apache acquired horses from the Spanish in the 1700s and some bands, like the Jicarilla of northern New Mexico, took on some of the cultural traits of the Plains tribes.

The best-known group, however, was the Chiricahua. Led by warriors such as Cochise and Geronimo, they were the last Indians in the Southwest to be pacified by yet another wave of immigrants – the white, English-speaking invaders from the East. ❑

LEFT: an ancient granary in the Grand Canyon.
RIGHT: a Navajo dancer photographed about 1904. The Navajo migrated into the region in the 15th century.

THE SPANISH ERA

Seeking mythical cities of gold and pagan souls, the Spanish planted
the seeds of European culture throughout the Southwest

A new chapter in Arizona's history began to unfold on February 22, 1540. Its main character was a young and by all reports dashing Spaniard named Francisco Vásquez de Coronado. He was leading an expedition of some 1,300 men and two or three women – Spaniards, Indians and Africans – heading north from Mexico on an important mission.

Coronado, governor of New Galicia in western Mexico, hoped to find the "Seven Cities of Gold." He was one of the conquistadores who followed in the wake of Columbus in that swashbuckling age sometimes known as the Spanish Century, their names once familiar to every Iberian schoolboy: Balboa, discoverer of the Pacific Ocean; Cortés, who wrested control of the Aztec empire in Mexico from Montezuma; Pizarro, the harsh ruler of Peru who exacted an immense ransom before killing off the Inca emperor; de Soto, whose own expedition traipsed across the American Southeast from Florida as far west as Oklahoma between 1539 and 1542.

Cities of gold

Coronado had been born into a wealthy Spanish family in the old university town of Salamanca about 1510. He became an assistant to the all-powerful viceroy in New Spain, António de Mendoza, and married into one of Mexico's wealthiest and most powerful families. It was Mendoza who picked him to head the expedition to the north. That region never held much appeal for Spanish colonials, but their interest could be piqued by any reports suggesting that the otherwise unpromising El Norte might turn out to be an El Dorado brimming with precious metals.

The notion of Seven Cities of Gold persisted in the imagination of those times. There were variations on the theme, but one basic Iberian

LEFT: Tumacacori mission, now in ruins, was founded in 1691 by Jesuit Father Eusebio Francisco Kino. **RIGHT:** missionaries were far more successful than military men at spreading Spanish culture.

legend involved Seven Bishops who fled the peninsula to escape persecution by Moorish infidels, crossed the Sea of Darkness, and wound up on an island named Antilia that was blessed with gold. One of those who helped keep that legend alive was Alvar Nuñez Cabeza de Vaca.

Sailing from Florida in 1528 after having survived one great shipwreck, Cabeza de Vaca became shipwrecked again in the Gulf of Mexico, off the land that would become Texas. He and three surviving companions were held as slaves by Indians before embarking on a long trek across Texas into the New Mexico–Arizona region. When, after eight long years, they met up again with Spaniards, Cabeza de Vaca and his companions recounted stories they had heard of supposedly great Indian kingdoms to the north.

The stories got back to Mendoza, who, before sending forth Coronado, dispatched two men on a reconnaissance mission. One was a

Franciscan friar, Marcos de Niza. The other, as guide, was Esteban, a North African slave who had accompanied Cabeza de Vaca. They set out in March 1539, traveling up the west coast of northern Mexico. Esteban, going ahead of the friar, crossed into southeastern Arizona, probably through the San Rafael Valley, and followed what is now the Arizona–New Mexico border. But his luck ran out. The Pueblo Indians he was now encountering were less pacific than those of the south,

> **SIZE MATTERS**
>
> Cárdenas, the first European to see the Grand Canyon, discovered a basic truth about the chasm: it's bigger than it looks. Failing to reach the bottom, he reported "what seemed easy from above was not so, but instead very … difficult."

discovery of the mouth of the Colorado River. And so Coronado set forth, amid much fanfare, a large financial investment by several parties and great expectations of a rich reward. After a public pledge of allegiance to Coronado, the expedition proceeded from southern Nayarit up the coast of the Gulf of California. It reached the Sonora River and followed it, then crossed the Gila River to Cíbola, in what is now western New Mexico. Unfortunately, there was nothing imposing

and they found much of Esteban's behavior – including his appetite for their women – objectionable and cut him to pieces.

Great expectations

Friar Marcos continued on and, according to his much exaggerated account, came upon the Zuni pueblo of Cíbola. He described it as a dazzling place that was larger than Mexico City, and his glowing report stirred new interest in the legend of the seven great cities. It was his report that prompted Mendoza to mount the ambitious Coronado expedition of 1540, plus two additional ships commanded by Hernando de Alarcón – a venture that resulted in the

about Cíbola, which turned out to be a plain Zuni pueblo. Coronado determined that Marcos de Niza had lied, and in disgrace the friar was ordered to return to Mexico City. The mission was a fiasco.

In actuality, it was the first systematic exploration of the Southwest and extended Spain's empire into North America. The expedition, en masse or in small groups dispatched here and there by Coronado, traveled as far into the interior as the land that would become central Kansas.

Coronado sent one of his lieutenants, García López de Cárdenas, and 25 comrades to search for a great river to the west that had been described by the Hopi Indians, and they became the first Europeans to encounter one of the world's great natural wonders – the Grand Canyon. For three days Cárdenas and his men tried to descend into that great abyss to reach the Colorado River, but the effort was futile and they turned back.

Also encountered for the first time were herds of buffalo, to which the Spaniards were directed by a Pawnee Indian guide they called El Turco. And there was another, though far more tragic, precedent – the first of many battles that would pit Indians against whites in what is now the United States was fought on July 7, 1540, in New Mexico.

El Turco spun a tale of a great city of gold called Quivira that also turned out to be illusory – it seems that Indians were finding it convenient to tell the Spanish intruders what they wanted to hear – and his mendacity cost him his life. Then, on December 7, 1541, Coronado was thrown from his horse during a race with one of his lieutenants and badly injured. Struck on the head by the horse's hoof, he was never the same again. The expedition returned home in 1542, without precious metals, and Coronado died 12 years later in Mexico City.

It would be 40 years before another exploration was undertaken. In 1582, Antonio de Espejo led a party of nine soldier-prospectors and a hundred or so Zuni Indians up the Rio Grande to what is now New Mexico in search of three missionary priests – they had been killed, as it turned out – and deposits of precious minerals. His party visited Hopi villages as Coronado's group had done four decades earlier, and the territory was officially claimed for Spain's King Philip II. Silver and copper were discovered in the area that came to be known as Jerome, east of modern-day Prescott. Three centuries later Jerome would be the site of a copper bonanza.

Spanish colonization of the Southwest began in earnest in 1598 under Juan de Oñate, a wealthy Mexican-born miner with important connections – his wife was a descendant of both the conquistador Hernán Cortés and Montezuma, the Aztec emperor. Oñate, who had received a contract from Philip II, led 130

families, 270 single men and several thousand head of cattle up the Rio Grande to an area just north of present-day Santa Fe, New Mexico. This was the first European settlement in the Southwest. The settlers were mostly Mexicans and half-Indian mestizos who had come in search of a new life.

Oñate traveled across Arizona and got as far east as Kansas, where he fought an unsuccessful battle against Indians. Meanwhile, a small troop of men under the command of one of his officers, Captain Marcos Farfán de los Godos, found a rich deposit of silver ore near present-day Prescott.

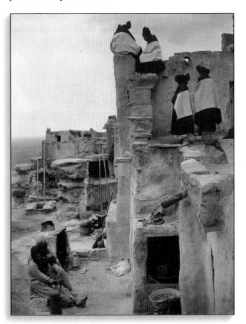

Heavy metal

Farfán and his eight companions, in addition to some Hopi guides, headed into the timberland of the Mogollon Rim. They encountered Jumana Indians who led them to the Verde River valley. Farfán's group came close upon the mineral deposits that had been discovered years earlier by Espejo and that were being mined by the Indians themselves. It was the Europeans' introduction to Arizona's mineral wealth. Farfán returned in 1604 with another expedition, and over the next two years the locations of much of the area's mineral deposits were found.

Oñate's major achievement was to solidify

LEFT: Indians bring gold to conquistadores in this 17th-century depiction of Spain's New World conquest.
RIGHT: the Hopi resisted Spanish dominance.

Spanish control over a vast area that encompassed Arizona, New Mexico, Texas, Colorado, Nevada, Oklahoma and Kansas. He has been called the Last Conquistador. After him, and for much of the 17th century, a missionary fervor took hold in the Southwest that sought to bring natives into the Christian fold through spiritual suasion and peaceful means.

Indian revolt

Three religious orders become dominant – Franciscans, Dominicans and Jesuits. The Franciscans came first, reaching Arizona about 20 years after Oñate's visit. Arriving at the Hopi villages in 1629, they established the first permanent structures erected for use by whites in Arizona.

Colonization was enhanced by the Catholic priests, their missions and their peaceable ways. But among some native tribes, such as the Hopi, resentment simmered. A major rebellion erupted in 1680 in the Pueblo Revolt, owing mainly to unhappiness over Spanish inability to protect the tribes against guerrilla attacks by nomadic Apache and Navajo warriors. The leader of the revolt, Popé, was determined to drive the Spaniards entirely out of northern New Spain. In a surprise, well-planned attack,

THE CROSSING OF THE FATHERS

Missionaries did a lot of traveling in the old days. A case in point is the journey made in 1776 by the Franciscan priests Silvestre Valez de Escalante and Atanasio Dominguez, who hoped to find a good route from Santa Fe to California. The priests journeyed north from New Mexico into Colorado and then over to Utah.

Disappointed, they headed for home, whereupon they became the first white men to encounter one of the few places along the 1,500-mile (2,400-km) Colorado River where it could be crossed on horseback. It is in northern Arizona, at Lake Powell, and known today as the Crossing of the Fathers – *El Vado de Los Padres*.

Pueblo Indians in Arizona and New Mexico arose. Some 400 settlers, including 22 priests, were slain, and the remainder were driven all the way back south to El Paso.

The most famous of the missionaries was Father Eusebio Francisco Kino, an Italian-born Jesuit who became legendary as the tireless "Padre on Horseback." He arrived in Mexico in 1681, established his first mission six years later, and first visited Indian villages in Arizona in 1691. Father Kino rode thousands of miles in the course of introducing European crops and teaching Indians how to farm and raise livestock, exploring and map-making in addition to tending to spiritual needs. By his death in 1711 he had started 25 missions, three of them between Tucson and Nogales in Arizona – including the future sites of the architecturally renowned San Xavier del Bac and San Jose de Tumacacori.

There were other major outbreaks of native violence. In 1700 Hopis killed priests and sacked Awatovi, ending Spanish colonization of northern Arizona. The Apache and Pima resisted the gradual entry of miners and farmers in Santa Cruz Valley. In 1751 a revolt by Pima warriors resulted in the death of a hundred or so people and the destruction of missions and farms. Spanish soldiers caught up to, and defeated, the Pima in the Santa Catalina mountains north of Tucson.

> **TRAILBLAZER**
>
> Father Kino was an explorer as well as a missionary. He searched for the source of the Colorado River, determined that Baja California was a peninsula, and developed a map of the Southwest that was in use for more than a century.

Holy mission

The Jesuit era in Arizona ended in 1767 when the powerful order was expelled by Spain's King Carlos III. Taking their place in the Southwest missions were the Franciscans, and the priest assigned to the Arizona missions was Francisco Tomás Garcés. Like Kino, he proved to be a tireless presence who established a strong rapport with the natives. He sought to establish a link with the missions newly founded in California by another Franciscan who would become equally renowned, Father Junípero Serra.

Garcés accompanied Captain Juan Bautista de Anza on two major expeditions to California in the mid-1770s. Garcés explored the westernmost reaches of the Grand Canyon and named the great tawny-looking river that coursed through it Río Colorado. He then headed east and reached the Hopi villages. His journey lasted 11 months and covered about 2,000 miles (3,200 km). Sadly, this popular priest who came to know Indian ways so intimately was martyred in the great Yuma Revolt of 1781 in which natives rebelled against their Spanish oppressors. The revolt effectively shut off the land route to California via Arizona, at the strategic Yuma Crossing, for four decades.

Tucson was chosen as the site for one of 15 presidios along a route stretching west from San Antonio, Texas. Construction was begun in 1775. Seven years later the fort was attacked by a large war party of Apaches. Under the able Don Pedro Allande, the presidio withstood the attack.

Apaches were always especially troublesome, but a Spanish policy initiated in 1784 by Viceroy Bernardo de Galvez took a new tack that sought to pacify them and all other tribes. Indians were now encouraged to settle near trading posts,

amply supplied with alcoholic beverages, and generally reduced to dependency on Spanish largesse. It was an effective, if cynical, strategy.

Nonetheless, the Spanish colonial phase was nearing an end. At the peak of its power, as historian David J. Weber observed, Spain claimed an area in North America alone, from ocean to ocean, that was larger than all of Western Europe. Now the tide was receding. And as political problems mounted for the Spanish governors in Mexico City, less attention could be paid to the outermost reaches of the empire. Shifts in power were looming that would reconfigure the political map of the American Southwest. ❏

LEFT: Navajo petroglyphs at Canyon de Chelly depict the coming of Spanish soldiers.
RIGHT: the interior of Mission San Xavier del Bac.

COWBOYS, INDIANS AND MINERS

Spurred on by nationalism and the promise of mineral wealth,
Americans take possession of a harsh and violent land

The 19th century brought a major change of identity for Arizona and the Southwest. What had long been a Spanish colonial outpost would now become an Anglo-American homeland. The old order of Iberian conquistadores, missionaries and remote bureaucrats yielded to an influx of North American gringos – the so-called mountain men at first, then miners and merchants, farmers and ranchers – driven by an imperative of materialism and Manifest Destiny.

Behind the transformation were such main historic currents as Anglo expansion and Iberian decline, an American self-confidence imbued with revolutionary fervor, even the nationalist sentiment of the tumultuous Napoleonic period. Those same nationalist winds of change that swept over all of Latin America were felt by Mexicans, who rebelled against their Spanish overlords in 1810 and achieved independence by 1821.

Oddly enough, the last years of Spanish rule in the Southwest had been relatively peaceful and productive. There had been good relations with the Pima. Farming and ranching activities were prospering, especially in the Santa Cruz Valley of southern Arizona. Minerals were discovered and missions erected – San Xavier del Bac was completed in 1797, San José de Tumacacori dedicated in 1822.

Mexican independence

This era of good feelings lasted about a quarter of a century, starting to dissipate about the time Mexicans began agitating for independence. When it was achieved, Arizona became Mexican territory. Ironically, the break with Spain helped open the Southwest to the gringos, who were at first welcome to enter the region. Mexico's regime, unlike the aloof and suspicious Spaniards, favored not only commercial rela-

tions with the Americans but settlement as well. In pre-independence Texas, for example, large tracts of land were made available – as long as prospective settlers swore fealty to Mexican rule and Catholic belief. For their part, what the Mexicans sought were large numbers of homesteaders whose presence would miti-

gate the threat of depredations by Apache, Comanche and other hostile Indians.

Anglos, disposed to free trade and commerce, began trickling into the territory. Many were trappers – beaver fur was profitable at a time when men generally wore that type of hat. The basic trade route, the Santa Fe Trail, became an American landmark. It stretched from St. Louis, Missouri, to Santa Fe, New Mexico. Some trappers added California to their itinerary, as did Christopher "Kit" Carson, who became a renowned frontier guide and Indian agent and served as a Union general in the Civil War. Traders came, mated – many with Mexican brides – and settled, laying down

LEFT: a Hopi man ascends a kiva ladder, *circa* 1897.
RIGHT: Christopher "Kit" Carson rounded up more than 8,000 Navajo and forced them on a "long walk" to an internment camp in New Mexico.

a foundation for a different Arizona that emerged after mid-century.

American takeover

The turning point came when war erupted in 1846. Mexicans had become unnerved by all the Americans they had once welcomed, and Texas was already lost. War was declared and the U.S. government sent troops, including an army headed by General Stephen Watts Kearny. It seized Las Vegas, a village on the Santa Fe Trail, and Kearny announced on September 22, 1846, that henceforth the United States was taking over New Mexico and the Arizona territory it included.

Kearny was assigned the task of opening up a wagon route across the Arizona wilderness to California, and the work was carried out efficiently by a specially formed unit of Mormon volunteers. Traveling more than 1,000 miles (1,600 km) in just 102 days, the Mormon Battalion of 340 men and a few women hacked out a road from Santa Fe through Tucson and on to San Diego. Some of the Mormons settled in Arizona, largely as farmers and ranchers.

Mexico lost a lot of ground – nearly half of her land – when the Treaty of Guadalupe Hidalgo ended hostilities on February 2, 1848. The lost acreage included Arizona north of the

ONE HUMP OR TWO?

Believe it or not, the U.S. Army once had a Camel Corps – not in some Arabian desert but in the American Southwest. It got started in 1855 when Congress assented to the old proposition that camels would be useful in exploring arid lands. Thirty-three camels were shipped to Texas, with a second shipment of 44 to follow. All were the one-humped dromedary type, as opposed to the 20 bactrians (two humps) later imported by mine owners in Nevada.

The camels were indeed well-equipped for their mission. They could haul heavier loads than mules, were fast, and could go for long periods without water. They came in handy when the Army opened a road west across the Arizona territory to the Colorado River. But, alas, these large, shaggy creatures also had a way of startling horses and mules, not to mention people, and they were disliked by Army cavalrymen. The camel drivers who were imported to handle them proved to be inept, although one of them achieved prominence – Hadji Ali, a Syrian known as Hi Jolly who was honored following his death in Arizona in 1902 with a grave monument. The camels themselves were generally mistreated and malnourished, miners pushing them beyond endurance. The Civil War caused the War Department to lose interest and the camels were sold at auction, many relegated to a nomadic existence.

Gila River. Six years later, the Gadsden Purchase brought all of the Arizona territory under U.S. control. James Gadsden, a railroad promoter serving as American minister to Mexico, purchased on behalf of the United States some 29 million acres in southern New Mexico and Arizona south of the Gila River. The cost: $10 million. The land was wanted, mostly, for a southern railroad route to California, but the project was never carried through.

Gold diggers

What really stimulated traffic across the Arizona territory was the gold rush, that frenzy which seemed to lure half the world to California after James Marshall found some bright metal in a stream at Sutter's Fort on January 24, 1848. The quest for mineral wealth attracted settlers to Arizona. Transportation was by wagon, stagecoach and even, on the Colorado River, steamboat. Tracks were laid by the Southern Pacific and the Atlantic and Pacific (later called Santa Fe) Railroads, and direct connection with the California coast was made in 1883, at San Diego. Arizona became inextricably linked to the rest of the United States.

Settlement remained sparse in the 1850s. In southern Arizona there were some mining communities but only two military posts (Fort Buchanan and Fort Breckinridge). The beginning of American occupation of the lower Colorado Valley occurred in February 1852, with the establishment of Fort Yuma on the California side of the Colorado River. More military forts would be constructed to protect travelers from attack by hostile Indians.

Most of the Anglos who were settling in Arizona were Southerners. With the outbreak of the Civil War, Confederate leaders noted that the territory was poorly defended by federal troops and sought to take advantage of that fact. Citizens of Tucson voted to join the secessionist cause, and Confederate troops occupied the town in February 1862. They withdrew, however, when Union forces from California arrived.

Most of the entire western half of the New Mexico territory was controlled by Indians, and they were not thrilled by the wave of fortune-

seekers intruding on their land like a plague of locusts. Before the Forty-niner fever ran its course, the region would be visited by an estimated 50,000 gold diggers and tradespeople.

Indian relations with settlers had waxed and waned ever since the Spanish arrival. The chaotic period that followed Mexican independence in 1821 brought a breakdown in relations, especially with Apaches. They made assaults on farms and ranches in Mexico's Sonora region and in southern Arizona, running off herds of horses and dislocating commerce and agriculture. There would be many notorious incidents. One of them, in 1837,

involved a group of Mexicans led by an Anglo settler, John Johnson, who abruptly ended two days of peace talks by suddenly gunning down their Apache counterparts, about 20 in all.

Apaches, fighting from mountain strongholds, had waged an especially fierce resistance against all invaders. To a Spanish missionary writing in 1630, they were "fiery and bellicose and very crafty in war," and so they appeared to the Anglo-Americans who inherited the territory and with it Indian hostility. Apaches were greatly skilled in handling the horse, a species introduced to the New World by Spaniards, and were accustomed to moving about freely. Now, however, their way of life was threatened –

LEFT: a stylized depiction of an Apache raid.
RIGHT: Indian scouts pursue Geronimo in a *Harper's Weekly* illustration by Frederic Remington, 1886.

miners were a particular nuisance – and they struck back.

Hostilities worsened in the 1860s. Bounties were paid for Indian scalps, and Arizona's territorial legislature called on the federal Department of War to carry out a policy of extermination. The request denied, a citizens' mob took it upon itself to slaughter 75 unarmed Apache women and children near Tucson.

Massacre of innocents

A more notorious incident occurred in the Camp Grant Massacre of April 1871. A posse organized in Tucson to avenge Indian raids rode

60 miles (95 km) northeast to the abandoned military camp, where Aravaipa Apaches were confined. The posse attacked at dawn, when most of the Apache men were out hunting, and caused as many as 100 deaths. Virtually all of the victims were women and children. The raiders were tried for murder in Tucson but acquitted. Bent on revenge, Apaches launched their own raids and ambushes against settlers and soldiers, with terrible atrocities committed.

In 1864, Colonel Kit Carson headed an army operation that rounded up some 8,000 Navajo at Canyon de Chelly in Arizona and forced them on an infamous 300-mile (500 km) "long walk" to a desolate area in New Mexico known as Bosque Redondo. Seven years later, the administration of President Ulysses S. Grant sent General George Crook to Arizona, and he proved adept at reining in roving bands of Apache marauders while at the same time winning greater Indian acceptance of the reservation concept.

The so-called Indian Wars in effect tied down America's military establishment before subjugation of Native Americans was completed by 1890. Three names are particularly prominent in most accounts of Indian leaders at this period in Arizona's history: Mangas Coloradas, Cochise and Geronimo. All were Chiricahua Apaches who fought fiercely against the takeover of their land and the subjugation of their people, though it was a struggle doomed to failure.

Mangas Coloradas ("Red Sleeves"), a giant of a man at 6½ feet (2 meters) tall, had conducted campaigns against Mexicans and even offered to help General Kearny when they met

A GRAND RIDE THROUGH THE CANYON

Exactly 100 years before Neil Armstrong became the first earthling to step on the Moon, a one-armed Civil War veteran was making his own fantastic voyage down the Colorado River to become a national hero of his day. Major John Wesley Powell, 35, and his boating expedition traveled 900 miles (1,450 km) from Green River, Wyoming, through the Grand Canyon in Arizona in 1869. It was a grueling, dangerous journey that had been considered impossible, even by Native Americans. Indeed, the expedition was given up as lost before Powell and five comrades emerged after three months from the mouth of the Virgin River. The date was August 30, 1869. Four men had dropped out

along the way, three of them killed by Indians in apparent retaliation, wrongfully, for the murder of an Indian woman.

Powell's right arm had been amputated after he was wounded at Shiloh, but he remained in active service on the condition that his bride, Emma, accompany him. After the war, she became the first woman to climb Pike's Peak, as part of a scientific expedition in Colorado headed by her husband. Powell, a geology professor, explored the Green and Colorado rivers again in 1870–71. He then took up the often frustrating duties of a government official, founding and directing the U.S. Geological Survey and later the Bureau of Ethnology, a post he held until his death in 1902.

in 1846. Turning in later years against Anglo-Americans, Mangas Coloradas attacked a 126-man army unit at Apache Pass in the Chiricahua Mountains and was wounded by gunfire. Captured in January 1863, he was imprisoned at an abandoned fort in New Mexico and gunned down by soldiers when he resisted being taunted with heated bayonets.

Cochise, who married a daughter of Mangas Coloradas, was captured in 1861 at Apache Pass by an army lieutenant named George Bascom who had pretended to be friendly. The notorious Bascom Affair involved the abduction of a 12-year-old boy from a ranch for

In 1877 he was arrested and confined to a reservation in Arizona. He broke free with a band of followers and for five years conducted raids that harassed army troops and terrorized southeastern Arizona and neighboring areas in Mexico and New Mexico.

General Crook pursued Geronimo and his Apache force and twice sat down with him to negotiate the terms of a surrender. A compromise allowing a return to the Arizona reservation was overruled by President Grover Cleveland, who suggested that Geronimo be hanged. The Apache warrior slipped away again. With his fourth and final surrender, this time to a less

which Cochise was wrongfully accused. Cochise escaped, but hostages on both sides were killed, including his brother and two nephews. Apaches took 150 lives in two months, and hostilities raged until 1872, exacting 4,000 casualties and causing entire settlements to be abandoned.

Geronimo was the last Indian to surrender to the United States, in 1886. Earlier in his life his mother, wife and children were killed in an attack by Mexican soldiers on an Apache camp.

sympathetic General Nelson Miles, harsh terms were imposed on the Apache warrior and his cohort. They were shipped in chains to a prison camp in Florida, and later to Alabama.

Late in life Geronimo performed in Wild West shows, took part in President Theodore Roosevelt's inaugural parade in Washington in 1905, dictated his memoirs for a biography published in 1906, and died three years later of pneumonia, still a prisoner of war, at Fort Sill, Oklahoma.

LEFT: John Wesley Powell confers with a Paiute scout.
ABOVE: Geronimo (fourth from left) discusses surrender with General George Crook (second from right), 1886.

Mining bonanza

If the Anglo-American takeover was Arizona's most important development in the 19th century, not far behind was the fact that the territory turned out to be so rich in precious metals – gold, silver and copper. Mining activity on a serious scale got under way right after the Gadsden Purchase fixed boundaries in 1854. The gold strike in California a few years earlier had made prospecting a popular activity in the region, and western Arizona was one of the nearby areas being searched.

Spaniards had made discoveries as far back as the 16th century, but the means of taking out the ore were limited. There were silver mines at Alamos, Zacatecas, Guanajuato and other places in New Spain. In 1736, a rich lode

excavation near the old Spanish presidio at Tubac and a booming business in silver. About $3,000 worth was extracted daily before the start of the Civil War in 1861 necessitated the removal of federal troops from the Santa Cruz area and, with no protection against hostile Indians, shutdown of the mines.

Poston pushed for territorial status for Arizona, going to Washington in 1862 to lobby. The territory and the name "Arizona" became official on February 24, 1863, and Poston was elected its first delegate to Congress. Whatever profit he accrued was dissipated by the time of his death in 1902.

of silver was found about 25 miles (40 km) southwest of what is now Nogales, Arizona, by a Spaniard who was guided to the site by a Yaqui Indian. Thousands of pounds of silver were mined.

One of the first of the latter-day Arizona miners to hit pay dirt was Charles D. Poston, a Kentuckian who came to be known as the "father of Arizona." Poston went to California about 1850 and four years later visited southern Arizona, taking ore samples at Tubac and Ajo. With him was Herman Ehrenberg, a German-born mining engineer he had met.

The high quality of the ore led to creation of the Sonora Exploring and Mining Company,

Another silver miner and Arizona promoter was Sylvester Mowry, an ex-soldier who built a thriving business in the late 1850s. He kept it operating despite the removal of troops at the start of the Civil War and in the face of harassment by Apaches. The Mowry Mine was one of the nation's richest silver producers early on, but wartime complications deprived its founder of any lasting fortune.

Arizona was found to have ample deposits of both placer gold, the surface kind easy to get at, and lode gold, which requires a large-scale mining enterprise. Placer gold became scarce after a relatively short period, and serious mining was left to the big companies. The territory's first gold rush occurred in 1858 when rich deposits of placer gold were discovered by Jake Snively, a Texan, about 20 miles (32 km) beyond the junction of the Gila and Colorado Rivers.

A boomtown known as Gila City arose, but by 1864 the site was virtually cleaned out. Another rich strike was made in 1862 at La Paz, some $8 million worth of gold being taken there before it too ran dry. The richest discovery was made in 1863 near what is now Congress Junction when in just three months

HONEST GOVERNMENT

Territorial governor Anson P. K. Safford returned all but $5,000 of a $25,000 bribe intended to secure a land grant for the Southern Pacific Railroad; the briber apparently overestimated the legislature's price.

shipped via Cape Horn all the way to Wales for smelting. Other large mining operations would be established at Bisbee, Clifton, Globe, Morenci, Bagdad, Tucson and other places.

Bisbee, in southeastern Arizona, turned out to be one of the richest copper areas in the world. Here the Copper Queen company began mining in 1880. The site had been chanced upon by an army scout from Fort Bowie, and ownership eventually passed to a San Francisco group of financiers.

more than a quarter million dollars in placer gold was found.

Rich copper deposits

There were many other gold and silver strikes worth millions of dollars in the latter years of the 19th century, but the precious metal that became Arizona's most valuable was copper. The first substantial effort at open pit mining was undertaken at Ajo in 1854 by the American Mining and Trading Company – the ore was

---

ABOVE: the town of Clifton (shown here in 1909), together with nearby Morenci, was part of one of the richest copper-mining districts in the country.

They formed the Copper Queen Mining Company, a huge deposit of rich ore was unearthed, and thus was born the boomtown of Bisbee, which took its name from the company's attorney, who never set foot in the place.

Now entering the picture was Phelps, Dodge & Company, a small metal importing firm based in New York that had been urged to set up mining operations in southern Arizona. It bought out Copper Queen and reaped a fortune. By 1908 copper totaling 730 million pounds (330 million kg) and worth millions of dollars was mined. Phelps Dodge became one of the nation's "Big Three" copper interests, the others being Anaconda and Kennecott. It has been estimated that by 1975 the Bisbee area alone produced gold, silver, copper, lead and zinc worth over $6 billion.

Great fortunes were made. James Douglas, the assayer-consultant who steered Phelps Dodge to Arizona and became president of Copper Queen Consolidated, was worth $20 million at his death in 1918. Douglas and Phelps Dodge did, however, miss out on one opportunity: a mine operation in Jerome that became the prodigious United Verde company.

Its principal figure was New York financier Eugene Jerome, whose offer to sell for $300,000 was met by the Montana mining tycoon and politician William A. Clark after Douglas held off one day too many. Clark eventually took in more than $100 million from United Verde. The company was bought by Phelps Dodge in 1935 for $21 million.

The town too tough to die

Most famous of all the boomtowns that grew out of the mining bonanza was Tombstone. Ed Schieffelin, who arrived in Arizona in 1876 with nothing to show after 20 years of prospecting, hit it rich in 1877. He discovered rich silver deposits in the San Pedro Valley about 70 miles (110 km) southeast of Tucson. Joining

THE ENIGMA OF TOMBSTONE

Hero? Villain? None of the above? Wyatt Earp is a hard man to pin down – buffalo hunter, gambler, gold-digger, sometime lawman who, craving excitement, lit out for Arizona and enduring notoriety. But one thing is certain: he had a knack for survival. He alone emerged unscathed in that bloody shootout near the O.K. Corral and then beat the rap – getting away with murder, as some people saw it – along with brothers Virgil and Morgan and their hot-tempered friend Doc Holliday. Then, when Morgan was mysteriously dispatched by a bullet while shooting pool, a second one went sailing by Wyatt. In another shooting, Virgil's arm was crippled. And in 1900, younger brother Warren was terminated by a bullet in an Arizona bar.

Wyatt outlasted all of his eight siblings. He and Josie Marcus, the showgirl who became his lifetime companion, knocked about mining camps in Colorado. They joined the Idaho gold rush in 1884, and ran a saloon in San Diego. In 1896, Earp took to the boxing ring in San Francisco to officiate at a match between heavyweights Bob Fitzsimmons and Tom Sharkey – in the process exposing the .45 Colt he packed under his frock coat. Then it was off to the Alaska gold rush and a profitable saloon-gambling venture. After further prospecting, Wyatt and Josie settled in Los Angeles, where he died in 1929, an 80-year-old Western legend. Among the pallbearers were film cowboy stars Tom Mix and William S. Hart.

him in the enterprise was his brother Albert and Dick Gird, an assayer who realized the value of the ore. Schieffelin was warned that the territory was Apache country and "all you'll find will be your tombstone." The name stuck.

With support from Eastern investors, the Tombstone Mining District was established. By 1888, some $30 million worth of silver had been taken out. At least 50 mines were lodged in the hills around Tombstone by 1886, and they employed hundreds of teamsters, millworkers and a host of other laborers in addition to miners.

Schieffelin and his brother Albert sold their claims for a half million dollars each in 1880, and Gird, too, cashed in handsomely the next year. Ed Schieffelin kept trying his luck over the years in various places, including Alaska. He died in a shack in Oregon and is buried in Arizona near the site of one of his strikes, a monument 25 feet (8 meters) tall towering over his grave. Tombstone's mines started to flood in 1883 and were shut down completely by 1909.

Frontier boomtowns like Tombstone attracted a variety of people, many with rough edges. Its population soared to 15,000 in a short time and the town acquired a notorious reputation – indeed, President Chester A. Arthur once threatened to impose martial law in the entire territory. Most notably, this was the heyday of the cowboy, that Anglo version of the vaquero character Spaniards introduced to the American West. Pulp fiction and Hollywood fantasy would tranform the drab, proletarian cowboy into a mythical hero-gunfighter.

Wyatt Earp is a good example. Born in Illinois in 1848, he worked at various jobs in the West, hunting buffalo, fighting Indians and occasionally running afoul of the law. In 1876 he was a deputy policeman in Dodge City, the wild and woolly Kansas cattle town. Here he met some characters now equally well-known in Western lore – Doc Holliday, Luke Short and Bat Masterson, a fellow deputy.

They, Earp and his four brothers gravitated to Tombstone, became known as the Dodge City Gang, and made political friends and enemies – Virgil Earp was appointed town marshal. Differences with the Clantons, a rowdy family of small ranchers and cattle rustlers, simmered into a poisonous enmity that finally exploded in a deadly shootout.

It happened near the O.K. Corral in Tombstone on the night of October 25, 1881. When it was over, three members of the Clanton faction lay dead, Earp's brothers Virgil and Morgan were wounded, and Holliday was creased by a bullet. Wyatt Earp was unhurt. The gunfight lasted less than 30 seconds but the legend has endured. Virgil later was wounded in an ambush and Morgan shot to death while shooting pool in a saloon.

Bloodier yet was the Graham-Tewksbury

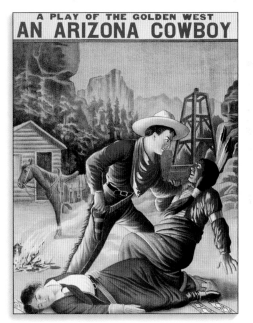

feud that raged for six years between cattlemen and sheepmen in Pleasant Valley, in the Tonto Basin, starting in 1886. It exploded when sheep by the thousands were allowed to graze in the valley despite a strict prohibition. Ambushes, shootouts and other violence left dozens of casualties, some of them innocent victims. One woman lost a husband and four sons.

Hollywood burnished the myth on screen in a steady flow of shoot-'em-ups – *Fort Apache*, *Arizona Kid*, *Broken Arrow* and, of course, *Gunfight at the O.K. Corral*. But the times were a-changin' for Tombstone and Bisbee and all the get-rich-quick boomtowns as another century dawned over Arizona Territory. ❏

LEFT: gallows at the county courthouse in Tombstone.
RIGHT: staged in 1907, *An Arizona Cowboy* romanticized the rigors of frontier life.

BIRTH AND REBIRTH

Reclamation projects, wartime industry and a cool new invention called
air conditioning powered Arizona through the 20th century

Gunfire flared in Arizona on St. Valentine's Day in 1912, but it wasn't triggering any Chicago-style gangland massacre, nor was it a resurgence of frontier lawlessness. It was a celebration of something happening in far-off Washington, D.C. A proclamation admitting Arizona to full-fledged membership in the Union was being signed there by President William Howard Taft.

After half a century as a territory, it was becoming the 48th and last of the continental United States. Taft's ceremonial signing was a good photo-op, as we say nowadays, so a motion-picture camera was on hand to film the historic moment. And who could blame the armed citizenry back in Arizona for being fired up? They had waited a long time. There were too many Democrats out there to suit the Republican gate-keepers in Congress, who had voted "Nay" on statehood in 1906, and who even considered wrapping Arizona and New Mexico together and labeling the package "Montezuma."

Taft had his own reservations about some progressive features in Arizona's new constitution. But the day finally arrived and the old territory became the so-called "Baby State." It was a new chapter in the Arizona story, and there would be more transforming moments ahead as this virtual desert started blossoming into a modern-day El Dorado for sun-seekers and fun-seekers who came and stayed in increasing numbers.

Bringing up baby

A year before admission to the Union, another important event occurred. Taft's predecessor as president, Theodore Roosevelt, came to Arizona to dedicate a great dam named in his honor. Roosevelt, champion of conservation, had been a vital force behind the Reclamation

LEFT: miners at work in a Bisbee tunnel. By 1900, Bisbee was Arizona's largest and wealthiest town. RIGHT: workers inspect a diversion tunnel during the construction of Hoover Dam, 1934.

Act of 1902 authorizing the federal government to build reservoirs and stimulate irrigation projects in the West. The first major effort was the Salt River Project in Arizona. It was the same area in which Hohokam Indians a couple of thousand years earlier had carried out their own irrigation project, building an extensive canal

system to bring water to their fields of corn, beans and squash.

Roosevelt Dam was built on the Salt River about 90 miles (145 km) upstream of Phoenix. Work began in 1905, and the dam was dedicated on March 18, 1911. It is the world's tallest masonry dam at 280 feet (85 meters), and it cost $10 million to build on rough terrain where it could get hotter than hell. It allowed for water to be stored, floodwaters controlled, arid land turned into an agricultural oasis, and Phoenix to bloom into a big city. Three more dams would be built along the Salt River and two on its major tributary, the Verde, storing water to irrigate vast acres of cotton, citrus, vegetables and other crops. The dams helped to spur farm acreage in the state by almost 400 percent between 1910 and 1920.

Also harnessed was the Southwest's mightiest waterway, the 1,450-mile-long (2,330-km) Colorado River, with the construction of Boulder, Glen Canyon, Parker and Davis Dams. Arizona is one of seven states served by Boulder Dam, which was dedicated by President Franklin D. Roosevelt in 1935 and renamed Hoover Dam in 1947 (the name changed back and forth for years). Arizona's claim to a major share of Colorado River water was affirmed by the U.S. Supreme Court in 1963.

the need to transport larger ore extractions, built their own connections when necessary, as Phelps Dodge did when it fought over terms with the transcontinental companies.

The livestock industry prospered as large ranches were established, their chief customer being the army forts. Mining companies thrived but were beset with labor problems – a shortage of manpower early on; ethnic and racial antagonisms involving Anglos, Mexicans, Chinese, Italians and others; union militancy. That militancy usually brought a harsh response from mine owners. When, for example, Mexican and Italian workers went on strike in 1903 at the

In 1968 Congress approved the Central Arizona Project, a grand federal undertaking to funnel water from the Colorado River to the state's populous central region, which includes Phoenix and Tucson. The total cost for the canal system is about $4 billion.

Prosperity and conflict

Railroads unified the state and stimulated its development starting in the late 19th century. North-south tracks were put down to connect the transcontinental lines – the Southern Pacific in Arizona's south, the Santa Fe in the northern part, where it was the dominant economic force. The powerful copper interests, faced with

Clifton-Morenci mines, Arizona's governor was enlisted to call out both the National Guard and the Arizona Rangers.

There were many labor-management conflicts in Arizona's mining areas during the early decades of the 19th century. Patriotic fervor during World War I engendered a fear of industrial sabotage and a hatred for militants like the "Wobblies"– the radical agitators, real or alleged, popularly associated with the Industrial Workers of the World.

The most notorious incident, known as the Bisbee Deportation, occurred in July 1917. As many as 1,200 people were rounded up by 2,000 "sheriff's deputies" and armed citizens, herded like cattle into railroad cars, shipped to Columbus, New Mexico, and unloaded in the dark of night.

More copper was produced in Arizona than in any other state in the Roaring Twenties, its mines supplying half of the total demand in the nation. The most productive year was 1929, when extractions totaled more than $155 million. Only a fraction of that was realized a few years later when the industry was hit hard by the Great Depression. The economic downturn

BORN LOSER

George Warren lost his claim to the Copper Queen Mine in a drunken bet that he could outrun a man on horseback. It later became one of the most productive mines in the history of the West.

from hostile Indians by army troops, farmland was irrigated, floodwaters restrained, cotton growers subsidized. And it was the federal government once again that played a prominent role in the state's phenomenal development, which started with the onset of the World War II period.

The war itself was a major stimulant. Defense plants and research laboratories launched operations in Arizona that created jobs and brought prosperity. Air bases and other military installations were established in

affected Arizona as severely as it hurt other places. Cotton had been the state's leading crop, but revenues now fell sharply. The cattle industry was hurt as well. Some of the copper mines were shut down, the communities they had spawned turning into ghost towns.

Wartime stimulus

Despite a reputation for rugged individualism, Arizona traditionally has benefited from a good deal of federal largesse – settlers were protected

the state out of fears for security posed by its location near the West Coast. (The federal government is the largest landowner in the state, possessing a major portion of its 113,642 sq miles/294,331 sq km.)

After the war, veterans returned to settle and start families. Homes went up, and businesses attracted by the labor pool opened plants, among them electronics giants like General Electric and Motorola. Mining production was revitalized in the war years.

Even before the war there were factors in play that opened Arizona to outsiders and made it the "Grand Canyon State." Railroad construction was at its peak between 1880 and

LEFT: Arizona, New Mexico and Oklahoma wait for their stars, signifying statehood, in a 1911 political cartoon.
ABOVE: striking miners are forced out of Bisbee, 1917.

1920, and brought many visitors. The automobile had an even greater impact, stimulating road-building. Great vistas and spectacular scenery, once the preserve of explorers and then the privileged class, began attracting masses of ordinary people.

Theodore Roosevelt had created Grand Canyon National Monument in 1908, seven years after a passenger train first brought tourists there. It became Grand Canyon National Park in 1919, drew 56,000 tourists the following year and three times that number within a decade (currently the park receives some 5 million visitors). Other national parks and monuments established in the 1906–08 period were Petrified Forest, Montezuma Castle, Tonto and Tumacacori.

Birth of the cool

Arizona was once regarded as so forbidding that General William Tecumseh Sherman recommended starting another war with Mexico to "make her take it back." But during the first two decades of the 20th century, the state began attracting people suffering from tuberculosis and other respiratory ailments. The dry climate had been sought out as early as the mid-1800s by a few health-seekers. But now churches and

MR CONSERVATIVE

He was either a plain-speaking hero or a loose cannon in scary nuclear times. Such were the depictions of Barry Goldwater (1909–1998), grandson of a Russian Jewish emigrant, who became the champion of an effort to outduel Soviet communism, revive American conservatism, and save Western Civilization. Goldwater gave up a career managing the family business in favor of public service. Starting out on the Phoenix City Council, he rose to become the Republican standard-bearer for president in 1964. He was defeated handily, returned to the U.S. Senate, and ultimately won the public's admiration for his steadfast conviction as "Mr Conservative."

other groups, especially in Phoenix and Tucson, were starting facilities that cared for the afflicted. The state's climate was giving Arizona a national reputation as a health haven.

Great change also came with the advent of air conditioning. In the 1930s, attempts were made to provide relief from the searing heat by evaporative devices. These so-called "swamp coolers" began appearing in windows and on roofs, and Phoenix billed itself as the "Air Conditioned Capital of the World." The city was a leading center for production of the artificial coolers, which were later replaced by the superior technique of refrigeration cooling. Air conditioning made work conditions more pleasant and were an inducement for out-of-staters to relocate in Arizona.

One of those attracted to Phoenix for health reasons played a major role in the Arizona transformation. Del Webb was born in California and moved to Phoenix in 1927. Forming the Del Webb Corporation, he entered the housing field and won fame and fortune by designing Sun City, a vast community of homes for retired people.

Encompassing 30,000 acres (12,000 hectares), it offered ranch-style houses with carports ,golf courses, swimming pools, shopping centers and other attractions. All were tailored to the needs of active senior citizens eager to enjoy the rewards of their "golden years" (a term invented by Webb) and possessing the resources to do so. It was a major innovation in the American social landscape.

Arizona was being transformed once again, propelled by an explosive growth in population that began intensifying in the 1950s and keeps on spiraling upward. The population ballooned from 335,000 in 1920 to 3.6 million in 1990, and a decade later it exceeded 5 million. In just seven years (1990–97) the state's population grew by 24.3 percent.

The most exceptional growth has been experienced by Phoenix, which did not exist until 1867 and now has nearly 3 million inhabitants. Its founding came as part of an effort to clean out the old Hohokam canals, an action seen as breathing new life into an ancient settlement, hence the adaptation of the name of the mythical Egyptian bird that rose from the ashes.

Phoenix, the capital since 1889, surpassed Tucson as Arizona's largest city in 1920. Both are among the fastest-growing in the nation. And both are burdened with helter-skelter urban development and suburban sprawl as well as the traffic congestion and smog that arise from a near-exclusive reliance on the automobile for transportation.

In the public spotlight

Several latter-day Arizonans achieved national reputations in the political realm. Barry Goldwater, a longtime U.S. senator and 1964 Republican presidential nominee, became the leading voice for American conservatism. Stewart Udall, scion of a pioneer Mormon family, was Secretary of the Interior in the Kennedy administration after he served in Congress, as did his equally liberal brother, Morris. Also highly regarded is Bruce Babbitt, a two-term governor who became Secretary of the Interior in the Clinton administration. Senator John McCain, who endured a long and harrowing captivity after his plane was shot down during the Vietnam War, was a favorite among many Republicans, independents and even Democrats during the presidential election of 1999–2000.

No one has played a more enduring role in Arizona's development, however, than Carl Hayden. He was present at the creation in 1912 when voters chose him to be the new state's first representative in Congress. He went off to Washington at the age of 34, and 56 years later he was still on the job. Hayden served in both the House and the Senate, his long career capped at its very end by congressional approval of the Central Arizona Project in 1968. His life stretched from the Indian Wars to the Vietnam War, and the family's history goes as far back as 1858, when his father, Charles, settled in Tucson and became a prominent merchant and civic leader. ❑

LEFT: suburbs sprawl around downtown Phoenix, now the sixth-largest city in the United States.
RIGHT: traffic is one result of exuberant growth.

THE CULTURAL LANDSCAPE

*A colorful combination of Indian, Hispanic and Anglo cultures
is enriched by immigrants from all over the world*

Early in 1856, an eastbound stagecoach arrived in a cloud of dust in Tucson, then a Spanish-speaking adobe village. Arizona had passed from Spanish to Mexican rule in 1821, and just two years before, as part of the 1854 Gadsden Purchase ending the Mexican War, become American territory. Papers signed thousands of miles away had little impact on residents of northern Mexico and southern Arizona, then as now united by a shared landscape and ancient cultural ties. Not until the arrival of the railroad in 1880 and the end of the Apache Wars in 1886 would Arizona Territory attract the flood of white settlers that dominate the state ethnically today. Statehood, granted in 1912, was still 56 years away.

Aboard that stagecoach in 1856 was one of Tucson's first Anglo immigrants. Sam Hughes, a 28-year-old Welshman, had been working in a bakery in a California gold-rush town. He was dying of tuberculosis and, in a last-ditch attempt to save his life, started making his way to Texas, hoping the warm, dry air would improve his health. The stage driver didn't share his faith. Expecting the sickly young foreigner with the sing-song accent to expire at any moment, he dumped him in Tucson. Of the 500 or so residents, Hughes was assured, five spoke English.

Founding father

Hughes didn't die. Just the opposite. Like the thousands who would later come here for their health, he was cured by the Arizona desert. Grit and determination made up for formal education in frontier Tucson, a town where, as journalist J. Ross Browne observed in 1864, "Every man went armed to the teeth, and street-fights and bloody affrays were of daily occurrence." Hughes's weapons were a steel will and a capacity for hard work. He made friends with

---

PRECEDING PAGES: San Carlos Apache Gaan dancer. **LEFT:** Mexican dancers perform at Tumacacori National Historical Park in southern Arizona. **RIGHT:** a mural in Tucson's historic El Presidio district depicts the Virgin of Guadalupe.

his Mexican neighbors, learned their language, married a young Sonoran girl, and had successful careers in ranching, real estate and politics. By the time he died, at the age of 88, he was considered one of Tucson's founding fathers.

At about the same time, in the opposite end of the state, Mormon colonists, recently settled in

Utah, were now setting their sights on Arizona. In 1858, Mormon missionary Jacob Hamblin traveled across the Arizona Strip to the Hopi Mesas in search of Indian converts and new farmland along the Little Colorado River. He was warmly welcomed at Moenkopi by Hopi chief Tuva, who became the first of many Hopis to convert to Christianity. Hamblin's trip laid the groundwork for settlements in the 1870s, when government persecution in Utah led Mormons to establish communities all the way down to St. David in the San Pedro River Valley. In one of the odd twists of history that seem to abound in this state, the Mormons were convinced that the Hopi spoke Welsh, and Hamblin brought with him a Welsh-speaking translator. Had they met, the translator and Hughes would undoubtedly have enjoyed the joke.

Opportunity knocks

For immigrants, Arizona has always been a land where dreams could come true, a "blank slate on which they could etch their visions of the future," according to historian Thomas Sheridan. Nor is this a recent phenomenon. Opportunity undoubtedly spurred the very first paleo-hunters to venture into Arizona's game-rich grasslands after the retreat of the Ice Age glaciers 12,000 years ago. It may have been

what motivated people from Mexico to travel north to Arizona and begin trading some 3,000 years ago. They mingled with Archaic hunter-gatherers in the Sonoran Desert and shared information about farming, pottery and religion that would be passed along to tribes throughout the state. Without this exchange among cultures, it's unlikely the Mogollon, Hohokam and Ancestral Pueblo would ever have come to dominate the prehistoric Southwest.

It must have been opportunity, too, that lured nomadic Athabascans – today's Navajo and Apache – from northwest Canada around the same time as Shoshoneans, the Utes and Paiutes, were also moving in from the Great Basin, probably in the 1400s. A couple of centuries later, it was the promise of gold and silver, timber and fertile land that lured first Spaniards and Mexicans, then Anglos and other immigrants to the state. Though they didn't always find what they were looking for, pioneers of every race stayed and made a life for themselves.

The trend continues. Arizona is the second-fastest growing state in the country, posting a growth rate of 40 percent between 1990 and 2000, and has an ethnic diversity rare even in the West. Of the state's 5.1 million residents, Hispanics constitute 25 percent, American Indians 5 percent, African Americans 3 percent. Most of the others are white people of various nationalities and religions. The result isn't so much a melting pot, in which ethnic groups are boiled down to a bland homogeneity, but a tossed salad in which distinct groups coexist and occasionally come into conflict.

The first Arizonans

Though American Indians are a relatively small minority, no other group is more closely identified with the state or, ironically, more misunderstood. For starters, there is no one overarching Indian culture. Each of the 21 tribes in Arizona has its own history, traditions and language, though almost all now speak English and many hold jobs off their reservations. While some tribal members have chosen to maintain traditional ways of life, the influence of modern culture is unavoidable and often produces unexpected and calamitous results.

Introduced diseases, substance abuse and domestic violence – while not uniquely Indian problems – have devastated many tribes already struggling to hold onto cultural identities after years of government-sponsored re-education, land reallocation and, during the 19th century, extermination. Tribal councils, introduced in the early 1900s, are frequently at odds with themselves or mired in the long debates that Indian people have traditionally employed to reach consensus. Casinos, resort developments and other businesses on Indian reservations have let tribes get ahead economically but also represent a compromise of traditional values.

Ironically, one of the keys to sustaining cultural values has been embracing positive change. Every tribe has borrowed cultural traits from its neighbors, creating dynamic societies that not only survive but, surprisingly, thrive in the face of change. Navajo kids use computers to learn their native tongue. Indian youth go away to law school, then return to the reservation to represent their tribes in centuries-old disputes over land and water rights, housing, subsistence hunting and gathering, and access to public lands for traditional religious uses. Reservation doctors and nurses combine modern medicine and traditional healing in the treatment of diabetes and other modern ailments.

The trick for most tribes is to engage the outside world without being overwhelmed by it. As more tribes take over the management of their institutions and natural resources, and

reservation that encompasses the mesas, canyons, black lava promontories and high-desert grasslands of northeastern Arizona, northwestern New Mexico and a sliver of southern Utah. A matriarchal society, where women own all the property and men move in with the wife's family, Navajo life is governed by complex clan relationships and the pursuit of traditional religious beliefs, often referred to as the Beauty Path. Modern Navajos still strive for *hozho*, a state of harmony with all things, taught by the Holy People who created First Man and First Woman, and later, Changing Woman, the ideal Navajo woman whose spirit is evoked in the *kinaalda*,

encourage the development of tribal businesses, there is a shift in decision-making from federal policy-makers to tribal governments. What Indian people will do with this new power is one of the great questions of the 21st century.

The Navajo

The 210,000-strong Navajo Nation, the largest in the country, grapples with this issue daily. The Navajo, or *Diné*, as they call themselves, live on a 25,000-square-mile (65,000-sq-km)

LEFT: a banner flies in Phoenix for the Day of the Dead, observed by much of the state's Hispanic community.
ABOVE: a Navajo silversmith works inside a hogan, 1915.

a puberty ritual observed by Navajo girls.

The ancestors of the Navajo were Athabascan nomads who migrated into the Southwest from Canada about 600 years ago. In addition to hunting and gathering, they raided Pueblo settlements, a practice that intensified after they acquired Spanish horses in the 1600s. But they also saw the merits of Pueblo agriculture and, during times of peace, intermarried, traded, learned weaving, and adapted some aspects of Pueblo religion. They were such proficient corn farmers that the Pueblo called them *Navaju*, a Tewa word meaning "great fields." Corn remains central to Navajo rituals, and corn pollen is used in all blessing ceremonies.

Conflict and cultural exchange

Though relations between Navajo and Pueblo people are cordial in most day-to-day interactions, tensions have simmered over the years – particularly between the Navajo and Hopi. In 1690, the Navajo united with Pueblo people in a revolt against the Spanish and, for a time, lived with them in small defensive pueblitos in New Mexico. But in 1868, after the Navajo's four-year incarceration at Fort Sumner, relations between the Navajo and Hopi soured fast. The reservation created for the Navajo was rapidly expanded to accommodate a rebounding Navajo population and its hungry livestock.

Eventually, Navajo grazing lands surrounded the compact cornfields and villages of the much smaller Hopi Reservation. A long and complex land dispute over boundaries and the relocation of families in some joint-use areas is still being adjudicated today, and there are ongoing concerns about how overgrazing of fragile desert grasslands by Navajo sheep and goats continues to exacerbate erosion on Navajo land.

What we now regard as traditional Navajo culture was also profoundly influenced by Europeans. The Spanish introduced not only horses but sheepherding, rug weaving and silversmithing. After the Long Walk, the Navajo

NAVAJO CODE TALKERS

Navajos have fought bravely in every major American military engagement in the last century, but their most important contribution came during World War II, when 400 Navajo Code Talkers served with the U.S. Marine Corps throughout the Pacific, sending and receiving messages in a disguised version of their native language. The code, which was never broken by the Japanese, is now recognized as having been one of the keys to victories at Iwo Jima and other major battles.

It was the brainchild of Philip Johnston, a white missionary's son who had grown up on the Navajo Reservation and spoke the language fluently. In 1942,

Navajo recruits at Camp Pendleton, California, devised their own code, using three Navajo words for each letter – e.g., ant, ax and apple for A, or badger, bear and barrel for B.

So secret was their work, Code Talkers didn't receive national recognition until 1982, when President Ronald Reagan proclaimed August 14 National Navajo Code Talkers Day. In 1999, President Bill Clinton visited the reservation and gave a speech that included a few words in Navajo code. For Navajos, the symbolism of that speech lay not so much in a recognition of their people's patriotism but in the use of a language that, for years, the U.S. government actively worked to stamp out as un-American.

adopted a version of the tiered Mother Hubbard dress they saw Army wives wearing at Fort Sumner and developed a taste for flour, canned goods and other consumer products. This created opportunities for merchants, who opened trading posts on the reservation in the 1870s. Early entrepreneurs like Lorenzo Hubbell in Ganado befriended the Navajo, became intermediaries between the tribe and federal government, and developed a market for Navajo weaving by suggesting improvements and selling finished rugs to eastern buyers. Rugs woven by women (and several men) all over the reservation now command top prices. Not far behind is the

surrounding the Pinal, Apache, Mescal and Catalina Mountains. The Eastern and Western bands of the White Mountain group occupied the area from the Pinaleno Mountains to the high plateau north and east of the White Mountains. The Cibecue, Southern Tonto and Northern Tonto groups lived in the high country from the Salt River north to present-day Flagstaff. Though they shared resources and recognized ties to each other, the bands owed no political allegiance to the larger group.

Conflicts with white settlers in the 1850s and 1860s led to the establishment of Fort Apache in the White Mountains in 1868. The White

beautiful silver jewelry made by Navajo artisans, along with pottery, kachina dolls and other crafts learned from the Pueblo people.

The Western Apache

The *Indé*, or Western Apache, are descended from the same Athabaskan stock as the Navajo and live in the mountains of Arizona. Historically, there were five groups of Western Apache. The four territorial bands of the San Carlos Apache inhabited the rolling high desert

LEFT: Navajo children learn from their elders.
ABOVE: a Pima activist protests freeway construction on the edge of the Salt River Indian Reservation.

Mountain and Cibecue Apache allied with whites and served as scouts in the wars against the Tonto, Chiricahua and Pai groups. Beginning in 1874, the federal government forced Apaches from four reservations to walk to the San Carlos Reservation, where tensions eventually arose between the 20 independent bands. In 1886, Victorio and Geronimo escaped with their bands of Chiricahua Apache and hid out in the Chiricahua Mountains and Mexico's Sierra Madre. They were forced to surrender in 1886 and were shipped to Florida. Most never returned to Arizona. Eventually, the White Mountain, Cibecue and Tonto groups were allowed to return to their own reservations. The

Tonto Apache population was much reduced, however, and merged with the Yavapai in the Verde Valley. Some members of the Eastern White Mountain band stayed on the San Carlos Apache Reservation, while others returned to the Fort Apache (now White Mountain) Reservation. The Cibecue group merged with the White Mountain Apache.

Today, Arizona's Apache live on three reservations and maintain strong links with the land. The White Mountain Apache Reservation has 10,000 tribal

PLACE YOUR BETS

Indian gaming already rakes in about $800 million annually. The figure is expected to exceed $1.3 billion – nearly a sixth of the state government's yearly budget – in the coming years.

The Tonto Apache are now officially known as the Yavapai Apache Tribe and inhabit a small reservation in the Verde Valley. While they were on the San Carlos Reservation in the 1870s, the Tonto lost most of their land to white settlers. Today, Cliff Castle Casino is the tribe's main source of income.

Like the Navajo, the Western Apache believe the world was made by the Creator, or Sun, and that it was first inhabited by animals, monsters and giants. Central to Apache belief are the *Gaan*, the Mountain Spirit

members and operates a successful logging and recreation economy. The adjoining San Carlos Reservation is slightly larger, at 1.8 million acres (730,000 hectares), but has only 8,000 residents. The San Carlos Reservation is known for its cattle and cowboys, a tradition that dates back to the 1870s, when some people accumulated their weekly allotments of beef to obtain a live steer. By the 1880s, the Indian agency was encouraging a cattle industry at San Carlos, which today has grown to some 20,000 head managed by five cattle associations. The reservation produces more cowboys than any area of comparable size in Texas or Oklahoma. The San Carlos Rodeo is one of the highlights of the year.

people, supernatural beings who live beneath sacred mountains like Mount Baldy. They serve as protectors, teachers and role models for the Apache. At puberty and healing ceremonies and other events, Gaan dancers with elaborate headdresses appear in groups of five – four *Gaan* representing each of the sacred directions and a messenger who communicates with them.

The Hopi

The Navajo and Western Apache are newcomers compared with the Hopi, whose ancestors – the *Hisatsinom* or Ancestral Puebloans – have lived on the Colorado Plateau for millennia. The Hopi moved to these stone villages, or pueblos, atop the Hopi Mesas beginning in the 1100s. Each village was founded separately during a period of contraction that saw many Pueblo clans seeking refuge in larger, more easily defended sites. Hopi identity is, therefore, complex: Hopis identify primarily with their village rather than with a single tribe. People in different villages speak different languages but have an overarching Pueblo culture centered around agriculture, seasonal ceremonies, and the making of pottery, basketry, jewelry and kachinas. Many Hopi have embraced education and professional jobs, but, unlike many Navajo, frequently stick to traditional dress and hairstyles, which, like so many aspects of Pueblo culture, have strong symbolic meaning.

Tohono and Akimel O'odham

If the Tohono O'odham (Desert People) and Akimel O'odham (Water People), who live on reservations in southern Arizona, are indeed descended from the ancient canal-building Hohokam, they rival the Hopi for ancient origins. We may never know. The Hohokam disappeared around 1400 and the O'odham encountered by the Spanish were hunter-gatherers who knew nothing of pottery making, city building and the construction of canals.

In historic times, Tohono O'odham, or Papago farmers relied on irrigation from the Santa Cruz River and dry farming at the base of bajadas, or mountain slopes. In the early 1900s, non-Indian settlers dug channels from the Santa Cruz River to intercept the water table, destroying O'odham agriculture in the process. Lawsuits filed by the tribe finally led to settlements in the 1980s that require the City of Tucson to negotiate with the O'odham on returning some of the water.

The Akimel O'odham, or Pima, who live on the Gila Indian Reservation with the Maricopa, south of Phoenix, were highly successful irrigation farmers along the Salt and Gila Rivers. They became the first agricultural entrepreneurs in Arizona during the U.S.–Mexico War, when they traded flour with the U.S. Army, and later supplied gold miners headed for California. They too saw their farms wither as white settlers dug canals and diverted water. By the late 1800s, the people who had once fed a

whole state found themselves poverty-stricken.

Coolidge Dam, constructed in 1924, was designed to return water to the Akimel O'odham but was an expensive failure. Built during a long drought, its reservoir not only never filled but prevented seasonal flooding, one of the last viable means of agriculture on the reservation. Today, the Akimel O'odham are beginning to farm again, using modified ancient methods supported by grants and outside funding.

The Colorado River Yumans

The struggle for access and control of the Colorado River was also at the root of fighting

between Quechan Indians and Spanish and later Anglo settlers. The Quechan, who had historically manned the ferry crossing at Yuma, were forced to cede control to Americans in the mid-1800s, after the construction of Fort Yuma. In the late 1800s, irrigation projects brought a wave of Anglo farmers to the desert and forced the Yumans to share newly created reservations with refugees from the Navajo, Hopi and other tribes.

The Yumans' ancestors covered their bodies in elaborate tattoos, wore shells in their ears, and made beautiful painted effigy pottery. They were guided by powerful dreams about every aspect of daily life, including institutionalized warfare. The most important battle waged by

LEFT: White Mountain Apache Rodeo.
RIGHT: a young Apache woman is painted with clay during a puberty rite known as the Sunrise Ceremony.

the Colorado River Tribes in recent times has been a legal one in the 1980s over zoning of tribal lands – a fight they won handily.

The Pai

The Yavapai, Havasupai and Hualapai tribes were nomads who once occupied nearly a third of northern and central Arizona. They speak closely related languages. The term Hualapai means Pine Tree People, Havasupai means People of the Blue Green Water, and Yavapai means People of the Sun. They believe themselves to be "the only true human beings on earth."

The Havasupai live in the western Grand

Canyon in one of the most beautiful and remote settings in the Southwest. Access to the village of Supai is by foot or mule from the rim of the canyon, or by boat from the river. The Havasupai receive provisions by mule but also farm in the canyons. Their neighbors, the Hualapai, live atop the rim and have embraced the modern world with a large-scale resort and airport. The Yavapai merged with the Tonto Apache in the Verde Valley. Both groups are known for fine basketry.

The Southern Paiute

The Southern Paiute are also superb basket makers. When encountered by John Wesley Powell during his 1869 and 1871 surveys of

the area around the Colorado River, they were still hunting and gathering seasonally on the North Rim and using tightly woven burden baskets for collecting seeds and plants, winnowing and headgear. Only the San Juan Paiute Tribe keeps the tradition alive today. They do a lively trade in Navajo wedding baskets, an essential part of Navajo nuptials. Arizona's Kaibab Paiute Tribe lives on a very small reservation north of the Grand Canyon and is embracing tourism as its main means of support.

Spanish legacy

Unlike New Mexico, which became the headquarters of Spanish government in the north in the 1600s, Arizona was never dominated by New Spain. The earliest explorers were mainly interested in finding the fabled Seven Cities of Gold. There were no such places in arid, overheated southern Arizona, only abandoned Hohokam towns melting back into the caliche soil. Poor Pimas and Papagos (today's O'odham people) wandered around the Sonoran Desert, hunting and gathering and sleeping in makeshift shelters. Warlike Yumans repelled the foreigners in the Mohave Desert along the Colorado River, and bands of Apache warriors hid in every corner of the mountains and staged lightning raids on livestock. To the north, there seemed to be nothing but mountains, mesas and the impenetrable Grand Canyon.

The conquistadores did not stick around. They hurried northeast to what is now New Mexico, where Spanish culture would change New Mexican pueblos forever, a fate that never befell Arizona's fiercely independent Hopi on their remote mesas in northern Arizona.

The mission era

Spanish missionaries returning to Arizona 150 years after the first Spanish explorers also found their work cut out for them. That Indian missions at Tumacacori and San Xavier del Bac in the Santa Cruz River valley south of Tucson were established in the 1690s was entirely due to the charisma of Father Eusebio Kino, an Italian-born Jesuit, who was warmly received in Indian communities throughout Sonora and southern Arizona. His respect for the Indians was largely undone by the Franciscan priests who replaced Jesuit missionaries in the 1700s. These priests taught Indians livestock ranching, farming, Old World construction techniques and the rituals, paraphernalia and icons of a paternalistic new religion. But this hardly mattered when the Indians were dying in huge numbers from introduced diseases and driven to exhaustion by the incessant demands of Spanish priests, soldiers and land grantees who expected the *encomienda*, or tribute, promised them by the Spanish Crown. Pima rebellions occurred twice, but even worse, Apache raiding constantly threatened the missions, even when garrisons, or presidios, were built to protect them.

In the end, Arizona proved too full of recalcitrant Indians and too wild a place for Spanish colonial efforts. When Mexico won its independence from Spain in 1821, the aristocrats who had sought their fortunes there headed home. Three hundred years after Spanish conquest, Mexico had become a country of Spanish-speaking Catholic Indians. It is this Mexican culture that pervades southern Arizona today.

Mexican influences

Ironically, Mexicans did not begin to filter up into Arizona until the land passed into American hands and U.S. soldiers were dispatched to

defend settlers from marauding Apaches. People from Sonora, many of them Yaqui Indians, now felt safe heading north to find new lands to farm, ranch and mine. The strong Sonoran influences that still pervade Tucson culture began during the early territorial period. Extended families lived in cool, thick-walled adobe compounds with saguaro and ocotillo rib ceilings, dirt floors, courtyards and shade ramadas like those preserved in downtown's colorful historic districts. People of all races socialized with each other, two-stepped to Norteña music played by mariachi bands, and ate *carne asada* (barbecued beef) and other typ-

LEFT: Hopi girls gather water, 1906. Their whorl hairstyles indicate that they are unmarried.
ABOVE: an O'odham boy at the O'odham Tash parade.

ically Sonoran dishes made with beef raised on the huge Spanish land grants along the border.

At the center of Mexican life was a deep Catholic faith, which, after being introduced by the Spanish, had taken permanent root with the miracle of the Virgin of Guadalupe, the dark-skinned madonna who appeared to an Indian man, Juan Diego, in 1531. The Virgin of Guadalupe is a ubiquitous presence throughout southern Arizona, in colorful murals, shrines and dedicated churches. The miracle of Guadalupe is celebrated every December 12 with food, music, prayer and a midnight Mass.

Most families still celebrate a daughter's *quinceañera*, the traditional puberty observance that probably dates back to Indian "coming of age" ceremonies not unlike those of the Navajo and Apache tribes. Another pre-Columbian ritual that remains popular is the Day of the Dead, held around November 1, All Souls Day. Celebrants honor the deceased, celebrate life, and acknowledge death by lighting candles, decorating graves, and offering food at altars, along with sugar representations of skulls. Other important festivities in Hispanic culture include Cinco de Mayo, the Fifth of May, which commemorates the Battle of Puebla, and Mexican Independence Day, or Fiestas Patrias, observed on September 16, the day in 1810 when Padre Miguel Hidalgo y Costilla called on Mexicans to throw off Spanish rule.

Unlike the Mexican peasants and laborers attracted to the agricultural fields of Phoenix, those who came to Tucson were often from ambitious, upper-class Sonoran families. One such immigrant was Federico Ronstadt, the son of a Sonoran mother and German father, who had trained as an engineer in his native land. Ronstadt opened a successful coach works in Tucson and, like Sam Hughes, became one of Tucson's founding fathers. Future generations of Ronstadts went on to fame and fortune, too. Federico's daughter was an opera singer with

A TASTE OF MEXICO

It's a balmy summer night at El Charro, Tucson's oldest Mexican restaurant. Waiters move through the old adobe bearing warm tortilla chips, guacamole and salsa – a piquant blend of chopped tomatoes, onions, jalapeño peppers and cilantro. Diners are tucking into platters of meat- and cheese-filled tacos, enchiladas, tamales, flautas, burritos and chiles rellenos, accompanied by rice, beans, flour tortillas and sopapillas, doughy deep-fried puffs doused with honey. The more adventurous are trying the house specialty, carne seca – sun-dried beef simmered with onions and peppers – and flan, a creamy custard.

Ranch-style, Sonoran beef dishes have been a staple since Arizona was part of Mexico. Chile colorado and chile verde (red and green chile beef stew) are longtime favorites. But other Mexican regional dishes are increasingly popular: huachinango à la Veracruzana, fish simmered in a sauce of garlic, tomatoes, capers and nutmeg from Veracruz; pan de cazon, a kind of shark-and-bean sandwich from the Yucatan; birria, a goat pot roast from Guadalajara.

At the heart of most dishes is the alpha and omega of Mexican spices: the chile pepper, which has been grown by Indians in Central America for thousands of years. Ranging from incendiary orange Habañeros to mild Anaheims, chiles add complexity to dishes that bring the tastebuds alive.

an international reputation. His great-granddaughter is the pop singer Linda Ronstadt.

Worldwide appeal

Arizona attracted a great variety of other immigrants as well, some seeking refuge, others seeking fortune or adventure in the far West. Even before the Civil War, African-Americans were escaping to Arizona to find a new life. Wiley Box and his wife came to Tucson from Louisiana in the 1850s. A runaway slave named Ben McClendon found gold in the Superstition Mountains in 1862. In territorial times, as many as a quarter of Arizona's cowboys were black.

soldiers." The 24th and 25th Infantry regiments, and 9th and 10th Cavalry regiments, were all stationed at Fort Huachuca, as was the first black graduate of West Point, Henry O. Flipper. Until the 1890s, blacks constituted 20 percent of all cavalry forces on the American frontier.

The promise of overnight riches drew prospectors from all over the world, making mining one of the most multicultural occupations in the West. A gold rush along Arizona's Gila River in the 1850s lured many hopefuls from California, including Chinese cooks, laundry workers and miners as well as Jewish traders, who set up shop in the boomtown of

They included John Swain of Tombstone, who rode with Cochise Sheriff "Texas" John Slaughter; Nat Love, who claimed to be Deadwood Dick, the fictitious hero of 33 dime novels; and Isom Dart, a black cowboy who was shot dead in 1903 for cattle rustling. Black soldiers were deployed by the U.S. Army during the Apache Wars and were also used by General George Pershing when he rode into Mexico to chase Pancho Villa. Their physique and character so impressed the Apache, they called them "buffalo

LEFT: Holy Trinity Monastery, St. David. Catholicism has a long tenure in southern Arizona.
ABOVE: mariachi band, St. Augustine Cathedral, Tucson.

Gila City. A 1918 survey in the copper-mining town of Jerome found that foreign-born mine workers outnumbered Americans by more than two to one. The nationalities listed on the report included 401 Mexicans, 393 Americans, 96 Slavs, 98 Spaniards, 60 Austrians, 57 Italians, 53 Irish and 32 Serbs. The ethnic makeup of Bisbee in southeastern Arizona was equally diverse.

Immigrants continue to pour into Arizona, some illegally, smuggled over the Mexican border by "coyotes" in order to labor namelessly in the underground economy, others attracted by high-tech jobs with executive salaries. Either way, it's a typically American story. Where opportunity lies, diversity is not far behind. ❏

American Indian Art: A Buyer's Guide

The quality of Indian craftsmanship varies from artist to artist and from piece to piece. Obviously, the finer the workmanship, design and materials, the more a piece is worth. And, while it's true that beauty is in the eye of the beholder — and that it is sometimes the imperfections of a work that make it most endearing — there are a few essential points you may wish to keep in mind when judging arts and crafts.

can fool an inexperienced eye. Jewelry should look clean and finished. Check the piece for file marks, sloppy soldering and other irregularities. Check the stones for cracks, pits or discoloration, and make sure the settings are adequate to hold the stones.

Pottery

Traditional Indian pottery is made by hand without a potter's wheel, painted with natural dyes, and fired over an open flame. The first thing you should ask about pottery is whether it is handmade or manufactured. Because the price of handmade pottery is so high, manufactured (or "ceramic") pots

Jewelry

Most Navajo and Hopi jewelry is made with silver and semiprecious stones. The Hopi are known for the "overlay" style in which a design is cut out of a sheet of silver and welded onto a blackened layer below. The Navajo are best-known for their work with silver and turquoise and such distinctive forms as "squash blossom" necklaces and concha belts. Be sure to ask what kind of silver you are buying. If it is sterling, there should be a small stamp on the back. Nickel silver, a lower grade alloy, is also sometimes used.

You should also ask the seller to identify the types of stones that are used. Be especially careful of turquoise; various forms of mock turquoise

have become quite common. They are often hand-painted in the traditional way and – so long as you know what you're buying – can be quite beautiful. Most Indian vendors make a point of distinguishing between handmade and manufactured pottery. Gift shops may not always be so scrupulous. Manufactured pots tend to be lighter in color and weight and uniform in size and shape.

If you're shopping for handmade pottery, look for a graceful, symmetrical form, fairly thin walls, and precise, neatly applied decoration. As always, watch out for irregularities: cracks, discoloration, bumps or pits in the clay, lopsidedness, slanted or uneven decorations. Keep in mind that firing clouds, which usually appear as dark smudges, are sometimes quite desirable, even though many potters consider them a problem.

Basketry

Fine, handmade baskets are quite rare these days, but there are still a few Indian people who are producing exquisite traditional work. First of all, make sure you are buying an American Indian basket. Imports from Africa, Latin America and Asia have found there way into the Southwest and occasionally crop up next to genuine American Indian work without any explanation.

There are basically two types of basketry: coiled and woven. In both cases, look for tight, even and

Some use a mixture of commercial products and traditional techniques. In any case, the finished product should be tightly woven, with a "balanced tension" of design and color.

The rug or blanket should have a smooth texture and the corners should not curl. It should also have fairly even edges (all four corners should meet when folded). Ask if the rug is 100 percent wool. Some weavers will use cotton or synthetic fibers in the warp. You should also know if the dyes are vegetal, commercial or both. Commercial dyes tend to give brighter, more saturated colors. Vegetal dyes are subtler and made by hand.

sturdy construction, a pleasing shape, and clear and even designs. To test the tightness of the weave, hold the basket up to the light. You should also check how the basket was started; the first coil should not stick out or be loose.

Weaving

Again, be absolutely sure you are buying Indian work. The popularity of Navajo rugs has created an entire industry of imitations. A few Navajo weavers still do their own washing, carding, dyeing and spinning, but most buy prepared wool.

LEFT: Navajo sandpainting; kachina doll.
ABOVE: pictorial-style Navajo rug.

Kachina carving

Although most often associated with the Hopi, kachina dolls are also made by other Pueblo people as well as by the Navajo. The most valuable kachina dolls are carved from a single piece of cottonwood root. Less expensive pieces may have separate arms or legs and possibly leather, feather or other adornments attached to the figure. Most reputable dealers will tell you if the figure is Hopi-made. Many people feel that Navajo kachinas are less authentic and therefore less valuable, but considering the high price of Hopi work (a good kachina doll will start at $300–$400), Navajo work may be a reasonable option. As with any purchase, let your eyes, conscience and wallet be your guide. ❏

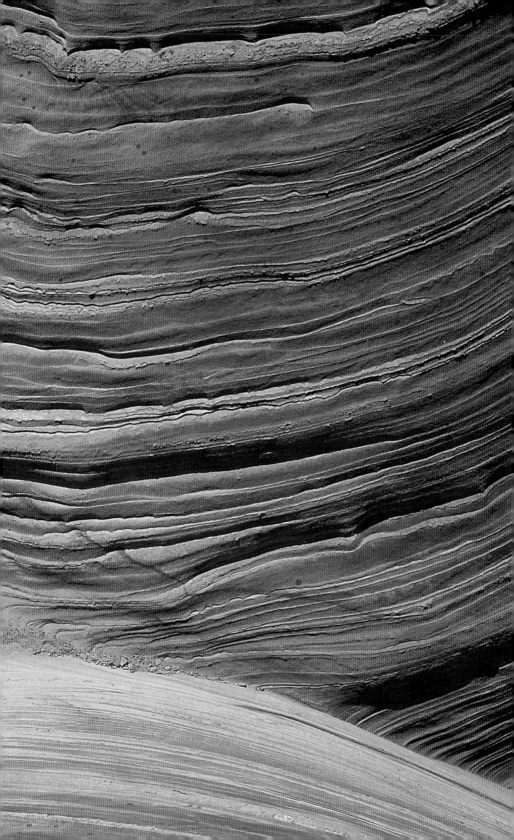

THE NAKED EARTH

Arizona bares its geological bones in some of
the West's most spectacular landscapes

For Arizona's Indian tribes, the state's mountains, mesas and eroded formations aren't just rocks; they are sacred touchstones. The Tohono O'odham believe their creator god lives on Baboquivari Peak near Tucson. Traditional Navajo rarely feel at home beyond the boundaries of the four sacred mountains that encircle their homeland and view rock formations as petrified gods, monsters or the settings of creation myths and legendary battles. Hopi dances honor the kachinas, spirit helpers whose summer home is the San Francisco Peaks near Flagstaff and whose intercession with the creator spirit ensures good crops and survival. The Paiute learn the song of every rock in the territory they "own" and act as caretakers of the natural world.

You don't have to be an Indian to feel the drama of this desert landscape. Thousands make pilgrimages to Sedona each year seeking to be healed by mud, crystals and the powerful vortexes said to vibrate out of the red rocks. Geologists make their own pilgrimages to view the world's oldest and best-preserved rock formations in the Grand Canyon. Miners continue to risk their lives to extract precious minerals from within the earth. A caver shines his headlamp through a tiny opening deep beneath the Whetstone Mountains, discovers an elaborate, untouched limestone cave system laid out in front of him, and spends 14 years fighting to protect it, as if it were his firstborn child.

A tale of two regions

Arizona's extraordinary geology can be explained partly by its geographic location between the faults that created the Rocky Mountains and Sierra Nevada, its diverse topography (a 12,000-ft/3,700-meter elevation span), and its dry climate, which leads to

PRECEDING PAGES: a backpacker relaxes in the petrified sand dunes of the Paria River region.
LEFT: Matkatamiba Canyon, Grand Canyon National Park.
RIGHT: Vishnu schist is the oldest rock in Grand Canyon.

unvegetated rocks that clearly show what's going on in the ground beneath our feet. The state divides neatly into two broad geological provinces: the basin-and-range country of southern Arizona's deserts and northern Arizona's Colorado Plateau region.

The Colorado Plateau, the dramatically

carved sandstone country of the north, covers 130,000 square miles (340,000 sq km) of Arizona, Utah, Colorado and New Mexico. A relatively stable, monolithic landmass a mile high and rising, it began to be pushed up about 75 million years ago, when the collision of the Pacific and North American Plates on which the continent sits reverberated east. This caused movement in faults that forced up the modern Rocky Mountains, a process known as the Laramide Orogeny. Localized uplifts split the region into distinct highland areas known as the Coconino, Kaibab, Kanab, Shivwits, Kaibito, Defiance, and Paria Plateaus.

The area has been subject to continued volcanism, visible as lava flows in the western Grand Canyon, along the southern edge of the plateau at the 2,000-foot-high (600-meter) Mogollon Rim, and as volcanic necks, dikes and other magma-intruded rocks and upwarps across the Navajo and Hopi Reservations. At Flagstaff, hundreds of cinder cones were thrown up in the large San Francisco Volcanic Field. The state's highest point, 12,633-foot (3,850-meter) Humphreys Peak, is part of the San Francisco Peaks, an ancient collapsed stratovolcano. To the east, Sunset Crater Volcano, which erupted between AD 1064 and 1065, was given its evocative name by geologist John

Wesley Powell, the first man to run the Colorado River through the Grand Canyon and explore the region in 1869.

Carving the canyon

The Grand Canyon, centerpiece of the Colorado Plateau, was carved by the Colorado River only within the past 4.7 million to 1.7 million years. The ancestral Colorado flowed south into Arizona from Utah, staying east of the Kaibab Upwarp. Another stream flowed west of the Kaibab Upwarp, cut back into the plateau, and "captured" the Colorado, which turned westward to its present position through the newer, steeper route. At this point, sediment-heavy

waters began to carve the Grand Canyon in earnest, deepening the chasm to its present mile depth. The Colorado, the "Red River" in Spanish, churned tawny and soupy with sediments that it carried all the way to the Gulf of California. Downcutting has slowed now that the river has reached resistant schists at the bottom of the canyon and its erosive force has been tamed by Glen Canyon Dam.

Different types of erosion – tributary streams, flashfloods, rockfalls, rain, ice, dust, wind, animal movements – have been responsible for widening the canyon to its 10-mile (16-km) width. Differential erosion of rocks of various composition, thickness and hardness have created ledges, cliffs, dramatic mesas, buttes, totems, spires and other features.

The Little Colorado River now runs along the ancestral course of the Colorado, which it joins within the canyon. The Little Colorado is today a major river on the Navajo Reservation, winding through the Painted Desert and tumbling over Grand Falls during heavy spring snowmelt. It has carved its own beautiful gorge, visible just west of Cameron. The Paria River, on the Utah–Arizona border, has also gouged out a distinctive course for itself through a uniform bed of sandstone, creating a picturesque 2,000-foot-deep (600-meter) slot canyon barely 30 feet (9-meters) wide, in which sunlight rarely reaches the sandy floor.

Sandstone is frequently stained with desert varnish, a shiny dark brown or black coating made up of manganese oxides (black) and iron oxides (reddish brown). It is unclear how the manganese and iron, which are derived from sources outside the rock, are bonded to the rock surface. Many geologists now believe that the process involves bacteria that oxidize minerals and cement them to the rock; others believe that a purely chemical reaction occurs between the iron, manganese and water. New evidence points to a combination of both.

Layer upon layer

Almost half of the earth's 4.5-billion-year history is contained within the horizontal layer cake of sedimentary rocks found in the Grand Canyon. The 1.7-billion-year-old Vishnu Schist in the Inner Canyon was laid down as sandstone, shale and limestone, interleafed with lava flows, in a sea that washed onto a shore at the western edge of the continent. These rocks were buried up to 12 miles (19 km) deep, then uplifted and folded into a mountain chain, injected with veins of molten rock, eroded to their roots, redeposited, and then uplifted and folded again. This created strata that are today banded and contorted in some places, and platey and shiny in others. The earliest fossils are found here – large mats of algae known as stromatolites.

Resting directly on top of the Vishnu Schist are sandstones that are only 545 million years old.

EARTH MOVER

Though restrained by Glen Canyon and Hoover dams, the Colorado River continues to rasp away at the Grand Canyon, transporting an average of half a million tons of sand and silt per day.

crinoids and trilobites up to 3 inches (8 cm) in size – the first organisms on the planet to have developed a skeleton.

During the Devonian Period (408–360 million years ago), the North American continent, which was slowly moving northward, straddled the equator, and a tropical sea covered much of the present-day Southwest. Fish with armored heads began to appear during this time, which has led geologists to call the Devonian the Age of Fishes.

old. What happened to the intervening 1.2 billion years of rocks? Were none deposited? Were they laid down and then eroded away? The Great Unconformity, as it is called, is one of the mysteries of the Grand Canyon.

These 500-million-year-old layers of sandstone were deposited at the start of the Paleozoic era, at the edge of a Cambrian sea. The Tapeats Sandstone, Bright Angel Shale, and Muav and Temple Butte Limestones contain fossil sponges, brachiopods, mollusks, corals,

The Redwall Limestone, formed in Mississippian times (365–330 million years ago), contains small invertebrate creatures known as crinoids, related to sand dollars and sea urchins, that looked like plants, with a base, a stem and a flowerlike top. It is a gray rock stained red by iron deposits in overlying Supai rocks, a group of siltstones and sandstones produced in a low, swampy environment, and the Hermit Shale, which was deposited about 280 million years ago.

Near the rim of the canyon is the yellow, crossbedded Coconino Sandstone, which was deposited in a desert filled with large sand dunes. The Toroweap and Kaibab Formations,

LEFT: petrified logs jam an arroyo in the Painted Desert. **ABOVE:** spring runoff sends a torrent of muddy water over the Grand Falls of the Little Colorado River.

laid down in Permian times (286–245 million years ago), make up the rim of the canyon. The fossil-rich Kaibab forms terraces that are cloaked with ponderosa pine forests across much of northern Arizona.

Where dinosaurs walked

Younger rocks of the warm, tropical Triassic era (245–208 million years ago) dominate the Navajo Reservation. The soft, banded Moenkopi Formation was born in a delta, when stream sediments mixed with limy marine deposits. It is barely distinguishable from the colorful overlying Chinle Formation, which is well exposed near Canyon de Chelly. A crumbly purple, yellow, and brown formation, the Chinle contains large quantities of uranium, produced from groundwater and likely leached out of volcanic ash. Certain plants, such as yellow feathery princes plume and milkvetches, are a good indication that uranium is present in soil.

The Chinle also preserves a lot of petrified wood, formed in a process similar to that of uranium, but with groundwater that was silica-rich, creating quartz. During this era, the first dinosaurs and mammals appeared. Fossilized dinosaur skeletons are often found preserved

TRIASSIC PARK

Her name is Gertie, and she is one of the oldest dinosaurs known to science. When her bones were found eroding out of the crumbling hills of Petrified Forest National Park in 1984, she had been resting silently beneath the Painted Desert for 220 million years.

Gertie was a chindesaur – a small, fast-moving dinosaur that ate flesh and walked on two feet – and she represented a world in transition, from gentle herbivores like the heavily armored aetosaur to giant carnivores. Even the 30-foot-long (9-meter) crocodile-like phytosaur, which patiently stalked its prey in the swamps, could not compete. Gertie, and descendants such as the three-toed,

10-foot-tall (3-meter) dilophosaurs, whose tracks are preserved in the red sandstone west of Tuba City, ruled the world for another 150 million years.

The park's Rainbow Forest Museum and the Museum of Northern Arizona in Flagstaff have exhibits of dinosaur skeletons and eggs. Arizona's southern deserts have also yielded their share of dinosaur remains. The 97 million-year-old *Sonorasaurus thompsoni*, a new species of brachiosaur, was recently found in the Sonoran Desert and will be displayed at the Arizona-Sonora Desert Museum. Mesa Southwest Museum, near Phoenix, is also worth a visit. It has one of the largest exhibits of dinosaur skeletons in the West.

in the Chinle Formation, while dinosaur tracks are nearly always found in the red Kayenta Formation, a rock that was laid down in damp, interdunal areas as the climate dried and desert sand dunes started piling up.

Deserts at the end of the Permian era, 260 million years ago, formed the De Chelly and Wingate Sandstones that make up the buttes, totems and mesas in Monument Valley. A significant period of desertification also took place during the Jurassic period (208–144 million years ago), when a Sahara-like desert of 3,000-foot-high (900-meter) sand dunes covered 150,000 square miles (390,000 sq km) of the

columbines, which also contribute to the destabilization of overlying rocks.

Volcanic remnants

Igneous intrusions of hot molten lava (magma) along faults beneath heavy layers of sandstone have pushed up and deformed much of the area in and around Monument Valley into anticlines (upwarps), monoclines (dropping on one side), and synclines (downwarps). Also clearly visible on the horizon are laccolithic ranges like Navajo Mountain, where magma has risen along a zone of weakness, spread laterally between sedimentary layers, pushed

West, eventually hardening into the beautiful pink Navajo Sandstone. Dune-formed sandstones have been eroded into distinctive shapes by the "exfoliation" process that occurs in porous sandstone. Groundwater passes easily through the rock and, when it encounters the impervious layers below, exits as dripping springs and seeps that undermine the sandstone, causing it to peel away like an onion.

Water-loving plants are attracted to these seeps, where they form hanging gardens of moss, maidenhair fern, monkeyflower and

ABOVE: the ruddy, water-sculpted walls of Oak Creek Canyon rise above the surrounding forest.

them up into a dome, and eventually been uncovered by erosion.

A San Juan River trip, from Mexican Hat to Clay Hills Crossing, offers an indispensable opportunity to view these rock strata and float through the Goosenecks of the San Juan, technically an entrenched meander, where uplift of the Colorado Plateau has caused an older river to cut down several thousand feet into its Cedar Mesa Sandstone course and form hairpin bends. Rivers won't meander for long without seeking a more direct route past obstacles in their way. In this case, the grinding action of the river currents punches a hole in a meander wall, widens it, and eventually leaves behind a natural bridge like those at nearby Natural Bridges and Rainbow Bridge National Monuments. Natural bridges are water formed; arches are formed by erosion along joints in sandstone, forming linear fins and eventually arches.

Basin and range

Southern Arizona's basin-and-range country is much younger and more mobile than the Colorado Plateau and largely the result of pulling apart, not pushing up. Starting about 20 million years ago, the Earth's crust beneath these deserts began to extend, stretch thin, overheat, and crack along a roughly north-south trend.

known as rhyolite. Subsequent erosion by water, ice and wind sculpted the rhyolite into columns, balanced rocks and hoodoos. Five to 13 million years later, lava and ash spewed out of a volcano in the southwestern part of the state. The light and dark rocks make up the Ajo and Bates Mountains of Organ Pipe Cactus National Monument.

Volcanic action along a northwest-southeast trend within sedimentary rocks, such as limestones, is thought to be the reason Arizona has such huge deposits of porphyry copper. One theory is that the continent drifted northwest over a hot spot in the Earth's mantle. Copper

Some blocks of earth started to break and tilt, forcing chunks of land to rise and others to drop. The ones that dropped formed the basins and began to fill with sediments washing down in huge alluvial fans called bajadas from the Huachucas, Chiricahuas, Dragoons and other sky island ranges. Some basins contain 15,000 feet (4,600 meters) of fill. Crustal movement along these faults continues to the present day.

One of southeastern Arizona's most violent volcanic events occurred 27 million years ago, when six ash flows shot out of Turkey Creek Caldera near present-day Chiricahua National Monument, producing a 2,000-foot-thick (600-meter) layer of dark volcanic rock,

ores may have been the last substances to crystallize out of the magma. Prior to crystallization, the copper-bearing minerals dissolved in the hot water that permeates most magma, making them able to penetrate narrow fissures and fractures in the channels of adjacent rocks.

Most significant copper deposits were injected by a molten granite batholith, or deep igneous intrusion, into nearby limestone rocks, such as the Mule Mountains around Bisbee, where beautiful turquoise malachite deposits have been found. ❏

ABOVE: erosion exposes bands of colorful sediments in Coal Canyon on the Navajo Reservation.

Arizona Volcanoes

When hot, molten rock, or magma, rises along vents and erupts at the Earth's surface, an extrusive mountain, or volcano, is created. Volcanoes that erupt violently and shower ash and lava over a large area are called composite, or strato, volcanoes and have a classic cone shape. Volcanoes that erupt in slow-moving lava flows and build up gradually are known as shield volcanoes.

Cinder cones erupt along side vents, which explains why they seem to cluster in chorus lines around the mother volcano. Magma that never reaches the surface forms an intrusive, domed mountain, or laccolith. Laccoliths are common on the Arizona–Utah border, at places like Navajo Mountain on the Navajo Reservation, where sedimentary layers are thick and hard to break through. Dark, jagged volcanic "necks" or "plugs" provide additional evidence of older volcanism on the Colorado Plateau. Erosion has uncovered the volcanic cores inside the sediments at places like Agathla Peak in Monument Valley, Church Rock in nearby Kayenta, and the Hopi Mesas.

Volcanic activity is greatest at the southern margin of the Colorado Plateau and may indicate that volatile basin and range activity in the southern part of the state is beginning to affect the relatively stable plateau along the Mogollon Rim, the 2,000-foot-high (600-meter) dividing line between the low deserts and the high country. Arizona's highest mountains are all found here. The highest, 12,633-foot (3,850-meter) Humphreys Peak, one of the San Francisco Peaks outside Flagstaff, is a stratovolcano that was built of lava and ash over a period of 1½ million years.

The Peaks stopped erupting about 400,000 years ago, but they are skirted by a 2,300-square-mile (6,000-sq-km) volcanic field – the largest in the United States – containing more than 400 younger cinder cones. The best known is 1,000-foot-high (305-meter) Sunset Crater. It was one of the last volcanoes to erupt, some 900 years ago, leaving behind lava flows that were used by the Sinagua Indians as mulch for their crops.

The state's second highest peak, 11,403-foot (3,476-meter) Baldy Peak, is at the center of the White Mountain Volcanic Field, which erupted 8 million years ago. The nearby 1,158-square-mile (3,000-sq-km) Springerville Volcanic Field is the third largest in the continental United States and contains 405 vents, craters, and shield volcanoes, which began erupting 3 million years ago. The state's third highest mountain, 10,912-foot (3,326-meter) Escudilla Mountain, is found here.

Just below the Mogollon Rim, 10,720-foot-high (3,270-meter) Mount Graham, the tallest of the Pinaleno Mountains, towers 8,000 feet (2,400-meter) above the cottonfields of Safford – the greatest vertical rise in Arizona. The most violent volcanic episode in southern Arizona's geological history, the eruption of Turkey Creek Caldera, occurred nearby about 27 million years ago. Ash covered a large area and settled as rhyolite, which

later eroded into the strange totems and balanced rocks of the Chiricahua Mountains.

Southern Arizona's Basin and Range topography has been described as a swarm of "giant caterpillars marching northwest," so linear are the Chiricahuas, Huachucas, Dragoons, and other volcanic ranges of this region. The Earth's crust is undergoing far more heating, extension and deformation here than anywhere else in the state. The result is younger and craggier mountains, rising as "sky islands" from flat desert basins. The clarity of the desert air has attracted astronomers, perhaps since ancient times. Powerful telescopes are found atop Kitt Peak in the Baboquivari Mountains, Whipple Observatory in the Santa Ritas and Mount Graham in the Pinalenos. ❏

RIGHT: cinder cones rise near the San Francisco Peaks.

DESERT LIFE

Though Arizona's deserts may at first seem stark and lifeless, they sustain a
fascinating array of plants and animals adapted to extreme heat and aridity

Spanning 118,000 square miles (306,000 sq km), and with elevations ranging from 70 feet (21 meters) above sea level at Yuma to 12,643 feet (3,854 meters) at Humphreys Peak near Flagstaff, Arizona is much more than the searingly hot desert flats, saguaro cacti and howling coyotes of popular myth. In fact, it is the most biologically diverse state in the American Southwest, with 137 species of mammals, 434 different species of birds, 48 snake species, 41 lizard species, 22 types of amphibians, thousands of arthropods and a stunning 3,370 species of plants.

Such diversity can be attributed to the state's wide range of habitats, which include four converging deserts – the Sonoran, Chihuahuan, Great Basin and Mohave – basin-and-range topography, and unusual ecozones, from lava flows to caves, where species have had to make special adaptations. In addition, a large number of plants and animals have migrated permanently north of the US–Mexico border to occupy protected niches in riparian canyon corridors.

Precious water

This is remarkable because when one thinks about Arizona, one instantly thinks of aridity. The Sonoran Desert of southern Arizona is found at the 30th parallel north of the equator, which creates atmospheric circulation patterns that affect world climate and lead to desertification. Another leading factor is that Arizona is a long way from the coast, too far to benefit from moisture. Moreover, any coastal moisture it might have received is effectively blocked by California's 14,000-foot (4,300-meter) Sierra Nevada, placing the Grand Canyon State in a rain shadow. Even high-elevation areas often receive less than 15 inches (38 cm) of precipitation a year – the high desert range.

Finding and holding on to water is what life

is all about here, especially for those plants and animals that, unlike people, birds and larger predators such as wide-ranging coyotes and mountain lions, cannot leave. Desert plants and animals have evolved a variety of strategies for survival, many so strange one can only marvel at nature's ingenuity. The kangaroo rat gets all

its water from seeds. Spadefoot toads encase themselves in slime in the bottom of dried-up potholes, or tinajas, and wait months for heavy rains. Cacti gave up leaves in favor of protective spines and large water-saving waxy trunks that also help them photosynthesize food.

"In the desert… the very fauna and flora proclaim that one can have a great deal of certain things while having very little of others," observed naturalist Joseph Wood Krutch in *The Desert Year*. "[T]hat one kind of scarcity is compatible with, perhaps even a necessary condition of, another kind of plenty… that plenty of light and plenty of space may go with a scarcity of water."

LEFT: a western patch-nosed snake slides across a cactus in pursuit of lizards and other snakes.
RIGHT: ringtail cats aren't cats at all but relatives of the raccoon that feed on small mammals, insects and fruit.

The lay of the land

The southern part of the state is "basin and range," a land of craggy, young volcanic mountains that form verdant "sky islands" above huge desert basins and ephemeral "playa" wetlands, such as those around Willcox, that attract thousands of migratory waterfowl each winter. By contrast, northern Arizona's Colorado Plateau soars from 5,000 to 12,000 feet (1,500–3,600 meters) in a sprawling high country of volcanic peaks and uplifted plateaus, expansive ponderosa pine forest, glittering lakes, alpine meadows and sandstone canyons carved by the Colorado River and its tributaries. In between,

at 3,500 to 5,000 feet (1,100–1,500 meters), are sweeping grasslands around the fast-growing communities of central Arizona's Payson and Prescott and the US–Mexico border around Patagonia (Arizona's historic cattle country), transitioning to pinyon-juniper dwarf forest between 5,500 and 7,000 feet (1,700–2,100 meters) in areas like Sedona on the Mogollon Rim.

Most of southern Arizona is in the Sonoran Desert, at 10,000 years old a relatively young desert, averaging 3,000 feet (900 meters) in elevation, that slices diagonally from the southwest quarter of Arizona down to the Sea of Cortez in Sonora, Mexico, as far as the Sierra Madre in the east and the lower southeast corner of California

on the west. Because of its location, the Sonoran receives moisture twice a year – summer "monsoons," as they are dubbed (incorrectly), from July to September, and winter storms – making it the greenest of the West's deserts.

In the drier west deserts, around Organ Pipe Cactus National Monument, dominant plants include foothill paloverde, saguaro, cholla, and ironwood; in areas with more moisture, such as the Arizona Uplands around Tucson, add to the mix blue paloverde, mesquite, catclaw, desert willow, and desert hackberry, and shrubs such as bursage, creosote, jojoba and brittlebush. When previous summer and early winter rains have been adequate, the Sonoran no longer seems a desert but a flower garden, with poppies, brittlebush, desert marigolds, lupines, fairyduster, fleabane and other beauties blooming in waves, beginning in February.

A lush desert

More than 100 species of cactus call the Sonoran home, including organ pipe, Mexican senita, cholla, pricklypear, beavertail, pincushion, claret cup, hedgehog, and the symbol of the Sonoran Desert: the many-limbed saguaro. Cacti like these are the most successfully adapted of all desert plants. They take advantage of infrequent but hard rains by employing shallow root networks to suck up water, which is then conserved, accordion-like, in the gelatinous tissues of their waxy trunks. Cacti use their broad trunks to photosynthesize sunlight for food and have modified leaves into spines, which are much more useful as protection.

Three-quarters of desert animals are nocturnal. Your best chance of sighting a javelina, coati, kit fox, raccoon, bobcat, badger, coyote or a rare desert bighorn sheep is to visit a water hole in the cool dusk or dawn hours, or pay a visit to the Arizona-Sonora Desert Museum, west of Tucson, to view desert creatures in naturally landscaped enclosures. More than 400 species of birds live in the Sonoran Desert and include the topknotted Gambel's quail, roadrunner (the state bird), mourning dove, phainopepla and birds that carve out cool nests in saguaro trunks, such as the Gila woodpecker, northern flicker, cactus wren, curved-bill thrasher and elf owl. Birds of prey and other avian species that can move easily from shade to sun are visible in daytime desert skies soaring on thermals. Often spotted are Harris's and red-tailed hawks, peregrine falcons and golden eagles on the lookout for darting jackrabbits, cottontails or ground squirrels.

Be careful where you walk and put your hands during daytime hikes. Mottle-skinned rattlesnakes, brightly hued collared lizards, whiptails, chuckwallas and the impressive-looking Gila monster, North America's only venemous lizard, keep cool under rocks and bushes during the day and don't become active until twilight, when they can regulate body temperature more comfortably. Lizards have a variety of strategies to evade capture, including detaching their tails when caught and later growing a new one. Gila monsters can live for several years on fat stored in their tails.

THE SCORPION'S STING

Only one of Arizona's 30 scorpion species, the bark scorpion, is considered life-threatening, though no deaths have been attributed to the species in the state for more than 30 years.

tively long, chilly winters, with occasional snowfalls that melt quickly. As with the Sonoran Desert, summer temperatures in the Chihuahuan exceed 100°F (38°C) but are cooled by violent summer monsoons, which drop 8–12 inches (20–31 cm) of annual rainfall in places like Bisbee, Tombstone and the Willcox Playa area. Limestone caverns, such as those at Kartchner Caverns State Park near Benson, are found in this area, which was inundated by a Permian Sea 250 million years ago. Ocotillo, pricklypear and

An unforgiving environment

Parts of southeastern Arizona are in the Chihuahuan Desert, two-thirds of which is found in Mexico. At a mean elevation of 3,500 to 5,000 feet (1,100–1,500 meters), this desert has rela-

LEFT: agave blossoms attract insects and birds.
ABOVE: the kit fox, a nocturnal predator about the size of a cat, uses its large ears to cool its body temperature.

cholla cactus do well in these calcium-rich soils. The signature vegetation of the desert is the lechuguilla agave, which has thick spikes rising from a rosette of fleshy, swordlike "leaves." After exiting the Mule Mountains tunnel, north of Bisbee, watch as the Chihuahuan Desert starts to blend with the Sonoran, with ocotillo and agave neighboring with saguaro.

Mohave and Great Basin

The Mohave Desert extends into Arizona along the Colorado River on Arizona's western border. The least colorful and most overheated of all the deserts in summer, the Mohave can transform overnight into a wildflower extravaganza with enough rainfall. Ironwood, desert holly, creosote, blackbrush and bursage are spaced evenly to take advantage of available moisture. The indicator species here is the shaggy Joshua tree, a giant yucca named by Bible-minded Mormons passing through in the 1800s. Relict palm trees have found a niche in a canyon in the Kofa Mountains, along with a thriving population of endangered desert bighorn sheep. A herd of about 500 bighorns lives in Cabeza Prieta National Wildlife Refuge, on the U.S.–Mexico border. Every June, as temperatures soar, volunteers count the sheep – the true calling of "desert rats."

The northwestern corner of Arizona is primarily Great Basin desert, which extends all the way to eastern Utah and Oregon. A cool desert, found at elevations of 4,000 feet (1,200 meters) or higher, the Great Basin was once dominated by lush, tall native bunchgrasses such as Indian rice grass, sideoats and blue grama. Today, most of these native grasses have given way to disturbance species such as sagebrush, saltbush, snakeweed, rabbitbrush and the ubiquitous cheatgrass after more than a century of grazing by cattle and sheep. Grasslands in protected parcels of southern Arizona like Las Cienegas National Conservation Area are beginning to recover.

SAGUAROS: GIANTS OF THE DESERT

The many-armed saguaro cactus seems as timeless as the Sonoran Desert it inhabits. Indeed, saguaros may live for more than 150 years, given warm southern exposures and sufficient rain on mountain slopes, or bajadas. They don't even begin to grow their famous appendages until they are 75 years old. Their shallow root network sucks up moisture into barrel-like torsos that swell like an accordion, storing as much as 200 gallons (750 liters) of water.

Saguaros take summer highs in excess of 100°F (38°C) and freezing winter temperatures in their stride. Spines protect them from intruders, trap cool air, provide shade, and along with the cacti's waxy coating, protect them from dehydration. Unlike leafy plants, saguaros photosynthesize food along their arms and trunks, the latter often reaching 35–40 feet (11–12 meters) in height. In spring, saguaros sprout glorious white blossoms that attract visiting Mexican long-nosed bats, which pollinate the cactus with their wings as they sip nectar. In late summer, saguaros sport ruby-red fruit that, for centuries, have been harvested and made into syrup and jelly by the Tohono O'odham. Their ancestors made shelters from saguaro ribs, glue from the flowers, and treated arthritis with saguaro poultices. Urban sprawl, pollution, vandalism and theft threaten saguaros. Millions are protected in Saguaro National Park, outside Tucson.

Animal magnetism

Arizona's southern desert "sky islands," with their higher elevations and thick stands of evergreen-deciduous forest, are a powerful magnet for living things trying to escape the heat of the desert. For every 1,000 feet (300 meters) gain in elevation, the temperature drops 4°F (2°C) and precipitation increases about 4 inches (10 cm). In the sheltered canyons of the Chiricahua and Huachuca Mountains, near the Mexican border, Arizona cypress and alligator juniper mingle with Mexican natives like Chihuahua and Apache pine, while at higher elevations, Douglas fir, aspen and ponderosa pine provide browse for white-tailed deer and cover for sulphur-bellied flycatchers, Mexican chicadees and long-tailed elegant trogons, which nest here every spring.

Wildlife (and human residents) in the desert borderlands are particularly drawn to cool riparian areas, where perennial streams offer that most precious of gifts: reliable water. Southeast of Tucson, places like Ramsey Canyon in the Huachucas and Madera Canyon in the Santa Ritas are oases, attracting 14 of 19 hummingbird species that winter in Mexico and nest in the huge sycamores, maples and oaks that line the creeks.

San Pedro River is one of the country's most important waterways, protecting cottonwood-willow bosques for hundreds of resident birds and literally millions of migratory waterfowl, such as sandhill cranes and snow and Canada geese, which also use flooded desert basins, or playas, in Sulphur Springs Valley, near Willcox in southeastern Arizona. In northern Arizona, bald eagles are often found wintering on alpine lakes and reservoirs near Flagstaff, where cold-water fish are plentiful.

Northern uplands

Glorious though southern Arizona's desert mountains are, the most spectacular area of Arizona is the canyon country of the Colorado Plateau, the uplifted region north of the Mogollon Rim that takes in the White Mountains, the San Francisco Peaks, and the Coconino and Kaibab Plateaus of the South and North Rims of the Grand Canyon. The largely sedimentary

layers of the monolithic Colorado Plateau began to be pushed up by faulting in the mid-Cretaceous period, some 50 million years ago. The area continues to rise and has been further uplifted and sculpted by local faulting into breathtaking high peaks and plateaus.

Even more extraordinary, the Colorado River has carved deep canyons through the uplifted plateaus creating the Grand Canyon, a vast abyss that drops from an elevation of 8,200 feet (2,500 meters) at the North Rim to 1,300 feet (400 meters) at the Colorado River. This kind of sudden elevation change has created a unique situation for wildlife, which has had to

adapt to vastly different environments, from desert to montane, and corresponding changes in temperature, moisture, soil type, slope angle and exposure to sun and wind.

The bottom of the Grand Canyon is as torrid as the Lower Sonoran Desert in summer, with temperatures exceeding 100°F (38°C). Life concentrates along the river, where willow and tamarisk form bowers for river runners and large numbers of songbirds, including the endangered Southwest willow flycatcher. Small canyon wrens flit around the rocks, their presence announced by their haunting descending songs.

It's a different story on the rims. Huge, airy

LEFT: Oak Creek supports a lush growth of reeds, grasses and other water-loving plants.
RIGHT: a gilded flicker nests in a saguaro cactus.

forests of ponderosa pine and Gambel oak sweep across the Coconino and Kaibab Plateaus, forming the largest ponderosa forest in the continental United States. The forests are home to noisy Steller's jays, mule deer and two species of related tassel-eared squirrels, the Aberts of the South Rim and Kaibab of the North Rim, whose destinies diverged millennia ago, when the Grand Canyon separated them. In high country, black bear are common, though grizzlies no longer roam the peaks. The last grizzly, nicknamed Bigfoot, was sighted on Escudilla Mountain near Springerville, in the White Mountains, in the 1930s.

Return from the brink

A number of endangered species are now once again roaming their natural habitats in Arizona. California condors were successfully introduced to the Arizona Strip area, 30 miles (48 km) north of the Grand Canyon, in 1996, after a 10-year captive breeding and release program guided by the Arizona Game and Fish Department, federal wildlife and land management agencies, and private conservation groups. California condors are the largest land birds in North America, with a wingspan of more than 9 feet (3 meters) and weighing up to 22 pounds (10 kg). Members of the vulture family, they are opportunistic scavengers, feeding exclu-

sively on carrion, traveling 100 miles (160 km) or more per day in search of food. The birds managed to maintain a strong population until the settlement of the West, when shooting, poisoning from lead and DDT, egg collecting, and general habitat degradation began to take a toll. Today, they may often be seen soaring over Marble Canyon and House Rock Valley in northern Arizona.

The reintroduction of another endangered species, the Mexican wolf, remains controversial. Mexican wolves once ranged from central Mexico to West Texas, southern New Mexico and central Arizona, but by the mid-1900s had been virtually eliminated from the wild by ranchers concerned about livestock predation. Since March 1998, six packs of radio-collared wolves have been released into Apache-Sitgreaves National Forest in eastern Arizona, after being bred in more than 40 zoos, then acclimated in large pens in Sevilleta National Wildlife Refuge and on Ted Turner's Ladder Ranch in southwestern New Mexico. There are currently about 30 wolves in the wild.

Although the program is going as planned, local reaction remains mixed, and some wide-ranging animals have been hit and killed by vehicles, several have been shot, and some pups have not survived.

Other reintroduction efforts include a black-footed ferret breed-and-release program in the Aubrey Valley, near Seligman, in northwestern Arizona, and the release of endangered Sonoran pronghorn antelope in the Buenos Aires National Wildlife Refuge, southwest of Tucson.

A move is also afoot to conserve the jaguar, the largest cat in the western hemisphere, which was listed as endangered in the United States in 1997. Jaguars have historically ranged from Central America's tropical forests into the arid oak-pine woodland corridors on the U.S.–Mexico border, where they prey on javelina, deer and a variety of smaller animals. Biologists consider that if the jaguars can make it into the United States without being shot in western Mexico, they stand a good chance of survival. Recent sightings of individuals in the Huachuca, Baboquivari and Chiricahua Mountains are cause for cautious optimism. ❏

LEFT: mountain lions are rarely seen. They are stealthy hunters that prey on deer and small mammals.
RIGHT: tadpoles crowd a seasonal water hole.

OUTDOOR ADVENTURE

Whatever your passion – backpacking, rock climbing, mountain biking, river running – Arizona has plenty of room to roam

The first thing to remember when contemplating an outdoor adventure is that *adventure* is a relative term. Look at the picture on the opposite page. How does it make you feel? Excited? Curious? If so, you probably have what psychologists call a high tolerance for risk. When it comes to exploring the outdoors, you're inclined to challenge yourself physically, find out what you're made of, test your mettle against the elements.

If, on the other hand, the picture makes you feel a little queasy, or you're more interested in the composition of the rock than the predicament of the climber, then you may prefer an adventure that emphasizes personal discovery instead of physical challenge. You're probably more interested in getting close to nature, exploring new places, and opening yourself up to novel experiences.

Either way, the opportunities for adventure travel in Arizona are more abundant than ever, and it's never been easier to get started. Schools and clubs are available that will teach you the basics of wilderness travel as well as adventure sports such as rock climbing and kayaking. There are also a growing number of tour companies that specialize in "light adventures" for people who want to experience the thrill and beauty of the outdoors without committing themselves to months of training or the hassles of planning a trip.

If you're a few years (or several pounds) past your prime, don't panic. Though the ads in outdoor magazines may lead you to believe otherwise, you don't need to be a latte-swilling 20-something with washboard abs and chiseled features. A minimal level of fitness may be required, but in most pursuits good judgment and a willing spirit count for more than brawn and bravado. Which is not to say you'll be dangling by your fingertips or wheeling

PRECEDING PAGES: a canyoneer scales the wall of a slot canyon on the Navajo Reservation.
LEFT: basalt cliffs offer excellent climbing routes.
RIGHT: hikers lend a hand in the Grand Canyon.

down a mountainside on your first day out. Making an honest assessment of your limitations – including your tolerance for danger – is an essential first step in any adventure, as is learning to say no when more experienced companions try to pressure you into situations that exceed your abilities.

A walk in the park

For some, hiking is adventure enough. They owe no apologies. A walk in the desert is not to be taken lightly, and even a short jaunt can turn ugly if you're not properly prepared.

What gets most people into trouble isn't snakebite, flash floods or falling off cliffs but the far more mundane risk of dehydration – a critical loss of moisture due to extreme heat and aridity. The condition is particularly insidious because in the desert even mild exertion, like hiking, can cause the body to loose moisture faster than the brain can generate an urge to drink. In other words, you become dehydrated before you feel thirsty.

Prevention is simple enough. Carry plenty of water and drink it at regular intervals, whether or not you feel thirsty. The rule of thumb is one gallon (4 liters) per person per day, but it's best to take more than you think you'll need just in case you want to extend your trip or you lose your way. Getting lost is notoriously easy to do in the desert, where the absence of trees and other landmarks leaves you with few reference points and the abundance of bare ground makes it easy to stray from even a well-marked trail. Coupled with the symptoms of mild dehydration – fatigue, light-headedness, disorientation – losing your way can quickly spiral into a life-

threatening situation. Carry a map and compass (or GPS unit) and know how to use them, and leave a travel plan with someone at home, so they know when and where to start looking if you don't turn up.

Other basics you'll need to take with you are a hat, sunglasses and sunscreen with a high SPF. The Arizona sun is unrelenting, and shade is scarce. Left unprotected, your skin and eyes will be fried in no time.

Foot notes

As a hiker, you will rely almost entirely on your feet, so keep them in good shape with the best hiking boots you can afford. Gone are the days of heavy leather clunkers that took forever to break in. Modern boots are lightweight but sturdy enough to protect your feet from cactus and thorny underbrush and need little or no breaking in, which helps avoid painful blisters. Wearing polypropylene liner socks under a thick pair of poly-wool outer socks will wick moisture away from your feet and prevent blisters. Avoid cotton socks, which soak up moisture and tend to be rough. If a hot spot develops, cover the area with moleskin (available at most camping supply shops) or white athletic tape and allow yourself extra time to rest.

Overnight trips are naturally more complicated to plan and require a rather daunting list of additional equipment, including a backpack, sleeping bag, tent, water-purifying kit and camping stove. The design and quality of camping gear has never been better, though choices (and prices) can quickly become overwhelming. Unless you have an experienced friend to show you the ropes, the best advice is to start by doing a little research in books and magazines and on the Web, then go to a reputable camping-supply retailer and work with a salesperson who's willing to take the time you need to make the right decisions.

Remember: comfort is key. Roughing it in the outdoors shouldn't be rough at all. The idea is to simplify your life, unload stress, and enjoy the place, people and moment, not aggravate yourself with ill-fiting or poor-quality equipment that leaves you cold, hungry, achy and generally miserable.

Now that you're properly equipped, you can begin making the tough decisions about where to go. Trail conditions, topography and weather vary widely in Arizona, so gathering accurate information about a destination – the length and difficulty of your route, the availability of water, the location of facilities – is essential for planning a successful trip. A summer hike into the Grand Canyon may seem like a good idea when you're enjoying a cool breeze on the South Rim, but it's another story when, a few hours later, your strength is sapped by the searing heat of the inner canyon and you're facing a long steep slog back to the top.

The best approach is to let your interests be your guide. Do you enjoy hiking in forests? Consider a trip through the aspen groves of the San Francisco Peaks or among stands of juniper and ponderosa pine on the Mogollon Rim. Have an interest in birding? More than 350 avian species, including a dazzling variety of hummingbirds, have been recorded at Madera and Ramsey Canyons in Coronado National Forest south of Tucson. Redrock country? Explore the swirling sandstone formations of Paria Canyon-Vermilion Cliffs Wilderness. Fly-fishing? Pull on your waders and cast a line into Oak Creek just north of Sedona in one of the state's most picturesque canyons.

DON'T DRINK THE WATER

Even clear streams can harbor parasites that cause severe gastrointestinal illness. All water from wild sources should be boiled for at least a minute, treated with iodine, or passed through a portable filter.

rugged riding machines designed to handle terrain that would reduce an ordinary bike to scrap metal. The advantages are obvious in a place like Arizona, where much of the backcountry is cross-hatched with logging and mining roads. You'll cover more ground on wheels than on foot, and, unlike motorized travel, biking is great exercise, is easy on the environment (so long as you stay on prescribed trails), and lets the landscape unfold at a speed that's more akin to hiking than driving.

Pedal power

The possibilities become even more enticing when you consider alternate modes of transportation such as mountain biking or rafting, which usually free you from the burden of lugging a backpack and open up territory that may have been unreachable on foot. Advances in the technology and design of mountain bikes, for example, make it easier and safer than ever to get started. The clunky, inflexible contraptions of 20 years ago have evolved into sleek and

LEFT: you can prevent blisters by covering "hot spots" with moleskin or medical tape.
ABOVE: bikers plot their course near Sedona.

While it can take months to master the subtleties of the sport, the basics aren't all that different from riding a garden-variety road bike. As long as you steer clear of extremely steep, tortuous or rocky routes and technically demanding single tracks (trails just wide enough for one bike), beginners shouldn't encounter too many difficulties.

Best of all, opportunities for mountain biking in Arizona are virtually endless. Even business travelers confined to offices in downtown Phoenix or Tucson will find good biking in classic Sonoran landscapes only a short drive from downtown. Farther afield, bikers can explore the alpine meadows of the White

Golfer's Paradise

G olf isn't usually considered an adventure sport, but in Arizona you can make it so. At the annual Cowboy Golf tournament in Springerville, a rural community in the White Mountains, you can play nine holes on a working cattle ranch. You ride horseback between holes and use cowpies as tees. There's the risk of having your "cart" gallop off while you're in mid-swing or twisting an ankle in a tumbleweed-filled arroyo.

In Apache Junction, east of Phoenix, there's a true desert course. The "greens" are sand (doused

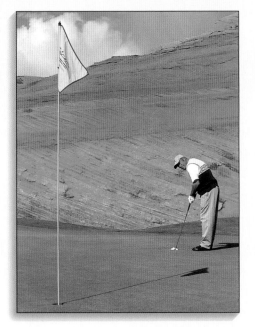

with recycled french-fry oil to keep the dust down), and golfers must make their way between creosote bushes and cacti. When you're done playing a hole, you have to drag a piece of carpet across the sand to erase your footprints.

Want more adventure? Book a tee time in Phoenix or Tucson at midday in July, when temperatures frequently reach 110°F (43°C) or higher.

For those who prefer the sport in its more genteel, traditional form, Arizona is a golfer's nirvana. The first official round of golf in the state was played in 1908, and it's been a growth industry ever since. There are some 320 courses statewide – more than 180 in metro Phoenix alone – and most are public. Couple that with more than 300

days of sunshine a year and mild weather between October and May, and you have plenty of opportunities to hit the links. Courses are active even in summer, with golfers booking tee times between dawn and 7am and driving golf carts rigged with giant ice-water jugs.

Golf courses are as varied as the terrain. Phoenix and Tucson feature dramatic courses set at the base of desert mountains, with greens surrounded by massive granite boulders and towering saguaro cacti. In the mountainous communities of northern Arizona, such as Flagstaff, Payson, Prescott and Pinetop, courses are surrounded by pine and juniper trees and cooled by mountain breezes. Still other courses are decidedly urban (and suburban), with office buildings or housing developments as backdrops. Older courses are lush with mature trees, such as the San Marcos course in Chandler, near Phoenix, which was established in 1912. The state's most challenging public course is said to be Las Sendas in Mesa, which has a rating of 73.8 and a 149 slope.

The cost to play 18 holes also varies, ranging from about $20 for a municipal course to $240 for Scottsdale's tony courses. If you want to learn golf or improve your game, there are plenty of golf schools and pros willing to help you sharpen your skills.

For some people, golf is strictly a spectator sport, and in Arizona, there are plenty of tournaments to watch. The three biggest tournaments are played in metro Phoenix during peak golf season. The PGA's Phoenix Open, held in late January, draws the nation's top golfers as well as more than 400,000 enthusiastic spectators, who come as much for the party atmosphere as the great game. In March, it's the women's turn with the LPGA's Standard Register Ping tournament, followed in April by the august members of the Senior PGA, who tee up for The Tradition.

There are still a few more ways to turn golfing into an adventure. Heli-golfing involves a chopper picking up a foursome in one town, dropping them off in a more exotic locale and returning in time for cocktails at the clubhouse. Then there's night golfing, which includes fluorescent golf balls and lighted fairways. But perhaps the most adventurous of all is encountering one of the state's wild residents on a green – a deer, a javelina, a coyote… maybe even a rattlesnake. ❑

● *For more information about golf in Arizona, contact the nonprofit Arizona Golf Association at 602-944-3035 or www.azgolf.org*

Mountains, the stark desert ranges of Organ Pipe Cactus National Monument, the slickrock trails of Sedona, the volcanic highlands of Coconino National Forest, and the "high, wide and lonesome" backroads of the Kaibab Plateau to little-known overlooks of the Grand Canyon and Colorado River.

Many of the same safety issues pertain to biking as to other wilderness travel. Bring plenty of water and nutritious food, keep abreast of weather conditions, and don't over-tax your skills or endurance. Carry a repair and first-aid kit, and be courteous to jeeps, horse-back riders and hikers who may be sharing the trail. Be particularly wary of logging trucks, which often barrel down backroads at break-neck speed, kicking up a giant plume of dust in their wake. Truckers may not be able to see you and probably can't stop in time if they do. Don't let your last thought be: "Funny, I didn't see that truck a moment ago."

Wet behind the ears

If, as naturalist Loren Eiseley wrote, there's magic in water, then the rivers of Arizona are truly a miracle. They bring life to sun-blasted deserts, sculpt rock into breathtaking canyons, and serve as natural corridors for travelers and wildlife seeking entrée to otherwise impene-trable wilderness.

The premier river trip in Arizona – and arguably in all of North America – is a white-water rafting trip through the Grand Canyon on the Colorado River. The full journey takes about two weeks (although motorized rafts take about half as long) and is filled with wild rides through heart-stopping rapids, long peaceful paddles between soaring canyon walls, and hikes into enchanting side canyons where ancient Indian ruins are sheltered by rocky alcoves, waterfalls plunge into aqua pools, and seeping springs sustain gardens of maidenhair fern and crimson monkeyflower *(see Colorado River Rafting, page 145, for details).*

The real beauty of the experience is that just about anyone can do it. Outfitters authorized by the Park Service handle all provisioning and navigation. About all you have to do – aside from paying the bill – is show up.

River running elsewhere in the state can be quite good depending on the season and ranges from boat-bashing whitewater to long stretches of calm water that can be floated in an inner tube. The Verde, Salt and Gila Rivers promise solitude, scenery and glimpses of desert wildlife, though water levels are often too low to boat. Flatwater enthusiasts can explore the countless red-rock gorges that feed into man-made Lake Powell, the watery caves and canyons of the lower Colorado River near Lake Havasu City and, farther south, the rich bird habitats of Imperial and Cibola National Wildlife Refuges.

Climbing the walls

The learning curve is far more precipitous for rock climbing, although even in this sport, in which technical skill and strength are para-mount, the opportunities for beginners are expanding. Not too many years ago, the only practical way to learn rock climbing was to tag along with experienced climbers. Today, it's much more common for newcomers to hone their skills at climbing gyms before they actu-ally put flesh to rock. "We can usually get peo-ple climbing within 20 or 30 minutes," says Eric Eaglstun, manager of the Phoenix Rock Gym in Tempe, although "there's only so much you can learn without being out on the rock."

LEFT: a golfer lines up a putt at a Page golf course.
RIGHT: a boater crashes through Lava Falls, one of the most challenging rapids on the Colorado River.

For that, he suggests contacting organizations like the Arizona Mountaineering Club, which runs a two-week course for novices that covers the fundamentals of climbing techniques, equipment and, above all, safety.

Climbing skills are also being used by a new breed of adventurers known as canyoneers, who combine hiking, rappelling and rock climbing to explore some of the least accessible canyons in the Southwest.

Much less technical but still challenging are the hundreds of peaks that rise from desert ranges scattered throughout the state. The degree of difficulty varies considerably from

one mountain to another, but most require no special skills or equipment and can be climbed in a single day. Those with little or no experience may want to set their sights on a modest goal – say, the 2,608-foot (795-meter) summit of Squaw Peak in Phoenix, one of the most popular hikes in the state. On the opposite end of the scale is the lung-searing trek to the top of 12,643-foot (3,854-meter) Humphreys Peak north of Flagstaff, where climbers will find the only patch of alpine tundra in Arizona.

Powder to the people

Arizona isn't particularly well known for skiing. In fact, most people – including quite a few

Arizonans – are surprised to learn that a place known for its eyebrow-singeing temperatures has skiing at all. Thanks largely to its basin-and-range geography, Arizona is one of the rare places where you can spend the morning schussing through fresh powder and the afternoon sunbathing at poolside.

Arizona has four ski areas – the Arizona Snowbowl and Williams Ski Area outside Flagstaff, the Mount Lemmon Ski Valley in the Santa Catalina Mountains near Tucson (the southernmost ski resort in the United States), and the Sunrise Ski Resort in the White Mountains. None has snowmaking capabilities, so they're entirely dependent on the whims of weather which, when generous, deliver mounds of dry, fluffy powder – as much as 250 inches (635 cm) or more a year.

The possibilities for cross-country skiing are even more extensive, with miles of trails at such facilities as the Flagstaff Nordic Ski Center and Mormon Lake Ski Touring Center, both in northern Arizona. For those who want to break their own trails, there are countless acres of snow-covered backcountry in Apache-Sitgreaves, Coconino, and Kaibab National Forests, including wilderness treks to the North Rim of the Grand Canyon for those with sufficient stamina and logistical know-how to make the 45-mile (72-km) journey from Jacob Lake, the nearest town with year-round access.

Elbow room

In the end, the deepest rewards of adventuring come not from mastering a particular sport but from simply being outdoors in places where, as Colin Fletcher wrote of the Grand Canyon, people can move "closer to rock and sky, to light and shadow, to space and silence." Thanks to farsighted citizens and politicians, Arizona has more than 5 million acres (2 million hectares) of legally protected wilderness.

What that means in practical terms is that, no matter how far or fast you hike, there will always be another canyon to explore, another hill to climb, another trail to follow. As a river guide said of her many journeys through the Grand Canyon, "the place is so huge, every trip feels like the first time." ❏

LEFT: a climbing guide teaches beginners the basics.
RIGHT: a camper enjoys the view from Toroweap Point on the North Rim of the Grand Canyon.

EXPLORING ANCIENT ARIZONA

You can tour prehistoric sites, visit some of the West's finest collections of artifacts, or join an actual dig under the supervision of a professional archaeologist

Land and people are deeply entwined in Arizona. Hike desert trails throughout the state and you'll soon come upon crumbling adobe dwellings, painted and pecked rock art, arrowheads, potsherds, and other reminders that people have been living here for thousands of years. Drive the highways and you'll pass ancient stone cities built into hills and cliffs. Float the Colorado River through the Grand Canyon and almost every side canyon will reveal sealed granaries and mud-walled dwellings that seem to have been abandoned only yesterday.

Arizona's wealth of prehistoric sites is one of its main attractions, and for many travelers the highlight of visiting the state is not only touring its many archaeological parks but getting involved in an actual dig. Not sure where to start? Four superb museums offer an overview of Arizona's ancient cultures and an easy way to get up to speed on the state's prehistory before hitting the road and visiting individual sites.

Getting started

Arizona State Museum, founded in 1915 at the University of Arizona in Tucson, is the oldest anthropological institution in the Southwest. An entire gallery interprets the prehistoric Hohokam and Mogollon cultures, first defined by famed university archaeologist Emil Haury in the 1930s. The museum also houses an important collection of prehistoric Southwest pottery.

The Heard Museum is, quite simply, one of the finest cultural institutions in Phoenix. It was founded in 1929 to display Dwight B. and Maie Bartlett Heard's large collection of Southwest artifacts and does an excellent job of tracing the prehistoric roots of present-day tribes. One of its most impressive exhibits is

LEFT: a Sinagua pueblo is tucked under a canyon ledge above Montezuma Well, a natural sinkhole.
RIGHT: sunrise streams through the window of a Salado cliff dwelling at Tonto National Monument.

the Barry Goldwater Kachina Doll Collection, which displays the country's most extensive collection of painted Hopi and Navajo religious carvings. Kachina dolls are traditionally fashioned into the likeness of individual helper spirits and given to Hopi girls during seasonal dances. Other exhibits chronicle the develop-

ment of pottery, basketry, weaving, jewelry-making and other arts from prehistoric times to the present.

The Museum of Northern Arizona in Flagstaff focuses on the Indian cultures of the Colorado Plateau. It was founded in 1928 by a Pennsylvania couple, archaeologist Harold Colton and his wife Mary Russell Ferrell Colton, who fell in love with the area and began excavating nearby Wupatki Pueblo. The museum houses artifacts from excavations throughout the Four Corners region and is an active research center.

Research is also the focus of the Amerind Foundation in Dragoon, southeast of Tucson, founded by archaeology enthusiast William S. Fulton in 1937. A large archive of ethnographic materials is available for scholars; casual visitors will be fascinated by the foundation's huge museum, which offers an excellent introduction to the cultures of the Southwest and northern Mexico, with an extensive collection of artifacts.

Can you dig it?

Ever wanted to don an archaeologist's battered hat and help dig up an important piece of the past? The romance of archaeology seems to infect everyone. Unfortunately, far more people want to take part in a professionally supervised archaeological dig than there are opportunities for them to do so. But a number of programs are available, with a limited number of slots open to volunteers.

The U.S. Forest Service operates two programs aimed at archaeology enthusiasts. Heritage Expeditions are tours of archaeological sites in national forests. The popular Passport in Time program (PIT) gives you the chance to participate in an actual archaeological excavation in one of the national forests. In recent years, PIT programs have included digs at Mogollon pueblos in Apache-Sitgreaves

FOOD FOR THOUGHT

The Southwest's most controversial archaeological debate rages around that most taboo of subjects – cannibalism. At the center of the debate is Christy Turner, who, with his late wife Jacqueline, spent 30 years researching cannibalism at Ancestral Pueblo sites after finding signs of butchering and cooking in human bones excavated in northern Arizona. In 1999, the Turners published their findings in *Man Corn*, an allusion to an Aztec word for a ritual meal of human flesh.

Though praised for its scholarship, the book's conclusions have been criticized even by supporters of the authors' work. The Turners suggest that an Aztec warrior cult from Mexico infiltrated Chaco Canyon in New Mexico about AD 900 and used ritual sacrifice to terrorize the local population into submission. The discovery of fossilized excrement containing human remains has prompted even more furor.

Violence is an understandably sensitive issue for the Hopi and other descendants of the Ancestral Puebloans, and two new studies are only adding fuel to the fire. A survey of Pueblo excavations conducted by archaeologist Stephen Le Blanc catalogues numerous examples of violence. Similarly, Polly Schaafsma recently published the results of her study of rock art depicting warfare, which makes clear that conflict was escalating in late Pueblo times.

National Forest and fieldwork in Tonto National Forest to map an Apache settlement from the historic period.

The Deer Valley Rock Art Center, run by Arizona State University, offers programs throughout the year that focus on rock art created by the Hohokam. Northern Arizona University, together with Coconino National Forest and other organizations, sponsors the Elden Pueblo Archaeological Project, one of the best participatory experiences in Arizona.

FINDERS AREN'T KEEPERS

It's illegal to remove or disturb archaeological remains on public land. If you stumble across rock art, potsherds or other artifacts, note the location and report them to the managing agency.

are another good bet for anyone interested in archaeology. The White Mountain Archaeological Center, located on a working ranch near St. Johns, offers tours of rock art sites, the chance to assist on a dig at the large Mogollon Raven Site Ruin, moonlit hikes in the surrounding area, and overnight ranch accommodations. Just east of Greer, the X Diamond Ranch also offers the chance to take part in a supervised excavation of a Mogollon ruin with a large kiva. Since 1983, Dr. E. Charles Adams

Educational programs include site tours, lab work, and excavation techniques and are offered to school groups and institutions between April and September each year at Elden Pueblo, a 60-to-80-room Sinagua ruin within Flagstaff city limits. The site is open for public participation during the Festival of Science in September and Public Field Days in summer, when visitors get a chance to take part in a supervised dig.

Not far from Flagstaff, the White Mountains

LEFT: volunteers get a closer look at Besh-Ba-Gowah, a Salado ruin in the town of Globe.
ABOVE: uncovering an ax head at Raven Site Ruin.

of the Arizona State Museum has operated a summer excavation program at Homolovi State Park near Winslow. The program relies heavily on college students, though volunteers 16 years or older are welcome. If you're interested, contact Earthwatch, a global environmental program. The Smithsonian Institution and National Geographic Society in Washington, D.C., also offer tours of Southwest archaeological sites and are worth contacting.

For a somewhat more formal experience, the Arizona Archaeological Society offers Professional Crew Member certification during summer programs at Elden Pueblo and Q Ranch, a large Mogollon ruin on a private cattle ranch in the White Mountains. Slots are few, there is a modest fee for the week-long digs, and you must be a society member.

Arizona State Parks organizes Archaeology Awareness Month, a program of events and activities involving more than 60 different government and private organizations, which takes place in March of each year. More than 100 events include prehistoric site tours, exhibits, open houses, lectures, demonstrations and other activities throughout Arizona. This is your chance to learn to use an atlatl, or spear thrower; weave a pine-needle basket; attend a lecture on the latest theories in southwestern archaeology; examine pottery rarely on public display; or take a ranger-led tour into backcountry areas that are usually off-limits.

In addition, the Museum of Northern Arizona, Heard Museum and Arizona State Museum all sponsor lecture series, special events, cultural programs and demonstrations, as well as occasional field trips to archaeological sites accompanied by experts.

Several Indian tribes now have their own archaeological resource departments and encourage culture tours led by tribal members. Entrepreneurs on the Navajo Reservation, for example, offer bed and breakfast in traditional Navajo hogans and horseback and jeep tours of nearby prehistoric sites at Canyon de Chelly and Monument Valley. Or you might stop at the Kaibab Paiute Tribal Headquarters next to Pipe Spring National Monument in the Arizona Strip and take a guided tour of rock art sites left behind by Virgin Anasazi and early Paiutes.

Serve and protect

A number of national parks now have Friends groups that raise funds and lobby for increased protection of their prehistoric sites. Site stewardship programs are also catching on fast with local archaeology enthusiasts. Arizona State Parks' highly successful Site Stewardship program trains volunteers to monitor archaeological sites for vandalism, conduct educational presentations about site preservation, and function as a trusted link between nearby communities and the State Historic Preservation Office. Arizona State Museum manages the training for the state parks, working with volunteers to monitor rock art sites east of Tucson.

Of particular interest is the Archaeological Conservancy, a nonprofit organization that purchases threatened archaeological sites across the country. The Conservancy is very active in Arizona, where, in 2000, it negotiated the donation of the Grewe Site, an early Hohokam community on land owned by Wal-Mart Corporation. Fragile archaeological sites are only opened periodically for member tours and volunteer days, but it's exciting to know that your membership dollars are making such a big difference in saving America's cultural heritage. ❏

ROCK ART

Rock art is found throughout Arizona, some dating back to Archaic times more than 2,000 years ago. Images may be pecked (petroglyphs) or painted with ground minerals like red hematite (pictographs) and depict hunting scenes, geometric patterns and fertility symbols that still have meaning to modern Pueblos. Some rock art had an astronomical purpose; it was used to mark the summer and winter solstices or equinox, indicating the best times to plant or have ceremonies. The most puzzling type may be the huge intaglios or "geoglyphs" that were made on the desert floor near the Gila and lower Colorado Rivers and are best viewed from above.

LEFT: the exact meaning of some rock art is a mystery.
RIGHT: Betatakin, occupied by Ancestral Puebloans in the 13th century, is set in the safety of Tsegi Canyon.

GHOST TOWNS

Abandoned mining camps and forgotten outposts are frozen in time,
offering insights into the lives of their long-gone inhabitants

Scores of abandoned mining camps that once housed several thousand people can be found throughout Arizona. Some are true ghost towns – mysterious names on a topographical map, completely unpopulated, with dilapidated buildings, empty schools, churches and collapsed mine works. Most, though, have a few residents who look after the buildings, conduct tours, and keep alive these forgotten places.

A few mining towns never really died. Bisbee, Clifton, Tombstone, Prescott and Jerome yielded billions of tons of copper, silver, gold, lead and other precious metals. They grew into the largest and wealthiest towns in the state and became politically important as seats of local and state government. Today, they are undergoing a metamorphosis.

Whole districts of Victorian mansions, company buildings, hotels, bars and bordellos are now on the National Register of Historic Places. Many have been restored by artists, retirees and local historical associations and turned into quirky homegrown museums, art galleries, bed-and-breakfasts, bars and restaurants filled with mine memorabilia and, as is the case at the Copper Queen Hotel in Bisbee, haunted by the restless spirits of working girls, former managers and other ghosts of the past.

Some ghost towns grew up to serve mining communities. Benson was the railhead for Bisbee and other nearby towns. The Verde Valley Railroad once carried mineral ore and passengers between Clarkdale and Perkinsville, serving mines at the hillside town of Jerome. These historic railroads are now the center of reborn communities, carrying thousands of tourists through the scenic backcountry.

Original buildings, colorful characters and bloody histories have attracted makers of movie westerns to ghost towns for decades. Many production companies took up permanent resi-

dence. Newly constructed "aged" buildings sit alongside original structures in an authentic boardwalk town at Old Tucson Studios, now one of the state's top tourist attractions, with staged gunfights and set tours. A movie set at Pahreah, an 1873 Mormon ghost town just over the Utah line, north of Lake Powell, was constructed for

John Sturges's 1962 comedy Western *Sergeants Three* and is now encompassed by Grand Staircase-Escalante National Monument.

The Lord giveth

Residents of the Copper State are proud of their mining heritage. Arizona's motto is "God Enriches." The state seal depicts a miner with a pick and shovel, the likeness of George Warren, the first prospector to hit it big in the Bisbee mines in the 1860s. Even the state's name is said to be derived from the abandoned silver mining town of Arizonac, just south of the Mexican border. Indian tribes were the first to mine turquoise, malachite and azurite deposits

LEFT: rusty vehicles and ramshackle buildings huddle around a dirt road at Gold King Mine near Jerome.
RIGHT: an adobe house melts back into the earth at Ruby, a desert mining town that died in 1941.

from marine-formed limestones. Later Spanish and Mexican miners found gold and silver near these beautiful blue minerals. In the mid-1800s, when Anglo miners reopened the Spanish diggings, they located copper seams – the mineral that put Arizona on the map.

It's hard to believe that these dusty ghost towns were once the sites of gold and silver bonanzas that attracted swarms of fortune-seekers – miners and merchants, clergymen and saloonkeepers, lawmakers and lawbreakers, of every nationality. Prospectors followed reports of gold and silver, staked claims, and hoped for a lucky strike. If successful, they usually sold

Spanish Jesuits. It was renamed when mine executive Sylvester Mowry bought it in 1859. Twelve furnaces reduced the rich ore to 70-pound (32-kg) bars and a reported $1.5 million was shipped. Mowry is now on private land, but FR 214 bisects the townsite and two small adobe ruins can be seen. Nearby are the walls of the mine and smelter site, with a collapsed shaft, powder house and large slag pile.

Sylvester Mowry was arrested for selling lead for bullets to the Confederates during the Civil War and lost his mine. He is also associated with the former ghost town of Tubac, the oldest European settlement in Arizona. When

their claims and moved on, leaving the actual hard-rock mining to companies that could afford to invest in the necessary machinery, labor and infrastructure. The bonanzas that fueled these boomtowns were dramatic, the decline often catastrophic. As mineral deposits played out and miners moved on, fortunes won turned quickly to fortunes lost, and boomtown became ghost town.

Cocktails at 30 paces

Mowry, between Patagonia and the U.S.–Mexico border, is one of the oldest mining camps in Arizona. The Patagonia Mine was worked by Mexicans in 1857 and perhaps even earlier by

Edward Cross, editor of the state's oldest newspaper, the *Weekly Arizonan*, criticized Mowry for his support of splitting off Arizona territory from New Mexico, Mowry challenged Cross to a duel with rifles. When each missed his mark, they ended up toasting each other's health.

Located in the Santa Cruz River valley, Tubac was founded as a presidio, or garrison, by the Spanish in 1752, then abandoned by Mexicans after repeated Apache raiding in 1848. It was reestablished in 1855 by American Charles Poston, a politician, entrepreneur and visionary often called the "Father of Arizona." Today, Tubac is no longer a ghost town. A state historic park preserves the remains of the presidio, and the town has taken on a new life as an art colony.

Tubac was the headquarters for Poston's Sonora Exploring and Mining Company, which reopened Spanish and Mexican silver diggings at Cerro Colorado ("red hill"), west of present-day Interstate 19, in the 1850s. The silver mine established there and named after company president Samuel P. Heitzelman was the outfit's most successful producer. Eventually, though, Apache raids, worker unrest and

HANG 'EM HIGH

Vulture has only one tree – a hanging tree. The mine supplied the Union with bullion during the Civil War, but miners "high-graded" (stole) as much as 40 percent of the gold. Eighteen were hanged for it.

dences and a miners' dormitory. Bandits from across the Mexican border killed four people during robberies in 1920 and 1921 in the now crumbling adobe store. Only one of the killers was captured, and it's conceivable that one or more are alive today.

The most famous murders of all were those that took place in the 30-second gunfight at the OK Corral in Tombstone in October 1881, killing Tom and Frank McLaury and Billy Clanton, known cattle rustlers, and wounding Virgil and Morgan Earp,

the murder of Poston's brother John closed the mine. Poston's grave is all that remains.

Bloody murder

Another ghost town with a violent history is Ruby, 30 miles (48 km) northwest of Nogales. A lead, zinc and silver mining town that died in 1941, Ruby has more than two dozen roofed buildings, including a jail, a school (with its basketball backboards still in place), mine offices, mill foundations, mine officials' resi-

---

LEFT: schoolhouses built in 1877 and 1936 still stand at the Vulture Mine near Wickenburg.
ABOVE: interior of the assay office at the Vulture Mine.

brothers of U.S. Marshal Wyatt Earp. Clanton and the McLaurys now lie beneath gravestones in the Boothill Cemetery and the infamous contretemps is commemorated daily in staged gunfights and exhibits at the red-brick 1882 Tombstone Courthouse State Historic Park.

Buildings like the courthouse are evidence that Tombstone's history is not all blood and guts, despite the obvious truth of its claim to being "the town too tough to die." It grew from the Tombstone and Graveyard mining claims filed by prospector Ed Schieffelin in 1877 into one of the largest and wealthiest towns in the West. Schieffelin is buried in a little-known grave west of town under a pyramid-like stone cairn that marks the spot where he spent two nights hiding from the Apache before making his famous strike.

The ghost town trail

East of Tombstone is one of the best concentrations of ghost towns in Arizona. The old copper mining town of Gleeson has the ruins of a jail, school and hospital. Farther up the road, in the Dragoon Mountains (the stronghold of Apache warrior Cochise), all that remains of Courtland is its jail, but before World War I the town had its own auto dealership and a population of 2,000. Neighboring Pearce, the site of an 1894 gold rush in the flat Sulphur Springs Valley, has several ruins from its heyday, including the 1884 post office, a school, a jail, a few ruins and foundations, and the Old Store, a large adobe mercantile building with a high false front and an elaborate tin façade. Just to the north, the almost deserted community of Cochise was founded in the early 1880s as a water and fuel stop along the Southern Pacific Railroad. Today, all that's left is the Cochise Country Store, a school, a boarded-up church, and the 1882 Cochise Hotel, which is, remarkably, still open for meals and lodging (both by reservation only).

RISEN FROM THE GRAVE

Arizona's colorful history has sparked its share of ghost stories. The spectres of Bisbee's Copper Queen Hotel are well known. A manager from the early 1900s still strolls the lobby and accompanies visitors in the old elevator. The ghost of Julia, one of many prostitutes who entertained men in the tiny "cribs" in neighboring Brewery Gulch, makes amorous advances toward male guests in a third-floor room that's come to be known as the Ghost Room.

"Soiled doves" and their clients also still seem to be having fun at Tombstone's Bird Cage Theatre. The theater sometimes smells of cigar smoke, and faint piano music can be heard. When the Bird Cage opened as a tourist attraction, a mannequin of Wyatt Earp was mistakenly placed in the Clanton family's favorite crib. Day after day, Earp's hat sailed mysteriously to the floor, knocked off by some unseen force, until he was moved to a crib of his own.

Guests at the 1917 Vendome Hotel in Prescott report sudden temperature drops, whispered conversations, objects being moved, and the appearance of Abby Byr, an owner who died of consumption in Room 16. The old hospital in nearby Jerome, now a hotel, also has a female ghost, perhaps a former nurse. "We hear voices," says the night clerk. "Feelings of cold air. Sometimes people have heard a name spoken, have turned around, and nobody's there."

Mining in the Verde and Prescott Valleys brought fortune hunters to central Arizona in the late 1800s, leading to the choice of Prescott as the first territorial capital in 1912. Gold deposits in the Bradshaw Mountains, southeast of Prescott, yielded $390,000 annually. By 1904, the Crown King mine had enriched its investors with $1.5 million in gold. Problems in reaching the smelter in Humboldt inspired entrepreneur George Murphy to construct what was dubbed "Murphy's Impossible Railroad," linking mining towns in the Bradshaw Mountains over impossibly steep terrain. Trestles, switchbacks and a tunnel were required in order to lay the tracks for the 51-mile (82-km) standard-gauge railroad. During its 23 years of operation, the railroad transported $1.1 million in gold and silver.

The former tracks now allow visitors to visit Humboldt, Mayer, Cordes, Bumble Bee, Cleator and Crown King, an easy loop west of Interstate 17. The latter is a popular getaway for Phoenicians, with cabins, camping areas, the century-old Crown King General Store and a saloon-restaurant that was packed in piece by piece from the mining camp of Oro Belle, 5 miles (8 km) to the southwest, in 1910.

Colorado River ghosts

Among the earliest Anglo settlements along the Colorado River were Forts Yuma and Mohave, which were built to safeguard gold seekers traveling to mining camps on steamboats that plied the river from 1852 to 1907.

The best-preserved ghost town along the Colorado River is actually on the California side. Picacho Mine has been worked intermittently since placer deposits were discovered in 1862 beneath 1,300-foot (400-meter) Picacho Peak. By 1907, the site was an "oasis of bustle," according to the *Los Angeles Times*, with a peak population of about 2,500. River damming in 1909 ended cheap transportation of ore and put paid to many mining towns, including Ehrenberg, La Paz, Castle Dome Landing, Hardyville, Aubrey Landing and Polhamus Landing. Much of Picacho was submerged behind Laguna Dam. Today, it is a state recreation area, with a relocated historic graveyard and a 2-mile (3-km) hiking tour that takes in the

Picacho cave jail and remnants of two mills.

Away from the river, other Mohave Desert ghosts still cling to life. The gold-mining town of Oatman, just south of Kingman, boomed to 10,000 people in 1913. The United Eastern Mine was one of the major producers in the area; the others, Goldroad and Tom Reed, sparked short-lived communities and no longer exist. Today, Oatman has less than 100 residents and is a popular stop for tourists traveling historic Route 66. Several original buildings still stand, including the renovated Oatman Hotel, Mohave County's only two-story adobe building, famous as the spot where Clark Gable

and Carol Lombard spent their honeymoon.

Three other ghosts can be found nearby, in the rugged Cerbat Mountains northwest of Kingman. Chloride, named for the silver chloride ore found there in the Silver Hill strike of the 1860s, is one of the earliest Arizona Territory mining camps. The town features a post office and false-front general store, built in 1928. Mineral Park was the seat of Mohave County in the mid-1870s but lost out to Kingman when the railroad arrived in 1887. Nearby Cerbat was settled in the early 1860s, not long after Chloride. Of its three mines – Golden Gem, Esmeralda and Vanderbilt – only the Golden Gem mill and headframe still stand. ❏

LEFT: sunset reddens the walls of Two Guns on old Route 66 east of Flagstaff.
RIGHT: old equipment is collected at Gold King Mine.

THE ARIZONA COWBOY

The cowboy mystique lives on at rodeos, dude ranches
and historic ranches, and in the lives of working buckaroos

On a crystal clear spring morning, the Sonoran Desert outside Scottsdale is carpeted with drifts of Mexican gold poppies, lupines, owl's clover and other wildflowers. In the distance, the 7,000-foot (2,000-meter) peaks of the Mazatzal Mountains are dusted with snow.

But three men and three women at the Arizona Cowboy College are oblivious to the scenery. They're hunched around the hind leg of a patient gray quarter horse as Rusty, a local farrier, gives them a detailed, three-hour, hands-on lesson on the art and science of horse shoes. The group is transfixed.

The six students have already spent a day learning horse basics, including saddling, riding and grooming; they've also learned the fundamentals of roping. Tomorrow, under the supervision of the cowboy college's instructor, they'll pack up gear, supplies and horses and head to a central Arizona ranch, where, for the following four days, they'll be at the beck and call of the rancher, doing everything from rounding up and branding cattle to mending fences and shoveling manure.

For a few days at least, these people will be real, working cowboys. And like real cowboys, their working conditions are pretty rough. At the college, they sleep together in an open, concrete-floored bunkhouse and share one bathroom; on the range, they sleep on the ground, eschew showers, and answer nature's call in the brush. And while real cowboys get paid for their efforts (though not much), this group of people – and many like them – pays good money for the experience. After a week of training, "graduates" could, ostensibly, work on a cattle ranch. Few do. Most come merely to fulfill a lifelong dream of cowboying.

Modern-day economics may not support many authentic ranches or cowboys, but in Ari-

zona, at least, the cowboy dream lives on. It's a rare visitor to this state who doesn't want to experience some form of cowboy culture, be it folk art or fashion, trail rides or steak fries, dude ranches, rodeos, or even something as advanced as the no-holds-barred program at the cowboy college.

The Spanish connection

Cowboy heritage – both real and legendary – runs deep in Arizona. The state's first cowboy was, arguably, Jesuit missionary Eusebio Francisco Kino, the "Padre on Horseback" who, in the late 17th century, planted the seeds of Spanish cattle ranching and farming throughout southern Arizona.

Cattle ranching during the Spanish colonial period was sporadic. Spain considered the region remote at best, and the missions were beset by disease, drought and Apache raids. After Mexico's independence in 1821, southern Arizona was home to numerous Mexican families who ranched on large land grants, with

LEFT: "Cowboys," wrote Walt Whitman, "are a strangely interesting class … with their swarthy complexions and broad-brimmed hats."
RIGHT: bronc riding at the Prescott Rodeo.

herds of cattle, horses and mules that numbered in the thousands.

The influence of early Mexican *vaqueros* on American cowboys is still felt today in ranching techniques, lingo and equipment. Arizona historian Marshall Trimble notes that a vaquero could "ride a horse through steep terrain, rope a cow, roll a smoke, sing a song and do it all with a smile on his lips."

By the 1830s, however, the Apaches had made it impossible for Mexican ranchers and their *vaqueros* to pursue a living; *los ranchos grandes* and the resident cattle were abandoned, while owners and workers moved into town.

Ranching takes root

After the Gadsden Purchase of 1853, Americans began to trickle into Arizona. Large herds of Texas cattle were driven across the state to supply military and mining concerns in California. After the drives, Texas cowboys brought back tales of southern Arizona's mild winter climate and stirrup-high grasslands.

In 1857, Bill Kirkland became the first American rancher in the state, bringing some 200 head of cattle to what was once a Mexican ranch south of Tucson. But between the outbreak of the Civil War and the continued hostilities of the Apaches, ranching remained in its infancy until Geronimo's surrender in 1886.

With the suppression of the Apaches, ranching flourished in both southern and northern Arizona, spurred on by the arrival of the transcontinental railroad in 1883. It wasn't unusual for large spreads to stretch for miles and support up to 60,000 head of cattle and hundreds of hired hands. Many early ranchers were from Texas and imported their own U.S.-born cowboys. Most of these "buckaroos" (a term derived from the Spanish *vaquero*) fit the same profile: they were young, unmarried, and without family or educational prospects. They worked from dawn to well after dusk in a dangerous profession, all for little more compensation than room and board.

Technically, early Arizona ranches didn't have cowboys at all. The term "cowboy" was a derogatory phrase reserved for cattle rustlers and outlaws. The early ranch hands who tended cattle were referred to as "herdsmen" or "cowpunchers," because they poked at cattle with prods to move them into corrals or railcars. The cowboy moniker didn't take on its present connotation until the turn of the 20th century.

Cowboys were hired hands and tended to move from one job to another as demand or whimsy moved them. Ranchers, on the other hand, often kept their business in the family for generations. Even today, old-time Arizona ranch families are regarded as a sort of royalty, whether or not they're still in the cattle business. Despite economic ups and downs and recurrent droughts, the industry became one of the "four Cs" at the cornerstone of Arizona's economy – cattle, cotton, copper and citrus.

Cowboys and Indians

It was about this time that rodeos became more prevalent statewide. What started out as a friendly test of cowboy skill became an organized event, complete with prize money. Both Prescott and Payson began having summer rodeos that continue today; Scottsdale's Parada del Sol Rodeo and Tucson's Fiesta de los Vaqueros are large winter events. Major rodeos also developed on Arizona's Indian reservations, particularly in the latter half of the 20th century. In an ironic twist, some of the state's best cowboys are Indians, particularly members of the Navajo and Apache Nations.

By the 1920s, though, cattle ranching changed forever. The state's once-abundant southern grasslands had been overgrazed, droughts had taken a heavy toll, prices dropped, and feedlots began to replace the open range. Where once fortunes could be made by ranchers, and a hard-working cowboy could always find work, there was now only hardship and broken dreams. Today, traditional ranches are few and far between, save for the most remote parts of the state and on some Indian reservations.

Fortunately, conservationists are now stepping in to rescue a few of the most vulnerable old spreads. The historic Slaughter

COWBOY'S LAMENT

An old cowboy song sums up the difficulties of adjusting to life on a dude ranch: "I'm a tough, hard-boiled cowhand with a weather-beaten hide, but herdin' cows is nuthin' to teachin' dudes to ride."

Bill, who romanticized the western lifestyle and took it on the road. Countless dime novels fired up the imaginations of city slickers, as did the western novels of Zane Grey, who lived in Arizona and set many of his stories here.

It wasn't long before Arizona attracted the attention of Hollywood producers. Westerns were big business between the 1920s and 1950s, and a great many of them were filmed in the state. Tom Mix, star of many a silent cowboy epic, made several movies in Arizona and died when

Ranch, near the Mexican border, for example, was saved from oblivion by preserving the 1890s ranch buildings as a museum. The San Rafael Ranch, also near the border, recently became a state park.

Birth of an icon

But despite the ranching industry's precipitous slide after World War I, the cowboy mystique never lost its appeal. The image was polished early on by popular entertainers like Buffalo

LEFT: a Navajo cowboy at the O'odham Tash rodeo.
ABOVE: John Wayne takes a swing at Montgomery Clift in 1948's *Red River*, shot on location in Arizona.

his car flipped on State Highway 79, south of Florence. There's a roadside memorial at the crash site – a metal statue of a riderless horse, which was one of the most-stolen "souvenirs" on Arizona's highways until it was permanently installed.

John Ford came to Arizona in 1938 to film the John Wayne classic, *Stagecoach*, in Monument Valley and returned for more than half a dozen other films, including *Fort Apache* and *She Wore a Yellow Ribbon*, making both Wayne and Monument Valley icons of the Western genre. Old Tucson, a "frontier town," was built in 1939 as the set for the epic *Arizona*, starring William Holden and Jean Arthur. The set remained as a desert film location, which, later, counted John Wayne as one of its business partners. Countless movies such as *Rio Bravo* and *The Outlaw Josey Wales* and television series such as *High Chaparral* and *Gunsmoke* were filmed there. The facility, still used as a movie location, is now a popular theme park.

Rex Allen, one of the last of the singing cowboys, was an Arizona native. Allen, whose career spanned radio, film and television, is honored in his hometown of Willcox in southern Arizona with an annual festival. Memorabilia from his performing career is exhibited at the Rex Allen Arizona Cowboy Museum.

Cash cows

Just as Hollywood was discovering the merits of Arizona as a movie set, tourism began to boom. The industry was boosted in its early days by the marketing efforts of Fred Harvey, who operated hotels and tourist programs throughout northern Arizona and New Mexico on behalf of the Santa Fe Railroad.

Before long ranchers discovered that accommodating guests could be as profitable as raising cattle, and the Arizona dude ranch was born. At first, they were primarily working ranches that took in guests as a way to supplement their income and offset market fluctua-

CHOOSING A DUDE RANCH

Arizona has scores of dude ranches, ranging from spartan, working cattle ranches to elaborate "resorts with horses." Picking the right one for your needs can save your dude ranch vacation from being one giant dud.

A personal recommendation is the best way to make a selection, but in the absence of firsthand information try searching the Web or calling the ranches directly *(see Travel Tips section for information)*. Be sure to ask about accommodations. Does the ranch have cabins, a bunkhouse, a lodge? Are meals included? How about the riding program? Do guests need to know how to ride or are lessons available? Does the ranch have a children's

program? Is accessibility an issue? Also, check the ranch's location. Tucson and Wickenburg, both in the Sonoran Desert, are dude ranch hot spots, but if you like mountains and pine trees you won't be happy there. Consider destinations in the White Mountains or around Flagstaff.

A few websites are useful. The Arizona Dude Ranch Association (www.azdra.com) lists comparisons of amenities and programs at their member ranches; Guest Ranches of North America (www.guestranches.com/usa/az.htm) offers profiles of more than 20 Arizona ranches; and the Dude and Guest Ranch Search Engine (www.dgma.com) lets you match seasons and activities to its 35 Arizona ranches. Happy trails.

tions, but by the 1920s facilities that catered strictly to tourists sprang up in and around Tucson, Wickenburg and, to a lesser degree, Phoenix. These guest ranches always kept a herd of quiet horses and plenty of steak and beans. As they grew more competitive, many offered Western-style entertainment, held "dudeos" (rodeos in which guests and staff compete against other guest ranches) and hay rides, and even added swimming pools and golf courses. Many of the old-time dude ranches are still open for the fall-to-spring season. In southern Arizona, these include the Tanque Verde Guest Ranch in Tucson and Rancho de la Osa in Sasabe, while in Wickenburg, it's the Flying E Ranch, Kay El Bar Guest Ranch, and the swanky Rancho de los Caballeros.

Developing at the same time were boarding schools that sprang up in central and southern Arizona, where the scions of New York and Philadelphia society were shipped West to learn the three Rs: reading, riding, and 'rithmatic. In addition to teachers who specialized in the usual subjects, the schools recruited local wranglers to instruct the young whippersnappers on cowboy basics. A few schools still exist, though, sadly, the Judson School, opened in Paradise Valley in the 1920s, was recently razed to make way for an upscale subdivision.

Living the legend

But those in search of a bit of the Arizona cowboy mystique don't have to stay at guest ranches, enroll in a boarding school, follow the rodeo circuit or, for that matter, endure the rigors of the Arizona Cowboy College. There are other, less time-consuming ways to soak up snippets of cowboy lore.

The Arizona Historical Society Museum on the grounds of the University of Arizona in Tucson has numerous exhibits that chronicle the state's ranching past. For art, the Desert Caballeros Western Museum in Wickenburg exhibits work by such celebrated cowboy artists as Frederic Remington and Charles Russell, as well as period rooms with furnishings that reflect the style of the desert frontier. Every October, the Cowboy Artists of America, an organization of noted Western artists formed in

Sedona in the 1960s, has a major exhibition of paintings and sculptures at the Phoenix Art Museum. In Prescott, the Phippen Museum specializes in the art of the American West.

For the literary-minded, cowboy poetry festivals abound throughout the state. Prescott hosts a major cowboy poetry gathering at the Sharlot Hall Museum in summer. The event includes music, too.

For cowboy duds you need only visit Stockman's Western Wear in Phoenix or Saba's, with several locations in the Phoenix and Scottsdale areas, both of which offer jeans, shirts, hats and cowboy boots. For something ultra luxurious, a

pair of custom-made boots may be in order, although a real cowboy wouldn't be caught dead in them. Paul Bond's boot company in Nogales has been making boots for decades, ranging from the utilitarian to the flashy. Customers include dudes, ranchers and movie stars (ask to see the company's attic, where wooden lasts are kept for the shop's celebrity clients). Stewart's Boots in Tucson also offers a wide range of custom footwear.

The romance lives on at dude ranches, at poetry gatherings, on trail rides, and at every bar in which a cowboy yodels a plaintive lament. The real cowboy may be scarce in Arizona, but cowboy culture lives on. ❑

LEFT: leading a packhorse through red-rock country.
RIGHT: ranch women reflect a depth of character forged by years of independent living and hard work.

PLACES

A detailed guide to the entire state, with principal sites
clearly cross-referenced by number to the maps

They came, they saw… they went home. That pretty well sums up the experience of the first Europeans to see the Grand Canyon, a contingent of soldiers dispatched by Francisco Vásquez de Coronado in 1540 to search for the fabled Seven Cities of Gold. Failing after several days to reach the Colorado River, they abandoned the effort and turned back, observing rather matter-of-factly that the canyon was not only big but difficult to cross.

The outcome was only slightly better three centuries later when Lieutenant Joseph C. Ives, leader of the first American expedition into the canyon, was shipwrecked on the Colorado River near the present site of Hoover Dam. Though Ives was awestruck by the "profound grandeur" of the great abyss, he couldn't imagine why anyone would willingly venture into such godforsaken country. "Ours has been the first and will doubtless be the last party of whites to visit this profitless locality," he reported in 1857, distinguishing himself forever after as the worst prognosticator in Arizona history.

Five million tourists visit the Grand Canyon every year, the vast majority congregating on the South Rim, creating one of the great ironies of the National Park System and one of its biggest headaches – traffic jams in the wilderness. With a peak of 6,000 autos vying for only 2,400 spaces, parking is an exercise in frustration. The Park Service has proposed remedying the situation by building a light-rail line from nearby Tusayan (to be completed, optimistically, by 2004), but until then it may be best to arrive by bus, ride the historic railroad from Williams, or head for the lightly visited North Rim.

Despite the crowds, the Grand Canyon lives up to its billing. You won't believe your eyes – nor should you – because the vision that sprawls before you is simply too vast to comprehend. It's a common problem in Arizona, where stunning landscapes crop up around every bend. Monument Valley, the Painted Desert, Canyon de Chelly, the Sonoran Desert. The list reads like the liner notes of *God's Greatest Hits.*

But there's more to do here than merely enjoy the scenery. Explore the dusty lanes of a ghost town, the graceful interior of a Spanish mission, the dramatic ruins of an ancient Indian village. Pamper yourself at a posh resort or play a round of golf on a world-class course. Ride horseback in a sun-drenched desert, cast a line into a cool mountain stream, go bird-watching in a secluded canyon. And get to know the people whose unique combination of Indian, Hispanic and Anglo cultures, as well as the cultures of recent immigrants, are as complex and colorful as a Navajo rug. ❑

PRECEDING PAGES: Havasu Canyon; aspens in autumn, Lockett Meadows, San Francisco Peaks; hikers on Echo Canyon Trail, Chiricahua National Monument. **LEFT:** wind sculpts the dunes of Monument Valley into ever-shifting patterns.

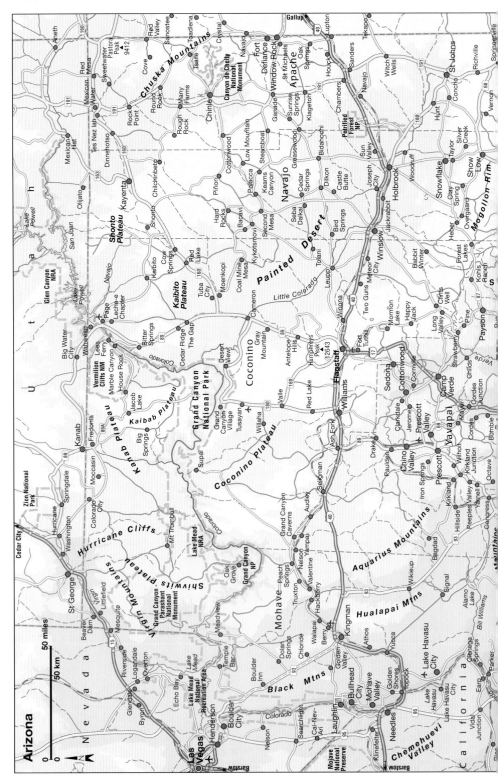

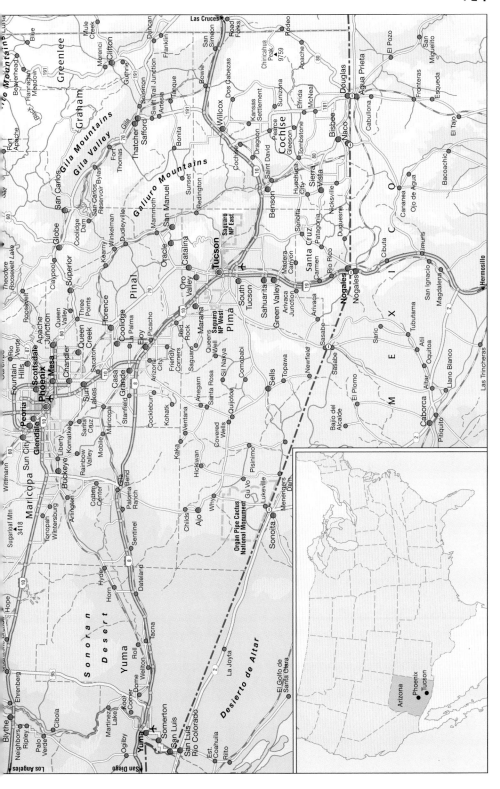

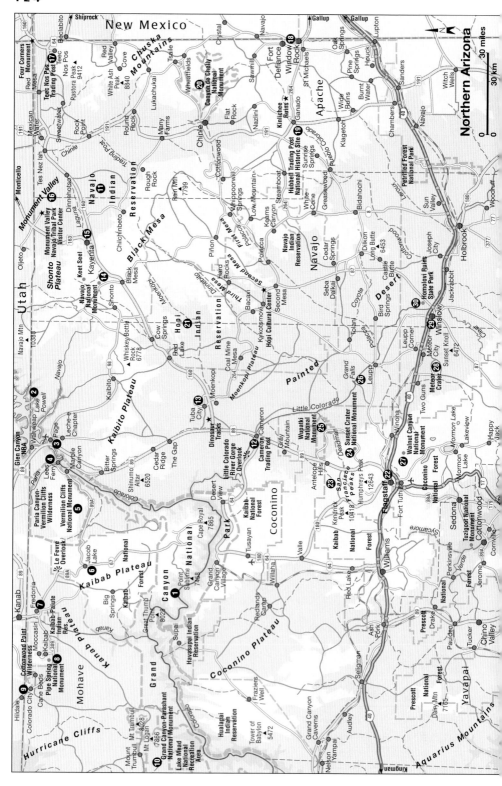

NORTHERN ARIZONA

Monumental landscapes, Indian cultures and a scrappy frontier spirit lure travelers to the canyon country of the north

The Colorado Plateau – a spectacular hunk of continental crust that sprawls across 130,000 square miles (337,000 sq km) of the Four Corners region – dominates northern Arizona. Its sandstone whorls and sinuous canyons give the landscape an animate quality not found elsewhere in the state. Warmed by the sun, rocks radiate heat long into the night. Water pulses through arroyos after heavy summer rains and weeps through fissures in canyon walls.

According to Navajo mythology, the land is indeed a living thing – *shimah*, mother – and the gargantuan stone formations that stand upon it are the petrified corpses of gods and monsters who inhabited the Earth before the coming of humans. To the Hopi, descendants of the Ancestral Puebloans whose abandoned villages are scattered throughout the plateau, every aspect of the natural world is infused with spiritual life. They regard the Grand Canyon as a place of emergence – *sipapu* – where their ancestors entered the present world before migrating to their mesa-top homes.

Though most visitors don't regard the region as a Holy Land in quite the same way that native people do, it's difficult not to be moved by its beauty and scale. The Grand Canyon is the most popular destination. About 5 million tourists make a pilgrimage to the park every year, though relatively few venture far from the main overlooks. Pity. Below the rim, the canyon unfolds like an inverted mountain, passing through a series of ecosystems as you descend into ever more ancient rock, transected by side canyons that lead into hidden worlds of waterfalls, hanging gardens, and narrow corridors of sculpted rock. Only the backpacker and river runner see this intimate side of the Grand Canyon or get a close-up view of the mighty waterway that created it.

Beyond the canyon, you'll find no lack of wondrous places and exciting activities. Pedal a mountain bike through the aspen groves of the San Francisco Peaks north of Flagstaff. Paddle a kayak into the tortuous, ever-narrowing canyons that feed into Lake Powell. Hike around the base of a 1,000-foot-high (305-meter) cinder cone in the country's largest volcanic field or stand on the rim of a 560-foot-deep (170-meter) crater blasted out of the bedrock by a meteor 50,000 years ago. Explore the ruins of ancient stone pueblos built in protected alcoves beneath soaring cliffs. Shop for silver and turquoise jewelry at a traditional Indian trading post. Ride horseback with a Navajo guide between the mineral-streaked walls of Canyon de Chelly. Or drive the rugged back roads of the Arizona Strip, the "high, wide, lonesome country" north of the Grand Canyon. ❑

PRECEDING PAGES: a hiker enjoys the view of a natural sandstone arch at Paria Canyon–Vermilion Cliffs Wilderness, a region of bizarre rock formations and dramatic slot canyons along the Arizona–Utah border.

GRAND CANYON NATIONAL PARK

Map on page 124

Humbling, exalting, beautiful beyond words – the canyon is undeniably one of the world's great sights and grows only more fascinating when you venture below the rim

The ancients spoke of the four basic elements of earth, water, wind and fire. But at the **Grand Canyon ❶**, another element must be added – light. It is light that brings the canyon to life, bathing the buttes and highlighting the spires, infusing color and adding dimension, creating beauty that takes your breath away. Where else are sunrise and sunset the two biggest events of any day? In early morning and late afternoon, the oblique rays of sunlight, sometimes filtered through clouds, set red rock cliffs on fire and cast abysses into purple shadow.

The Grand Canyon, in northern Arizona, is rightfully one of the seven wonders of the world. Nearly 5 million people a year arrive at its edge and gaze down into this yawning gash in the earth. But the approach to the canyon gives no hint of what awaits. The highway passes a sweeping land of sagebrush and grass, through dwarf pinyon and juniper woodland, and into a forest of tall ponderosa pines. Then, suddenly, the earth falls away at your feet. Before you stretches an immensity that is almost incomprehensible.

The canyon is negative space – it's composed as much by what's not there as what is. After taking time to soak in the scene, one's eyes rove down to the bottom, where there appears to be a tiny stream. Though it looks small from this distance, 7,000 feet (2,100 meters) above sea level, it is in fact the **Colorado River**, one of the great rivers of the West. And unbelievable though it may seem, the river is the chisel that has carved the Grand Canyon. The Colorado rushes through the canyon for 277 miles (446 km), wild and undammed. Over several million years, it's been doing what rivers do – slowly but surely eroding the canyon to the present depth of one mile (1.6 km).

An awful canyon

To the east, the scalloped skyline of the **Palisades of the Desert** defines the canyon rim. To the north, about 10 miles (16 km) as the hawk flies, is the flat-lying forested **North Rim**. To the west, the canyon's cliffs and ledges, cusps and curves extend as far as the eye can see, with only distant indigo mountains, nearly in Utah, breaking the horizon. **Grand Canyon National Park** is more than a million acres (400,000 hectares) of land, and this view encompasses only about a fourth of the entire canyon.

People's reactions to their first sight of the Grand Canyon vary. Some are speechless. Some are brought to tears. Still others, such as early visitor Gertrude B. Stevens, have been overcome in other ways: "I fainted when I saw this awful looking cañon," she declared. "I never wanted a drink so bad in my life."

PRECEDING PAGES: sunrise illuminates the canyon rim. **LEFT:** Toroweap Overlook, North Rim. **BELOW:** hikers at Nankoweap Canyon.

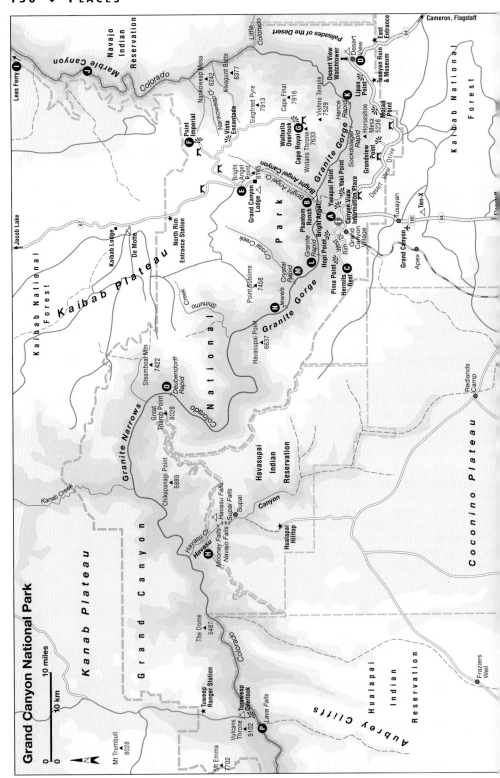

But with more than the average four-hour stay, a person can begin to explore this miraculous place, savoring different moods throughout the hours of the day, as the light constantly changes the face of the canyon.

Map on page 130

The South Rim

Most visitors first see the Grand Canyon from the South Rim, the area that is open year-round and offers the most ample accommodations. The best place to start is at the **Canyon View Information Plaza ⒶＡ**, accessible by free shuttle bus. This open, spacious center features wall-size maps, exhibits and books that set the canyon in a larger context and help orient visitors. Park rangers there can answer specific questions. From the plaza, it's a short stroll out to **Mather Point**, for that virgin glimpse of the canyon.

TIP

Cars at the South Entrance Gate often back up during peak summer hours. Traffic tends to be lighter at the East Entrance Gate.

Back at the plaza, buses run at frequent intervals all day to many overlooks along the rim. Other buses go to trailheads to drop off day hikers and backpackers. By extending the public transportation system, the Park Service is aiming to get people out of their cars, and get cars and development away from the rim, seeking to restore that invigorating sense of discovery. Now, the ravens are taking back their rightful place, soaring over the dizzying abyss and croaking their calls of greeting.

The historic buildings on the rim, most of them of native stone and timber, will stay, however. One is the **Yavapai Observation Station**, on the next point west of Mather. One entire wall of this small museum and bookstore is glass, affording a stupendous view into the heart of the canyon – slices of the Colorado River, a 1928 suspension bridge, and **Bright Angel Campground** and **Phantom Ranch ⒷＢ** tucked at the very bottom.

BELOW: Bright Angel Trail is the most popular route into the canyon.

Hermits Road

From here, a paved path along the rim leads to the village area, where shuttle buses head out along 8-mile (13-km) **Hermits Road** (also called **West Rim Drive**). Constructed in 1912 as a scenic drive, it offers several overlooks along the way. At **Trailview Point**, you can look back at the village and the **Bright Angel Trail** switchbacking down to the river. **Indian Garden**, a hikers' campground shaded by cottonwoods, is visible 4½ miles (7 km) down the trail. The Bright Angel Fault has severed the otherwise continuous cliff layers that block travel in the rest of the canyon, providing a natural route for hikers.

In the morning, mule trains plod into the canyon, bearing excited greenhorns who may wish they'd gone on foot when the day is done. The trail is also the route of a pipeline that pumps water from springs on the north side up to the South Rim. The benefit of that reliable water supply makes the Bright Angel Trail favored among canyon hikers, especially in the heat of summer. Big flashfloods have washed out parts of the trail and the pipeline, hampering delivery of that most precious commodity in this semiarid land.

Other recommended points along Hermits Road are **Hopi**, **Mohave** and **Pima**. From each vista different isolated buttes and "temples" present themselves. There is the massive formation called the **Battleship**,

Mule rides have been a tradition at the canyon for more than 90 years but are not for the faint of heart. Reservations should be made several months in advance; call 303-297-2757.

best seen from **Maricopa Point**. There's **Isis** and **Osiris**, **Shiva** and **Brahma**. These overblown names were bestowed by Clarence Dutton, an erudite geologist with the early U.S. Geological Survey and protégé of Major John Wesley Powell. Dutton's classical education inspired names with this Far East flavor. He wrote that all the canyon's attributes, "the nobility of its architecture, its colossal buttes, its wealth of ornamentation, the splendor of its colors, and its wonderful atmosphere … combine with infinite complexity to produce a whole which at first bewilders and at length overpowers."

At **Mohave Point** on a still day, you can hear the muffled roar of crashing waves in **Granite** and **Hermit Rapids** on the Colorado. With binoculars, it may be possible to spy boaters bobbing downriver in rubber rafts. The road ends at **Hermits Rest ⊙**, with a gift shop, a concession stand and restrooms. This is also where hikers head down the **Hermit Trail**, one of the more accessible backcountry trails beyond the main corridors of Bright Angel and South Kaibab. It's about 8 miles (13 km) down **Hermit Canyon** to a lovely streamside camp for overnight hikers.

The Santa Fe Railway built the camp as a destination for tourists who arrived on mules, while supplies were shuttled 3,000 feet (900 meters) down a cable from the rim. In those days, according to author George Wharton James, the camp furnished accommodations "to meet the most fastidious demands." The "hermit" was a Canadian prospector named Louis D. Boucher, who settled at an idyllic spot called Dripping Springs, off the Hermit Trail. Known for his flowing white beard and a white mule named Calamity Jane, Louis kept mostly to himself. He prospected a few mining claims, escorted tourists now and then, and by all accounts grew amazing fruits and vegetables down in the canyon.

Desert View Drive

Returning to the village, another road, **Desert View Drive**, follows the canyon rim for 25 miles (40 km) to the east. Overlooks along the way display still more spectacular canyon scenery. From **Yaki Point**, the panorama includes the massive beveled surface of **Wotans Throne**, and beside it graceful, pointed **Vishnu Temple**. The other main hiking route, the 7-mile (11-km) **South Kaibab Trail**, departs from near Yaki Point, snaking down the side of **O'Neill Butte** through a break in the Redwall Limestone, down to Bright Angel Campground and Phantom Ranch.

Farther east, **Grandview Point** looks down on **Horseshoe Mesa**, site of early copper mines. The **Grandview Trail** starts here, built by miners to reach the ore. But even a short walk will reveal that no matter how pure the ore, hauling it out was not a profitable enterprise. Grandview was among the first destinations for early tourists to the canyon, who stayed at Pete Berry's Grandview Hotel. One of the regulars there was old John Hance. He arrived at the canyon in the 1880s and built a cabin near Grandview. For a time, John worked an asbestos mine on the north side of the river but quickly realized that working the pockets of "dude" visitors was more lucrative. "Captain" Hance regaled rapt listeners with tales of how he dug the Grand Canyon, how he snowshoed across to the North Rim on the clouds, and other fanciful yarns. His stamp remains on the canyon – there is a Hance Creek and Hance Rapid, and the Old and New Hance Trails, rugged routes that drop down into the canyon from Desert View Drive.

In addition to great views and good stories, the drive in this area also gives a look at stands of splendid old ponderosa pines. These cinnamon-barked giants grow back from the rim, here benefiting from slightly higher elevation and

Map on page 130

TIP

The Grand Canyon Chamber Music Festival in September stages three weeks of concerts at a South Rim auditorium. Call 928-638-9215 for information.

BELOW: tourists take in panoramic views from Mather Point on the South Rim.

Mule wranglers take a cigarette break.

increased moisture. Their long silky needles glisten in the sunlight, and a picnic beneath their boughs is a delight. Grazing mule deer and boisterous Steller's jays may be your companions, along with busy rock squirrels looking for handouts. (Resist the temptation; feeding wildlife is strictly prohibited.) The trees growing on the very brink of the rim are Utah junipers and pinyon pines. Sculpted by the wind, they cling to the shallow, rocky soil, never attaining great heights though they can be very old. The warm, dry air rising up from the canyon explains their presence.

In certain good years, pinyon pines produce delicious, edible brown seeds. People gather them, but so do many small mammals and birds. One bird – the dusky-blue pinyon jay – shares an intimate relationship with the tree. The jays glean nuts from the sticky cones, eating some and caching others. Inevitably, some of the nuts are forgotten and grow into young pinyon pines.

The eastern tip

Just to the east of Grandview is the entrance to the **Tusayan Ruin and Museum**, which preserves the remains of masonry structures constructed some 800 years ago by Ancestral Puebloans. These early farmers were by no means the first humans to inhabit the canyon. Archaeologists have found a tantalizing stone point nearly 13,000 years old left by big-game hunters in the waning days of the Ice Age. For another several thousand years, hunter-gatherers made a living on canyon resources. About 4,000 years ago, they split willow twigs and wound them into small animal figures. They left the figures in caves in the canyon, where modern-day archaeologists have discovered them.

Lipan Point, farther east, provides one of the most expansive views of the

BELOW: an ancient granary is built into a cliff ledge in Nankoweap Canyon.

canyon and Colorado River from anywhere along the rim. The river makes a big S-turn, with **Unkar Rapid** visible below. A little farther downstream is Hance Rapid, punctuating the entry of the Colorado River into the Inner Gorge.

In autumn, hundreds of hawks – Cooper's, sharpshins, redtails and others – migrate over Lipan Point on their way south. Nearby, in 1540, a detachment of Francisco Vásquez de Coronado's Spanish entrada tried but failed to reach the river. They are believed to be the first Europeans to enter the canyon proper, though Native Americans had long preceded them.

The final destination on this drive is **Desert View ❻** itself. Here the canyon opens out into the wide Marble Platform and east to the huge Navajo Reservation. The **Little Colorado** meets the main Colorado a few miles upstream. And an interesting circular tower stands out on the edge. Mary Jane Colter, architect for the Fred Harvey Company and Santa Fe Railway, designed it. (She also designed Bright Angel Lodge, Hopi House, Lookout Studio, Hermits Rest and Phantom Ranch.) Colter was heavily influenced by Puebloan architecture, and the **Desert View Watchtower** is modeled after structures she'd seen in the Four Corners area. It was built in 1932 of native stone, and on the interior walls are murals painted by Hopi artist Fred Kabotie.

Map on page 130

The North Rim

At times, especially during the summer, the concentration of people on the South Rim can get to feel a little crowded. The place to turn is the **North Rim**, the peaceful side of the Grand Canyon.

From the South Rim, it doesn't look terribly far, but the North Rim is 215 miles (346 km) away by road. Leaving Desert View, join Highway 89 and head

BELOW: Desert View Watchtower, built in 1932 by the Fred Harvey Company, rises from the edge of the canyon.

BELOW: a hiker explores Nautiloid Canyon, named for the fossil creatures that are embedded in its rock.

north across the **Navajo Reservation** and part of the **Painted Desert**. Take Highway 89A, cross the bridge over the Colorado River at **Marble Canyon**, and allow time for the 5-mile (8-km) detour to **Lees Ferry**, put-in for Grand Canyon river trips and a vortex of Southwest history. This is the only place for nearly 300 miles (480 km) where you can get down to the river, sit on the shore, and marvel that this is the same insignificant-looking stream you saw from the rim.

Back on Highway 89A, drive west across the wide-open, lonesome stretch of **House Rock Valley**, where keen-eyed travelers may glimpse a giant California condor soaring over the **Vermilion Cliffs**. The road then climbs up the east flank of the **Kaibab Plateau**, reentering pinyon-juniper forest and ponderosa pine. At **Jacob Lake**, Highway 67 winds 45 miles (72 km) through the forest to the rim.

To the Paiute Indians, who lived on this side of the canyon, Kaibab means "mountain lying down." The North Rim's elevation does qualify as a mountain. It averages 8,000 feet (2,400 meters), 1,000 feet (300 meters) higher than the South Rim, making for a very different forest environment. Here grow dense stands of spiky dark spruce and fir, along with quaking aspen and big grass-filled "parks," or meadows, where coyotes spend their days "mousing." The limestone caprock also holds a few small sinkhole lakes. This forest supports a different variety of wildlife too – the handsome Kaibab squirrel, a tassel-eared tree squirrel of the ponderosa pines, is found only here; there's also blue grouse; a larger population of mule deer; and a consequently larger number of mountain lions, the main predators of the deer. The North Rim is buried in snow in winter, and the entrance road is closed from the end of October through mid-May.

Because of the short season and isolation, the North Rim has never been as

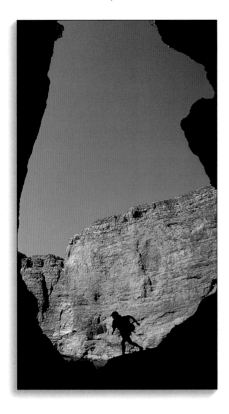

THE CANYON IN WINTER

Winter weaves a magic spell over the Grand Canyon. In this season the rim is softened by a mantle of ermine snow, and the chilled air bristles with crystals. Pine needles are glazed with frost, and gossamer clouds snag on the tops of pointed buttes. Sounds are muffled, and hectic summer days are a memory.

During the holidays, the fireplace in the lobby of El Tovar Hotel is surrounded with poinsettias. It's tempting to spend the day indoors by the fire, sipping hot chocolate. That's certainly an option, especially if the winds are buffeting the rim. But the outdoors beckons, and with proper clothing and footwear you can walk along the rim path and find yourself nearly alone with the canyon.

Juncos, nuthatches and finches flit in the tree branches. Ravens two-step out on improbable promontories, oblivious to the gaping abyss below. Tracks in the snow hint at dramatic encounters between hawk and rabbit.

Diligence is needed near the rim, though, for snow can hide a slippery drop off and trails may be icy. A ski pole or boots with instep crampons can be helpful. Beware of hypothermia, too. It can strike suddenly in wet, cold, windy weather when you're tired from exertion. Dress in layers, keep a supply of dry clothes, and drink plenty of water.

Map on page 130

fully developed as the South Rim. There is a campground, small cabins, a visitor center, cafeteria, and the **Grand Canyon Lodge** , which perches on the canyon's edge. One of the prime activities is to nab a rocking chair on the veranda of the lodge and engage in serious canyon watching.

The road to transcendence

From the lodge, a short trail goes to **Bright Angel Point**. Though you're still looking at the same canyon, the north side's greater depth and intricacy are immediately apparent. This is due partly to the Grand Canyon's asymmetry: the Colorado River did not cut directly through the middle of the Kaibab Plateau but slightly off-center to the south. Also because of its greater height and southward tilt, more water flows *into* the canyon here than *away* from it as on the South Rim. Thus the northern side canyons are longer and more highly eroded. The **North Kaibab Trail** along **Bright Angel Creek**, for example, is 14 miles (23 km) long, twice the distance of the corresponding trail on the south side. While many people take the North Kaibab all the way down to the river for overnight stays, this trail also lends itself to wonderful day hikes. Other shorter walks on the rim include the **Transept, Widforss** and **Ken Patrick Trails**.

A drive out to **Point Imperial** 🅕 and **Cape Royal** 🅖, on the only other paved road, is well worth the time. At 8,800 feet (2,700 meters), Point Imperial is the highest prominence on either rim of the canyon. Its eastward-facing view showcases **Mount Hayden, Kwagunt Butte** and **Nankoweap Mesa** in the Marble Canyon portion of Grand Canyon. From there, the road goes out to Cape Royal, where it ends. Clarence Dutton also named this promontory; his description of sunset there strains even his exuberant prose: "What was grand

BELOW: cross-country skiers enjoy a view from the North Rim.

before has become majestic, the majestic becomes sublime, and ever expanding and developing, the sublime passes beyond the reach of our faculties and becomes transcendent."

Go vertical

With the first step down into the Grand Canyon, the horizontal world of the rims turns decidedly vertical. A walk down a trail, even for a short distance, is really the only way to begin to gain a fuller appreciation of the canyon's great antiquity and sheer magnitude.

A word to the wise, though. Adequate preparation for this backcountry experience is essential. A Grand Canyon trek is the reverse of hiking in mountains: the descent comes first, followed by the ascent, when muscles are tired and blisters are starting to burn. And no matter what trail you follow, the climb out is always a long haul against gravity – putting one foot in front of the other and setting mind against matter. For first-time hikers, the maintained corridor trails are recommended: the Bright Angel, or the South or North Kaibab. Also be aware that all overnight hikes require a Park Service permit; day hikes do not.

There are two other critical considerations – heat and water. As you descend into the canyon, you pass from a high-elevation, forested environment into desert. Temperatures in the inner canyon are routinely 20 degrees warmer than the rim – from June to September that means upwards of 110°F to 120°F (43°–49°C) down below. That kind of unrelenting, energy-sapping heat, coupled

BELOW: Havasu Indian boys play in Havasu Creek.

with a shortage of water, can spell disaster for the unprepared. In summer, each person should carry – and drink – a minimum of a gallon (4 liters) of water apiece. Along with water, a hiker should eat plenty of high-energy foods and take frequent rest stops. A hat, sunscreen and sunglasses are necessary items. To avoid the extreme heat, hike in early morning and early evening. Or avoid summer altogether and go in spring or fall, which are the best times for an extended canyon hike.

The Inner Canyon

Dropping below the rims into the canyon's profound silence, you enter the world of geologic time. Recorded in the colorful rock layers is a succession of oceans, deserts, rivers, and mountains, along with hordes of ancient life forms that have come and gone. The caprock of the rims, the Kaibab Limestone, is 250 million years old. It is the youngest layer of rock in the Grand Canyon; every layer beneath it is progressively older, down to the deepest, darkest inner sanctum of black schist that rings in at close to 2 billion years.

As you put your nose up against the outcrop, you'll notice that this creamy-white limestone is chock ablock with sponges, shells and other marine fossils that reveal its origin in a warm, shallow sea. The next obvious thick layer is the Coconino Sandstone. Its sweeping crossbeds document the direction of the wind across what were once dunes as extensive as those in today's Sahara Desert. It isn't hard to imagine because already, even in this first mile of the trail, the canyon begins to look and smell like the desert – dusty and sun-drenched. Beneath the Coconino is the Hermit Shale, soft, red mudstone that formed in a lagoon environment. Underlying the Hermit is the massive Supai Formation, 600 feet (180 meters) thick in places, the compressed remains of mucky swamp bottom 300 million years past. The Redwall Limestone is always a milestone on a Grand Canyon hike, passable only where a break has eroded in the 500-foot-high (150-meter) cliffs. Beneath the Redwall are the Muav Limestone, Bright Angel Shale, and Tapeats Sandstone – a suite of strata that indicate the presence of, respectively, yet another ocean, its nearshore, and its beach. Throughout most of the canyon, the tan Tapeats reclines atop the shining iron-black Vishnu Schist, the basement of the Grand Canyon and arguably its most provocative rock.

At the bottom, embraced in the walls of schist, are the tumbling, swirling waters of the Colorado River, the maker of this, its greatest canyon. The river, aided by slurries of rock and water sluicing down tributary canyons, has taken only a few million years to gnaw down into the plateau to expose almost 2 billion years of earth history.

Soak hot feet in the cool water. Listen to boulders grinding into gravel on their way to the sea. Consider these old rocks in this young canyon. Ponder our ephemeral existence in the face of deep time.

Havasu Canyon

Havasu **H**, a side canyon in the western Grand Canyon, has been called a "gorge within a gorge." Within it flow the waters of **Havasu Creek**, lined with emerald cottonwood trees and grapevines and punctuated by travertine falls and deep turquoise pools, paradise in the midst of the sere desert of the Grand

Map on page 130

Coyotes are often heard yipping and howling at sunset.

BELOW: Havasu Falls spills into a turquoise pool. The water takes its color from calcium carbonate.

Map on page 130

Canyon. A visit is an unforgettable experience, a gentle introduction to the Grand Canyon and to the Havasupai Indians, the "people of the blue-green water," who have made their home here for at least seven centuries.

Getting there is no easy matter. The journey requires a 62-mile (100-km) drive north of Route 66 (about 190 miles/300 km from the South Rim) to a remote trailhead, then an 8-mile (13-km) hike or horseback ride to the small village of **Supai** on the canyon bottom.

The pace at Supai is slow and easy. Development is limited to a small café, general store, post office, school, tourist lodge and tribal museum. Mail and supplies arrive by mule or horse (and these days by helicopter and Internet). In past times, the Havasupai partook of what the land offered. Evidence is seen along the trail in large rock piles, the pits used year after year for roasting the sweet stalks of agave. In their rocky homeland are distinctive natural features that hold great significance to the Havasupai. Rising high above the village is a pair of sandstone pillars known as Wigleeva. To the Havasupai, these are their guardian spirits; as long as they are standing, the people are safe.

About 1½ miles (2.5 km) beyond the village is the first of the famous waterfalls – **Navajo Falls**. A short distance beyond is 100-foot-high (30-meter) **Havasu Falls** and the campground. The trail continues on to **Mooney Falls**, known as the Mother of the Waters to the Havasupai. To go farther down canyon requires a steep descent next to the falls on a water-slickened cliff face, with the aid of a chain railing. It's another 3 miles (5 km) to **Beaver Falls**, a popular day hike for boaters coming up from the river to frolic in the beautiful pools. Those who make the journey know why Havasu is often called the Shangri-la of the Grand Canyon. ❏

BELOW: a hiking party follows a desert trail. Water, sunglasses, a hat and sunscreen are essential for even short excursions.

The Return of the Railroad

In 1883, cowman William Wallace Bass was out chasing doggies south of the Grand Canyon, when he found himself on the brink of the chasm "scared to death." Two years later, he set up cabins on the rim at Havasupai Point, where tourists came to see the great sight. From the small town of Williams, they boarded stagecoaches and bounced along the 72 miles (116 km) to the camp, where Bass escorted them into his "dear old Canyon home."

His competition in those days was Pete Berry's Grandview Hotel out at Grandview Point. There, tourists arrived after an 11-hour trip from Flagstaff aboard the Grand Canyon Stage and stayed at Berry's hotel or at John Hance's cabins nearby.

But things changed. On September 18, 1901, the Grand Canyon Railway's Locomotive 282 pulled up to the budding Grand Canyon Village on the South Rim. Passengers found the three-hour train ride from Williams far preferable to the dusty daylong stage trips. The arrival of the railway spelled the end of Bass's and Berry's tourist headquarters. With construction of the Bright Angel Lodge and Fred Harvey's five-star El Tovar Hotel, Grand Canyon Village became (and has remained) the center for visitors to the South Rim.

El Tovar's patrons were treated to fresh meals, prepared and served by Harvey girls dressed in white starched aprons. Accommodations were luxurious, and rocking chairs on the spacious porch permitted a classic canyon view with little exertion.

Despite the Harvey Company's dominance on the rim, other entrepreneurs came on the scene. Ralph and Niles Cameron staked mining claims and ran the Bright Angel Trail as a toll route for a time. In 1904, brothers Emory and Ellsworth Kolb built their photographic studio at the trailhead. They took pictures of people departing on mule trips in the morning, ran 4 miles (6 km) down to a water source at Indian Garden to develop the film, and were ready with prints when the tourists returned. In 1911, the Kolb brothers made a film of their wild trip down the Colorado River, which visitors watched in their studio for 65 years.

Again things changed as Americans embraced the automobile, ending the era of rail service to the Grand Canyon in 1968. But another entrepreneur stepped in, restored the tracks, cars and locomotives, and relaunched the Grand Canyon Railway in 1989. Once again, locomotives chug out of the Williams station each morning, making the 135-minute, 65-mile (105-km) run to the canyon. Passengers have a choice of restored coaches or the more opulent club or parlor cars. The three-hour canyon layover allows plenty of time for lunch, a bus tour or a stroll along the rim.

A night at the canyon is also an option. It's a relaxing ride back, complete with crooning cowboy troubadours and mean hombres who stage a hilarious mock holdup.   ❑

● *For more information, contact the Grand Canyon Railway at 800-843-8724 or www.thetrain.com/*

RIGHT: the first passenger train to the Grand Canyon gets ready to depart, September 1901.

COLORADO RIVER RAFTING

*The West's mightiest river transports
boaters on a breathtaking journey through the
heart of the Grand Canyon*

Map
on page
130

O n a hot July day, a flotilla of rubber rafts floats down a serene stretch of the **Colorado River** in the **Grand Canyon**. A high-pitched buzz echoes off the sun-drenched cliffs. It's a peregrine falcon sounding an intruder alarm as it swoops down to the water, then soars back up into the blue sky.

For boaters, the sight of this majestic raptor is an awesome spectacle, and one of the many reasons that a journey through the canyon is such a singular adventure. Here boaters enter the heart of the Southwest's remaining great wilderness and one of the planet's deepest gorges. They encounter wild creatures, pass in wonder through stunning desert canyons, and ride some of the biggest whitewater in the West.

The Rio Colorado courses wild and free through the million acres (405,000 hectares) of **Grand Canyon National Park** in northern Arizona. From the launch point at **Lees Ferry ❶**, the only way out in the next 227 miles (365 km) is by foot on long, steep trails up to the canyon's rims.

Summer is prime season for running the "Grand," and while private individuals with the proper gear and experience are allowed to make the trip, a Park Service permit can take years to obtain. That's why most of the 22,000 people who boat the canyon each year go as paying passengers with outfitters licensed by the Park Service. On these trips, experienced guides row the boats, and the company furnishes all the food and gear. The guides know the river, the best places to hike and camp, and the canyon's stories. It's a tough job – part navigator, part tour guide, part entertainment director. They're up before dawn to make the coffee, they rig and row the boats, they lead hikes and side trips, and they strum their guitars under the stars.

Rules and risks

Even with seasoned guides, passengers need to know a few rules and risks. The rules are: wear shoes on shore, don't use soap in the water, drink plenty of fluids, never litter, and most important, wear life jackets at all times on the river. Helping in camp and kitchen is welcome but certainly not mandatory.

The risks are: boats can flip, and they do once in a great while. Should this happen, the best advice is to keep your feet up and point them downstream. The reason is twofold: first, to ward off rocks with your feet rather than your head and, second, to prevent your feet from getting trapped on the bottom, which can cause you to be dragged under by the current. Get back in the boat if possible; if not, swim to shore and wait for your party to pick you up. The water temperature hovers around 50°F (10°C), and even a short dip can be a numbing experience.

PRECEDING PAGES:
a river guide crashes
through a "hole" on
the Colorado River.
LEFT: rafters stop at
Vasey's Paradise.
BELOW: a dory
noses through
Houserock Rapid.

The Grand Canyon is a remote and wild place; emergency help is more than a phone call or a short drive away. But if you're armed with proper information and take sensible precautions, the journey can be safe and pleasurable for everyone.

Martin Litton, a seasoned river guide and ardent conservationist, guides a dory down the Colorado.

BELOW: dories give a "dry ride" even through big water and can be steered with amazing precision.

Choosing a vessel

Many companies run both oar-powered and motorized boats. Oar boats are smaller, holding four or five people, and trips usually last two weeks (though partial trips are an option). Motor trips last a week or less, and each boat carries many more passengers. Purists eschew the motors because they disturb the canyon's sublime silence. Others who go by motor swear their journey could not have been more profound. As one riverman put it, you could go down the Colorado in a bathtub and still have a peak experience.

Yet another option is a dory – an elegant, wooden, oar-powered boat that is reminiscent of (though much more river worthy than) the vessels used by such early explorers as Major John Wesley Powell, who first ran the Colorado River in 1869.

No matter what kind of boat you choose, you're guaranteed a white knuckle ride unlike any river you may have paddled elsewhere in the West. Though most of the Colorado's rapids aren't technical in the sense that they require a rapid-fire succession of precise maneuvers, the sheer size of the waves packs a mighty wallop and should never be underestimated. Unlike other rivers, which are rated on the familiar International Scale of White water Difficulty, the Colorado has its own rating system, 1 being the most tranquil, 10 the most challenging.

Canyon time

Canyon trips start at Lees Ferry, a desert outpost where a road goes down to the river's edge. It's a busy place on summer days, with several parties rigging at the same time. Tanned, muscled guides lash bags, coolers and metal ammo cans onto boat frames and laugh and joke with their pals. Then, a big bus or van pulls up, disgorging passengers, many of whom have never met before but who will be sharing perhaps the most intense two weeks of their lives together. It's hard to imagine, standing by the gentle, gurgling water, just what the Colorado has in store for them.

With everything neatly stowed and ready, the passengers buckle on life jackets and climb aboard. The boats push off from shore and bounce through the Paria riffle. Everyone stares up at **Navajo Bridge**, 300 feet (90 meters) overhead, the last bit of civilization they'll see for many, many miles.

Around lunchtime, **Badger Rapid** bellows its presence. Boats slide easily down the shining tongue at the top, and passengers squeal with shock and delight at their baptism in the river's chilly water. The trip continues down through **Marble Canyon ❶**, past canyon walls rising ever higher.

The river routine sets in – eat breakfast, pack boats, travel downriver for a few miles, walk up to an ancient Pueblo granary or stop to view a historic inscription on a boulder, lunch under a shady tamarisk, boat a few more miles, then pull up onto a sandy beach for the night. Change into dry clothes, enjoy social hour and dinner, then hit the sleeping bag under a starry sky.

By the third or fourth day of a trip, the sense of being in and of the earth is palpable. Skin toughens to the sun and dry air, people start to talk more about what they're seeing around them than what the stock market is doing

Map on page 130

TIP

It can take 10 years to get a private permit, but you can bypass the process by signing on with one of the commercial outfitters who support kayakers wishing to pilot their own boats.

BELOW: the rigid frame and long oars of an oar raft give pilots power and maneuverability.

back home. Wristwatches and worries are shed as canyon time takes over

Past the scalloped cliffs of the **Desert Palisades**, the stone tower at **Desert View** punctuates the rim skyline. Soon, the aquamarine waters of the **Little Colorado River** interweave with the main Colorado. Guides often pause here to let their passengers enjoy a swim in the Little Colorado's relatively warm turquoise waters, slather themselves with mineral-rich mud, or hike to the remains of a hermit's cabin.

A little farther on, at Mile 77, the canyon walls change from colorful sandstones and limestones to the ominous dark black schist of the **Inner Gorge**. Here is **Hance Rapid** , the first big drop on the river. Its predecessors were only teasers. Hance is a long jumble of rocks and waves, featuring a nasty hole midway through called the **Mixmaster**. At low water it earns a rating of 10.

A camp chef prepares a salmon feast after a long day on the river.

As the canyon closes in, boaters gear up for another series of rambunctious rapids including **Sockdolager**, translated as "the knock-out punch." A taste of rustic civilization rears its head briefly at **Phantom Ranch**, where people can sip an ice-cold lemonade, watch backpackers toiling into camp, and send home a postcard that will be carried out of the canyon on the back of a mule.

This is the point at which an interchange of passengers may occur. Some hike out of the canyon, while others join the trip. They have no idea what's in store for them below Phantom Ranch, because rapids that heretofore inspired awe and fear will soon pale in comparison to those ahead.

Whitewater quartet

BELOW: umbrellas provide welcome shade. Summer temperatures on the river can reach 115°F (46°C).

At lunch, the usually garrulous guides get a little serious. Furrowed brows, furtive conversations, gear tied down a little tighter. Then it's **Horn Creek**,

Map
on page
130

hort, sweet jolt. At lower water levels, when the vicious rocks, or "horns," are howing, this rapid requires a precise entry and one or two strategic oar strokes.

A few miles downstream, the roar of **Granite Rapid** ❶ drowns out jokes and ughter. Formed by boulders washed in from **Monument Creek**, Granite is a haotic flume of monstrous waves issuing off the right wall, along with a few rushers coming in from the left, not to mention dreaded **King Edward**, a major ddy at the bottom. A left entry into Granite is desirable, but the river often has ther ideas, as all the current piles into the right. Granite's been known to flip few boats, so everybody's happy to be right side up at the bottom and beyond e clutches of King Edward.

Hermit Rapid awaits – a series of five beautiful, standing waves – pproached head on, right down the middle. The fifth wave, the granddaddy f them all, can grab a raft and hold it in a watery grip for a few seconds – hough it feels like an eternity – as it decides whether to permit passage or to apsize the prisoner.

With adrenaline nearly exhausted, some guides elect to stop for the night on pleasant little beach before attempting the last of the quartet – infamous **Crys- al Rapid** ⓜ. Crystal – the name is pronounced with reverential dread – eserves its 10-plus rating and is generally regarded as one of the most danger- us rapids on the Colorado. Before 1966, Crystal was a mere riffle. But during storm that winter, a flash flood deposited a mass of boulders in the riverbed, ransforming Crystal into one of the two toughest runs on the river.

A far-right entry in this rapid is almost mandatory. A faulty start can send a oat into the frightening maw at center-left, which may result in a trip through he strainer known as the **Rock Garden** down below.

LEFT: a river guide negotiates a formidable series of standing waves in Granite Rapid.
BELOW: most river trips leave plenty of time for relaxation.

Heart of the Earth

Once all the excitement is over, passengers can enjoy the beauty of the Inner Gorge, surrounded by walls of fluted, blue-black Vishnu schist gleaming like forged iron. The Vishnu, nearly 2 billion years old, is the oldest rock in the canyon. All the rock on top, and all the rock since leaving Lees Ferry, is younger. The Grand Canyon lays out in textbook fashion a neat chronology of the Earth's history, one of the most complete records anywhere, from 2 billion through about 250 million years ago, with only a few gaps.

The rock is old, but the canyon is young. It took the Colorado River less than 6 million years, and maybe as few as 1–2 million, to carve the mile-deep Grand Canyon. It wasn't merely flowing water that that did the work, however. The Colorado once carried millions of tons of sediments in its waters. That heavy load of sand, gravel and large boulders acted like a giant rasp, grinding against the streambed, abrading the rock, and carrying it bit by bit to the delta at the Gulf of California. The river is still trying to cut deeper, but the old, hard, crystalline schist is resisting mightily.

Altered environment

Another major impediment has slowed the work of the river. **Glen Canyon Dam**, 15 miles (24 km) above Lees Ferry, was completed in 1963. This 710-foot-high (216-meter), 10-million-ton concrete plug now holds back the waters of the Colorado in **Lake Powell**. The hydroelectric power generated at the dam electrifies cities all over the West. The water that goes through the turbines is pulled out of the lake about 200 feet (60 meters) below the surface. For boaters downstream, that means cold, clear, green water. In the old days, the Rio

The Colorado is the soul of the desert... Brave boatmen come, they go, they die, the river flows on forever.

– EDWARD ABBEY

BELOW: Redwall Cavern, created by river erosion in a layer of limestone, is a favorite place to stop and rest.

Colorado was choked thick with mud and silt, but no more. Also, electricity demand now determines water levels on the Colorado, which has caused more stable and predictable levels over the course of the year, though daily fluctuations can be dramatic. In some cases boats are left high and dry on beaches in the morning when the water level drops precipitously during the night.

Glen Canyon Dam has also been the single most important influence on the river ecosystem in modern times. Native fish and plants, like humpback chubs and willow trees, have given way to introduced trout and tamarisk. Altered though it may be, the river corridor still harbors a wealth of wildlife – bighorn sheep perched on impossibly sheer cliffs, coyotes coming down to the river to drink, great blue herons standing stock-still on a mudflat, Bell's vireos calling from the thickets, bats fluttering overhead at dusk, collared lizards scampering from boulder to boulder in search of shade, canyon wrens warbling their distinctive liquid trill.

While the river remains the focus, each day brings new places and new discoveries. Boaters frequently stop and walk up side canyons, paradises in the desert with year-round flowing streams, pools reflecting canyon colors, waterfalls where hummingbirds hide, and freshwater springs lush with maidenhair ferns and crimson monkeyflowers. The names of these places are legendary among river rats. **Redwall Cavern**, where a sandy beach is sheltered by an enormous rock alcove, frames glorious views of the canyon; spring water pours hundreds of feet down the mineral-stained walls of **Vasey's Paradise**; **Nankoweap** is known for ancient Pueblo granaries tucked into the canyon 600 feet (180 meters) above the river; **Shinumo Creek** is favored for its inviting swimming hole and the ruins of an old mining camp; **Elves Chasm** and

Map on page 130

A waterfall cascades into one of the many side canyons along the river.

BELOW: a rafter on a hiking expedition fills her water bottle at Dutton Spring, Deer Canyon.

Map on page 130

Matkatamiba Canyon have trickling streams, beautifully eroded rock formations, and lush hanging gardens of water-loving plants.

Lava and beyond

Moving ever downstream, boaters soon come to a stretch of the river below Crystal Rapid known as the **Jewels ⓝ**: **Agate**, **Sapphire**, **Turquoise**, **Ruby**, **Serpentine**, **Garnet**. Boats swirl peacefully past the colonnade of **Conquistadore Aisle**, down to Mile 130 and **Bedrock Rapid**, and below it to **Deubendorff ⓞ**, a long rapid to be run before camping for the night. **Tapeats** and **Deer Creeks** are fine places to linger before facing **Upset Rapid** with its sharp surprises. On to Mile 157 and **Havasu Canyon**, "place of the blue-green waters," home of the Havasupai Indians, where river trips often spend the better part of a day exploring the canyon's travertine ledges and splashing in the plunge pool at the base of **Beaver Falls**.

Farther on, the rocks assume a new form. Black volcanic rocks fill side canyons and form etched pillars. **Vulcan's Anvil**, a remnant of basalt standing in the middle of the river, is an ominous marker of what lies just ahead.

Lava Falls ⓟ is yet another Grand Canyon legend, the one the guides have been talking about ever since the trip began. It's a frightful maelstrom of foaming, seething turbulence stretching the width of the river, and it's rated a 10 at all water levels.

After a scouting session that seems to last forever, everyone walks back down the hot, dusty trail to the boats, hushed and sobered. Life jackets are buckled tight, the guides check every loose line, cameras and binoculars are securely stowed. This one's for real, and everyone seems to know it.

BELOW: a hiker scrambles up Matkatamiba Canyon.
RIGHT: a lone dory drifts through Marble Canyon.

Untied, the boats swing into the current. The guide stands up for a better view, searches for the proverbial "bubble line" that marks the entry. "Hang on," he says, and the passengers clutch whatever handhold they can find. The boat slips down the tongue. Slam! A wave hits the bow like a two-ton truck. Then the boat drops down into a trough of air and climbs up the front of another wave. In a brief second, people stare over into the gargantuan hole formed by Lava's famous V-wave. The boat just kisses it, and the guide shouts, "Get ready!" Another slam of water engulfs boat and passengers. Seconds later, the boatman whoops and orders: "Bail! Bail!" The passengers oblige, tossing bucket after bucket of water back into the Colorado.

Relief. Exultation. Joy. Camp below Lava is always a big celebration. Of course, the trip isn't over. This is only Mile 179.6. There are still another 50 miles (80 km) to go. The terrain changes again as the canyon widens and the river drops into even more austere desert. Finally, **Diamond Peak** spears the horizon. The trucks wait at the **Diamond Creek** take-out. Boats are unpacked one last time, the fine canyon sand sloshed away. It will be a while, though, before all the sand and all the memories are washed clean. Dreams of diving falcons and the sweet songs of canyon wrens will fill many nights to come. Dreams of the canyon and river may last forever.

PAGE AND THE ARIZONA STRIP

*A modern town built to harness the power of
the Colorado River is a gateway to the lean and lonesome
country north of the Grand Canyon*

Map
on page
124

Phoenix

Tucson

High, wide, lonesome country" is what cowboys called the **Arizona Strip**. Even many Arizonans have never heard of this quiet stretch of high desert on the Arizona–Utah border, sandwiched between the **North Rim f the Grand Canyon** and the **Vermilion Cliffs**. For most visitors, it's the ighway 89A Grand Canyon corridor, connecting the communities of north-rn Arizona with those of southern Utah via the only road bridge over the Colorado River in 600 miles (970 km).

To the Kaibab Paiute Tribe, whose small reservation surrounds Pipe Spring National Monument, the Strip was once a bountiful homeland of tallgrass rairie, sunflowers and hundreds of other food plants. Some 5,000 of their ncestors roamed long distances seasonally, living in wickiup brush shelters nd weaving beautiful baskets to gather pinyon nuts, seeds and other foods. n summer, they hunted deer and elk on the Kaibab Plateau, then returned to tone houses beside springs to harvest corn and squash like their predecessors, the Virgin River Anasazi. Springs "belonged" to individual families, vho acted as caretakers on behalf of the natural world, learning the songs of ach rock and tree, much as Australian aborigines ollow "songlines" across the Outback. "They cannot lescribe a country to you," wrote explorer John Wesey Powell, who mapped this area with Paiute guides n 1871, using Pipe Spring as his base. "But they an tell you all the details of a route."

PRECEDING PAGES:
Horseshoe Bend,
near Page.
LEFT: Paria River
Canyon.
BELOW: Great Basin
rattlesnake.

he road to recovery

Che Kaibab Paiute were almost wiped out by 18th-entury Spanish diseases and 19th-century Navajo nd Ute slave trading. Then, in the 1860s, Mormon olonists took over water sources and traditional unting and gathering lands for farms, ranches and ettlements, and very quickly, Kaibab Paiutes lost heir self-sufficiency and became poverty-stricken nd dependent on the newcomers. The situation has hanged today, thanks largely to education, successul legal challenges over self-determination and ccess to water, and modest commercial developnent on the reservation.

Things look less rosy for the land itself. The huge attle drives of the 1870s and 1880s badly overgrazed he Strip. Lush grasslands have been replaced by sagerush and erosion of deep arroyos, and despite better tewardship of the land under the watchful gaze of he Bureau of Land Management (BLM), it struggles o recover. Although ranching, logging and mining re still in evidence, tourism and outdoor recreation

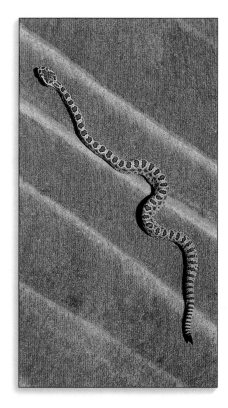

are becoming more important economically. Four-wheel-drivers, river runners, hikers and other outdoor-lovers can explore some of the most beautiful and little-traveled backcountry in the state in **Grand Canyon National Park**, four national monuments, and eight wilderness areas.

Unnatural beauty

Given this abundant natural beauty, it's ironic that the area's most popular attraction is unnatural. Some 130 miles (210 km) north of Flagstaff, on Highway 89, is 180-mile-long (290-km) **Lake Powell ❷**, the second largest man-made lake in the Western Hemisphere. The lake is formed by 710-foot-high (220-meter) **Glen Canyon Dam**, downstream at **Page ❸**, which generates 1,200 megawatts of hydroelectricity for the megalopolises of Phoenix and environs – and ample controversy.

When it was begun in 1956, the dam had the blessing of almost everyone concerned. By the time it was finished in 1963, conservationists like the Sierra Club's David Brower and writer Wallace Stegner had belatedly recognized that Glen Canyon, "the place no one knew," was comparable in grandeur to anything – including the nearby Grand Canyon – on the Colorado Plateau. Today, many people believe that the drowning of Glen Canyon and its rich natural and cultural history was an unspeakable ecological tragedy and are advocating the eventual dismantling of the dam. In the meanwhile, both biologists and politicians are investigating ways to mitigate the effects of the dam on the downstream environment.

That said, Lake Powell, administered by the National Park Service as **Glen Canyon National Recreation Area** (open daily 8am–7pm; tel: 928-608-6404), is a stunning place to waterski, fish and explore the shoreline. Miles of blue water and a 1,961-mile (3,156-km) shoreline of carved sandstone cliffs make the lake a photographer's dream. Houseboats, popular with vacationers, may be rented at any of the five marinas, along with fishing tackle and powerboats. Sea kayaks, ideal for exploring the dozens of side canyons that spill into the lake, are also available.

Carl Hayden Visitor Center (open daily 7am–7pm in summer; 8am–5pm rest of year; tel: 928-608-6404; admission fee), next to the dam in Page, has exhibits, interpretive presentations and information on hiking, side canyons and river trips. It offers frequent self-guided and guided tours of the dam and powerplant, which is operated by the U.S. Bureau of Reclamation.

There are four campgrounds, numerous undeveloped sites along the shoreline, and camping on the southern shore of Lake Powell with permission from he Navajo Nation. Also on Navajo land is 290-foot-high (90-meter) **Rainbow Bridge National Monument** (open daily; tel: 928-608-6404), the world's tallest known natural bridge. The bridge may be reached by boat trip directly from Glen Canyon, but the site is sacred to the Navajo who control overland access on the two rugged trails leading to the bridge. For hiking and camping permission, contact the Navajo Nation, Recreational Resources Dept., Box 308, Window Rock, AZ 86515. Hiring a Navajo guide is also recommended for trips into **Antelope Canyon**, one of the easiest slot canyons in the area to reach and explore.

You'll find equally stunning vistas at the **Horseshoe Bend** viewpoint, which is set on the cliffs over a hairpin loop in the Colorado River, known to geologists as an entrenched meander. It's roughly a half mile (800 meters) to the overlook from the trailhead, which is about 5 miles (8 km) south of the Carl Hayden Visitor Center on Highway 89.

Lake Powell was named for explorer John Wesley Powell, whose 1869 and 1871–72 river-running trips were the first to explore the Green and Colorado River Gorges. **John Wesley Powell Memorial Museum** (open Mon–Sat 8am–6pm; tel: 928-645-9496; donation) has old drawings and photos about Powell's life and voyages, geological displays, and Indian artifacts. The museum is located in downtown Page, which has grown from a makeshift shantytown for dam workers into far northern Arizona's largest community, with a variety of mainstream lodgings, restaurants and gas options.

To enter the Arizona Strip itself, head back south to the junction of Highway 89 and 89A, at **Bitter Springs**, and drive west via **Marble Canyon**. When it opened in 1929, the narrow, 467-foot-high (142-meter) **Navajo Bridge** over the Colorado River was the highest steel structure in the world. A wider bridge

Map on page 124

LEFT: Antelope Canyon is one of the most accessible slot canyons in the Page area.
BELOW: the Glen Canyon Bridge spans the chasm just below the dam.

was opened in 1997, and you can walk across the old structure. The small **Navajo Bridge Visitor Center** is an impressive piece of desert architecture, with pueblo-style sandstone walls and a fine little bookstore.

Behind the dramatic Vermilion Cliffs is **Lees Ferry ❹**, once a ferry crossing operated by John D. Lee, a prominent Mormon elder. Lee was sent here personally by Mormon Church President Brigham Young after being implicated in the 1857 Mountain Meadow Massacre of an emigrant wagon train bound for California. At the mouth of the **Paria River**, Lee's old homestead, **Lonely Dell Ranch** is a pretty spot with a log cabin, a blacksmith shop, ranch house and shady orchards, a good place to while away an hour or two, watching the river runners putting in on the Colorado River.

Canyons and crossings

The 293,000-acre (119,000-hectare) **Vermilion Cliffs National Monument ❺** incorporates **Paria Canyon–Vermilion Cliffs Wilderness**, which has no fewer than three spectacular slot canyon hikes. The most popular is the 38-mile (61-km) hike through the narrow, 2,000-foot-deep (600-meter) **Paria River Canyon** to **Paria, Utah**, a trip of four to six days. The southern trailhead is at Lees Ferry. Day users must register before setting out; all overnight trips are by permit only, with daily quotas in force. The best time to do this river hike (which requires wading in places) is mid-March to June. This is not a place you want to be during a flash flood in the summer monsoon season.

Hiking tips, permits, and up-to-date weather information can be obtained from the BLM office in **Kanab, Utah** (open Mon–Fri 7:45am–4:30pm; tel: 435-644-26720), which also sells a booklet on hiking the canyon.

BELOW: erosion exposes intricate cross-bedding at Vermilion Cliffs National Monument, a legacy of its birth as a field of sand dunes.

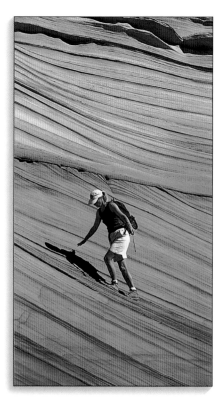

BUFFALO JONES

Jesse "Buffalo" Jones was an aging buffalo hunter who had participated in the mass slaughter of the shaggy beasts on the Great Plains in the 1870s. In 1906, realizing the buffalo were close to extinction, he drove a herd of survivors to the Arizona Strip, where he set up a buffalo preserve and tried unsuccessfully to breed "cattalo," a cross between buffalo and cattle.

Writer Zane Grey was introduced to Jones in 1907, while the colorful frontiersman was on a fundraising tour of the East Coast. Jones, clad in fringed buckskin, held audiences spellbound with stories of lassoing wild mountain lions in the Grand Canyon and other tales of life on the frontier. Grey, who had honeymooned in northern Arizona the year before, was intrigued. He traveled to Arizona and witnessed Jones's lion-hunting skills firsthand, which became a key inspiration for *Last of the Plainsmen* and other stories.

Although Grey admired Jones, he was dismayed by Jones's ruthless pursuit of his prey. "He shore can make animals do what he wants," wrote Grey in *Don, the Story of a Lion Dog*. "But I never seen the dog or horse that cared two bits for him." Descendants of Jones's original buffalo herd may still be seen in House Rock Valley today.

The first white men to see the mouth of the Paria River were Spanish Padres Dominguez and Escalante whose expedition left Santa Fe, New Mexico, in 1776, hoping to forge an overland route to Monterey, California. They were forced to turn back near St. George, then tried, unsuccessfully, to cross the Colorado River at Lees Ferry. Eventually, they found a good ford, 40 miles (64 km) upriver, at a spot known as the Crossing of the Fathers (it has since been flooded by Lake Powell). The **San Bartolome Historic Site** marker on the north side of Highway 89A, marks one of their campsites. You'll find it west of the 1890 **Cliff Dwellers Lodge**, a tiny redstone oasis built beneath a huge boulder, with overnight lodging, a decent restaurant, a gas station, a small store and stunning views.

A Navajo taco: fried dough heaped with chili, cheese, etc.

The Vermilion Cliffs support desert bighorn sheep, pronghorn, mountain lion and, since 1996, California condors, which were reintroduced at **House Rock Valley**, a grassy break in the cliffs. House Rock Valley was home to Mormon pioneer Jim Emett, who operated Lees Ferry in the early 1900s. Emett and his neighbor, frontiersman Jesse "Buffalo" Jones *(see sidebar)*, guided Zane Grey on his first mountain lion hunting trip to Arizona in 1907, when they spent time at both ranchers' homesteads on the Strip and explored **Surprise Valley**, near the Grand Canyon. Grey later wrote that Emett was "the man who influenced [me] most," noting Emett's love of the West and all living things despite "so few of the joys commonly yearned for by men." The frontier spirit embodied in men like Emett became recurrent themes in such classic Grey novels as *Riders of the Purple Sage* and *Last of the Frontiersmen*.

BELOW: the *Canyon King* offers sunset, dinner and short scenic cruises on Lake Powell.

The road winds onto the 8,000-foot (2,400-meter) **Kaibab Plateau** through old-growth ponderosa pine forest. The turnoff for the North Rim of the Grand

The prickly pear cactus usually blooms May to June

BELOW:
Rainbow Bridge,
considered sacred
by the Navajo,
can be reached by
tour boat from
Wahweap Marina.

Canyon is at **Jacob Lake ❻**, named for Mormon missionary Jacob Hamblin, whose exploring party came through in the 1860s. Starting in 1866, Franklin Woolley, followed by his brother Edwin "Dee" Woolley, explored the plateau's potential for lumber, grazing and Mormon settlements and hatched numerous schemes for development.

Woolley's most extravagant caper came in 1892, when he and Brigham Young's son John, on a mission in England, hired Buffalo Bill, whose famous Wild West Show was currently in London, to escort a party of wealthy English nobles interested in game hunting and ranching in the region. None of the Brits decided to purchase ranches, but they stopped at Jacob Lake, where Buffalo Bill reputedly said grace at one meal, offering thanks for many blessings, specifically "Emma Bentley's custard pie."

Excellent homemade pies and milkshakes are still served at historic **Jacob Lake Inn**, operated by descendants of Edwin Woolley. **Jacob Lake Visitor Center** has exhibits and information on visiting the rough backcountry of **Kaibab National Forest**. One of the best hikes here is in **Snake Gulch**, where you'll see remarkable Virgin River Anasazi rock art. Camping and horseback rides are also available near the inn.

From Jacob Lake, the road spirals 3,000 feet (900 meters) off the plateau, descending from ponderosa pine into pinyon-juniper dwarf forest. Views of the western Arizona Strip and southwestern Utah's Color Country are breathtaking. It's hard to drive and goggle at the scenery, so pull off at **Le Fevre Overlook**. From here, you can see the geological formation known as the **Grand Staircase**, including the **White Cliffs** of Navajo Sandstone in **Zion National Park**.

At the base of the Kaibab Plateau, the small Mormon community of **Fredonia ❼**

(a contraction of the English word "Free" and the Spanish word "Dona" to signify a free woman – a reference to the town's polygamous past) is a good place to spend the night, with small motels, Mexican restaurants, gas stations, and convenience stores. If you're heading south, you can also pick up information on Kaibab National Forest at the U.S. Forest Service headquarters.

Map on page 124

Mormon outpost

Turn west on Highway 389 and continue to **Pipe Spring National Monument** ❽ (open daily; tel: 928-643-7105; admission fee), a small 1870 fortified ranch where the Mormon-owned Canaan Cattle Company ran the Church's large tithe cattle herd. The two-story fort was ostensibly built to enclose springs from the nearby Sevier Cliffs and to keep out Navajo raiders; in reality, there was more to fear from government officials hounding polygamous families (including Dee Woolley and his young wife Flora). The women were kept busy making pies, bread and stews for travelers, explorers, miners and, after the St. George Temple had been completed, Mormon newlyweds who had been "sealed" and were returning home on the Honeymoon Trail. John Wesley Powell used the West Cabin as a headquarters during his 1872 survey, which ascertained that lands originally thought to be in Utah were actually in Arizona, creating the area we know today as the Arizona Strip.

In summer, rangers in period costume offer fascinating living-history demonstrations of pioneer life. Year-round tours leave from the visitor center and pass through the heavy wooden doors of the fort into two buildings joined by a catwalk. Spring water was piped into a ground-floor spring room where milk was kept cool, then processed into butter and cheese. Milk, meat, butter and cheese

BELOW: heavy doors protect the entrance to Winsor Castle, the main building at Pipe Spring National Monument.

Map on page 124

were sent by the wagonload to St. George, Utah, every two weeks to feed workers constructing the new St. George Temple. A second-floor room housed Arizona's first telegraph. A self-guided tour through the orchards has a push-button oral history by Maggie Heaton, a hired hand at Pipe Spring in 1898. The Kaibab Paiute Tribe, whose reservation surrounds the monument, participates in the management of the site. The tribe runs a campground, offers guided tours of rock art sites, hikes and cultural activities, and holds a powwow every October. Many tribal members work at the tribe's new gas station and convenience store or at tribal headquarters opposite the visitor center, and live in nearby Kaibab and Moccasin.

All in the family

The Arizona Strip tends to attract nonconformists. **Colorado City ❾**, on the Arizona–Utah border, is one such town. Its massive, half-finished houses with more than one door, bonneted wives, and young girls in quaint leggings and floral shifts are just a few outward signs of the polygamous lifestyle still practiced here. Once subject to government raids (the last was in 1957), the residents of Colorado City are no longer harassed by the authorities and are beginning to interact with tourists needing gas, food and other services. A small city park has steep trails into the 6,500-acre (2,600-hectare) **Cottonwood Point Wilderness**, which contains 1,000-foot (300-meter) multihued cliffs, pinnacles and canyons.

Views to the south take in an area of spare beauty that includes the **Shivwits Plateau**, **Mount Trumbull** and **Mount Logan Wildernesses**, **Grand Wash Cliffs Wilderness** and **Paiute Wilderness** in the **Virgin Mountains**. All of these are now part of the newly created 1.1-million-acre (450,000-hectare) **Grand Canyon–Parashant National Monument ❿**. The monument expands the geological story of the Grand Canyon by including volcanic landmarks like 8,028-foot (2,447-meter) **Mount Trumbull** (which provided the wood for the St. George Temple). It is also an ecologically unique area where the Sonoran, Great Basin and Mohave Deserts intersect, providing critical habitat for endangered California condors, desert tortoises, Southwest willow flycatchers, desert bighorn sheep and pronghorn antelope.

Long, very rough dirt roads are the norm in this undeveloped monument. Avoid them during the summer monsoon season, and don't travel here without several gallons of backup gas and water, food and spare tires. The monument's size and the long distances required to reach its features are intimidating, but adventurous travelers will enjoy the 60-mile (100-km) kidney-bruising drive to 6,393-foot (1,947-meter) **Toroweap Overlook**, where the Grand Canyon drops away 3,000 feet (900 meters) right below your feet. **Tuweep Ranger Station**, about 6 miles (10 km) before the overlook, is open year-round and has information on hiking, camping and road conditions.

The BLM's excellent Arizona Strip map offers an overview of the region and is essential for navigating the monument's backcountry roads. For more information, contact the BLM's Arizona Strip Field Office and Information Center in St. George, Utah (open Mon–Fri 7:45am– 4:30pm; tel: 435-688-3200). ❏

BELOW: the hooves of desert bighorn sheep are adapted to scrambling over bare rock and narrow ledges. **RIGHT:** sandstone formations swirl around a hiker in the Paria Canyon–Vermilion Cliffs Wilderness.

Desert Blossoms

Arizona has two main wildflower seasons – the result of steady winter rains and violent summer "monsoons" that awaken first delicate annuals and later hardy perennials. As a result, flowers are blooming somewhere in Arizona from late January all the way to October, starting with low-elevation deserts and ending with the high country of the White Mountains and San Francisco Peaks near Flagstaff.

But it is the brilliant March displays of brightly colored annuals below an elevation of 6,000 feet (1,830 meters) that catch the headlines and send photographers scrambling for their cameras. With the right balance of rain and sunshine between October and January – an event that occurs only every five years or so – expect a wildflower extravaganza the following February to May. Displays of annuals are unpredictable. To find out what is blooming and where, check in with wildflower reports on the Web and at local parks, in newspapers like the *Arizona Daily Star*, and the 602-542-4988 Arizona Wildflower Hotline set up each spring.

In February, Organ Pipe Cactus National Monument and other low-elevation spots in the west deserts are the first to bloom, in delicate waves of desert chicory, bladderpod, desert marigolds, and verbena. They are followed by showy displays of sulfur yellow brittlebush, a shrub that, like creosote, appears to die in summer heat, only to releaf a few days after consistent rains.

In late March and early April, trails along hillsides in Catalina State Park and Picacho Peak, north of Tucson, are carpeted with Mexican and California poppies in shades of gold, yellow and peach, interwoven with bunches of white-purple Coulter's lupine, blue toadflax, pink owl clover, white desert phlox and yellow evening primrose.

By May, pricklypear, hedgehog, claret cup and cholla cactus begin wearing topknots of neon red, purple haze and acid yellow to attract birds for pollination and to spread their seeds through juicy fruits. Green-barked

LEFT: a mass of brilliant red flowers adorn a claret cup cactus. **BELOW:** house finches alight on creamy white saguaro blossoms.

paloverde trees are decked out in a golden rain of blossoms; long-lived ironwood trees erupt into a riot of lilac blooms. Living fences of ocotillo branches, rooted in the ground, are tipped with red blooms in villages all over Sonora, Mexico.

Just as low-elevation wildflowers start to wilt under triple-digit temperatures in the deserts, the race to reproduce is heating up in the reawakening high country. After wet winters, look for outrageous displays of penstemons atop the rocky limestone and volcanic soils around Flagstaff, including one species that grows only at Sunset Crater Volcano National Monument.

Monsoons saturate the soil, and by August, wildflowers are drinking up moisture greedily. Flame-colored Indian paintbrush, a parasitic beauty, roots atop other plants. Five-fingered purple lupines "wolf" down nitrogen. Red skyrocket gilia and a variety of salvias, or sages, attract hummingbirds. Along shady streams and washes, bog iris, Rocky Mountain columbines, nodding bluebells, pink shooting stars, and jolly yellow and red mon-

keyflowers keep their feet wet, while in open sandy areas, like those on the Navajo Reservation, vetches and princes plume occupy sandy ridges rich in selenium.

Yellow sunflowers and purple asters are the summer stars of the high country. They line roadsides and form joyful throngs in meadows, allowing tits and finches to stock their larders with seeds before the first snows of October once more blanket the mountains.

Surrounded by such beauty, it's easy to forget that wildflowers are actualy engaged in a competitive struggle to reproduce. Their shape and color are designed to attract the animals they rely on for pollination and seed dispersal. Night-blooming white flowers are a magnet for visiting Mexican long-nosed bats and hawkmoths; pastel purples and pinks attract butterflies; yellow flowers lure carpenter bees; red trumpet flowers advertise for hummingbirds. It's all part of an evolutionary scheme that links one living thing to another. As is always the case in nature, the survival of any one species depends on the health of the whole ecosystem. ❑

BELOW: Dune evening primrose and sand verbena bloom in spring in the Sonoran Desert.

NAVAJO AND HOPI RESERVATIONS

At home in remote and sacred valleys and mesas, the Navajo and Hopi tread a path between centuries-old rituals and modern lifestyles

Map on page 124

T ravel anywhere in Indian Country and you will encounter beauty. It haunts the eerie rock formations, deeply etched canyons, sacred peaks and serpentine rivers that give form and meaning to the Navajo and Hopi homelands. Life in such huge, empty, dry country seems ephemeral – a question of chance. What is really required is adaptation and a deep understanding of the land, the seasons and the rituals that help humans remember their place in the cosmos.

Both the Hopi and Navajo understand this. The Hopi say that, after being expelled from three lower worlds because they fell out of harmony with the Creator Spirit, the people entered this Fourth World and encountered Masaw, the caretaker of the Earth. Masaw offered them a short ear of blue corn, from which they realized that life would be difficult, and, in order to cultivate the corn, they would have to learn humility, cooperation, respect and earth stewardship. The Hopi clans migrated for countless generations, traveling in all four directions in search of the Center of the Earth. They finally settled on this arid plateau between the Rio Grande and the Colorado River, a place so barren they would be forced to depend on prayer for rain and food. Never again would they forget to be thankful to the Creator.

PRECEDING PAGES: Navajo herders, Monument Valley. **LEFT:** Navajo dancer, Navajo Nation Fair **BELOW:** Navajo rug, Hubbell Trading Post.

Indian country gateway

Begin your tour of the 25,000-square-mile (65,000-sq-km) **Navajo Nation ⓫** and much smaller adjoining **Hopi Reservation** north of Flagstaff, on Highway 89. In about 30 miles (50 km), the elevation drops from 7,000 to 6,000 feet (2,100–1,800 meters), with a corresponding change in scenery from ponderosa pine forest to sagebrush rangeland dotted with pinyon and juniper. The road passes through the large volcanic field that gave birth to **Sunset Crater Volcano** and the 12,000-foot (3,600-meter) **San Francisco Peaks**, revered by both the Navajo and Hopi. To the east are the pastel-hued badlands of the **Painted Desert** and the distant **Hopi Mesas**.

Ahead is the **Little Colorado River**, which rises on Mount Baldy in the White Mountains and flows northwest to its confluence with the Colorado River in the Grand Canyon. A good view of the river can be had from the historic **Cameron Trading Post ⓬**, left of the highway bridge, established by Mabel and Hubert Richardson in 1916. Still in the Richardson family, there's now a 65-room motel, a gas station, a post office and an art gallery. The original trading post retains its authentic atmosphere, with creaky wood floors and dry and canned goods traded for rugs, jewelry and the other Indian arts and crafts sold here.

Skip the cheap souvenirs in the front rooms and head for the stone gallery, where big-ticket, museum-quality artifacts are sold. The dining room serves a tasty Navajo frybread taco (voted Arizona's state dish in a 1995 *Arizona Republic* poll). It's a good idea to get here early to avoid the tour bus lunch crowd and to obtain a room, if you wish to spend the night.

Drive east on Highway 160 through a spectacular landscape of rocks laid down during the Time of the Dinosaurs, 200 million years ago. Handmade signs lead north of the highway to the famous **Dinosaur Tracks** in the red Kayenta Formation, where, for a few dollars, a young Navajo guide will show you the three-toed tracks of dilophosaurus, a "running dinosaur." This dinosaur weighed 1,000 pounds (450 kg), stood 8 to 10 feet (2.5–3 meters) tall, and ran on its powerful hind legs. It used short forearms and clawed fingers for grasping and tearing apart its prey. Claw marks can be seen in the tracks.

Mormon way station

To the north is **Hamblin Ridge**, named for Mormon missionary Jacob Hamblin, who was sent by Church President Brigham Young to make contact with the Hopi and Navajo and assess the area's potential for colonization in 1858. Hamblin farmed here for several years, after befriending Hopi Chief Tuuvi, who subsequently converted to Mormonism. **Tuba City ⑬**, founded by Mormons in 1877, honors this chief. The town was used as a way station for Mormons traveling south from Utah to develop communities on the Colorado River and still displays the Lombardy poplars that typically marked such settlements.

Even before the Mormons arrived, Charles Algert had opened the **Tuba Trading Post** in 1870. This unusual octagonal trading post, built in 1906 to

BELOW: tracks record the presence of dinosaurs more than 150 million years ago.
RIGHT: a mechanized coal line runs from Black Mesa.

resemble a traditional Navajo hogan, is a good place to buy a Storm Pattern rug, the signature design of the western Navajo Reservation, with symbols that vividly recall the landmarks and colors of this dramatic area.

Map on page 124

The Mormons never obtained clear title to the land on which Tuba City was built, and in 1903 it was withdrawn by the U.S. government and added to the Navajo Reservation. In 1905, the Bureau of Indian Affairs built the large two-story sandstone complex of Tuba City Boarding School. Schools like this one aimed to assimilate Indian children by taking them from their families, cutting their hair, forbidding them to speak their language, and enforcing military-style discipline. Today, despite 50 years of educational reform and a renaissance in Indian culture, only half of the 210,000 tribal members speak Navajo, although reservation schools have been required to teach the language since 1984. Sixty percent of the Navajo Nation is now between the ages of 19 and 38 and exposed every day to the more materialistic Anglo culture. Many, though by no means all, see little value in the old land-based traditions.

South of the highway, between Red Lake Trading Post and Kayenta is 8,210-foot (2,500-meter) **Black Mesa**, the largest single land form in northern Arizona. Peabody Western Coal Company operates two of the largest open pit strip mines in the country here and pays royalties to both the Navajo and Hopi tribes. Coal from the Black Mesa Mine goes to the Mohave Generating Station on the Nevada–Arizona border through the Black Mesa Pipeline, which uses a billion gallons of pristine aquifer water a year to slurry the coal more than 273 miles (440 km) around the Grand Canyon. This has prompted a great deal of concern by residents about spring depletion, and alternatives are now being explored.

Happily may I walk.
May it be beautiful
before me.
May it be beautiful
behind me.
May it be beautiful
below me.
May it be beautiful
above me.
May it be beautiful
all around me.
In beauty it is finished.
– NAVAJO NIGHT CHANT

BELOW: Keet Seel Ruin, Navajo National Monument.

Navajo girl, about 1910, in traditional skirt and velveteen blouse.

The ancient ones

North of Black Mesa, a 10-mile (16-km) drive on Highway 564 leads through swirling pink slickrock country to **Navajo National Monument** (open daily, May–Sept 8am–6pm, closes earlier rest of year; tel: 928-672-2366; free admission), which protects some of the largest and best preserved prehistoric cliff dwellings in the nation. Snugged into a 450-foot-high (140-meter) alcove above **Tsegi Canyon**, the 135-room pueblo of **Betatakin** ("Ledge House") was built in AD 1250 and housed about 135 people for 50 years. It harmonizes so perfectly with its surroundings, visitors standing at the overlook at the end of the short Sandal Trail usually don't see it at first. Five-mile (8-km) hikes to Betatakin are led by rangers each morning and are limited to 25 hikers. To avoid disappointment, stay in the monument's delightful 30-site campground and high-tail it to the visitor center first thing in the morning to pick up a ticket.

A second, larger pueblo, **Keet Seel**, lies 8 miles (13 km) in the backcountry and requires a permit and challenging overnight hike to view. A limit of 20 visitors per day is strictly enforced; make reservations before your trip and be sure you're up to it. Temperatures reach 100°F (38°C) in summer. Wear a hat, sunscreen, sunglasses and sturdy boots, and carry high-energy food and at least a gallon (4 liters) of water.

Monument Valley

Kayenta is a large prosperous town with good food and lodging. It has benefited from its proximity to the Black Mesa Mine and **Monument Valley** (open daily, 8am–7pm, winter to 5pm; tel: 928-871-6647; admission fee), the crown jewel of the Navajo tribal park system. Begin your tour at the visitor

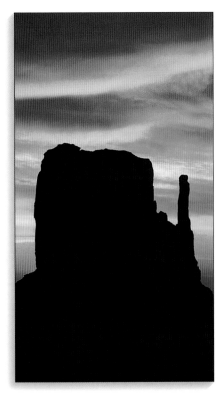

NAVAJO–HOPI LAND DISPUTE

The Navajo and Hopi tribes have had their differences over the years, especially regarding the disposition of tribal lands and resources. The Hopi, whose mesa-top homes are completely surrounded by the larger Navajo Nation, have long claimed that the expansion of the Navajo reservation in several stages during the 19th and 20th centuries was made at the expense of Hopi land.

Tensions seriously escalated in 1974, when the U.S Congress passed the Navajo–Hopi Relocation Act. The law which divided nearly 2 million acres (800,000 hectares) between the tribes, was supposed to compel 11,000 Navajo and about 100 Hopi to leave homes they had known for generations. Many of the Navajo moved to new government housing; others still resist relocation.

In recent years, public attention has been focused on a resolution of the so-called Bennet Freeze, a decree passed down by the U.S. Department of Interior in 1966 that prevents Navajo living on contested land from building new homes or making substantial repairs to old ones. The ruling affects as many as 7,000 Navajo living on a 1½-million acre (607,00-hectare) disputed area, only 10 percent of whom have running water and 3 percent have electricity, according to a Navajo survey.

center, 24 miles (39 km) north of Kayenta on Highway 163, which has exhibits about the Navajo, or Diné, way of life, a gift shop, restrooms and water. This is the place to watch the world's most awe-inspiring sunrise illuminate the Owl, Mittens, Totem Pole and other fiery sandstone landmarks familiar from such John Ford Westerns as *Stagecoach*, *She Wore a Yellow Ribbon* and *Cheyenne*. Local Navajo pose for photos in traditional dress, but always ask first and offer payment. Families rely on tourism income.

A tour booklet has information on 11 scenic overlooks along the 17-mile (27-km) unpaved scenic drive, including John Ford Point, the most famous view in the valley. You'll need to hire a Navajo guide to go into the back-country. Horseback and van tours usually include a visit to the hogan of a Navajo rug weaver, a traditional Navajo lunch, and the chance to view some of the more than 200 Ancestral Pueblo ruins and petroglyphs in the valley.

Make arrangements at the visitor center or at the 62-room **Gouldings Lodge** (tel: 435-727-3231). The old 1930s trading post started by Harry Goulding and his wife Mike is now a museum filled with memorabilia from Harry's friend-ships with John Ford, John Wayne and other Hollywood celebrities. The lodge offers the only accommodations actually set in Monument Valley. The restau-rant serves up Navajo and American fare, but it's the view, not the food, that leaves the biggest impression.

Monument Valley isn't a valley at all but the Monument Upwarp, a geolog-ical uplift, or monocline, riddled with faults. It stretches from Comb Ridge and the San Juan River on the Arizona–Utah border to the north and Black Mesa to the south. Restless earth movements have created all kinds of strangely tilted cliffs (long mined for valuable minerals) and major landmarks. Looming on

Map on page 124

BELOW: an elder demonstrates traditional Navajo weaving outside a hogan in Monument Valley.

the northern horizon is 10, 416-foot (3,175-meter) **Navajo Mountain**, sacred to the Navajo and Hopi, and the twin buttes called the **Bear's Ears**. At the valley's southern perimeter is craggy **Agathla Peak**, a dark basaltic volcanic neck bared by erosion that once marked the southern boundary of Ute territory. The only camping in the park is in the Mitten View Campground, which has about 100 sites but no facilities.

Four Corners

Highway 160 continues east from Kayenta on the south side of **Comb Ridge** (try to do this drive at dusk when the oblique rays of the sun turn the sandstone blood red). In 64 miles (103 km), you'll reach historic **Teec Nos Pos Trading Post**  ("cottonwoods in a circle"), a good place to get gas, have a quick bite to eat, and view superb examples of large, intricately patterned Teec Nos Pos rugs. Many say the design is reminiscent of Persian rugs – with a price tag to match. A brief detour north takes you to **Four Corners Monument Navajo Tribal Park** (open daily 7am–8pm; admission fee), the only place in the United States where you can stand simultaneously in four states – Utah, Arizona, New Mexico and Colorado.

Highway 191 heads south on the west side of the **Carrizo**, **Lukachukai** and **Chuska Mountains**. So many of the reservation's overscaled, fantastically shaped rocks seem alive. Indeed, Navajo legends state that many of these formations were once fearsome, human-devouring monsters, slain by the mythic Hero Twins – Monster Slayer and Born for Water – thereby freeing the Navajo to pursue the Beauty Path in the Fourth World. The Chuskas, Lukachukais and Carrizos are said to be the head, torso and feet of the male god Yootzill.

BELOW: a young Navajo cowboy. **RIGHT:** a Navajo rug weaver at Hubbell Trading Post.

avajo capital

orthwest of **Window Rock** ⓮ is **Fort Defiance**, the site of an 1851 fort built
y the U.S. government to calm tensions between Navajo and newly arrived
nglo residents. By 1863, things had deteriorated to the degree that U.S. Army
aptain Kit Carson, under the orders of General James Carleton to "solve the
oblem," instigated a five-year scorched-earth campaign to drive out the
avajo. Homes and possessions were burned, fruit trees cut down, and livestock
aughtered. As many as 8,000 Navajo were sent on a 300-mile (480-km) forced
arch to Bosque Redondo (Fort Sumner) on the Pecos River in New Mexico,
hile several thousand others hid in remote Canyon de Chelly, the Grand
anyon and Monument Valley.

Although many Diné starved or died of diseases in confinement, survivors of
e Long Walk were eventually allowed to return to a fraction of their original
>meland in 1868. They quickly rebounded in numbers and livestock holdings
id began to thrive. The government built a Bureau of Indian Affairs agency at
ort Defiance in 1868, followed by the first reservation boarding school.

A few miles to the south is Window Rock, the capital of the Navajo Nation.
▪ 1923, after vast oil reserves were found underneath the Navajo Reservation,
ie federal government created the Navajo Tribal Council to facilitate negotia-
ons of lease agreements with oil companies. Later discoveries of oil, gas and
ranium further concentrated the power of the tribal council, and eventually
idespread corruption necessitated a complete reorganization in 1991. It now
is 88 delegates from 110 chapter houses, or local councils, across the reser-
ition, which meet four times a year (and on many special sessions) in the
eautiful Navajo Nation Council Chambers, constructed in the shape of a

Map
on page
124

BELOW: the hands
of a Navajo weaver
and sheepherder
reflect years of
hard work.

Navajo rugs, some costing thousands of dollars, are displayed at Hubbell Trading Post.

BELOW:
Navajo riders gallop through Canyon de Chelly.

traditional hogan. Delegates speak in Navajo while the council is in session, and visitors are welcome to observe the proceedings. A colorful mural recounts the history of the Diné.

Navajos fought bravely in World War II, Korea, Vietnam and other recent conflicts. Their finest hour may have been when Navajo Code Talkers foiled Japanese codebreakers by transmitting important communications among allies in Navajo. Commemorating the tribe's distinguished military service is the **Navajo Nation Veterans Memorial Park** in **Window Rock Tribal Park**, a pleasant spot for a picnic and a closer look at Window Rock itself, a geological opening in the Cow Springs Sandstone.

Stop at the Navajo Nation Parks and Recreation Department (open daily; tel 928-871-6647) off Highway 264 to pick up information on Navajo tribal parks and visitor permits for hiking, camping and fishing. Next door is the delightful **Navajo Nation Zoo**, which exhibits mountain lions, coyotes, Mexican wolves, churro sheep and other native animals, interpreting them from the Navajo point of view. Well worth a look, too, is the adjoining **Navajo Cultural Center**, an oversize, hogan-style building with permanent and revolving exhibits.

Historic trading post

Highway 264 leads west to **Ganado**, named for Navajo leader Ganado Mucho, a friend of trader Lorenzo Hubbell, who, in 1876, opened a trading post here. The still operational **Hubbell Trading Post National Historic Site ⓭** (open daily 8am–6pm, to 5pm in winter; tel: 928-755-3475; admission fee) is a fine place to learn about the important role of trading posts in the late 1800s.

Hubbell became a powerful political figure in Arizona, hosting Theodore Roosevelt and other dignitaries. He is best remembered, though, as a loyal friend and mentor to the Navajo, whom he encouraged to make heavier, better designed rugs and use new artificial dyes from back east. The trading post is known for the Ganado Red blanket, a bright red design with a diamond or cross in the center. Pottery, baskets and renderings of rug designs by famous artists hang in the Hubbell Home next door. Daily tours are limited to 15 people. Navajo rug weavers and silversmiths demonstrate in the visitor center.

Sacred canyons

About 30 miles (50 km) north of Ganado, off Highway 191, is **Chinle**, headquarters of 130-square-mile (340-sq-km) **Canyon de Chelly National Monument ⓴**, where the Rio de Chelly has carved 1,000-foot deep (300-meter) **Canyon de Chelly** and **Canyon del Muerto** into the Defiance Plateau. Scenic drives along the North and South Rims offer heart-stirring views into inner canyons and historic overlooks, such as the one above **Massacre Cave**, where 90 men and 25 women and children were massacred by Spanish Lieutenant Antonio de Narbona in 1805. The 1½-mile (2.5-km) **White House Trail** down Chinle Wash is the only route accessible without a Navajo guide. It leads to the multilevel pueblo cliff dwelling called **White House**. These canyons were home to Ancestral

Map on page 124

...eblo farmers for centuries before the arrival of the Navajo around AD 1400. ...he trail is a wonderful introduction to this most beautiful of Southwest ...nyons. Swallows swoop down to the wash from the clifftops. Raven caws ...nd the silence. And in summer, you'll encounter Navajo residents tending ...rn near hogans on the canyon floor.

...If you have a four-wheel-drive vehicle, consider hiring a Navajo guide who ...n accompany you deeper into the canyons to see cliff dwellings like **Antelope ...uin**, **First Ruin** and **Junction Ruin**, remarkable rock art on canyon walls ...om the Ancestral Pueblo, Spanish and Navajo eras, and stunning formations ...e **Spider Rock**, a sandstone spire that rises 800 feet (240 meters) from the ...nyon floor. Guides are available at the 1902 **Thunderbird Lodge**, a beauti-...l historic building with lodgings, reasonably priced rugs and other artwork, ...d a popular cafeteria. Half- and whole-day tours in large, jostling open-air ...hicles (jokingly referred to as "shake-and-bakes") also depart from here.

...opi homeland

...ighway 264 continues west to the **Hopi Reservation ㉑**, which is made up of ...series of 12 compact, autonomous stone villages atop windswept **First**, ...**econd** and **Third Mesas** and **Moenkopi**, several miles to the west, near Tuba ...ity. The Hopitu, the "peaceful people," are the descendants of the Ancestral ...uebloan culture, which they call Hisatsinom. A proud, private people, the Hopi ...ve a very different kind of life than their Navajo neighbors, whose much larger ...servation completely surrounds theirs. Their east-facing villages have changed ...tle since late Pueblo times. Hopi men dry-farm untilled plots of corn, melons, ...quash and other crops at the base of the cliffs and in terraces that catch the

BELOW: a Navajo girl plays at the family sheep camp on the northern edge of the reservation.

Blue corn is a staple of traditional Hopi cooking.

scant 10 inches (25 cm) of rain that falls here each year. Women make potter and baskets. Children play in dusty streets. Visiting the villages is about a close to stopping time as you may ever experience – which is, of course, it greatest attraction to travelers and, ironically, one of the biggest threats to th Hopi way of life.

It is believed that the Bear Clan was the first to arrive on the mesas. I time, other clans arrived from their migrations, and each was asked to cor tribute a different skill or ceremony to ensure the well-being of people o earth. From this, a complex seasonal ceremonial calendar was devised, wit sun priests in each village determining the timing of ceremonies based on th positions of the sun, moon and planets.

The most important ceremony of the year is the Niman, or Home Dance, i July, when the kachinas, serving as supernatural intermediaries between th Creator Spirit and the people of Earth, return to their winter home in the Sa Francisco Peaks after blessing the crops and bringing rain. The hypnoti singing and dancing of the kachinas symbolize the harmony of good though and deed necessary for a balanced life and to bring the blessing of rain.

Sacred dances

BELOW: Spider Rock rises about 800 feet (245 meters) from the floor of Canyon de Chelly.

Though the crowd may seem nonchalant, Hopi dances are deeply spiritual an should be accorded the same respect as any other religious event. Dancers a required to undergo extensive preparations for their roles. Spectators have role, too: they contribute their prayers to the successful completion of th dance's mission. Disrespect by outsiders means that some dances have bee closed to non-Hopis. If you are lucky enough to attend a dance, men and wome

ould dress modestly; refrain from talking, asking questions, or following the chinas; and never photograph, sketch, videotape or record the dances. formation on current dances is available at the **Hopi Cultural Center** (open on.–Fri. 8am–5pm, Sat.–Sun. 9am–3pm; closed weekends in winter; tel: 928-34-6650; admission fee to museum) on Second Mesa, the best place to orient ourself to the reservation.

Map on page 124

rtistic specialties

side the Cultural Center is the **Hopi Museum**, which has modest but effective splays on Hopi art and culture. Each mesa specializes in a particular craft. First lesa is known for its pottery, which women coil by hand, smooth with a pol- hing stone, and fire outdoors, usually with dung. The pots are then hand- ainted with intricate designs using fine yucca-fiber brushes and natural paints. econd and Third Mesas are renowned for basketry, one variety made of woven icker, the other of coiled yucca. Kachina dolls, perhaps the best known of the opi crafts, are made by craftsmen on all the mesas and carved from cotton- ood roots. Hopi silversmiths specialize in the distinctive overlay style, though a number of talented jewelers are now branching off into inlay and annel work with turquoise, jet, corral, shell and other semiprecious stones, d a few jewelers work with gold settings. Many craftspeople work out of eir homes and sell directly to the public.

The cultural center offers tours that include workshops, craft stores, villages d other places of interest. The villages of **Shungopavi** (home of artist Fred abotie, who painted the mural inside the Grand Canyon's Desert View Tower), **hipaulovi** and **Mishongnovi** all feature dances.

BELOW: the Hopi are known for crafting exquisite handmade pottery.

Map on page 124

The 33-room motel next to the Hopi Cultural Center (tel: 928-734-2401) fills up quickly in summer. A restaurant serves all-American fare as well as Hopi specialties, such as paper-thin blue corn piki bread and traditional stews, though these will seem bland to most palates. The blue corn pancakes are the best bet. You can also stay at **Keams Canyon**, an administrative town east of the Hopi Mesas. Before 1860, it was known to the Hopi as Peach Orchard Springs. It was renamed in honor of English trader Thomas Keam, who established a trading post there in 1875 and defended the Hopi from repressive government practices.

Ancient villages

Behind Keams Canyon is the abandoned 12th-century village of **Awatovi** on Antelope Mesa. Awatovi was the only Hopi village to be converted by Spanish missionaries, who built a church here in 1629. In 1680, the Hopi joined their New Mexican Pueblo neighbors and killed or exiled the Spanish. When the mission was reestablished in 1700, the Hopi grew so angry over the continued Christian influence, they destroyed Awatovi, massacred all the men of the village, and removed the women and children to other villages. You'll need a permit and a Hopi guide to visit.

Of all the Hopi villages, be sure not to miss **Walpi**, atop First Mesa. A traditional village, with no running water or electricity, residents live much as they have since prehistoric times. The village may be entered only with a Hopi guide on free 40-minute walking tours that leave from Ponsi Hall in **Sichomovi** or from the tourist booth at Walpi parking lot. Interestingly, **Hano**, the first village you reach, is not Hopi; it's a Tewa village built by people from the Rio Grande region of New Mexico, who sought refuge here during an unsuccessful revolt against the Spanish in 1696. The village at the base of the mesa is **Polacca**, also a latecomer, made up of residents of the three villages on First Mesa.

Old Oraibi, on Third Mesa, constructed in AD 1120, is often dubbed the oldest continuously inhabited community in the United States. The ruins of a Spanish mission built in 1629 are visible north of the village. By 1900, Old Oraibi had one of the reservation's largest populations (800), but disputes between chiefs caused many to leave. In the first major dispute, in 1906, two leaders staged a "push-of-war" contest, where two groups pushed against each other until one side crossed a line marked in the dust. The loser, You-ke-oma, left with his followers and established **Hotevilla**, 4 miles (6.5 km) away. Eventually, some tried to return to Old Oraibi, but were ousted again in 1909. They settled a new site called **Bacavi**, opposite Hotevilla. Other residents moved to join New Oraibi, at the foot of the mesa, otherwise known as **Kykotsmovi**.

Today, Kykotsmovi is the location of the modern Hopi tribal government, which has itself been the source of a continuing conflict among the traditional, self-determined villages ever since it was created by the federal government in the 1930s. "One is not born Hopi," explains one tribal member, when asked what it means to be Hopi. "One becomes Hopi."

BELOW: Hopi cornfields sprawl around the village of Moenkopi.
RIGHT: White House Ruin, set at the bottom of Canyon de Chelly, can be reached via a steep trail from the rim.

FLAGSTAFF AND ENVIRONS

*Ancient Indian ruins, a historic observatory and one
of the state's most beautiful mountain ranges are just a few of the
attractions in and around this former frontier outpost*

Map
on page
124

O n the road up **Mars Hill**, there's a pull-off where you can look out over
Flagstaff ㉒. The railroad tracks weave a steel ribbon through the middle
of town. Famed **Route 66** parallels the tracks, and sturdy brick and stone
buildings line the road. From this vantage point, Flagstaff looks for all the world
like a toy railroad town, just like those miniature cardboard villages that came
with your model train set.

And so it should, for the railroad made Flagstaff and has been its beating heart
for more than a century. Freight trains rumble through like clockwork all day
long, their whistles echoing through town, and Amtrak's passenger train, the
Southwest Chief, stops twice a day, eastbound in the morning, westbound at night.

In the 1850s, government surveyors plotted a railroad route along the 35th
Parallel. By the early 1880s, loggers rolled their big wheels into the ponderosa
pine forests of northern Arizona, felled the tall trees, then sawed and stockpiled
nearly a half million ties for the rails, as they blazed west. A spring at the base
of Mars Hill furnished precious water for advance crews, and in 1882 the Santa
Fe Railway arrived there at the first depot, a boxcar. The steep uphill grade
soon mandated a move back to flatter terrain a half mile east, from Old Town
to what soon became known as New Town. Across the street, a thirsty man
could find not only a cup of water but stronger brew
as well in this wild and woolly newborn burg.

PRECEDING PAGES:
Wupatki National
Monument.
LEFT: Lowell
Observatory.
BELOW: Aspens, San
Francisco Peaks.

Crossroad town

A few Anglo-Americans had preceded the railroad.
The Boston Party, a group of colonists who under-
took an arduous westward journey in response to
claims of good, cheap farmland, celebrated the
nation's centennial in 1876 by hoisting the flag up a
pine tree on the Fourth of July. Though their patriotic
act gave Flagstaff its name, few of the immigrants
stayed. Disillusioned, they discovered that the glowing promises of agricultural possibilities were so much
promotional puffery.

Stockmen found the grasslands fine, though. A handful of them, such as Thomas McMillan and John Clark,
settled in. Another pioneer, merchant P. J. Brannen,
had faith in the railroad. He erected his store across
from the New Town depot. Soon thereafter came five
brothers from Cincinnati, Ohio, by the name of Babbitt. Through their efforts, and others, Flagstaff was
on its way to becoming an established town.

Now a small and growing city of nearly 60,000,
Flagstaff hosts a lively, eclectic mix of small business owners, students, writers and artists, travelers,
cowboys and Indians, river runners and Rastafari-
ans, old-timers and newcomers. It's been character-
ized as a crossroads and a destination. Millions from

all over the world pass through on their way to the Grand Canyon each summer. Big-city folks wander up on weekends, sampling the small-town feeling. Students stay for a few years to obtain an education at **Northern Arizona University Ⓐ**. The rest – hearts captured by the town's friendliness and the surrounding beauty of forests, mountains and canyons – find themselves permanent Flagstaffians.

The Babbitt Building, downtown Flagstaff

Art and history

Downtown Flagstaff is a good place to start a visit. **Heritage Square Ⓑ** is the center of downtown. This outdoor plaza features an amphitheater where concerts are presented nearly every weekend through summer and fall. Diagonal to the square is the landmark **Weatherford Hotel**. Judge John Weatherford opened this elegant establishment on New Year's Day 1900. Like many downtown structures, the hotel is built of locally quarried sandstone called Arizona Red. The present owners have faithfully restored the hotel's original face, including a restored balcony that wraps around the second story; it's a perfect place to sip a cold drink and view the parade of humanity on the sidewalk below.

For a more in-depth look at downtown's many other turn-of-the-century stone buildings, two publications will help: *Flagstaff Historic Walk* and *Stone Landmarks*, both available at the **Visitor Center Ⓒ** (open Mon–Sat 7am–6pm, to 5pm on Sun; tel: 928-774-9541) in the train station a block from the Weatherford Hotel or at local bookstores.

Flagstaff is no Santa Fe, but in recent years a slew of galleries has opened downtown. On the first Friday of each month, several stay open between 6pm and 8pm for the **First Friday Art Walk**. Visitors have a chance to meet the

BELOW: Old Number 12 sits idle outside the Arizona Historical Society's Pioneer Museum.

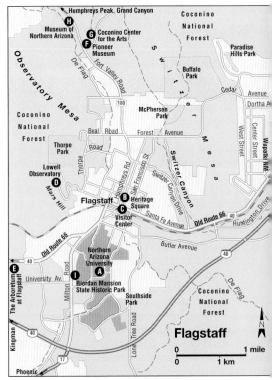

Flagstaff

artists, many of them local, who produce fine art and crafts in glass, wood, cloth and other media.

Map on page 188

Lowell's legacy

A trip up to **Lowell Observatory** ⑩ (open 9am–5pm daily, 12pm–5pm in winter) just west of downtown affords that toy-town view of Flagstaff from Mars Hill. Wealthy Bostonian Percival Lowell chose the hill as the site for his observatory, where he ordered a telescope erected to view the planet Mars. Lowell arrived in 1894 in time to make those observations and lived part-time there for the rest of his life. The planet Pluto was discovered at Lowell in 1930, and astronomers continue to make significant contributions in their various specialties. The **Steele Visitor Center** and the **Slipher Building** contain fascinating interactive exhibits on the work of astronomers and the history of the observatory. With the clear, dark sky bursting with stars, it is a distinct treat to attend a nighttime viewing through Percival's original Clark telescope.

Flagstaff is also a center of other scientific pursuits. A branch office of the U.S. Geological Survey is located in town and is the place where the late Eugene Shoemaker founded the discipline of astrogeology. A ten-day **Festival of Science** is held each fall, with a constant round of public events. Recognizing the area's botanical diversity, the **Arboretum at Flagstaff** ⑥ (open 9am–5pm daily Apr–Dec 15) features native plant gardens, nature walks, and other activities on the grounds on Woody Mountain Road, 4 miles (6.5 km) from town.

The Arizona Historical Society's **Pioneer Museum** ⑥ (open 9am–5pm Mon–Sat) displays interesting artifacts from Flagstaff's past. To visit, follow Highway 180 (Fort Valley Road) north to a white stone building, originally the

BELOW: Percival Lowell, founder of Lowell Observatory, believed that "canals" on Mars were built by intelligent life.

LOWELL AND THE RED PLANET

Percival Lowell may have seen little green men on Mars, but he never said so. What he did say was that life probably existed on the red planet. His belief in Martian life was based on observations of lines radiating from various points on the planet's surface, which he thought were a network of canals.

The canal idea had been posed some years earlier. Italian astronomer Giovanni Schiaparelli claimed to have seen such lines, which he called *canali*, or channels. Lowell expanded on this, writing that "A mind of no mean order would seem to have presided over the system [of canals] we see." Because Mars was presumably an arid place, an irrigation system would have been necessary to gather water from melting polar ice caps and dew or frost. Lowell also suggested that Mars had an atmosphere, thin and cloudless but adequate to support life.

Percival Lowell wasn't shy about publicizing his findings. The press picked up the stories, sometimes poking fun at them. Support from astronomers was mixed at first but later soured into scathing criticism. If Lowell were alive today, he might find some vindication in recent photographs of Mars that show signs of water in old riverbeds and possible evidence of organic material in rocks.

TIP

Hankering for live country music? Check out the Museum Club (928-526-9434) on old Route 66, a classic log roadhouse known as the Zoo for the stuffed animals and trophy heads that adorn the walls.

BELOW: scores of cinder cones and craters are scattered around the San Francisco Peaks Volcanic Field.

county hospital, that locals once called "the poor farm." Along with housing the small staff, the hospital had room for about a dozen patients. In 1908, the local newspaper described the new building as "a substantial one of stone, fitted up with hot and cold water in each of the airy rooms, located among the pines on a small hill overlooking the rich little valley to the south."

Outside the museum stands old **Number 12**, a shiny black steam locomotive put into service in the Northwest woods in 1929 and used in the Flagstaff area in the 1950s. Inside, individual rooms contain artifacts of early medicine, logging and transportation in northern Arizona. A display of old dolls, games, children's books, tea sets, quilts and more – called Playthings of the Past – is held each holiday season. The museum's two big events each year are the **Wool Festival** on the first weekend in June, and the **Independence Day Festival** marking the Fourth of July, with live demonstrations at each.

Immediately behind the Pioneer Museum is the **Coconino Center for the Arts ⑥** (open 11am–5pm Tues–Sat; tel: 928-779-2300), exhibiting the work of local artists and providing a venue for live music and other programs. Next door is the **Art Barn**, location for classes and opportunities for resident artists.

Family treasures

A mile farther out Highway 180 resides the **Museum of Northern Arizona ⑪** (open 9am–5pm daily; tel: 928-774-5213). Dr. Harold Colton, his wife Mary-Russell Ferrell Colton, and other community members founded this institution in 1928. This gem of a museum, standing amid ponderosa pines beside the Rio de Flag, shares the wealth of geology, biology and culture of the Colorado Plateau, the geologic province in which Flagstaff is located. Rotating exhibits

showcase some of the museum's extensive collections of basketry, pottery, paintings and kachina carvings. Mrs. Colton, an accomplished artist in her own right, encouraged Native American artists in their work. Her legacy continues at the museum to this day, with a series of shows and marketplaces in summer and early fall featuring some of the best arts and crafts produced in the region.

Back in town near Northern Arizona University, another piece of Flagstaff's history has been preserved in a state park. **Riordan Mansion ❶** (open daily 8.30am–5pm May–Oct, 10.30am–5pm Nov–Apr; tel: 928-779-4395) was the home of businessmen and brothers Michael and Timothy Riordan.

The 40-room, 13,000-square-foot (1,200-sq-meter) house, designed by Charles Whittlesey, architect of the the Grand Canyon's El Tovar Hotel, was built in 1904. Stone, plank and shake construction was used; some of the wood was scrap ponderosa pine from the nearby Arizona Lumber and Timber Company mill, which the Riordans owned. The two brothers married the Metz sisters, and each family had separate living areas in the mansion, connected by a common space called the "cabin room." The Steinway piano, Tiffany stained-glass windows, velvet upholstered seats, and six-car garage show what life was like for the "upper crust" in Flagstaff in the early years. But the Riordans weren't immune to grief. In daughter Anna's bedroom is her hoop dress, which she wore as a young woman. On the night of her engagement party in 1927, she was stricken with polio and her life was cut short.

Sacred peaks

The **San Francisco Peaks ㉓** sweep up behind Flagstaff, a small range as far as mountains go, but an extremely captivating one. The Peaks are sacred

Map
city: 188
area: 124

BELOW: a bicyclist cruises through downtown Flagstaff.

Spurs give a musical ring to a cowboy's step. Horseback riding is offered by several stables in the Flagstaff area.

BELOW: Kachina Peaks Wilderness, Coconino National Forest.

mountains to nearly everyone who has felt their attraction – considered so by the Hopi, Navajo and many other Native Americans and non-Indians as well. The Peaks rank as the highest mountains in Arizona – 12,643 feet (3,854 meters) at the windswept tundra atop **Humphreys Peak**. A trio of separate summits complete their impressive profile: **Agassiz**, **Doyle** and **Fremont**.

Franciscan friars who saw the mountains from the Hopi Mesas in 1629 named them in honor of their founder, St. Francis. Early travelers headed for the springs that issue from them, and a fledgling Flagstaff relied on those water sources for the town's sustenance. Now people flock to the mountains for recreation and inspiration. They hike the trails in summer, gawk at golden aspens in the fall, sled and ski in winter, and watch for the first candytuft to bloom in spring. Botanists search the alpine tundra for rare plants, hunters scan the ridges for elk and woodcutters load up logs for their stoves.

Geologists classify the Peaks as a "stratovolcano." Numerous explosions piled layer upon layer of lava, cinders and ash to an elevation of nearly 16,000 feet (4,800 meters) about 400,000 years ago; on the north side, the mountain collapsed into a huge bowl called the Inner Basin.

Mountain wilderness

The uppermost reaches of the San Francisco Peaks are protected as the **Kachina Peaks Wilderness Area**. While no motorized or wheeled vehicles are allowed, hikers walking the wilderness may be rewarded with the sights and sounds of gray fox, Mexican owls and bugling elk. Two popular trails, the Humphreys and Kachina, can be reached by driving to the **Arizona Snowbowl** (open 9am–4pm daily; tel: 928-779-1951) 17 miles (27 km) from town off Highway 180. The

Humphreys Trail ascends steeply through dense evergreen forest to the rocky tundra of the highest summit. The **Kachina Trail** is a gentler path that follows the lower slope. Northward stretches the grassy expanse of **Hart Prairie**, home to a Nature Conservancy preserve. Forest Road 151, accessible from Highway 180, is a scenic unpaved drive that gives unending views of the Peaks.

Map on page 124

Ski country

With the first dusting of snow on the Peaks in early winter, Flagstaffians rejoice at the prospect of downhill skiing. The sport arrived here in 1915. That winter, with 6 feet (2 meters) of snow on the ground, Ole and Pete Solberg strapped on homemade wooden skis and swooshed down Mars Hill. Townsfolk gathered to watch, and the local paper exclaimed, "They call it 'skiing'!" In the 1930s a local ski club formed to foster the sport, and the first lodge was built at what is now the Arizona Snowbowl. It's music to skiers' ears when the snow report reads "67 inches of packed powder at Midway, all runs open." The Snowbowl's four lifts serve beginner to advanced skiers. (In summer, one lift operates as a scenic skyride, taking riders to an elevation of 11,500 ft/3,500 meters.)

Without snow-making equipment, the Snowbowl depends on what mother nature provides. In dry years the season can be short; but in average years, with 260 inches (660 cm) of snow possible, the slopes are open from mid-December through March.

For a lower-tech experience, the **Flagstaff Nordic Center** (open 9am–4pm daily; tel: 928-779-1951) is the place to go. On Highway 180, 8 miles (13 km) past Snowbowl Road, the center offers a variety of groomed cross-country and snowshoe trails through the forest and meadows. Cross-country skiers will also

BELOW: cross-country skiers at the base of Humphreys Peak.

BELOW: a mountain biker pedals through rugged volcanic terrain around the San Francisco Peaks.

find a nearly endless supply of backroads, most of them closed in winter, in **Coconino** and **Kaibab National Forests** that provide a wealth of possibilities for winter trekking.

During the entire month of February, a kind of cold-weather mania grips Flagstaff during **Winterfest.** All manner of snow-related activities are scheduled, including skiing, dogsledding, snowshoeing, ice skating and skijoring (a cross between cross-country skiing and dogsledding), not to mention the Snowball Slide and Icicle Walk and Gawk. An array of music, food and dance events complements the more vigorous endeavors.

Volcanic origins

Like the San Francisco Peaks, the landscape around Flagstaff owes its character to a long period of volcanism. Hundreds of cinder cones are scattered throughout the grassy plains surrounding town. And though some of the cones date back several million years, the most recent is less than 1,000 years old. That one is **Sunset Crater ㉔** (open 8am–5pm daily; tel: 928-526-0502). This black 1,000-foot-high (300-meter) cone was formed when hot ash and lava exploded from a vent around AD 1064–65. It continued erupting for 150 years or so pouring out fiery lava and other volcanic debris that has frozen into a black, jagged moonscape.

To see Sunset Crater up close, travel 12 miles (19 km) north of Flagstaff on Highway 89 and turn at the national monument sign. After a stop at the visitor center, continue on the loop road at the base of Sunset Crater. Though the crater itself is now off-limits to hikers due to erosion, you can walk around it on the mile-long **Lava Flow Trail.** Along the way you'll see the many byproducts of

SOUTHSIDE

South of the tracks, along South San Francisco and South Beaver Streets in Flagstaff, is what's known a Southside—a funky neighborhood of ethnic restaurants coffee shops, dance studios, sport shops, youth hostels historic churches and modest homes.

Southside has always been the working-class side c town. Its residents claim a mixture of Mexican, Basque an African-American heritage. They moved here between th 1870s and 1930s to escape revolution in Mexico and t find jobs, mostly as sheepherders and mill workers.

They built modest stone cottages and frame bungalow and gathered at Zaragosa Hall on South San Francisco fc dances and boxing matches. Billiards and handball playe at a traditional Basque *pelota* court (which still stands o South San Francisco Street) provided other pastimes.

Today, the grandchildren of those early pioneers still liv in the same houses and run family businesses. The street are filled with the scent of fresh tortillas and roasted coffe Diners can enjoy every kind of cuisine from Chicago-styl hot dogs to hemp burgers. On most days, some of th 15,000 students at Northern Arizona University pedal an skateboard through this down-home neighborhood tha relishes its individuality and history.

he eruption – football-shaped volcanic bombs, upturned slabs of lava descriptively called squeeze-ups, and the entrance to an ice-filled lava tube.

Map on page 124

After the eruption

When the volcano first erupted, the people living in the vicinity must have thought the world was coming to an end. But the fine cinder mulch the volcano deposited, along with a favorable period of precipitation after the eruption, lured them back. Harold Colton, founder of the Museum of Northern Arizona, named these people the Sinagua, which means "without water," for their arid homeland. He and other archaeologists believed the "new" volcanic farmland lured thousands of settlers into northern Arizona.

Ancestral Puebloans were probably among them. Their stunning architectural stonework is on display at **Wupatki National Monument ㉕** (open daily 8am–5pm, to 6pm in summer; tel: 928-679-2365), 22 miles (35 km) beyond Sunset Crater on the loop road. Several beautiful pueblos have been excavated and are open to visitors. The largest is namesake **Wupatki Pueblo**. From the visitor center, a half-mile self-guiding path leads through this four-story dwelling built of sandstone slabs set in mud mortar. Some of the masonry resembles that of Chaco Canyon in New Mexico. Wupatki Pueblo's more than 100 rooms ramble without any apparent plan, and recent work suggests it was built in several phases from the mid- to late 1130s through the early 1200s. Cached in several rooms were remains of such tropical birds as scarlet macaws and thick-billed parrots. These and other finds have led archaeologists to suggest that Wupatki was a site of high political or spiritual significance. Other intriguing sites in the park – **Wukoki**, the **Citadel** and **Lomaki** – certainly support this thought.

BELOW: spring runoff laden with silt spills over the Grand Falls of the Little Colorado River.

Map on page 124

Wupatki is located in the high-desert valley of the **Little Colorado River**. For a real backroad trip, take a ride to the **Grand Falls** ㉖ of the Little Colorado. The river's muddy brown waters tumble over a 185-foot (56-meter) ledge, a virtual Niagara in the desert. Keep in mind, however, that Grand Falls flows only seasonally, when the river is running with springtime snowmelt or summer storm water, and requires quite an undertaking to reach.

Take Highway 89 just north of Flagstaff, turn right onto the Townsend–Winona Road, go 8 miles (13 km) to Leupp Road, turn left and go another 15 miles (24 km) to the boundary of the Navajo Nation. Turn left (north) onto Navajo Route 70, a good gravel road when dry, but impassable when wet. In another 9 miles (15 km), you'll spot picnic ramadas and find yourself at Grand Falls.

Relics of the past

Returning to Flagstaff, head east on Interstate 40 for 10 miles (16 km) to the area's third national monument – **Walnut Canyon** ㉗ (open daily 8am–5pm, to 6pm in summer; tel: 928-526-3367). The Sinagua lived here too, though in a totally different setting than Wupatki. They tucked their living quarters beneath limestone ledges in a deep canyon. Descend the **Island Trail** to the small rooms and smoke-blackened walls of their abodes. A host of plants along the stream-course, on the drier hillsides and on the forested rim sustained them with wild foods and material for clothing and other utilitarian items. By building small rock dams across gullies, the Sinagua gathered pockets of soil where they grew corn, beans and squash. Some of these are visible along the **Rim Walk**, a fine place to gaze into Walnut Canyon or up into the sky for soaring hawks and eagles.

BELOW: Meteor Crater was blasted from the Earth's surface about 50,000 years ago. **RIGHT:** wildflowers carpet a meadow in the San Francisco Peaks.

Continuing on Interstate 40 another 25 miles (40 km), there's a big hole in the ground about 6 miles (10 km) south of the highway that interests many people. And well it should. About 50,000 years ago, a chunk of iron traveling at about 40,000 mph (65,000 kph) hit the Earth. With the force of about 20 million tons of TNT, it blew out a depression known as **Meteor Crater** ㉘ (8am–5pm daily, 6am–6pm in summer; tel: 928-289-2362; admission fee). This natural landmark – 4,000 feet (1,200 meters) across and 560 feet (170 meters) deep – is open for guided tours, or the crater can be viewed through windows at the fine museum on the rim.

Another 25 miles (40 km) beyond Meteor Crater is the railroad town of **Winslow** ㉙. Beside the tracks stands **La Posada**, a grand hotel that dates to the heyday of American passenger trains in the 1930s. Private owners have superbly restored the huge mission-style structure and it is well worth a visit.

A few miles north of town is **Homolovi Ruins State Park** ㉚ (8am–5pm daily; tel: 928-289-4106). Situated atop high mounds overlooking the **Painted Desert** are 14th-century pueblos. Certain Hopi clans claim Homolovi as the home of their ancestors, the *hisatsinom*, who made this their last stop before arriving at present homes on the mesas about 60 miles (100 km) to the north. Homolovi sites I and II are accessible to visitors. Hiking trails, a campground, picnic areas and a chance to watch archaeologists at work are features of the park. Check at the visitor center for the latest information. ☐

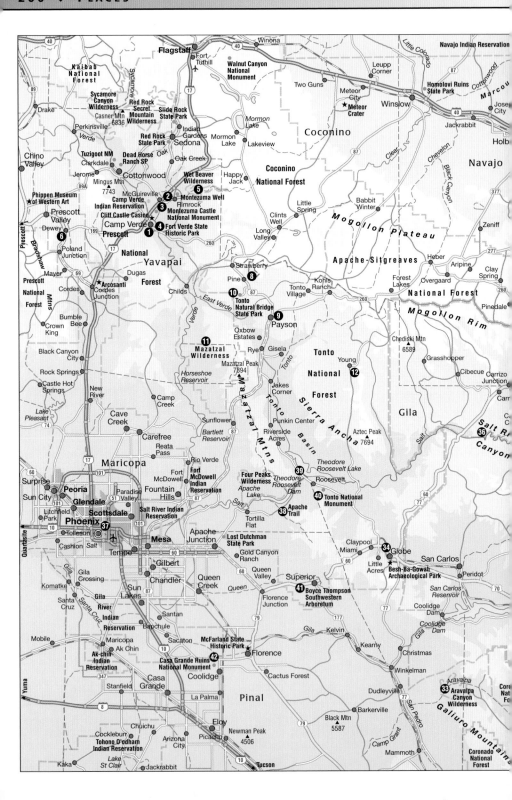

The map on this page shows part of Central Arizona and New Mexico, including the following labeled features:

Gallup, Chambers, Sanders, Navajo, Zuni Pueblo, Tekapo, Leroux, Sun Valley, Witch Wells, Ojo Caliente, Arntz, Petrified Forest National Park, Woodruff, Milky, Apache, Zuni Indian Reservation, Zuni, Hunt, New Mexico, Little Colorado, St Johns, howflake, ylor, Conchó, Black Mesa, Shumway, Silver Creek, Cerro Hucco 6511, Richville, Lyman Lake State Park, Lyman Dam, Lyman Lake, Socorro, Raven Site Ruin, Vernon, Coyote, Lakeside, Casa Malpais National Historic Landmark, Springerville, Sipe White Mountain Wildlife Area, Pinetop, Antelope Mtn 9003, Eagar, Hon Dah, McNary, Greer, Milligan Knoll, Escudilla Mtn 10912, Hawley Lake, Sunrise Ski Area, Baldy Peak 11403, 8800 Nutrioso, Apache-Sitgreaves, hite Mountain che Reservation, White Mountains, Three Forks, Alpine, Luna Lake, Luna, San Francisco, Whiteriver, Sprucedale, Fort Apache, Odart Mtn 8525, National, Beaverhead, Rancho Grande Estates, Hannagan Meadow, Blue, San Carlos Apache Reservation, Willow Mtn 7817, Blue Vista, Forest, Greenlee, Maple Peak 8294, Alma, Glenwood, Elevator Mtn 7113, Graham, Silver City, Stargo, Mule Creek, Emery, Morenci, Clifton, Fort homas, Gila Box Riparian National Conservation Area, Guthrie, York, Glenbar, Central, Pima, Sheldon, Thatcher, Solomon, Safford, Cactus Flat, Roper Lake State Park, Coronado National Forest, Mount Graham 10720, Swift Trail Junction, Artesia

Central Arizona

0 — 20 miles
0 — 20 km

CENTRAL ARIZONA

Phoenix, Arizona's urban heart, anchors a region of varied charms

P
hoenix and its suburbs, known collectively as the Valley of the Sun, form the nucleus of central Arizona. Built upon the bones of an ancient Hohokam settlement, the city has grown from a drowsy desert outpost to a booming metropolis of more than 1.3 million souls – the sixth largest in the country. It has never been a cultural heavyweight, but two new sports venues and a cluster of museums, theaters, parks, shops and restaurants in the downtown area – long derided for its nonexistent nightlife – have given the city a much-needed center of gravity.

Beyond the Valley of the Sun is a region that too many travelers overlook in their dash to the Grand Canyon. In the White Mountains, for example, you may hardly suspect you're in Arizona at all. Ponderosa pine and Douglas fir tower above you, cool breezes tousle your hair, and cold streams feed the headwaters of the Salt River.

To the northwest, in another dramatic change of scenery, are the red-rock formations of Sedona, whose reputation for "spiritual hot spots," known as vortexes, and trendy shopping have made it a popular weekend getaway. It's about 50 miles (80 km) and yet another set change to historic Jerome, a former mining town.

Far to the west, where the Colorado River has been fashioned into a series of reservoirs, is Arizona's "West Coast," a 350-mile-long (560-km) water world with resort towns, wildlife refuges, and an abundance of boating and fishing. There's also the state's second most popular tourist attraction, the London Bridge, which, as an extravagant marketing gimmick, was shipped to the desert brick by brick and rebuilt on the banks of Lake Havasu. ❑

PRECEDING PAGES: having fun at a rodeo, Whitewater Apache Reservation.

ARIZONA'S WEST COAST

Map on page 206

The Colorado River forms a 350-mile coastline on the state's western border, with palm-shaded beaches, excellent boating and fishing, wildlife refuges and, improbably, the London Bridge

t seems a misnomer at first. After all, Arizona's "west coast" is far from any ocean, in a desert so hot and dry that rain often evaporates before it can reach the ground. In the eyes of newcomers, this harsh landscape may seem completely devoid of life. Yet first impressions can be deceptive. There are, in fact, many life-forms that thrive here, including humans, along the all-important coastline of the **Colorado River**.

"Where you see a barren wasteland, we see a supermarket," a member of one of the area's indigenous groups once told an anthropologist. Indeed, the Hualapai, Yavapai, Mohave, Quechan, Chemehuevi, Cocopa and Maricopa cultures flourished here for millennia, hunting and gathering wild foods as well as cultivating gardens. Descendants of some of these early residents remain, commingling with Hopi and Navajo who have migrated from northeastern Arizona. The secret of their survival is the Colorado's delivery of the region's most precious commodity – water.

In 1540, Hernando de Alarcón became the first European to sail the Colorado. The Spaniard navigated its broad delta and, near present-day Yuma, met Quechan Indians with facial tattoos "covering their faces almost entirely" and ear piercings "in which they placed beads and shells." Juan de Oñate pushed farther upstream 64 years later, encountering the Mohave and other tribes. In 1699, the peripatetic Father Eusebio Kino crossed the river and paused to name it. *Colorado* means *red* in Spanish, a reference to the iron-laden silt the waterway historically carried from the north.

PRECEDING PAGES: canoeing on the lower Colorado. **LEFT:** Lake Havasu. **BELOW:** Hopi girl at the Colorado River Indian Reservation.

Troubled crossing

Over the next two centuries, the Spanish developed trails that linked their settlements in California and New Mexico. Following their official exit from the area in the early 1800s, western Arizona drew Mexican farmers and American adventurers. In 1849, thousands of fortune-seekers used Yuma Crossing, where the Gila Trail met the Colorado, en route to California's goldfields. This had a devastating effect on the Quechans, who had historically controlled the ford and gathered food nearby. Americans took over the crossing, established a fort, and allowed their livestock to eat most of the mesquite beans that Quechans depended on for sustenance. Similar incursions to the north routed the Mohave people from their homelands.

Eventually, the mighty Colorado was tamed and the remaining indigenous people were granted reservations along the river: Fort Mohave, Chemehuevi, Colorado River and Yuma. Now that the Colorado is the most harnessed river in the United States, thousands of acres of farmland have been developed along its course with the use of elaborate irrigation systems.

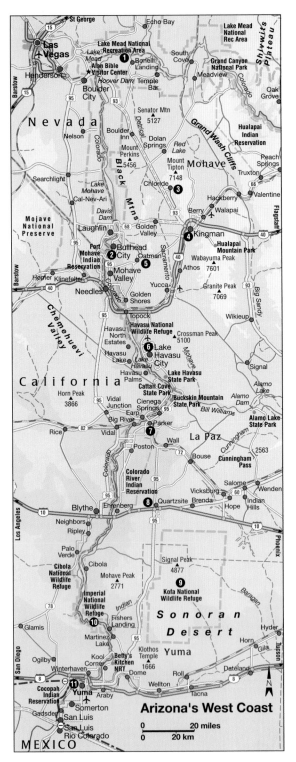

Arizona's West Coast

0   20 miles

0   20 km

The lure of water

Today, Arizona's West Coast is an aquatic playground in a land that averages a mere 3 inches (8 cm) of rain annually. Snowbirds and retirees are attracted by the year-round sunshine, carefree lifestyle, easy access to casinos and endless outdoor recreation. Thousands of vacationers converge from Las Vegas, Phoenix and Los Angeles, most heading for the reservoirs formed by a series of dams along what is now a tame stretch of the once-unpredictable Colorado.

Thankfully, at least a small percentage of the river's extraordinary biodiversity is protected at several wildlife preserves, which maintain vital wetland habitats used by migrating birds as well as resident flora and fauna.

Three east-west interstate highways traverse western Arizona and connect it with the Southwest's major cities. Interstate 40 bisects the state via Kingman as it connects central California with Flagstaff and points east; Interstate 10 links Phoenix and Los Angeles through Quartzsite; Interstate 8 flows through Yuma, halfway between San Diego and Phoenix. In the northwest, U.S. Highway 93 links Kingman with Las Vegas, Nevada. State Route 95 follows a north-south axis, roughly parallel to the Colorado, from Davis Dam (straddling the border with Nevada) through Parker and Yuma to Mexico.

Recreational oasis

The tour begins in Arizona's northwest corner along U.S. Highway 93 at **Lake Mead National Recreation Area ❶**, which encompasses the largest reservoir in the United States (twice the size of Rhode Island). Created by the impoundment of the Colorado River at **Hoover Dam**, Lake Mead extends more than 100 miles (160 km), nearly into the Grand Canyon. The reservoir, which straddles the Arizona–Nevada line and is stocked with gamefish, has six marinas and more than 500 miles (800 km) of shoreline that have made it a sun-drenched mecca for those keen

Map on page 206

on boating, water-skiing, fishing, sunbathing, picnicking and RV or tent camping. Boats and sports equipment can be rented in many locations, and you'll also find numerous tackle shops, restaurants, motels and groceries.

Scenic tours leave from **Boulder Beach**, 2 miles (3 km) north of Highway 93 on Nevada State Route 166. The three-deck steamboat *Desert Princess* makes a two-hour cruise six times a day from the main **Lake Mead Marina**, also on Route 166. From the Arizona side, the reservoir is accessible from Highway 93 at **Temple Bar** (via Temple Bar Road) and **Meadview** (via Dolan Springs-Meadview Road). The **Alan Bible Visitor Center** (open daily 8.30am–4.30pm; tel: 702-293-8907) is at the intersection of Nevada State Route 166 and Highway 93, 4 miles (6.5 km) west of Hoover Dam. Free literature is available, along with fascinating, fact-filled videos about desert ecosystems and wildlife and the dam's construction.

Without Hoover Dam's water and power, not only would Lake Mead not exist but the neon-lit oasis of Las Vegas (30 miles/48 km northwest) would have remained a tiny settlement. The structure is the keystone of the Colorado River Reclamation Project, which serves millions of users in Nevada, Arizona and California. U.S. Highway 93 passes over this edifice, at 726 feet (221 m) the highest concrete arch dam in the Western Hemisphere. Hoover was completed in 1935 (by 5,000 men working in 24-hour shifts) and can retain some 30 million acre-feet of water.

The site has parking, exhibits and a viewing area. Tours last 35 minutes and are offered several times each day except Thanksgiving and Christmas (tel: 702-294-3523, fee). Motorized raft trips can be taken from a dock below the dam to and from Willow Beach, about 20 miles (32 km) downstream.

BELOW: spring-break revelers work on their tans at Lake Havasu.

The longest remaining stretch of legendary Route 66 runs through western Arizona.

BELOW: burros roam freely in Oatman; they are descendants of the animals used by gold miners.

Services are available in nearby **Boulder City**, the Nevada town created by the U.S. Bureau of Reclamation for those who built and continue to manage the dam. (Boulder is the dam's original name, changed in 1947 to honor former President Herbert Hoover.)

About 50 miles (80 km) below Hoover is **Davis Dam**, one of three smaller dams that control the river's flow along the rest of Arizona's West Coast. Davis creates **Lake Mohave**, a part of Lake Mead National Recreation Area accessible from both banks but relatively undeveloped.

Boom and bust

Below Davis Dam are the twin cities of **Bullhead City ②**, Arizona, and **Laughlin**, Nevada, about 20 miles (32 km) east of U.S. Highway 95. As recently as the 1980s, these communities barely existed. They have since morphed into a bridge-connected metropolis with more than 10,000 hotel rooms, scores of restaurants, and, in Laughlin, a dozen major casinos, including a few on old-fashioned riverboats. These cities provide gaming and other amenities (notably golf) to those who don't want to drive another 100 miles (160 km) to Las Vegas or who simply prefer a less glitzy atmosphere.

Switching from the modern to the historic, the colorful mining legacy of western Arizona is well preserved in **Chloride ③**, 20 miles (32 km) north of Kingman on U.S. Highway 93 and another 4 miles (6.5 km) east via Chloride Road. Home to as many as 2,000 people during its 1860s boom, Chloride's name derives from the silver-chloride ore extracted from mines in the nearby **Cerbat Mountains**. Only a few hundred residents remain in the rustic, frontier-style buildings, but at the end of June each year the town comes alive during Old Miners Day. Festivities are marked by burro rides, a swap meet, a crafts fair and a parade. An old-time melodrama is performed at the **Silverbelle Playhouse** (tel: 928-565-2204, free) on the first and third Saturday of the month (Mar–May, Sept–Nov).

Honeymoon suite

The sprawling city of **Kingman ④** extends from the intersection of Interstate 40 and U.S. Highway 93, 48 miles (77 km) east of the California border in the brown plain of the **Hualapai Valley**. Established as a turquoise-mining center and railroad stop, the town now mainly serves highway travelers and retirees. Learn about the region's history from prehistoric times to the present at the worthwhile **Mohave Museum of History and Arts** (400 W. Beale St., open Mon–Fri 9am–5pm, Sat–Sun 1pm–5pm; tel: 928-753-3195; fee). See a detailed replica of a Mohave Indian village, an impressive collection of carved turquoise, and an entire room dedicated to the memory of Kingman's most famous native son: "good guy" actor Andy Devine, who died in 1977.

Adjacent is the **Kingman Visitors Center** (open Mon–Fri 8am–5pm, Sat 9am–4pm, Sun 10am–3pm) offering information about several historic sites in the area. Fourteen miles (23 km) southeast is **Hualapai Mountain Park** (tel: 928-757-3859, fee), a pine-rested enclave that rises to 8,500 feet (2,600 meters) above sea level, with enic hiking trails, a campground and picnic areas.

A scenic detour from Kingman takes you to the old mining town of **Oatman ❺**, out 25 miles (40 km) southwest on Historic Route 66 (Oatman Road). atman's single dusty street is lined with tourist-oriented curio shops, loons, cafés and hotels. Among the more venerable institutions is the ramackle **Oatman Hotel**, a virtual museum of century-old memorabilia where ollywood legends Clark Gable and Carole Lombard spent their wedding ght in 1939, after getting hitched in Kingman. Wandering throughout the wn are good-natured burros (a prospector's favorite helper), eager for handts of carrots and similar goodies. Fake shoot-outs are staged on the main rag on weekends and holidays.

ondon Bridge

ollow Interstate 40 and State Route 95 about 60 miles (95 km) south of ingman to the improbable "instant city" of **Lake Havasu City ❻**, developed n the Colorado River during the early 1960s by the late tycoon Robert 1cCullough. McCullough's chain-saw factory moved from here to Tucson ears ago but not before his town acquired its greatest single attraction: ondon Bridge. Yes, the same graceful, arched structure built in 1824 across e River Thames in England. When replaced in 1971, it was sold for $2.5 illion and shipped in numbered pieces to the Arizona desert, where it was :assembled on a peninsula jutting into the lake.

Despite its unlikely relocation, this is an authentic piece of history: note the rafing scars left on the stones by German bombers during World War II. Next

Map on page 206

TIP

Look for colorful murals painted by artist Roy Purcell on boulders outside of Chloride. Follow Tennessee Avenue into the hills about a mile from town.

BELOW: kitsch is king at a Route 66 hamburger stand.

OUTE 66: THE MOTHER ROAD

or generations, U.S. Route 66 drew hundreds of thousands of travelers to the Southwest, providing a ncrete trail between Los Angeles and Chicago for those search of a better life. Most of Route 66 was destroyed create Interstate 40, and many communities along the ghway nearly died. But nostalgia and shrewd promotion vived interest in "the Mother Road," now commemorated places like Kingman and Flagstaff, where Route 66 is ill the main thoroughfare.

The longest remaining stretch of the highway is open etween Topock (east of the Colorado River) and Ash Fork. esides spectacular desert scenery, Route 66 provides ccess to the Hualapai Indian Reservation on the edge of e Grand Canyon. Near Peach Springs is Grand Canyon averns, where you can take an elevator 21 stories into the arth for a 45-minute tour (tel: 928-422-3223). A fun stop Seligman is the Snow Cap Drive-In, a popular hamburger int that has changed little over the past 40 years.

Free literature about this stretch of highway is available om the Historic Route 66 Association of Arizona, located the Kingman Visitor Center (tel: 928-753-6106). Nearby Mr. D's Route 66 Diner (106 Andy Devine), a 1950s-era atery filled with memorabilia from the road's glory days.

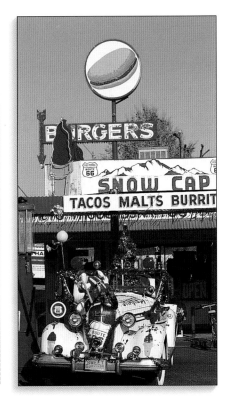

*Mohave girl, 1903.
The tribe numbered
about 6,000 at the
arrival of the first
Europeans.*

to the 900-foot (275-meter) span is **English Village**, a tourist-oriented promenade of shops and restaurants decked out in an "old London" theme.

The city itself has thrived and become home to more than 45,000 year-round residents, including many retirees. A full spectrum of water recreation, golf courses, tennis courts and related services is available. Although you can hike up nearby **Crossman Peak**, most of the action is on Lake Havasu, a 45-mile-long (72-km) artificial lake. Be advised that, like others on Arizona's West Coast, this reservoir is extremely popular with the spring break crowd during March and April, when thousands of party-hungry college students arrive.

Those favoring more sedate pursuits may wish to visit nearby **Buckskin Mountain State Park**, **Bill Williams National Wildlife Refuge** or **Lake Havasu National Wildlife Refuge**, each protecting scenic areas and key ecosystems along this stretch of the river. The parks provide a mix of boat-launch ramps, campgrounds, swimming beaches, picnic areas and hiking trails.

Parker Dam, which impounds the Colorado about 20 miles (32 km) south of Lake Havasu City, is not as stunning as Hoover, although workers were required to dig an amazing 230 feet (70 meters) into bedrock below the river in order to make the structure secure. Free, self-guided tours are available on the west side of the dam (open daily 8am–5pm, tel: 760-663-3712).

Another 15 miles (24 km) downstream is the small town of **Parker ❼**, headquarters of the **Colorado River Indian Reservation**, which extends about 40 miles (64 km) south to **Ehrenberg** and across the border into California. The reservation is unusual in that it is open not only to those whose ancestors (mainly the Mohave and Chemehuevi) lived here traditionally but to members of other tribes whose homelands are hundreds of miles away. A complicated legal

istory has also resulted in a number of non-Indians owning land and living on he reservation. Residents derive much of their income either from farming or by catering to tourists attracted to **Lake Moovalya**, a reservoir below Parker Dam. Crowds here are smaller than those at Lake Havasu and Lake Mead but increase dramatically during spring break.

Parker is home to the **Colorado River Indian Tribes Museum** (Second and Mohave streets, Mon–Fri 8am–5pm, Sat 10am–3pm; tel: 928-669-9211, free), a terrific place to learn about the indigenous people who have made this part of Arizona their home. The museum displays an impressive collection of baskets, pottery, jewelry and historical artifacts. There's a craft shop, and a casino dominates the adjacent shopping center.

State Route 95 veers east of the river south of Parker and, 35 miles (56 km) later, intersects Interstate 10 at **Quartzsite ⑧**. This scruffy, unincorporated hamlet is home to about 2,000 year-round residents and 200,000 snowbirds, who migrate from the cold north in their RVs and mobile homes during the winter months. Most of these sun-worshippers alight in the surrounding desert, which is public land.

Rock show

Throughout the winter, Quartzsite's single main street is an amazing flea market, where a motley crew of vendors hawks everything from anvils to zithers. The season's biggest events, however, are the week-long **Quartzsite Powwow Rock & Mineral Show** (tel: 928-927-5600, free) and a series of smaller gem fairs which draw as many as a million visitors during January and February. Sellers offer precious or collectible stones of every size, shape and description. Concurrent

Map
on page
206

BELOW:
reconstruction of
London Bridge was
completed in 1971.
The channel
beneath was
dredged afterward.

Map on page 206

The thermometer failed to show the true heat because the mercury dried up. Everything dries; wagons dry; men dry; chickens dry; there is no juice left in anything, living or dead.

– J. ROSS BROWNE, 1864, ABOUT SUMMER IN YUMA

BELOW: Yuma Territorial Prison was built by the inmates themselves.

events include a rodeo, parade, and both camel and ostrich races. Despite the quirky independence, the encamped snowbirds organize themselves well enoug to hold dances, hoedowns and potluck dinners to which the public is invited.

Continuing south on State Route 95, the remote **Kofa** and **Castle Dom** ranges loom as jagged escarpments to the east. Much of this pristine desert protected by 665,400-acre (269,000-hectare) **Kofa National Wildlife Refuge** (tel: 928-783-7861), accessible via dirt roads and unimproved trails. Campe and backcountry hikers face primitive conditions and rough, waterless terrain b may be rewarded with a glimpse of some of the state's few remaining dese bighorn sheep. Rare California palm trees – the only palms native to Arizona are found in the refuge's rugged, secluded canyons. Some botanists specula that the palms were stranded here at the end of the last Ice Age.

Bordering the refuge is the military's **Yuma Proving Ground**. Seconda roads cross through this restricted area into **Cibola** (tel: 928-857-3253) an **Imperial National Wildlife Refuges** ⑩ (tel: 928-783-3371), which prote wetlands along the Colorado River north of Imperial Dam and Martínez Lak offering birding, hiking, boating, fishing, hunting and camping.

A sense of Yuma

State Route 95 returns to the Colorado at **Yuma** ⑪, a farming and militar community of about 65,000 where an important ford has existed since lor before Europeans first visited. The Spanish presence here was brief, terminate by an uprising of the native Quechan in 1781. A riverside fort on the Californ bank, now **Fort Yuma Quechan Museum** (open Mon–Fri 8am–5pm, S; 10am–4pm; tel: 619-572-0661; fee), was built to protect travelers five yea before the area fell under U.S. control under the term of the 1854 Gadsden Purchase. This was followed t construction of the penitentiary that is now **Yum Territorial Prison State Historic Park** (Prison Hi Road, open daily 8am–5pm; tel: 928-783-4771; fee Known as the Hell Hole, the prison housed 3,06 convicts before its closure in 1909. Its best-know resident was Pearl Hart, the prison's only fema inmate, sentenced to five years for robbery. She w: released two years early when it was learned that sh was pregnant, presumably by one of her guards. Oth attractions include **Yuma Crossing State Histor Site**, which preserves the original ford and quarte master depot (Fourth Avenue at the river, open dai 9.30am–5.30pm; fee). Living-history demonstratio are offered by docents, recalling the bygone era whe paddlewheel steamers plied the Colorado.

Day-trip options include boat rides, date farm ar camel ranch tours, and the **Yuma Valley Railwa** excursion train (tel: 928-783-3456, fee), which fo lows a two-hour, 22-mile (35-km) route downrive Not a restaurant but a recreation site, **Betty's Kitche** (past Laguna Dam, 14 miles/23 km north of Yum; offers hiking, birding, picnicking and fishing in a lus shady spot. A word of warning: this part of the Sonor; Desert is uncomfortably hot in summer, and man tourist businesses close – wisely – until relativel cooler weather returns in autumn.

Water Issues

"**T**oo thick to drink, to thin to plow."
That's what they used to say about the
Colorado River. Not anymore. The
1,450-mile-long (2,330-km) Colorado, rising
in the Rocky Mountains and draining an
area the size of France, has been tamed –
dammed, diverted for irrigation and power,
and so heavily used by the states it flows
through that it is no longer a river by the
time it passes over the Mexican border. The
river once known as the Grand is now a
managed resource, not the wild, churning,
seasonally flooding Great Unknown that so
intimidated John Wesley Powell's 1869 and
1871 river expeditions.

Historically, the Colorado was a warm river
that swelled into a red, silty, roaring froth
when snow in the high country melted. Two
thirds of its volume comes from the Green
River, which confluences with the Colorado in
what is now Canyonlands National Park in
Utah. The Colorado then rages in a series
of whitewater rapids through the narrow
confines of Cataract Canyon.

Plants and animals in the Grand Canyon,
carved by the Colorado, evolved to deal with
seasonal surges in the river. Humpback chub
appeared in the warm waters of the Colorado
some 3 million to 5 million years ago, when
the river first cut through the layer-cake
strata of the uplifted Colorado Plateau. Now,
warm-water fish like the chub and razorback
sucker struggle to survive in the colder
waters exiting Glen Canyon Dam, which has
created Lake Powell. In the words of environmental analyst Stephen Corothers, the
Grand Canyon is now a "naturalized" environment rather than a natural one, meaning
that the ecosystem has changed to suit man-
made conditions.

The greatest challenge today is to provide
for the needs of a burgeoning Southwest population in the nation's fastest-growing region
while conserving its natural habitats, such as
those of the Grand Canyon and the lower Colorado. Daily surges in demand for power in
large metropolitan centers like Phoenix once

drove dam releases, creating damaging high
and low river levels. This has been improved by
the passage of the 1992 Grand Canyon Protection Act, which requires the dam's operators to smooth out flows to ensure that the
natural habitat downstream is not subjected to
extreme fluctuations.

On the other hand, infrequent great floods
were once a feature of the Colorado and may
have a place in the downstream environment. In 1996, the floodgates at Glen
Canyon were opened to allow the river to run
unchecked through the Grand Canyon.
Beaches were quickly renewed, old vegetation whisked away, and habitat improved in
the week-long flood.

As former Secretary of the Interior Bruce
Babbitt put it: "When the dam was going
up in the 1950s, it never occurred to any-
body that they needed to think about what
would happen a hundred miles downstream
because we tended to see the landscape as
fragments and each one of them independent. What we've learned... is that nature
doesn't operate that way." ❑

RIGHT: kayakers put into the Colorado
River below Hoover Dam.

SEDONA AND VERDE VALLEY

Map on page 218

Spectacular red-rock formations surround this popular getaway town, known for its dining, shopping and New Age vibrations

I n 1996, a Northern Arizona University study found that 64 percent of visitors coming to **Sedona** ❶ were seeking a "spiritual experience." Of those, 43 percent specifically mentioned the area's male and female "vortexes," unusual power points in the earth where energy flows freely, affecting living things with their vibrations.

In case you haven't heard, the New Age is big business in this community of 14,000 in west-central Arizona's Red Rock Country. You can take Jeep tours to vortex sites, read all about the latest local UFO sightings and abductions, experience a sweat lodge with a genuine Native American healer, have your aura tuned, your chakras aligned, crystals placed on your body, be rebirthed, cover yourself from head to toe in the sacred healing mud of Sedona, even buy a T-shirt hand-dyed with Sedona Red Dirt "believed to bring good luck to the wearer." And still have time to shop at Sedona's tony Mexican-style marketplace, **Tlaquepaque**, before sunset sets the rocks afire.

It would be easy to write off Sedona as Arizona's answer to Santa Fe. But what both places have in common, beyond their sometimes wacky offerings, is a stunning natural setting and a quality sought after by all the weary urban refugees, wealthy retirees, artists and spiritual seekers who have moved here since the 1980s: Inspiration. They seem to find it. The Cowboy Artists of America was established in Sedona, and today, more than 50 galleries offer some of the most sophisticated art in the Southwest. The town is home to an array of world-class artists, writers, photographers, musicians, and others who ensure that Sedona maintains a jam-packed cultural calendar.

PRECEDING PAGES: biking near Sedona. **LEFT:** Cathedral Rocks, Red Rock Crossing State Park. **BELOW:** a Sedona psychic.

Natural splendor

But the main reason to visit Sedona is to get outdoors and enjoy the scenery. At this 4,000-foot (1,200-meter) elevation, temperatures stay above freezing year-round. Summer months see 90°F (32°C) days at low elevations, but relief is always just a hike away in thousands of acres of cool, high-elevation national forest. Spring arrives early, with newly leafed cottonwoods and wave after wave of poppies, lupines and other wildflowers on the desert floor. Summer brings drenching monsoon rains and ephemeral waterfalls in the canyons. By October, fall leaves in **Oak Creek Canyon** ❷ are peaking. In January, the **Mogollon Rim** is dusted with snow, but down in the valley the crowds have evaporated and locals have taken back the trails. The best remedy for cabin fever, say residents of Flagstaff, 30 miles (48 km) to the north, is a drive to Sedona.

The route of choice from Flagstaff is spectacular **Highway 89A**, which spirals down off the ponderosa-

TIP

Sedona's dramatic setting and artsy atmosphere lend themselves to a lively schedule of special events, including the Sedona International Film Festival in March, the Chamber Music Festival in May, and Jazz on the Rocks in September.

BELOW:
sunset casts long shadows in the red-rock country outside Sedona.

pine-clad Colorado Plateau into Oak Creek Canyon. The road descends stratum by stratum from pale Kaibab Limestone into the variegated Supai Group, the Hermit Formation and the Schnebly Hill Formation. Differential erosion has carved a fantasyland of rock formations here: alcoves, arches, hoodoos, buttes and mesas with anthropomorphic names like Cathedral Rock, Coffee Pot Rock, Bell Rock and Vultee Arch.

Oak Creek Vista is a good place to stop and get a first look at the canyon described by Zane Grey in *The Call of the Canyon*, as "a gigantic burrow for beasts, perhaps for outlawed men – not for a civilized person." Civilization, for better or worse, finds its way into the canyon regularly now: an astounding 3 million visitors a year make the drive. But before Arizona's first designated scenic highway was built in the 1940s, early residents remember Oak Creek Canyon as a gloomy, isolated place, home to deer, elk, bobcats, black bear and at one time grizzlies.

The first permanent homesteader in the canyon was Irishman Jim Thompson who, in 1876, built a log cabin at Indian Gardens, where Tonto Apaches had only recently been raising corn, squash and beans. Homegrown produce is still one of the main attractions at **Garland's Oak Creek Lodge** (open Apr.–mid-Nov.; tel: 928-282-3343), a 1930s cabin resort located 7½ miles (12 km) north of Sedona. It's almost impossible to get a room reservation here, but don't miss a stroll in the gardens (a popular wedding venue) and one of the lodge's famous dinners, a chef's choice of whatever is fresh that day, served family style, in a warm, friendly atmosphere.

Two miles (3 km) south of Garlands, is 55-acre (22-hectare) **Slide Rock State Park ❸** (open daily, 9am–8pm; tel: 928-282-3034; fee). In 1907, Frank

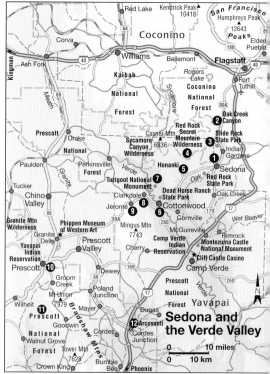

Pendley built a home and planted an apple orchard in the meadow above Slide Rock that is still producing today. *Life* magazine named Slide Rock one of the Top 10 swimming holes in the United States, and the park attracts some 1,600 bathers on a typical hot July day. But even if you don't want to whoosh down the natural rock chute (it's hard on the rear), stop here for a stroll along the creek, which is home to more than 20 fish species. There are many shady picnic spots under sycamore and oak trees.

Map
on page
218

Red-rock trails

Slide Rock may also be your best bet for trailhead parking during peak seasons. Several spectacular hikes – including the 3-mile (5-km) **West Fork of Oak Creek Trail**, which follows the creek through a narrow slot canyon – take off near here into the 44,000-acre (17,800-hectare) **Red Rock–Secret Mountain Wilderness** ❹. It's easier to find solitude in the backcountry. Better still, connecting trails allow you to begin in Oak Creek Canyon and end up in **West Sedona**. One possibility is **Sterling Pass Trail**, which connects with **Vultee Arch Trail** for a 4-mile (6-km) one-way hike. Five small campgrounds line Highway 89A in Oak Creek Canyon (only one is year-round); they fill quickly and reservations are essential. The Sedona Ranger District of Coconino National Forest (tel: 928-282-4119) has complete hiking information.

Sedona has suffered from a very visible, unregulated real-estate boom, which, to its present regret, allowed runaway development and overscaled homes to blight its famous red-rock vistas. Since then, new zoning has led to environmentally sensitive, smaller-scale public buildings like the attractive little Sedona Library. Outside the library is an engaging bronze statue of Sedona's founder,

LEFT: Slide Rock State Park is crowded with swimmers on hot summer days.
BELOW: the Chapel of the Holy Cross, completed in 1957, rises from a bluff on the south side of town.

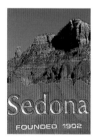

FOUNDED 1902

The town's name is etched on a slab of its signature red rock.

Sedona Schnebly, a Missouri pioneer, who with her husband T. C. began farm ing 80 acres (32 hectares) on the west bank of Oak Creek in 1902. Some of the most spectacular vistas in Sedona lie along **Schnebly Hill Road**, a dirt road that winds onto **Munds Mountain**. It's closed in winter, but for careful drivers this makes a scenic alternative to Interstate 17.

For lessons in how to live harmoniously with the environment, look no far ther than the Sinagua Indians who lived in Sedona a thousand years ago. They farmed along Oak Creek and built warm, south-facing cliff-side pueblos in the red rocks that blend seamlessly with their surroundings.

Hundreds of ruins are secreted away in the red rocks, but the easiest to visi are **Palatki** and **Honanki** ❺ on the north side of the valley. To reach them drive Highway 89A west 9½ miles (15 km) from the Y intersection with High way 179. Turn right on FR 525, drive 6 miles (10 km) to where FR 795 branche to the right, and take FR 795 2 miles (3 km) to a dead end. For Honanki, con tinue on FR 525 another 3¼ miles (5 km) beyond the intersection with FR 795 Forest Service rangers offer tours daily.

Prehistoric crossroads

The Verde River Valley is increasingly a bedroom community for those who'c rather live in Sedona but can't afford the rent. One such town is **Cottonwood** ❻ 17 miles (27 kim) southwest of Sedona. Picnicking, camping, canoeing and fishing for trout, bass and catfish are available at 320-acre (130-hectare) **Dea Horse Ranch State Park** (open daily; tel: 928-634-5283; admission fee) Nearby is **Tuzigoot National Monument** ❼ (open daily, 8am–7pm in summe to 5pm in winter; tel: 928-634-5564; admission fee), a large Sinagua pueblo buil

BELOW: a guitarist serenades shoppers at Tlaquepaque, designed in the style of a Mexican village.

FIRST LADY OF ARIZONA LETTERS

Rancher and writer Sharlot M. Hall was "a genuine youn frontierswoman," wrote Charles F. Lummis, her editor an friend. "Not of the cheap drama and Sunday-edition counter feits, but a fine, quiet, loveable woman made strong and wis and sweet by life in the unbuilded spaces."

This love of "unbuilded spaces" began early. The firs white child born in Kansas, in 1870, Sharlot and her famil traveled west along the Santa Fe Trail in 1882 and buil up a ranch on Lynx Creek near Prescott, which Sharlc continued to run until 1928, when she began her museum She retained a love of adventure, the outdoors and free spirited living until her death in 1943.

In 1906, she helped defeat a congressional bill to mak New Mexico and Arizona a single state by using her epi poem *Arizona* to sway the U.S. Congress. In July 1911 while serving as territorial historian (the first woman t serve in the territorial government), she and famed guide A Doyle spent 10 weeks journeying by wagon through th remote Arizona Strip. Her glowing accounts of the trip le Congress to include the area when statehood was grante in 1912. She wrote 10 books and more than 500 articles stories and poems and was the first woman to be inducte into Arizona's Hall of Fame.

Map
on page
218

on a high ridge above the **Verde River**. Begun as a small pueblo in AD 1000, Tuzigoot grew to 110 rooms in the 1200s, as Sinagua refugees from drought-stricken northern areas moved south. The fertile, well-watered Verde Valley became an important prehistoric crossroads for traders, but eventually over-population, diminishing natural resources, and epidemics seem to have taken a toll. The pueblo took on a defensive appearance and began to store more food. By 1425, all the residents had moved away.

Tuzigoot is a Tonto Apache word meaning "crooked water," a reference to a crescent-shaped lake near the monument. The Apache are still a strong presence in the Verde Valley, where they have intermarried with Yavapai Indians to such a degree that the two groups have merged into the Yavapai–Apache Nation. They live together on three separate tracts of land on the 560-acre (225-hectare) **Yavapai–Apache Reservation** and operate the successful **Cliff Castle Casino** (Montezuma Castle exit 289, off Interstate 17) in **Camp Verde**, now the Verde Valley's main employer. Even if you don't gamble, stop at this casino for a look at the tribe's administrative offices, which were designed by Hopi architect Dennis Mumkena in the shape of a kiva. The interior (not open to the public) is decorated with symbols connected to Hopi legends.

Before Tuzigoot National Monument was deeded to the National Park Service, in 1939, it was the property of the United Verde Copper Company, the Verde Valley's primary industry, from 1882 to 1953. Two miles (3 km) north-west of Cottonwood is the old smelter town of **Clarkdale ❽**, which is sputtering back to life with the revival of the historic **Verde Valley Railroad** (excursions 11am daily, Sat. starlight rides June–Oct; tel: 800-293-7245; reservations required). The Verde Valley Railroad carried ore and passengers – the Verde

BELOW: at its height in the late 1300s, Tuzigoot had more than 100 rooms and perhaps 225 residents.

Bikers pay Jerome a visit; the town is known for attracting an eclectic and off-beat crowd.

BELOW: houses cling to Jerome's Cleopatra Hill.

Mix, it was called. Today, it's strictly tourists, with about 60,000 passengers a year boarding the old locomotive for the four-hour, 40-mile (64-km) round-trip from **Clarkdale** to **Perkinsville**. With its bright blue engines and obvious family appeal, the railroad is a pleasant way to spend an afternoon. It also offers a unique opportunity to view **Sycamore Canyon Wilderness**, a 21-mile-long (34-km) gash in the earth, with 700-foot-high (215-meter) red cliffs, huge cottonwoods, endangered wildlife, and bald and golden eagles in winter.

Sin City

The Verde Valley Railroad was financed by Senator William A. Clark, owner of the United Verde Mine in **Jerome ❾**. Jerome began life as a mining camp in 1876 and eventually yielded $1 billion of copper, gold, silver, zinc and lead during its 77 years of operation. Seeming to defy gravity as it clings to the side of 7,743-foot (2,360-meter) **Mingus Mountain**, quaint little Jerome could be a miniature Bisbee, with its stacked Victorian "painted ladies," narrow streets and innovative art galleries. But it beats it hands down for breathtaking scenery, with vertiginous views of the Verde Valley all the way north to the San Francisco Peaks. Entranced by such beauty, it's easy to forget the reality. Between 1895 and 1935, 150 miners lost their lives in the 4,650-foot-deep (1,420-meter) shaft. Even in the 1940s, remembers the son of a mine executive, "the miners were in rubber boots, working in water about a foot deep. It was humid, and very, very hot… They could work only 20 minutes without rest."

Despite this sad history, by 1900 Jerome had 2,681 residents, making it the fifth-largest town in Arizona Territory. Americans and immigrants from Mexico, Spain, Italy, Austria, Ireland and Eastern Europe vied for lodging, often having

o bunk in shifts. Prostitution was so common it was intermittently legalized. Saloons, opium dens and gambling houses did a roaring trade, leading the *New York Sun*, in 1903, to dub Jerome "the Wickedest Town in the West" and to express the opinion that "the best thing that could happen to Jerome would be a nice, big, citywide fire."

Mud slides, floods and devastating blazes did destroy much of the town between 1894 and 1925, but somehow it has never given up the ghost. A handful of artists, retirees and others looking for cheap digs began restoring individual buildings in the 1960s, and now the whole town is listed on the National Register of Historic Places. Jerome's interesting art galleries are its best feature today. **Jerome State Historical Park** (open daily 8am–5pm; tel: 928-634-5381; admission fee), located in the 8,000-square-foot (750-sq-meter) 1916 home of "Rawhide Jimmy" Douglas above his Little Daisy Mine, has a model of the mines, an assay office, old photos, mining tools and mineral displays.

Capital idea

By contrast, upstanding Victorian values seem to ooze out of **Prescott** ❿ (pronounced PRES-cut), a tidy little town cradled in a forested basin beneath the **Bradshaw Mountains**, south of Jerome. Prescott itself has a population of 30,000, but mushrooming subdivisions in neighboring Prescott Valley have pushed the total population to 90,000, making it one of Arizona's fastest growing towns. Tree-shaded streets, solid Victorian buildings and an elegant courthouse make Prescott's town center a delightful place to linger on a sleepy summer afternoon. Several historic hotels offer lodging, including the 1927 **Hassayampa Inn**, a gorgeous grande dame in the old style, recently renovated and featuring antiques, painted ceilings and plush furnishings.

Prescott had noble aspirations from the get-go. When President Lincoln made Arizona a territory in 1863, Governor John Goodwin and other appointed officials toured the territory for three months, looking for a site for the new capital that had lands rich in mineral wealth and grazing but was relatively free of Confederate sympathies. The party based itself at Fort Whipple and chose gold-rich Granite Creek for the new settlement, which they named Prescott, after the historian noted for his work on Mexico. Government buildings were built in 1864, at the height of the campaign against the Tonto Apache and Yavapai Indians. As with the Verde Valley, the shoe is on the other foot these days. **Bucky's Casino**, operated by the small Yavapai Indian tribe, is one of Prescott's booming new businesses.

Prescott lost the capital to Tucson in 1867 (it eventually ended up in Phoenix), but quickly consoled itself with gold mining and large cattle ranching operations on the surrounding grasslands. The town became legendary as a hard-drinking haven for cowboys spending their pay on a Saturday night. By the early 1900s, 40 saloons lined Montezuma Street, or **Whiskey Row**, as it was known. Working cowboys from surrounding ranches are still very much in evidence and have been known to down a whiskey or two at the **Palace Saloon**, one of the last honky-tonks

Map on page 218

During one of three fires that swept through Jerome in the late 1890s, Jennie Banters, a local madam, encouraged firemen to save her bordello by offering her services for free.

BELOW: signs warn visitors of the dangers of open mine shafts.

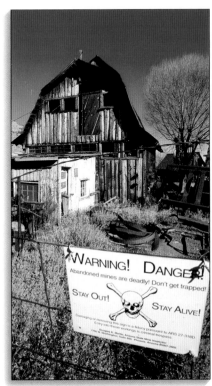

Map on page 218

on Whiskey Row. What's billed as "the world's oldest rodeo" takes place in July (Payson also claims that honor). And a popular **Cowboy Poets Gathering** attracts several hundred saddlestruck bards to the town in August.

Western visions, past and future

Six miles (10 km) north of Prescott, just north of Highway 89A, the **Phippen Museum of Western Art** (open daily, except Tues 1–4pm; tel: 928-778-1385; admission fee) honors western artist George Phippen, founder of the Cowboy Artists of America. The museum has a good selection of paintings, sketches and bronzes by up-and-coming as well as established Western artists. Arizona's territorial history is beautifully told at the **Sharlot Hall Museum** (open Mon.–Sat. 10am–5pm, Sun. 1–5pm; tel: 928-445-3122; donation), housed in the 1864 Governor's Mansion and 11 other buildings. It was founded in 1928 by former territorial historian Sharlot Hall, a pioneer Prescott rancher, travel writer and, not incidentally, cowgirl poet.

BELOW: a hiker strides across a rocky bluff in the Granite Mountain Wilderness.
RIGHT: Arcosanti reflects the "arcological" philosophy of its founder, architect Paolo Soleri.

Trails lace **Prescott National Forest ⓫**. One of the most popular is 1.7-mile (3-km) **Thumb Butte Loop Trail**, which winds through ponderosa pine, then crosses pinyon-juniper and oak forest for good views of Prescott and the surrounding countryside. **Granite Mountain Wilderness** is also popular with hikers and rock climbers. For information, contact Prescott National Forest's **Bradshaw Mountain District** (tel: 928-445-7253). A beautiful drive north through the grasslands of **Chino Valley** takes you to Ash Fork and Interstate 40. Highway 69 heads south past dirt roads leading to old mines and historic ranches before connecting with Interstate 17 at **Cordes Junction**, the turnoff for **Arcosanti ⓬**, the futuristic concrete city founded by visionary architect Paolo Soleri. ❑

Arcosanti

"U nless we reinvent the American dream in terms of the physiology of it, then it's not going to be a dream, it's going to be doomsday," Italian-born architect Paolo Soleri told an interviewer in 1995. Soleri was talking about the pollution, congestion, social isolation and enormous waste of resources caused by Americans' pursuit of the good life at the expense of the rest of the planet. Furthermore, states Soleri, "We would be in need of 40 planets by the year 2050, if the American dream becomes the planetary dream."

Soleri's solution? Arcosanti, an experimental city on 25 acres in the high country of Cordes Junction, 70 miles (115 km) north of Phoenix. Since 1970, Soleri's Cosanti Foundation has been building the new community, which incorporates large, siltcast, concrete structures and solar greenhouses. It is a strange vision in the midst of sweeping grasslands surrounded by mountains, prompting everything from praise for its far-reaching vision to horror from one critic who labeled it "a social experiment that has more to do with totalitarianism than harmonious living."

When complete, Arcosanti will soar 25 stories high, house 7,000 people, and include apartments, businesses, studios and performance venues in an urban setting that emphasizes privacy linked to accessible public spaces. The complex is designed in accordance with the concept of "arcology" (architecture+ecology) developed by Soleri. In such a system, artificial structures and living things interact as organs do in the human body, with efficient circulation of people and resources, and solar orientation for lighting, heating and cooling.

Soleri began developing his arcological concepts after spending 18 months studying with famed architect Frank Lloyd Wright at Taliesen West in Scottsdale and Taliesen East in Wisconsin. Taking to heart the famous edict, "Form ever follows function," he returned to Italy and began building large ceramics, using processes that led to the award-winning windbells of ceramic and bronze that are sold to support his experi-

mental work, as well as the siltcast architectural structures at Arcosanti. Soleri returned to Arizona and began constructing his first experimental village, Cosanti, in Paradise Valley in 1956, which remains his permanent home today.

Volunteers and students from around the world, many with no previous design experience, undertake a five-week workshop that teaches building techniques and arcological philosophy, while continuing the city's construction. Residents are workshop alumni who continue the work of planning, construction and teaching. They produce the world-famous Soleri Bells as well as host 50,000 tourists each year. Daily tours ($6 fee) introduce visitors to the site, and concerts and other events are held regularly in the Colly Soleri Music Center, named for Soleri's late wife. Shows include dinner and are often followed by a light show on the opposite mesa. Tours of Cosanti in Paradise Valley are also available. ❏

● *For more information, contact Arcosanti at 928-632-7135 or www.arcosanti.org/*

Bird-Watching

Birds are big business in Arizona and for good reason. More than 500 species live in or migrate through the state, many of them visitors from Mexico and other points south that are rarely found elsewhere in the country.

Mention bird-watching to a non-birder, however, and you're likely to be met with a blank stare. The arcane terminology and not-entirely-inaccurate image of birders obsessed with extending their "life lists" has a way of turning off the uninitiated. It's a shame, because birds are not only fascinating in themselves but a gateway to a larger understanding of the natural world.

Even a rank amateur on a casual visit to the Grand Canyon can spot and identify large raptors like golden eagles and turkey vultures, which are often seen soaring on thermals that rise from the canyon. The golden eagle (actually brown with gold highlights) usually flies alone, its 6-foot (2-meter) wing-span held flat or in a slight V. It can tuck its wings and dive after prey, plummeting at speeds of up to 100 miles per hour (160 kpm). Turkey vultures look more wobbly in flight and often circle in groups. They are unmistakable up close, with a bald head, hunched profile and hooked beak used to pick flesh from carrion.

The small birds that dart through the air at the canyon's edge are white-throated swifts and violet-green swallows chasing after insects. The swift has a black-and-white body and peculiar way of flying that makes it appear as if the wings are alternating strokes. The swallow has a white breast and round body and is more steady in flight.

Consider yourself lucky if you catch a glimpse of a California condor. They're difficult to miss. With a wingspan of 10 feet (3 meters), they're the biggest things in the sky – and one of the rarest. Had it not been for the intervention of biologists in the 1980s, the species may have gone extinct. Nine captive birds were released at the Vermilion Cliffs in 1996 and occasionally glide through

LEFT: red-tailed hawks prey on small mammals, reptiles and other birds. **BELOW:** an elf owl nests in saguaro cactus cavity.

the canyon on daily foraging trips of 50 to 100 miles (80–160 km) or more.

It's in the desert ranges of southeastern Arizona, however, that birders find the greatest diversity of bird life. Hummingbirds are a specialty of the region. It's not unusual to see as many as 15 species in late summer, when drenching rains set off a profusion of blooming wildflowers. Moist, sheltered canyons are hot spots. Places like Ramsey Canyon in the Huachuca Mountains and Cave Creek Canyon in the Chiricahuas are legendary for hummers as well as a dazzling variety of other subtropical species such as sulphur-bellied flycatchers, red-faced warblers, and painted redstarts that are at the northernmost limit of their range.

Another subtropical species, the elegant trogon, is a specialty of Madera Canyon, which spills down the flank of the Santa Rita Mountains. The male is the most colorful, with a red belly, an emerald head and chest, and a squared-off, coppery tail. It's call isn't nearly as lovely as its plumage – a low croak that's been likened to a pig's grunt.

Prime birding continues along the San Pedro River near Sierra Vista, where about 350 bird species have been recorded in the riparian forest and grasslands.

In the Sonoran desert, saguaros are a magnet for bird life, providing food, shelter and moisture for a host of species. Gila woodpeckers and gilded flickers peck nests into the trunks, which are later inhabited by elf owls. Red-tailed hawks and curve-billed thrashers build nests in the protection of spiny arms, and an array of birds, including white-winged doves and cactus wrens, feed on the saguaro's nectar and succulent fruit.

Birders will want to remember two events: the Southeast Wings Birding Festival in mid-August and the Wings Over Willcox Sandhill Crane Celebration in January, when nearly 10,000 cranes descend upon the marshes and fields around Willcox Playa. ❑

● *For more information, contact the Southeastern Arizona Bird Observatory at 520-432-1388 or www.sabo.org/; or the Tucson Audubon Society at 520-629-0510 or its website, www.tucsonaudubon.org/*

LOW: the bill an Ana's ummingbird adapted to nectar m tubular wers. They e especially tracted to d blossoms.

MOGOLLON RIM AND TONTO BASIN

Map on page 200–201

Once roamed by the Apache, this land of rugged beauty encompasses ancient pueblos, historic forts and reminders of a violent past

Captain John G. Bourke, an Apache fighter under the command of General George Crook in the 1880s, described the **Mogollon Rim** as "a strange upheaval, a strange freak of nature, a mountain canted up on one side. One rides along the edge and looks down two and three thousand feet into what is termed the 'Tonto Basin,' a scene of grandeur and rugged beauty."

Bourke was equally impressed by the way the Apache lived so harmoniously with this rugged terrain. "The Apache was a hard foe to subdue, not because he was full of wiles and tricks and experienced in all that pertains to the art of war, but because he had so few artificial wants and depended almost absolutely upon what his great mother – Nature – stood ready to supply."

But the lessons of the Apache, brave fighters whom Bourke and Crook admired, were mostly lost on the white settlers whose lands they were charged with defending. Attracted initially by gold, then by timber, rivers and rich lands that could sustain ranches and farms, those who came to the Mogollon Rim and **Tonto Basin** found themselves locked in an epic struggle of possession – with nature and their fellow men. Nowhere in Arizona saw more bloody battles between Indians and white men, ranchers and rustlers, homesteaders and rogue wild animals.

It was this authentic Wild West quality that led western novelist Zane Grey to fall in love with the area in the early 1900s. "For wild, rugged beauty, I had not seen its equal," he wrote. Grey built a hunting lodge near Payson and returned year after year to hunt bear and mountain lion with local guides like Babe Haught and Al Doyle. More than half of Grey's novels are set in the Tonto Basin, earning the area the official moniker Zane Grey Country.

Early inhabitants

This tour begins at **Camp Verde ❶**, off Interstate 17, where the **Verde River** meanders through the stark Verde Valley basin. Farmers from the Prescott area founded the first Anglo settlement here in 1865, but 1,000 years earlier prehistoric farmers were raising corn, beans, squash, cotton and other crops on these riverbanks, using technology perfected by the Hohokam to the south. A rare 12th-century Hohokam-style pithouse can be viewed at **Montezuma Well ❷**, 11 miles (18 km) north of Camp Verde, along with irrigation ditches and pueblos built by the northern Sinagua culture. The Sinagua were adept dry-land farmers who moved into the Verde Valley from the Flagstaff area in the 1100s, following the eruptions of Sunset Crater Volcano.

PRECEDING PAGES: cowboy and mount. **LEFT:** hikers on the Mogollon Rim, Apache-Sitgreaves National Forest. **BELOW:** fallen agave.

Montezuma Well is a detached unit of **Montezuma Castle National Monument ❸** (open daily, 8am–7pm summer, 8am–5pm winter; tel: 928-567-3322; free). The "castle" is really a beautifully preserved five-story, 13th-century Sinagua cliff dwelling above Beaver Creek. It so impressed early settlers they erroneously thought it the palace of Aztec leader Montezuma. An adjoining pueblo, Castle A, has collapsed, but most of Montezuma Castle's limestone walls and 20 rooms have survived, protected in an alcove high in the cliffs. Visitors may view the dwelling from a trail below but aren't permitted to enter.

By the time Spaniard Antonio de Espejo rode through the Verde Valley in 1583, these early farming cultures had disappeared. Strong but inconclusive evidence indicates the Sinagua may have moved back north into the Hopi and Zuni pueblos in the 1400s. In their place were hunter-gatherer Yavapai Indians, related to the Havasupai and Hualapai of the Grand Canyon, and small bands of Tonto Apache. The latter proved so troublesome during an 1863 gold rush on the Hassayampa River and the subsequent settlement of the Verde Valley that the U.S. Army was dispatched to build Fort Lincoln, later called Fort Verde.

Agave is adapted to arid desert conditions, blooming only once in its lifetime.

Apache campaign

The fort became a staging area for General Crook (known as "Gray Eyes" by the Apache) and his army's successful Tonto campaign, which resulted in the defeat of Chief Chalipan and 2,300 Tonto Apache in the winter of 1872–73. As part of the peace agreement with the Tonto Apache, the honorable Crook promised to provide jobs, farmland, and a police force and immediately had the Indian workers begin digging a 5-mile-long (8-km) irrigation ditch, planting 57 acres (23 hectares) of melons and other crops. **Fort Verde State Historic Park ❹**

BELOW: surgical instruments from the 19th century are displayed in Fort Verde's infirmary.

WRITER OF THE PURPLE SAGE

Pearl "Zane" Grey was born in Zanesville, Ohio, in 1872 and trained as a dentist before finding his calling as a self-taught Western writer and avid outdoorsman. Between 1903 and his death in 1939, Grey wrote 56 Western romances, 13 outdoor books, seven juvenile stories, three historical novels, a novel set in Ohio, one set in Tahiti, two screenplays and numerous short stories and nonfiction articles collected in some 20 anthologies.

Sales of his novels have exceeded 100 million copies, and at least 100 of his books and stories have been adapted to film. Much of their appeal lies in the portrayal of simpler times, authentic settings and classic characters like the lone gunman Lassiter of *Riders of the Purple Sage*, a rugged individual who achieves redemption by wrestling with the ghosts of his past. Almost all of his tales reveal a West where man is engaged in an epic struggle with his environment and is either redeemed or destroyed by it.

Although Grey loved Arizona, he, wife Dolly and children moved to Altadena, California, in 1918, where Dolly handled her husband's business deals, freeing Grey to write, scout movie locations, and take extended hunting and fishing trips every fall using his Payson, Arizona, cabin as a base.

(open daily, 8am–5pm; tel: 928-567-3275; admission fee) preserves four surviving fort buildings, including General Crook's adobe headquarters. Exhibits include 1880s-era furnishings, old saddles, Indian crafts, letters and uniforms belonging to cavalry, infantry and the Apache scouts Crook used to understand and outmaneuver his opponents.

Map on page 200–201

Forest trails

North of Camp Verde, hiking and swimming are popular activities at 6,700-acre (2,700-hectare) **Wet Beaver Wilderness** ❺, a lush oasis with sycamore-, cottonwood-, and ash-lined riverbanks. Trails follow the river and climb the 2,000-foot-high (610-meter) Mogollon Rim above. This is a popular area in summer, with swimming holes that provide respite from temperatures in the 90s°F (30s°C). The **Beaver Creek Ranger District** of the **Coconino National Forest** (I-17, Sedona exit 298; tel: 928-567-4501), north of Camp Verde near Beaver Creek Campground, has information on trails throughout the Mogollon Rim area.

The **General George Crook Trail**, which starts in **Dewey** ❻, near Prescott, proceeds east through Camp Verde, up along the Mogollon Rim, and finally ends at Cottonwood Wash near **Pinedale** ❼, is an Arizona State Historic Trail that passes through three national forests – Prescott, Coconino and Apache-Sitgreaves – over its 138-mile (222-km) length. The trail was blazed in 1871 by Crook and his men and used for 22 years to patrol the northern boundary of the Apache Reservation. Connecting trails at the west end join the **Highline Trail** at the base of the Mogollon Rim in **Tonto National Forest**, allowing you to hike from desert scrub to pine-fir forest. The Crook Trail is best hiked in spring or fall; portions are open for cross-country skiing in winter.

BELOW:
llamas are used for pack trips in Tonto National Forest.

Air-traffic control in Payson.

BELOW: float trip on the Verde River.
RIGHT: horseback riding is the best way to travel the remote reaches of the Mazatzal Mountains.

To access the eastern section of the trail, drive east on Highway 260 from Camp Verde, turn north on Highway 87, then east on unpaved Forest Road 300, the 1928 logging road that parallels the Crook Trail for 42 miles (68 km) along the forested rim. Views are breathtaking from this perched route, with range after range of hazy mountains, emerald forest basins and valleys, and heart-stopping drops below limestone outcrops. All is not beauty and light, however. The remains of the devastating 1990 Dude Fire, which blackened 24,000 acres (9,700 hectares) and killed six firefighters, can still be seen.

Also along the road are monuments to the major conflicts of the Apache campaign: the Battle of Skull Cave (1872), the Battle of Turret Butte (1873), and the final showdown, the Battle of Dry Wash (1873), which resulted in the deaths of 22 Apaches and the flight of the rest, clearing the rim country for white settlers.

Rim country

Scenic Highway 87 drops down from the Mogollon Rim into the heart of the Tonto Basin. Historic homes, antique shops and galleries line the main street of the little Mormon settlement of **Pine ❽**, while nearby **Strawberry** (named for the wild strawberries that used to grow here) preserves Arizona's oldest one-room log schoolhouse. Built in 1885, it is open on summer weekends and by appointment (call Strawberry Lodge at 928-476-3333 for information).

Busy little **Payson ❾** started out as a gold mining camp in 1881 but is now more popular as a shopping center, a getaway destination for Phoenicians and a base for exploring the cliffs of the Mogollon Rim, which loom majestically over the town.

Limestone deposited at the bottom of an ancient ocean forms the cliffs

surrounding the Tonto Basin. Mineral springs at **Pine Creek**, northwest of Payson, have carved the rock into the world's longest natural bridge, preserved at **Tonto Natural Bridge State Park** ❿ (open daily 8am–6pm Apr–Oct, 9am–5pm Nov–Mar; tel: 928-476-4202; admission fee). At 400 feet (120 meters) wide, with many limestone formations similar to those found in caves farther to the south, the bridge is a beautiful little oasis off the main highway and a bonus on any trip into the rim country.

Map on page 200–201

Saddle up

What is advertised as the West's oldest rodeo (begun in 1884) takes place in Payson every August. Get in the saddle yourself or hike a trail in some of the state's most glorious forests. Tonto National Forest's **Payson Ranger District** (1009 E. Hwy. 260, Payson; open daily 7:45am–4:30pm May–Oct; Mon–Sat Nov–Dec; Mon–Fri Jan–Apr; tel: 928-474-7900) has information on hiking, horseback riding and camping in the surrounding forest and the 252,000-acre (102,000-hectare) **Mazatzal Wilderness** ⓫, whose highest point, 7,894-foot (2,406-meter) **Mazatzal Peak**, dominates the southern skyline. You can arrange private horse packing trips into the Mazatzals (pronounced MAT-a-zals) at the Forest Service office. One of the most popular entry points into these steep, rocky mountains is the 6¼-mile (10-km) **Barnhardt Trail**, near the little town of **Rye**. The trail joins the 29-mile (47-km) **Mazatzal Divide Trail**, which runs along the crest of the Mazatzals and features stunning views of the Sierra Ancha Wilderness to the south and the San Francisco Peaks near Flagstaff to the north.

On the western side of the range is the 28-mile (45-km) **Verde River Trail**, which follows a wild and scenic stretch of the **Verde River**. Float trips are

TIP

The Mazatzal Divide Trail has been incorporated into the Arizona Trail, which will eventually stretch the length of the state from Mexico to the Utah border.

BELOW: the Verde River supports a rich growth of riparian vegetation such as cottonwood and willow.

Map on page 200–201

possible on the river, though water levels vary considerably depending on spring runoff and summer rains and, in some years, may not be high enough to boat. However you choose to explore the Mazatzals – on foot, on horseback, or by boat – be prepared for a hot, dry, rough country. Bring plenty of water, food and appropriate clothing.

Long pack trips were a mainstay of life in the Tonto Basin for Zane Grey, who made the Payson area his base. In 1921, his longtime guide Babe Haught, scion of Payson's first pioneer family, sold Grey several acres of land and built him a hunting cabin. The Zane Grey Lodge burned to the ground in the 1990 Dude Fire, but the Gila County Historical Society, which runs the sweet little **Rim Country Museum** (open Wed–Sun 12pm–4pm; tel: 928-474-3483) on Main Street, is raising money to build a replica on its grounds. The museum, housed in a 1907 forest ranger's house, has a marvelous display of Grey memorabilia that survived the fire (including the author's tooled leather saddlebags, first editions of several of his books, and an embroidered waistcoat) as well as exhibits on the area's forests and Indians.

BELOW: a swimming hole on Wet Beaver Creek is an inviting spot for a picnic.
RIGHT: sacred datura blooms at the base of Montezuma Castle.

Family feud

Grey visited the Tonto Basin every fall, hunting and fishing with Haught and writing detailed notes about the landscape, the people, and the historic events that have given the rim country its unique character. No event has had more impact than the 1887 Pleasant Valley War, one of the most bloody and violent range wars of the frontier era, which pitted the Tewksbury family against the Graham family. Details vary, but the feud was between sheepmen and cattlemen and the Grahams' cattle rustling activities. Adding fuel to the fire was the presence of cowboys from the Hashknife outfit who had been chased out of the Holbrook area. By the time the smoke cleared five years later, 30 people were dead, including 12 Grahams and three Tewksburys. And residents of rim country weren't talking – even to famous authors.

Grey's novel, *To the Last Man*, wove fact with fiction. To try to uncover more of the truth, history buffs won't want to miss visiting **Pleasant Valley**, located between the rim country and the remote little settlement of **Young ⓬**. Hard to reach over rough dirt roads (turn off Highway 260 at Milepost 284, about 33 miles/53 km east of Payson), Young is one of Arizona's last cow towns. In keeping with a long tradition of feistiness, local folks are independent types with little use for authority or development. Check out the **Antlers Bar and Café** (open daily, tel: 928-462-3265), which serves three squares daily and has walls displaying everything from old saddles and mining gear to dusty stuffed bears.

Clair's Gallery and Museum (open Fri–Sun 10am–6pm; tel: 928-462-3402) is also unusual. It's housed in an 87-room pueblo ruin occupied between 1100 and 1350 by the Mogollon and Salado cultures. The first victim of the Pleasant Valley War, a Navajo sheepherder, is buried 5 miles (8 km) north of Young. A white cross and sign mark the spot on Forest Route 200, a mile (1.6 km) west of the road. ❑

WHITE MOUNTAINS AND EAST CENTRAL ARIZONA

Forest-clad slopes offer stunning mountain drives, an abundance of recreational opportunities and welcome relief from desert heat

n his classic *A Sand County Almanac*, naturalist Aldo Leopold describes the **White Mountains** in the early 1900s as "the exclusive domain of the mounted man: mounted cowman, mounted sheepman, mounted forest offi-cer, mounted trapper, and those unclassified mounted men of unknown origin and uncertain destination always found on frontiers."

A century later, rugged individualism is still a way of life in the White Mountains, but ever since Arizona's oldest roadway, Route 666, linked "the palms to the pines" along the Arizona–New Mexico border in 1926, isolation has been more a matter of choice than necessity. Newer paved highways have shrunk the time it takes to reach the White Mountains. As a result, carloads of overheated city slickers now make the pilgrimage on summer weekends, and almost every sleepy town is happy to host them, offering the gamut from rustic lakeside cabins, historic inns and homegrown museums to roundups, rodeos and hands-on archaeological digs.

Visitors are lured to these skyscraping peaks, sapphire lakes and ice-melt streams by a laid-back western lifestyle, temperatures in the 70s°F (20s°C), and some of the Southwest's best trout fishing, winter sports and mountain biking. Arizona's second- and third-highest mountains are found here – 11,403-foot (3,476-meter) **Baldy Peak**, sacred to the White Mountain Apache on whose reservation it lies, and 10,912-foot (3,326-meter) **Escudilla Mountain**, on the adjoining 2-million-acre (809,000-hectare) **Apache–Sitgreaves National Forest**.

Silent Indian ruins are reminders that east-central Arizona also sits on a cultural frontier – a frontier breached by U.S. Army soldiers sent to quell the Apache in the 1870s but never entirely subdued, as can be seen in the spirit of self-determination displayed in the San Carlos and White Mountain Apache Reservations today. Equally strong are the Mormon communities founded during the same period, which prospered by trading meat and vegetables with the troops at Fort Apache. Descendants of pioneer families still work the land, trade with travelers, and exert political clout from their mountain stronghold.

PRECEDING PAGES: Salt River Canyon. **LEFT:** White Mountain Apache *Gaan* dancer. **BELOW:** cowboy, Whiteriver Rodeo.

When cattle was king

Holbrook ⓑ, 92 miles (148 km) east of Flagstaff on Interstate 40, is a convenient place to start your explorations. Founded as a railroad town in 1881, the vast surrounding grasslands quickly attracted cattlemen, and the town became a major ranching center. The Hashknife outfit was one of the most famous cattle companies, running 60,000 cattle on a million acres (405,000 hectares) an becoming the third-largest cattle empire in the United States. Rustling and poc management eventually shut down the ranch in 1900, but not before Hashknif cowboys had become celebrated for their whoop-'em-up Saturday-night way in upstanding Mormon towns to the south. Situated near the Navajo, Hopi an Apache reservations, Holbrook is a good place to pick up silver-and-turquois jewelry, pottery and Apache baskets at a local trading post or attend India dances held nightly on the lawn next to the old courthouse in summer. In Januar or February, you can post a letter via Hashknife Pony Express, which carries th

Living wood becomes petrified when its cellulose is slowly replaced with silica.

mail on horseback from Holbrook to Scottsdale.

Trees of stone

The town is surrounded by the **Painted Desert**, a highly atmospheric backdro of buttes, mesas and banded pink, gray, brown and purple badlands that have a unearthly glow at sunset or after a heavy rain. To explore this evocative lanc scape, drive southeast of Holbrook on Highway 180 to the south entrance c 147-square-mile (381-sq-km) **Petrified Forest National Park ⓮** (open dail 7.30am–5pm in winter, extended summer hours; tel: 928-524-6228; admissic fee), set aside in 1906 to protect one of the world's most abundant deposits c petrified wood. The southern section of the park contains the best examples c these highly prized gems. Resist the temptation to slip a few samples into you

BELOW: the Long Logs section of Petrified Forest National Park.

pocket. Regulations strictly prohibit rock collecting in the park and, anywa petrified wood is sold for pennies outside the park.

Exhibits in the **Rainbow Forest Museum** explain that petrified wood bega forming 225 million years ago, when North America was about where We:

frica is today. The warm tropical climate sustained enormous reptiles and mphibians (look for the fearsome crocodile-like phytosaur and "Gertie," a inosaur found here in 1984), cycad ferns, and conifers up to 200 feet (60 ieters) tall. When these trees toppled into rivers, they were washed in logjams ito swamps, then buried by silt and ash from volcanoes to the south. Silicates radually mixed with groundwater and replaced woody cells with the jasper, methyst and smoky quartz so prized today.

Map on page 200–201

A 27-mile (44-km) scenic drive, accessed at either end of the park, has pull-its, interpretive trails and picnic areas. The middle section contains a number f Ancestral Pueblo ruins, including **Agate House**, an unusual 900-year-old ructure made of petrified wood, and the 100-room **Puerco Pueblo**, occupied round AD 1400. Look for the spectacular petroglyphs here, one of which marks ie summer solstice. The **Painted Desert Inn**, built in 1924 as a lodging, is ow a national historic landmark and has exhibits and a bookstore. There are no ampgrounds, but you may hike and camp by permit in the park's 43,020-acre 17,410-hectare) **Painted Desert Wilderness** and 7,240-acre (2,930-hectare) ainbow Forest Wilderness. Bring a hat and plenty of water, food and sun-creen; summer is hotter than Hades in this relatively undeveloped park.

long the rim

Iighway 77, south of Holbrook, passes through a pair of oddly named Mormon owns. **Snowflake** ⓯ isn't named after the winter storms that occasionally blow irough town but the combined surnames of Mormon elders William J. Flake nd Erastus Snow who, in the 1870s, escaped government persecution of olygamists in Utah and headed south to Arizona to settle and convert Indians.

BELOW: backpackers enjoy the view from the Mogollon Rim.

bout 19 miles (31 km) to the south is **Show Low** ⓰, small commercial center on the edge of the White Iountains, at the junction of Highways 77, 260 and). Show Low's odd name apparently dates from 870, when the legendary Corydon Cooley, a former ir trader and Indian scout at nearby Fort Apache, hallenged Marion Clark, his business partner, to a ard game to settle differences over the ranch they o-owned. "Show low and you win," Clark reputedly aid. Obligingly, Cooley pulled out an unbeatable euce of clubs and won the ranch. The gaming site Cooley's kitchen) eventually became the town's Iormon Church. Its main street is called the Deuce of lubs, where you'll find the town's motels, restaurants nd gas stations.

Stop between mileposts 347 and 348, 7 miles (11 m) southeast of Show Low on Highway 260, to get our first look at the Mogollon Rim, the escarpment iat sharply divides the Gila–Salt River watersheds nd the mile-high Colorado Plateau. Stroll along the ile-long **Mogollon Rim Overlook** and **Nature Trail** r scenic vistas of forested peaks and shadowy val-eys. Signs offer information on the ponderosa and inyon pine, Douglas fir, three types of juniper, and iambel and scrub oak that make up the forest.

Lakeside–Pinetop ⓱, 8 miles (13 km) southeast of how Low, is the largest resort area in the White Iountains, with a wide range of developed lodgings

The White Mountains are laced with tough bike trails.

and restaurants. Lakeside (elevation 6,745 ft/2,056 meters), founded by Mor mons in 1880, was originally called Fairview but changed its name to reflec its abundance of lakes. Soldiers laboring up the Mogollon Rim from For Apache often stopped to rest at Pinetop (elevation 7,279 ft/2,219 meters) and gave the town its name. All around are forest roads, hiking and horsebac trails, and lakes and streams stocked with trout. The community was also voted the third-best mountain biking town in the country. Forest Route 300 a dirt logging road, begins here and heads west along the Mogollon Rim fo nearly 200 miles (320 km). It's impassable in winter.

For information on trail and road conditions, contact the **U.S. Forest Servic Lakeside Ranger District** (202 White Mountain Blvd.; tel: 928-368-5111) and if you're planning on spending a day or two here, borrow the two cassette-tap audio tours interpreting the area's forest, wildlife, geology and history.

Apache homeland

Just south of Lakeside–Pinetop is the 1.6-million-acre (650,000-hectare) **Whit Mountain Apache Reservation** ⓲. An abundance of outdoor activities i available on the reservation, which offers a quiet, natural and very spiritua setting for those wanting to get away from the all-American ambiance o adjoining areas. Permits for outdoor sports and visiting Indian ruins on triba land are available at **Hon Dah** ("Be My Guest" in Apache) at the junction o Highways 260 and 73 about 5 miles (8 km) south of Pinetop-Lakeside, a attractive roadside complex with a log motel and restaurant, casino, grocer store and gas station. Or you can drive south on Highway 73 to the Game an Fish Department (tel: 928-338-4385 or 338-4386) at tribal headquarters i

BELOW: a princess is crowned at the Apache Tribal Fair in Whiteriver.

RODEO-CHEDISKI FIRE

The whole place looks like death," said a Show Low res ident surveying the charred remains of her home. Th house was one of 400 buildings destroyed by the Rode Chediski Fire of 2002, the biggest in Arizona history.

Actually, the fire began as two separate blazes tha merged into one monster conflagration. The first was starte by a part-time firefighter hoping for work, the other by lost hiker signaling for help.

Fueled by a buildup of deadwood and fanned by warn gusty winds, the 15-day fire consumed nearly half a millic acres (200,000 hectares) in Apache-Sitgreaves Nation Forest and the White Mountain Apache Reservation an forced the evacuation of more than 30,000 people from towns, including Show Low and Pinedale.

Among the hardest hit, in addition to those whose hom and businesses were burned, was the White Mounta Apache Tribe, which lost more than 700 million feet (20 million meters) of timber, one of the reservation's ma resource. Evidence of the fire will be visible for years the charred landscape around Cibecue, site of the tribe principal mill, but the economic fallout will last even long "This devastation will effect our kids for two or three ge erations," said tribal president Lorin Henry.

Vhiteriver **⑲**, where you'll find a motel, trading post, restaurants, a shopping center, hospital and tribal offices.

While you're in Whiteriver, be sure to visit **Fort Apache**, the former U.S. rmy post built in 1870 as a supply base for soldiers sent to keep an eye on the White Mountain Apache and prevent white settlers from encroaching on Indian nd. The fort was later used as a staging area for campaigns against the Tonto id Chiricahua Apache. The army relied on friendly Apache scouts, of whom ie most famous was Alchesay, who assisted Indian fighter par excellence eneral George Crook in making peace with Geronimo in 1886. The commanding officer's quarters, adjutant's office, and officers' row still stand. xhibits and photographs of the old fort are on display at the **Apache Cultural enter** (open Mon.–Fri., 8am–5pm.; extended summer hours; tel: 928-338-525; free), 4 miles (6.5 km) southwest of Whiteriver.

now trails

he White Mountain Apache also own and operate the popular **Sunrise Ski rea ㉑**, 20 miles (32 km) east of Hon Dah, on 10,700-foot (3,260-meter) **1ount Ord**, which has three peaks – Sunrise, Apache and Cyclone Circle – ith 11 lifts and 65 ski runs. For diehard powder bunnies, there's an onsite ɔtel, restaurant, marina and sports center offering ski, snowshoe and mountain ɪke rentals. A quieter option is to stay in the tiny community of **Greer ㉑** (pop. ɔ0), 15 miles (24 km) east as the crow flies. It's hardly a straight shot for ɪivers: continue on Highway 260 for 10 miles (16 km), then drop south on ɪighway 373 for 5 miles (8 km) until it dead-ends in the village. But Greer, ɛstled at an elevation of 8,500 feet (2,600 meters) in a beautiful valley at the

Map
on page
200–201

TIP

Anglers will find lots of rainbow, brown and brook trout as well as an occasional Apache trout and Arctic grayling in the lakes and streams of the White Mountains. A tribal fishing license is required for the White Mountain Apache Reservation.

BELOW: an Apache rodeo cowboy limbers up.

headwaters of the Little Colorado River, is worth the trip. It's the kind o stopped-in-time place with local characters and friendly innkeepers that seem to have stepped right out of the mythical Brigadoon.

Small-town memories

TIP

Hikers and mountain bikers can hitch a ride up the mountain at Sunrise Ski Resort in the off-season. Chairlifts run on weekends from late May to mid-October.

Greer was originally called Lee Valley after Mormon pioneer Willard Lee, wh founded the town as a farming community in 1879. The name was changed i 1898, at the request of the post office, to honor America Vespucius Greer, prominent Mormon. It was the generous hospitality and good cooking of towns people like Molly Butler, however, that attracted famous guests like Presiden Theodore Roosevelt and writer Zane Grey, who spent days hunting cougar an bear in the backcountry guided by Molly's husband John. True, the 1908 **Moll Butler Lodge** hasn't been quite the same since Aunt Molly died, although new owners are trying to breathe some life into the aging hostelry. But no matter. Yo can have a fish fry or a steak here for old times' sake and stay at one of the othe lodges in the valley. The down-home **White Mountain Lodge** is a good choice It's housed in the 1892 Lund Home, Greer's oldest residence, and offers gues rooms and modern log cabins on the edge of a beautiful riverside meadow **Greer Lakes Recreation Area**, which surrounds Greer, has cross-country ski ing and hiking trails and four campgrounds with fishing.

BELOW: bold black-on-white designs are a common feature of Mogollon and Ancestral Puebloan pottery.

Memories of John and Molly Butler remain strong for Wink Crigler, Molly' granddaughter, who, with her sister Sug (short for Sugar), now operates th family's 1889 X Diamond and MLY Ranch over the hill from Greer. Flyfishing horseback riding, roundups, an archaeological dig and even a day spa are offere on this 20,000-acre (8,100-hectare) working ranch, 7 miles (11 km) west o

FATHER AND SON TEAM

Civilization? I have always avoided it whenev possible." So said explorer, naturalist and writ James Willard Schultz, author of 37 books, who, in 191 moved into a cabin in Greer, where he wrote, among oth books, *In the Great Apache Forest: The Story of a Lor Boy Scout*, a tale inspired by the World War I adventures Molly Butler's children, George and Hannah Crosby.

Schultz, a refugee from a wealthy East Coast fami had lived for many years among the Blackfoot Tribe Montana, the subject of his first book, *My Life as a Indian* (1907). He dubbed his new home Apuni Oy (Butterfly Lodge) and was soon joined by his hal Blackfoot son, Hart Merriam, or Lone Wolf, a popul American Indian artist.

Lone Wolf found inspiration here for paintings ar sculptures of western scenes, purchased by su luminaries as Herbert Hoover and Mrs. Calvin Coolidg Lone Wolf inherited the cabin in the mid-1920s and live here on and off until his death in 1970. Butterfly Lodge now on the National Register of Historic Places and h been converted into a museum (open summer weeken only; tel. 928-735-7514) containing Schultz's writi desk, Lone Wolf's paintings and other memorabilia.

Map
on page
200–201

agar ㉒, off Highway 260. Don't pass up a chance to visit **Wink's Little House Museum** (tours Thur–Sun or by reservation; tel: 928-333-2286; admission fee). Begun in 1990 as a memorial to her late husband Oscar, a rodeo champ, the museum's collection of finely tooled saddles and trophies has swelled to include pioneer tools, the buggy used in John Wayne's 1960 movie *The Alamo*, and vintage clothing. The *pièces de résistance*, however, are the antique music machines, including nickelodeons, pianolas and one of only 700 Violin "virtuosas" in the world, which Wink plugs in and brings to toe-tapping life during her two-hour tour. If the Smithsonian is America's Attic, the Little House Museum is surely Arizona's.

Mogollon ruins

The Little House Museum is one of the undiscovered delights of the White Mountains, and so is the large number of relatively unvisited prehistoric Mogollon Indian ruins throughout the mountains. The Mogollon culture originated in the mountains of southwestern New Mexico, where they lived on ridges and farmed corn, beans and squash in the valleys, supplementing their diet with deer, antelope, rabbit and other game.

They were the first people in the Southwest to make pottery, which they learned from their trading partners to the south. Beautiful black-on-white pottery decorated with images of lizards, traders, macaws and other daily scenes characterize the Mimbres branch of the Mogollon culture and is highly prized among collectors today. After AD 1000, the Mogollon moved north to Arizona's east-central mountains, where they merged with the Ancestral Pueblo culture. Archaeologists can still identify their settlements by the presence of their

BELOW: an archaeologist works at the Raven Site Ruin, a Mogollon pueblo above the Little Colorado River.

signature pottery style and other cultural traits such as the construction of rec tangular kivas, or ceremonial chambers.

Springerville in Round Valley is situated in the heart of Mogollon country, wit one of the most important ruins, **Casa Malpais National Historic Landmar** ㉓, 2 miles (3 km) north of downtown, perched on five basalt terraces abov the Little Colorado River. The 14-acre (6-hectare), two-story **House of the Bad lands**, as it was called by 19th-century Spanish-speaking residents, is one of th most complex Mogollon communities yet discovered and caused excitement in th archaeological world when excavations began there in the 1940s. The site wa occupied between AD 1266 and the late 1400s by an estimated 300 people. Unusu features include a large rectangular kiva, evidence that sacred ceremonies and bur als took place in natural fissures throughout the site, and a solar calendar.

Tours of the pueblo are conducted daily (weather permitting) and begin : **Casa Malpais Museum and Visitor Center** on Main Street (open dail 9am–5pm; tel: 928-333-5375; call for reservations; fee), which has exhibits c Casa Malpais and Springerville, a film about excavations at the pueblo, an information on the area. Wildlife lovers won't want to miss the relatively unpul licized 1,362-acre (551-hectare) **Sipe White Mountain Wildlife Area** ㉔ (ope daily, tel: 928-942-3000, free), 2 miles (3 km) south of Springerville. Admir istered by Arizona Game and Fish, Sipe Ranch is an old ranch homestead th. was purchased to protect the threatened Little Colorado spinedace, a tiny nativ fish. It also provides winter range for up to 800 elk and 175 acres (70 hectare: of wetlands used by hundreds of bird species, including migratory avocet sandpipers, white-faced ibis and other waterfowl. Ask for information on ho to reach the Mogollon petroglyph panel near the old homestead.

BELOW: grassy plains around Nutrioso attracted cattlemen in the late 19th century; several large ranches remain in the area.

The source of the basalts used in construction of Casa Malpais is obvious when you stand atop the pueblo and look south. The **Springerville Volcanic Field**, the third-largest volcanic field in the continental United States, covers 1,158 square miles (3,000 sq km) and contains 405 vents, craters and shield volcanoes, which began erupting 3 million years ago. To the south of Greer is the older **White Mountain Volcanic Field**, created by a different type of volcanism 8 million years ago. Baldy Peak, sacred to the Apache, is at its center. The youngest lava flows are from Twin Knolls, northwest of Springerville, a double volcano that erupted twice.

Map on page 200–201

Detour 12 miles (19 km) north of Springerville on Highway 191 toward St. John's to view a young lava flow, which erupted about 700,000 years ago, and a second important Mogollon site, **Raven Site Ruin** ㉕. The 800-room Raven Site Pueblo is interesting because it was occupied for more than 400 years between AD 1000 and 1450, contains two kivas, and displays both Mogollon and Ancestral Pueblo features. **White Mountain Archaeological Center** (open May-Oct. 5; tel: 928-333-5857; programs by reservation; fees vary) runs daily tours of the pueblo and petroglyph panels. It also runs public digs that last from a day to a week and overnight programs on an old Mormon ranch.

The roads less traveled

Two breathtaking but white-knuckle drives wind precipitously from the mountains to the low desert. The first, the 123-mile (198-km) **Springerville to Clifton Highway** (Route 666/191), follows the eastern edge of Apache-Sitgreaves National Forest and the Arizona–New Mexico border. It reaches an elevation of 9,000 feet (2,700 meters) at Hannagan Meadow, then drops into the copper mining towns of Morenci and Clifton – a plummet of 5,000 feet (1,525 meters). The route, one of the country's first federal road projects, opened in 1926, with 5,000 dignitaries puttering into the high country in their Model T Fords for the ribbon-cutting festivities, which included barbecued bear. Things have quieted down considerably since then. This is now one of the state's most beautiful but lonesome highways, driven only by a handful of motorists each day.

The road has long been promoted as the route that Spanish conquistador Francisco Vásquez de Coronado took through the mountains into New Mexico in 1540. Some historians now dispute that, including former Interior Secretary Stewart Udall, who grew up in St. Johns and is an authority on Coronado's route through the Southwest. Udall believes the Coronado expedition took a route 40 miles to the west, in the gentler topography of the Natanes Plateau.

Check road conditions before starting out. Snow may make sections of the road impassable in winter. The road leaves Springerville and heads south through **Nutrioso** ㉖, another odd local name derived from the Spanish words for beaver *(nutri)* and bear *(oso)*. It was home to Arizona's first forest ranger at the turn of the century, when Apache National Forest was part of Black Mesa Forest Reserve. The next community is 8,050-foot (2,450-meter) **Alpine** ㉗, originally known as Bush Valley, near the headwaters of the San

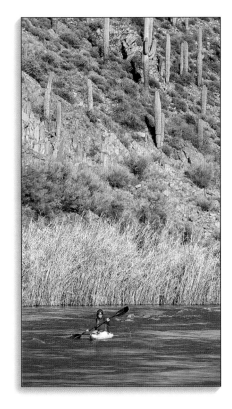

BELOW: kayakers can expect solitude and spectacular scenery on the Salt River, though water levels are sometimes too low to boat.

The western diamond-back rattlesnake is responsible for more bites than any other snake in the country.

BELOW: more than 200 bird species have been recorded in Aravaipa Canyon Wilderness.

Francisco River, where Escudilla Mountain, which features prominently in Aldo Leopold's writings, dominates the horizon. There is good camping at **Luna Lake**, a wildlife refuge where you can see bald and golden eagles and look for Luna agate. Dog sled races are held here in January.

The road's halfway point is **Hannagan Meadow ㉘**, named for Robert Hannagan, a Nevada miner who had a cattle ranch here in the 1870s. Legend has it that Hannagan racked up $1,200 in debt to some neighbors, who chained him to a tree until his son arrived from New Mexico to bail him out.

Hannagan Meadow Lodge, renovated in 1996, was built at the same time as the road for travelers making the two-day trip into the high country; it's still a logical place to gas up, stop for lunch, or spend the night in one of the rustic cabins. **Hannagan Meadow Cross-Country Ski Trail** starts nearby and has 12 miles (19 km) of backcountry paths.

South of Hannagan Meadow, the road begins to live up to its reputation as one of the best "serious-drivers' roads in America," with sharp hairpins that make a slalom course look straight. Step out of the car for some calming breaths at the Blue Vista overlook, on the edge of the 2,000-foot (600-meter) Mogollon Rim, and look down into the pinyon-juniper forests and savannah grasslands of the upper Sonoran ecosystem, 4,000 feet (1,200 meters) below.

To the east are the **Blue Range Mountains**, where, since 1997, several packs of Mexican wolves have been released. The Blues contain the last designated primitive area in the National Forest System and are a fine place to lose yourself for a while on foot. Simply turn off, park, and start walking. Perhaps you'll get lucky and hear a wolf howl, glimpse one of the resident herds of Rocky Mountain bighorn sheep, or surprise a blue heron on a creek.

Copper country

Twelve miles (19 km) farther and the road drops below the Mogollon Rim into copper country. **Morenci ㉙** is a mining town owned by the Phelps Dodge company (free tours are given on weekdays by appointment). Arizona isn't called the Copper State for nothing, and Morenci is the leading copper producer in North America. But at a cost. The open pit mine, built in 1937, gradually swallowed the old town of Morenci; today's community is a modern replacement. **Clifton ㉚**, on the other hand, retains much of its historic charm. Nestled in a rugged canyon carved by the San Francisco River, the former copper mining town still has a number of historic buildings, including the 1912 Southern Pacific Depot, Clifton Jail (which was blasted from a cliff face), and the Chase Creek Historic District with its outstanding Territorial architecture.

From Clifton, continue south to the junction with Highway 70 and head west through the cotton-growing town of **Safford ㉛**. Looming more than 8,000 feet (2,400 meters) above Safford is 10,720-foot (3,270-meter) **Mount Graham ㉜**, home of **Mount Graham International Observatory**. Still under construction, this University of Arizona observatory has been controversial from the start because it impinges on the habitat of the Mount Graham red squirrel. The 35-mile (56-km) **Swift Trail Parkway** ascends the mountain; camping, hiking and fishing are available in Coronado National Forest en route. Back among the cottonfields, the Mount Graham visitor center is in **Discovery Park** (open daily; tel: 928-428-6260; admission fee), Safford's new science, culture and education center, which has a 12-passenger spaceship simulator that gives visitors a virtual tour of the solar system and a 20-inch telescope available for public viewing.

North of Safford is an unpaved road leading west into **Aravaipa Canyon**

Map
on page
200–201

LEFT: high-tech instruments probe the universe at Mount Graham International Observatory.
BELOW: cooling off in the Gila River.

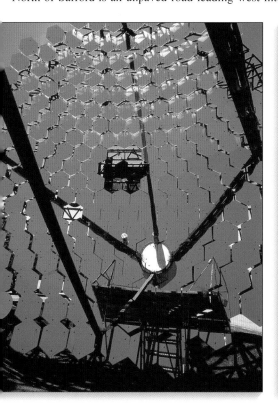

Map on page 200–201

Wilderness ③③ (open daily; tel: 928-828-3443). The Nature Conservancy protects 7,000 acres (2,800 hectares) of this magical 10-mile-long (16-km) canyon, where author Ed Abbey wrote movingly of encountering a mountain lion along Aravaipa Creek at dusk. You can reserve the Nature Conservancy guest house and hope for a precious encounter with one of the big cats or perhaps a less intimidating bobcat, a rare bighorn sheep or more than 200 bird species. Camping and hiking are allowed throughout this remote canyon with a permit from the Bureau of Land Management in Safford (tel: 928-428-4040).

Globe and the Salt River Canyon

Highway 70 continues to **Globe** ③④, the site of enormous silver and copper deposits, which led to boom growth between 1870 and 1920 and the success of the Old Dominion Copper Company, one of the world's largest copper mining operations. You won't miss the enormous man-made terraces on the north side of town; they look almost extraterrestrial. Globe's name actually came from the extraction of a large, globe-shaped piece of silver with what appeared to be a rough outline of the continents upon it. Downtown Globe retains a 19th-century feel, and you can take a historic walking tour of 25 buildings ranging from the 1906 Gila County Courthouse (now the Cobre Valley Center for the Arts) to the "Oldest Woolworths in the West" (1916). Homely Globe was one of contrarian Ed Abbey's favorite Arizona towns.

The main reason to stop in Globe is to view the large Salado ruin known by the Apache name **Besh-Ba-Gowah**, or House of Metal, for the abundance of precious metals that attracted newcomers in the late 1800s. Besh-Ba-Gowah was begun in 1225 and abandoned around 1400. The 200-room pueblo was first excavated in the 1930s, but excavation has been sporadic ever since. Now partially stabilized, the ruin is still revealing its secrets. Large quantities of beautiful polychrome pottery have been uncovered at the site and are on display in the small museum.

North of Globe, Highway 60 skirts the **San Carlos Apache Reservation** ③⑤. Globe was originally part of the reservation, but when silver was found there in 1870 the boundaries were redrawn, causing prolonged bitterness with the San Carlos Apache, who allied themselves with Geronimo and other warring Apache leaders. The San Carlos Apache now hold the popular **Apache Days** in Globe in October and a rodeo in November in **San Carlos**.

Highway 60 follows a dramatic twist-and-turn route through the **Salt River Canyon** ③⑥. The Jesuit missionary Padre Eusebio Francisco Kino visited this canyon in 1698, naming it Salado for the salt springs in the area (eventually that name would also be applied to the prehistoric people who once lived here). The bridge over the Salt River and the beginning of the climb into the White Mountains marks the boundary between the San Carlos Apache Reservation and White Mountain Apache Reservation, which lies to the north. This is the second of the beautiful scenic byways on this tour and a perfect sunset drive, when lengthening shadows in the canyon deepen the drama of the colorful formations. ⌐

BELOW: Besh-Ba-Gowah has been partially restored.
RIGHT: White Mountain Apache (Das-Luca, Skro-kit and Shus-El-Day) pose for a picture in 1909.

PHOENIX AND ENVIRONS

*Summer heat can purge the mind of lucidity, but air conditioning –
and a booming economy – have made the Valley of the Sun
one of America's fastest-growing metropolitan areas*

Maps:
Area: 200
City: 258

When Frank Lloyd Wright first saw the Salt River Valley in the late 1920s, it struck him as a "vast battleground of Titanic natural forces." Like a revelation to Wright were its "leopard spotted mountains… its great striated and stratified masses, noble and quiet," its patterns modeled on the "realism of the rattlesnake." Here, thought Wright with the zeal of someone moving in, if Arizonans could avoid the "candy-makers and cactus-hunters," a proper civilization could be created that would "allow man to become a godlike native part of Arizona."

Wright's architectural work in Arizona sought that lofty aim, though it has hardly happened. But aggressive irrigation – which has been in use both in ancient and modern times in this area – and air conditioning have nurtured a metropolis of nearly 3 million people – **Phoenix ❸**, America's sixth-largest city. Unfortunately, there is a nearly total dependence on automobiles that results in both traffic headaches and smog. Water is sucked up from deep aquifers to keep green the metropolitan area's 190 golf courses, upon which 2 million tourists and half a million locals play 11 million rounds of golf each year.

PRECEDING PAGES:
Superstition
Mountains.
LEFT: blacksmith at
work on sculpture.
BELOW: T-rex, Mesa
Southwest Museum.

Risen from the ashes

A civilization adapted to the harsh conditions of the Salt River Valley preceded Wright's idealistic visions by some 2,500 years. As early as 500 BC, the Hohokam people developed an intricate system of canals for irrigating fields of corn, beans, squash and cotton. Remains of that ancient system were absorbed and expanded in 1868 by the Swilling Irrigation Canal Co., the first Anglo organization to stake claims in the long-deserted valley. The following year, their settlement was named Phoenix by an Englishman who saw a new civilization rising like the mythical bird from the ashes of the vanished Hohokam.

What rose from the ashes was an aggressive ranching community that catered to miners and military outposts. Canals were extended through the alluvial valley, watering fields of cotton and alfalfa, pastures for cattle, and rows of citrus to the horizon's edge. Water storage began on a grand scale with construction of Roosevelt Dam, dedicated in 1911 and still the world's largest masonry dam, on the Salt River some 90 miles (145 km) upstream from Phoenix. Three more dams on the Salt, and two on its major tributary, the Verde, allowed agriculturalists to send water where they liked. The Salt River itself became the driest place in the region.

Residents with long memories recall the 1930s as a Phoenician golden age. Those who couldn't afford the Biltmore found it too snobbish anyway and frequented a lively downtown that still retained a Spanish-

American flavor. In summer, when temperatures climbed over 110°F (43°C) and daytime highs did not dip below the hundreds for months, locals complained less about the heat than they boasted of tricks to stay cool. It was common sport to be pulled on an aquaplane along the canals, holding a rope from a car.

Phoenix was transformed forever by World War II. The open desert was ideal for aviation training, and much of Phoenix became something of an extension of nearby Luke Air Force Base. Aviation equipment companies moved into the valley and even the cotton fields turned out silk for parachutes. It is less known that Phoenix had internment camps for German prisoners of war, and many of the prisoners, as susceptible to the desert's allure as anyone else, remained in the area after the war to become a part of the community.

The military revolutionized Phoenician life with a device called air-conditioning. The city had previously seen use of the evaporative or "swamp" cooler, but now there was genuine refrigeration. Suddenly Phoenix was a year-round possibility for those who couldn't stand the heat. The great migration was on. Camelback Mountain, at whose feet lay the most elegant dude ranches, was engulfed by suburbia. To the east, greater Phoenix swallowed up the once-isolated communities of Scottsdale, Tempe, Mesa and Apache Junction. Golf courses replaced dude ranches and resorts sprouted like desert flowers after a thunderstorm.

The stereotype newcomer over the past decades has been the snowbelt retiree living in rule-bound planned communities of upscale houses or proletarian acres of mobile homes. In fact, however, the more recent influx of career-oriented young people in high-tech industries has so altered the population in the past couple of decades that the average resident within city limits, contrary to popular belief, is younger than the national average.

A grand garden, the like of which in sheer beauty of space and pattern does not exist, I think, in the world.

– FRANK LLOYD WRIGHT
ABOUT THE DESERT

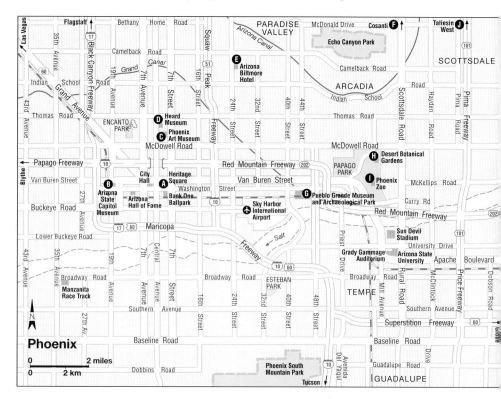

Downtown Phoenix

The geographical setting of Phoenix is impressive, especially when the air is not veiled with smog. To the east soar the massive Four Peaks and the flank of the Superstition Mountains, while the Sierra Estrella rides the southwest horizon in dorsales of blue silk. Hemming in the city north and south are lower ranges of Precambrian gneiss and schist, framing the Phoenix trademark of Camelback Mountain – a freestanding, rosy, recumbent dromedary with a sedimentary head and granitic hump.

And what of the city itself? Even by American standards, Phoenix is a young city and, like others of its age, lacks a strong personality, seeming at times to be rather sterile in ambiance, especially when many of its residents retreat into the air-conditioning in summer. Most of downtown is not a place that encourages casual strolling and people watching, especially in the scorching heat of summer, and at night one may find more happening at the motel than downtown. And unlike other older cities and towns in the Southwest, Phoenix lacks an Old Spanish undercurrent. Still, like many other cities with the same downtown identity problem, Phoenix has invested considerable energy in locating museums and cultural venues in the downtown area.

Heritage Square A (open Tues.–Sat. 10am–4pm, Sun. from noon; tel: 602-262-5029; free), a block east of the **Civic Plaza**, is what remains of the city's Victorian heritage and is part of downtown's **Heritage and Science Park**. Most striking of Heritage Square's 11 buildings – some of them, like the Lath House Pavilion, quite modern – is the **Rosson House** (admission fee), built in 1895 and once one of the most prominent homes in Phoenix. Some of the other houses here, dating from the early 1900s, were moved from other locations to save

Map on page 258

Temperatures in the Phoenix area exceed 100°F (37.8°C) on more than 90 days a year, with an average scorching high in July of 106°F (41°C).

BELOW: Bank One Ballpark, known locally as BOB, is home to the Major League Arizona Diamondbacks.

them from demolition. Also part of Heritage and Science Park are the **Phoenix Museum of History** (open daily 10am–5pm, Sun from noon; tel: 602-253-2734; admission fee), with interactive exhibits of the city's development, and the **Arizona Science Center** (open daily 10am–5pm; tel: 602-716-2000; admission fee), which is a $50 million hands-on funhouse of science, embellished with a planetarium. In particular, the center highlights Arizona's contributions to technology and the sciences. Fascinating exhibits on aviation, including a flight simulator, make this a good choice for antsy children tired of the mundane.

The Fallen Warrior *by Tempe artist Jasper d'Ambrosi is part of the Vietnam Veterans Memorial on the capitol grounds.*

Seat of government

Arizona's modest state capitol building lies 1½ miles (2.4 km) to the west of downtown, along Washington Street. The **Arizona State Capitol Museum** ❸ (open Mon–Fri 8am–5pm, Sat 10am-3pm; tel: 602-542-4581; free) uncovers some of the building's secrets. The capitol building was constructed in 1899 to house the territorial government; its dome was covered in 1976 with 15 tons of copper donated by the state's mining interests. Atop the dome is *Winged Victory*, a quarter-ton statue dating from 1899 that turns with the wind. Much of today's governing is done in adjacent modern structures, but the restored Senate and House of Representatives chambers are open to visitors. Furnishings and ornamentation throughout the building date from 1912, when Arizona became a state.

The **Phoenix Art Museum** ❻ (open daily 10am–5pm except Thur and Fri, to 9pm, closed Mon; tel: 602-257-1222; admission fee) at Central Avenue and McDowell Road, 1 mile (1.6 km) north of Heritage Park, supplements a sometimes obscure permanent collection with splendid rotating shows and owns a choice group of recent Mexican works. Galleries include American and Asian

Map
on page
258

works, and a decorative arts gallery exhibits ceramics, metalwork and furniture covering a diverse spectrum of cultures and time periods. Art of the American West is represented by the works of Thomas Moran and Frederic Remington.

The **Heard Museum ⊙** (open daily 9.30am–5pm, Sun noon–5pm; tel: 602-252-8848; fee) is one of the must-sees in Phoenix, even for travelers who aren't particularly fond of museums. It was founded in 1929 to house the Heard family's collection of American Indian art and artifacts, and it remains an exceptional collection. The 1999 revamp of the museum, located on Central Avenue a few blocks north of the Phoenix Art Museum, enhanced the visitor experience.

Contemporary art of the last few decades is displayed in the Edward Jacobson Gallery of Indian Art, while the Crossroads Gallery has changing exhibits of today's new artists. Also on the courtyard level (the original museum, just one-eighth the size of today's, encircled the modest courtyard) are the Native Peoples of the Southwest Gallery and Katsina (Kachina) Doll Gallery, which help to place the Southwest tribes in a historical and cultural context. Everywhere in the Southwest visitors will see kachina dolls in souvenir shops, but the Katsina Doll Gallery features almost 500 authentic dolls, a number of them from the collection of Arizona's late senator, Barry Goldwater. Many of the nearly dozen galleries have rotating exhibits. An excellent book and gift shop is worth a look, and the Ironwood Cafe is convenient for a break.

A great monument to another period is the **Arizona Biltmore Hotel ⊜** (tel: 602-955-6600), 5 miles (8 km) northeast of downtown and Heritage Park. With a slack economy to begin with, Phoenix hardly noticed the Great Depression of the early 1930s, living off its own agriculture and catering in fine style to those tourists who managed to keep their money. Built just before the crash of 1929,

BELOW:
redevelopment of
downtown Phoenix
has given the city
much-needed
venues for sporting
events and the arts.

the Biltmore sailed in splendor through the bleakest of times. It is to the Biltmore that Phoenix owes the arrival of Frank Lloyd Wright. The hotel was originally designed by Albert Chase McArthur, a former student of Wright, who summoned the master for help. Wright came, and then stayed to create Taliesin West.

Wright probably gave more help than required, for the result was a masterpiece of textile block construction and is a delight for the eye – geometrically tidy, quietly whimsical and aesthetically inspiring. Gutted by fire in 1973, the interior was refurnished with furniture and textile designs from all periods of Wright's career. The visitor who enters no other building in Phoenix should make it to 24th Street and Missouri to inspect the Arizona Biltmore.

A contemporary architect today who has caught worldwide attention is Paolo Soleri, an Italian who has lived in Arizona since 1956. In Scottsdale, Soleri's **Cosanti ❻** (open daily 9am–5pm; tel: 480-948-6145; free) offers a broad-brush overview of Soleri's architectural philosophy and of a grander site 65 miles (105 km) north of Phoenix, Arcosanti. Cactus and olive trees are scattered amid Cosanti's earth-formed concrete structures, designed to maximize both ecological efficiency and use of space.

Frank Lloyd Wright left an indelible mark on the Phoenix streetscape.

Pueblo Grande Museum and Archaeological Park ❼ (open daily 9am–5pm, Sun from 1pm; tel: 602-495-0901; admission fee) is sited just outside of the central city, wedged in between an interstate highway and the international airport. It is a confounding juxtaposition, but this ancient pueblo site is worth a look. A wheelchair-accessible trail, just over half a mile long, encircles the ruins and has numerous, well-written interpretive displays. The visitor center has artifacts from the Hohokam culture and this pueblo site.

BELOW:
Doug Hyde's
Intertribal Greeting
welcomes visitors to
the Heard Museum.

The Hohokam people lived in southern Arizona until around AD 1450. Experts at cultivation, the Hohokam developed a complex system of irrigation canals extending hundreds of miles; some of these canals remain today. Bad weather and internal conflicts resulted in the abandonment of the Salt River Valley, home to Phoenix, in the 1400s.

The Pueblo Grande mound is actually two smaller mounds dating from around AD 1150. Less than 200 years later, the two mounds were combined into a mound the size of a football field and about 30 feet (9 meters) high. Many of the buildings once on top of the mound were probably used for other purposes, including ceremonial. Immediately north of the mound, accessible by a walkway, is an excavated ball court similar to those found at ancient Maya sites in Mexico.

East and north of downtown

To the east of downtown, increasingly surrounded by the expansion of greater metropolitan Phoenix, the **Desert Botanical Garden ❽** (open daily; tel: 480-941-1225; admission fee) is said to be the world's largest collection of desert plants living in a natural environment. Several trails lead through the plants, displays and balmy air. The garden emphasizes, as one might expect, the Sonoran Desert of southern Arizona. Not far away on the same road, the **Phoenix Zoo ❾** (open daily; tel: 602-273-1341; admission fee) offers the Arizona Trail, which features the flora and fauna of the Southwest.

Taliesin West ❶ (open daily 9am–5pm; tel: 480-860-2700; admission fee), in northeastern Scottsdale, was the personal residence and architectural school of architect Frank Lloyd Wright. In fact, most of the buildings and facilities were intended to be an ongoing, hands-on educational exercise for architectural students. New techniques in the use of natural materials were developed here, often after the many failures that Wright considered part of the educational process. Rocks from the desert and sand from dry washes were melded into foundations, walls and walkways, all the while following geometrical proportions that stayed constant from the smallest ornamental detail to the dimensions of the buildings themselves. Some of Wright's trademark techniques, such as the squeeze-and-release of a cramped entranceway opening into an expansive room, are apparent here. But from a distance, the buildings are barely apparent.

Around Phoenix

Development leapt to the northwest when **Sun City**, America's first fully-planned retirement community, was pitched by the Del Webb Corporation in 1960. More recently, cactus forests to the north of Phoenix have been bull-dozed for a realty bonanza, and Phoenix and Scottsdale have competed in annexing the area under the pretext that they are trying only to control development. Expansion has taken such forms as trailer parks to the east, tract housing to the west and walled-in mazes of simulated adobe ranchettes in the newly populated areas to the northeast.

For those preferring humanity untrammeled by nature, there are the sumptuous resorts north of Scottsdale – itself rich with resorts – and the three mountainside Pointe resorts on the north and south edges of Phoenix. Gone is any

Map on page 258

TIP

Wright's works in Phoenix include half a dozen homes, the Arizona Biltmore, First Christian Church on North Seventh Avenue, Grady Gammage Auditorium in Tempe and Taliesin West.

BELOW: lounging by the pool at the Arizona Biltmore.

FRANK LLOYD WRIGHT

When Frank Lloyd Wright (1869–1959) was in his sixties, an age when other men are retiring, he was designing buildings that continued to revolutionize architecture, dismissing the stagnation found in much architectural design. Indeed, the older he got, the more innovative and revolutionary his designs became. His Guggenheim Museum in New York City, for example, was completed in 1959, the year he died at the age of 90. From his earliest days as an architectural student in the Chicago area in the 1890s, Wright remained true to his philosophy of "organic architecture," which stated that a building should be an integral part of its natural surroundings.

"We must recognize the creative architect as poet and interpreter of life," he wrote. "This enrichment of life is the cause of architecture, as I see it." Lewis Mumford wrote in 1929: "Wright has embodied in his work two qualities which will never permanently leave it – a sense of place and a rich feeling for materials." Wright's works in Phoenix, including Taliesin West and the Biltmore Hotel, on which he served as a consultant, revealed his belief that architecture should enhance both person and environment. Taliesin West, Wright's winter home and studio from 1937 to 1959, was also a school that encouraged experimentation.

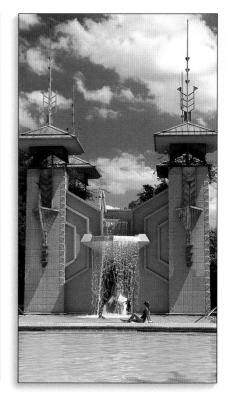

pretense of the dude-ranch culture common before World War II, and the only reference to cactus may be worked into the macrame in the lobby. Offering golf, tennis, saunas, pools with underwater bar stools, French restaurants, night-clubs, discos, refrigerated suites and a clientele armored in platinum credit cards, these are not desert hideaways but total-concept luxury resort complexes.

Apache Trail

Of the desert drives outside Phoenix, the most spectacular is the **Apache Trail** ❸. As an Arizona initiation rite, locals like to take visiting friends and relatives out for a drive along the curvy route. During this desert ritual, in-the-know motorists will turn to passengers just before a series of steep, hairpin turns and hoarsely whisper something to the effect that the brakes are out, just to get a giggle out of the ensuing screams.

Wooden indians stand guard in Scottsdale's 5th Street shopping district.

If you can avoid having a local jokester at the wheel, a drive along the Apache Trail is a day well spent. Bad brakes notwithstanding, most of the chills and thrills come from the spectacular scenery along the way, including mountains, sheer cliffs, canyons and a series of large lakes. The 45-mile-long (72-km) trail – actually a section of State Highway 88 – snakes its way past the **Superstition Mountains** and along the edge of the **Four Peaks Wilderness** in **Tonto National Forest**, just east of metro Phoenix.

BELOW: Cosanti artists cast signature bronze bells.

The Apache Trail's moniker reflects its Native American history. Attracted by the availability of water from the Salt River and Tonto Creek, the Salado people inhabited the area as early as AD 1150. Many farmed along the flat land on the water's edge and built cliff dwellings in the mountainous terrain. Later, nomadic Apache and Yavapai Indians found sanctuary in the canyon lands.

By the 1860s, Anglo-European traders and prospectors drifted into the mountains. One such entrepreneur was German-born Jacob Waltz, who periodically came into the fledgling community of Phoenix with sacks of gold nuggets that he claimed were from his secret mine in the Superstition Mountains. Waltz died without revealing the location of his mine, and the enduring legend of the Lost Dutchman Mine worked its way into local folklore. (Back then, apparently, nobody knew the difference between Dutch and Deutsch).

By the early 20th century, Phoenix's influential farmers and ranchers saw gold in the form of a steady water supply at the confluence of the Salt River and Tonto Creek. The federal government agreed, and the site was chosen to be one of the first major reclamation projects in the West. Funds for **Theodore Roosevelt Dam** ❸ were approved in 1903 – as was money for the construction of a roadway linking the outskirts of Phoenix to the dam site. The roadway, of course, was the Apache Trail, which followed portions of the old Indian pathway. By the time the dam was completed in 1911 (and dedicated by its namesake), millions of pounds of freight had been hauled up the road by mule teams and wagons, and tourists, too, had gotten their first glimpses of the wild and beautiful landscape of the Superstition Mountains.

No need to worry about encountering mule teams today, although you might pass some grazing cattle or wildlife, including coyotes, rattlesnakes, various bird species and even elusive bighorn sheep. The plant life includes the usual suspects of the upper Sonoran Desert – saguaro, prickly pear and cholla cactus – as well as striking century plants. Look for pockets of deciduous trees along the washes and creek beds; in spring, after a rainy winter, roadsides are ablaze with lupines, Mexican gold poppies, owl's clover and other wildflowers.

Coming from Phoenix, most visitors drive the Apache Trail south to north, picking up State Highway 88 off U.S. 60 in **Apache Junction**, a suburban community (this is a good place to get gas – there aren't any service stations along the scenic part of the road). The scenery starts just outside Apache Junction, where the road is flanked on one side by **Goldfield Ghost Town** and on the other by **Lost Dutchman State Park**. The ghost town – once an actual mining hamlet – has been recreated as an amusing Old West town, complete with shootouts, a narrow-gauge railroad, gift shops and a restaurant, while the park offers hiking and interpretive trails, ranger-led programs, picnic areas and campsites.

About 7 miles (11 km) from the park is an overlook for **Canyon Lake**, the first of the three lakes created by the Roosevelt and other dams. Against a backdrop of ocher- and rust-hued cliffs, the lake is visually striking but often crowded on warm weekends. You can rent a boat from the marina, cruise the lake aboard a steamboat, or hike one of several trails.

A few miles beyond Canyon Lake is **Tortilla Flat**, once a rest stop for freight operators and construction workers traveling to Roosevelt Dam. Today, it's a series of false-front buildings that lures tourists with burgers and chili, drinks served in mason jars, and a gift shop stuffed with souvenirs. For good luck, pin a dollar bill to the wall of the restaurant or gift shop (the walls sport

Map on page 200–201

BELOW: a "sheriff" lays down the law in Goldfield Ghost Town, a recreated mining camp on the Apache Trail.

Map on page 200–201

To see more of the work of the Hohokam and their canals, visit the many sites along the Salt River, including those in the path of a long-planned crosstown freeway held up, in part, by research work on the canals.

BELOW: lupin and brittlebush bloom in the Superstition Mountains.
RIGHT: Salado ruins at Tonto National Monument.

thousands) and buy a T-shirt that begs the question, "Where the hell is Tortilla Flat?"

At this point, many travelers turn back, but the most beautiful scenery begins beyond Tortilla Flat. A few miles up, the pavement ends, but the gravel road is well maintained (watch for flash flooding during heavy rains) and suitable for all vehicles except RVs and cars pulling trailers. Here, the road begins its precipitous descent into **Fish Creek Canyon**, the scenic high point of the drive and the spot where the no-brakes story usually unfolds. As the road twists downward, cliffs, mountains and the creekbed (usually dry) become visible. Parking areas and hiking trails are at the bottom of the hill.

About 5 miles (8 km) farther, you will get your first glimpse of **Apache Lake**, the most remote of the man-made lakes, hence the quietest and, some say, the loveliest. Against painted cliffs, the lake is 17 miles (27 km) long and rather narrow. You can take a boat almost to the foot of Roosevelt Dam at the lake's eastern end. A small marina offers boat rentals, bait, supplies and light meals.

At the end of the Apache Trail is the mighty Roosevelt Dam, which, at 280 feet (85 meters), is the highest masonry dam in the world. There are several points from which to view the dam and **Roosevelt Lake**, the largest man-made lake in central Arizona; a visitor center, boat ramps and campgrounds are on the lakeshore.

Closing the circle

At this point, you have several choices. You can return the way you came, head back to Phoenix via Highways 188 and 87, or make a full loop around the Superstition Mountains by continuing southeast on Highway 88 and then west on U.S. 60.

The latter option offers the most attractions, including **Tonto National Monument** ⓴ (open daily 8am–5pm; tel: 928-467-2241; fee), site of well-preserved cliff dwellings occupied by the Salado from the 13th to early 15th centuries. Set in natural limestone alcoves, the apartment-like structures were built of rough quartzite mortared crudely with mud. These were topped with mud-and-wood roofs, many of which can still be seen, as can the ghostly handprints of the workers in the mud. Examples of fine Salado pottery and woven textiles are exhibited in the visitor center.

It's a scenic drive around the eastern side of the mountains through the little mining towns of **Miami** and **Superior** to the **Boyce Thompson Southwestern Arboretum** ⓸ (open daily 8am–5pm; tel: 520-689-2723; fee), a showplace for desert plants and wildlife founded in the 1920s by mining magnate William Boyce Thompson. Self-guiding trails wind through 35 acres (14 hectare) of beautifully landscaped grounds. A stone house listed on the National Register of Historic Places serves as an interpretive center.

A 25-mile (40-km) detour on highways 79 and 287 leads to **Casa Grande Ruins National Monument** ⓺ (open daily 8am–5pm; tel: 520-723-3172; fee), a prehistoric village occupied by the Hohokam until about AD 1450. The central structure is a four-story "great house" (now protected by a modern roof). Though its function remains a mystery, the presence of holes aligned with the sun on the equinox and solstices suggest that it may have been used as an observatory. ❏

SOUTHERN ARIZONA

Successive cultures – Indian, Hispanic, Anglo – have left their mark on the region's desert landscapes and quirky small towns

Tucson, Arizona's second-largest city and the focal point of the southern tier of the state, has a maverick streak that's characteristic of the region as a whole. Tucsonans value individuality. They tend to be politically more liberal and culturally more daring than their conservative neighbors, and, as a community, identify themselves more closely with the city's Hispanic roots.

They also share an awareness of the environment. Ringed by mountain peaks and bracketed by parklands, Tucson embraces its desert setting. A short drive from downtown leads into Tucson Mountain Park or the twin units of Saguaro National Park. A bit farther on are the breezy heights of Mount Lemmon and the Santa Catalina Mountains or, to the south, the cool recesses of Madera Canyon.

An independent and enterprising spirit is evident elsewhere in the south, too, from the ranchers who cling to family spreads to the "desert rats" who scratch a living from the earth with little more than muscle and wit. In the old mining town of Bisbee, a coalition of artists, entrepreneurs and urban refugees have transformed decaying saloons into shops and restaurants and have breathed new life into the "painted ladies" once occupied by the town's thriving middle class.

A similar revival occurred in Tubac, the state's oldest European settlement, founded about 1723 and later overrun by Apache raiders. Had it not been for the vision of various artists and business people, the village – now a popular arts colony – might have been left to the elements. The atmosphere in Tombstone is far more commercial but no less vital. The "town too tough to die" has capitalized on Wyatt Earp's fateful encounter at the OK Corral, with staged shootouts, stagecoach rides and an entertaining, if hokey, Old West ambiance.

But the towns of southern Arizona are merely grace notes on the landscape. The Sonoran Desert is the dominant presence. Sky islands like the Chiricahua Mountains, hideout of Geronimo's fugitive Apaches, offer relief from the sere lowlands. The lush grasslands that so enticed Spanish *rancheros* now support Arizona's small but scenic "wine country," and wetlands ranging from desert springs to the San Pedro River sustain a profusion of plant and animal life, including the thousands of migratory waterbirds that flock to the seasonal marshes of Willcox Playa.

The population grows thinner and the landscape more austere west of Tucson, where dark volcanic mountains jostle the sky and desert vegetation asserts itself over the parched terrain. This is the homeland of the Tohono O'odham, the Desert People, whose descendants were the original masters of drawing life from this unforgiving land. ❏

PRECEDING PAGES: a rider on a pack trip leads his mount across the Salt River.
LEFT: the cool waters of Seven Falls reward overheated hikers in Bear Canyon, part of the Sabino Canyon Recreation Area on the outskirts of Tucson.

TUCSON AND ENVIRONS

Smaller and more liberal than Phoenix, with a streak of feisty independence, Arizona's "Old Pueblo" embraces its Hispanic roots and scenic desert setting

Maps:
Area 292
City 276

Tucson ❶, or the Old Pueblo, as it's known locally, is a modern metropolis of some 834,000 souls that has insinuated itself across 500 square miles (1,300 sq km) of southern Arizona's Sonoran Desert between five encircling mountain ranges. Warm winters, low year-round humidity, an unbeatable desert setting, hundred-mile vistas and perhaps the easiest access to hiking, biking, camping, horseback riding, rock climbing and skiing of any city in the nation have lured visitors for decades. Four-star resorts, spas, dude ranches, elegant historic inns and gourmet restaurants nudge up against nature parks, Wild West towns, Indian reservations and Mexican border towns in a classic Old West meets New West setting.

To get oriented and enjoy a killer sunset view, drive up **Sentinel Peak Ⓐ**, the dark volcanic hill west of downtown Tucson with the whitewashed "A" (the work of University of Arizona students since 1915). Used as a lookout by Mexican soldiers between 1821 and 1853 (hence the name), the peak now known as "A" Mountain offers sweeping views of the burgeoning city, nearby mountains, and the basin-and-range topography all the way into Mexico, 65 miles (105 km) away.

Long before Spanish, Mexican and Anglo settlers arrived, the Sonoran Desert was home to the Hohokam Indians, irrigation farmers who left behind pecked petroglyphs on basaltic boulders, such as those at Signal Hill in Saguaro National Park West. By the time of Spanish conquest, in 1540, the Hohokam had been replaced by ancestors of today's Tohono O'odham ("People of the Desert," formerly known as Papago) and Akimel O'odham ("People of the Water," also known as Pima) tribes, whose modern reservations adjoin Tucson. O'odham people lived in a *rancheria*, a scattering of huts built from mesquite limbs, saguaro ribs and thorny ocotillo, along the now-dry Santa Cruz River at the base of "A" Mountain.

A rough beginning

The O'odham referred to their village as Stjukshon (*stjuk* means "black"; *shon*, "hill"). This word was roughly transliterated to "Tucson" by Colonel Hugo O'Conor, an Irishman in the service of the Spanish Crown, when he was ordered to build a new garrison to protect nearby San Xavier Mission. The Tucson presidio replaced the one at Tubac in 1775, after its former commander, Juan Bautista de Anza, left to find an overland route to Alta California.

El Presidio de San Agustín del Tucson, located just east of "A" Mountain, was heavily fortified with adobe walls 12 feet (4 meters) high and 750 feet (230 meters) long, but soldiers found little protection here

PRECEDING PAGES:
Presidio Historic District, Tucson.
LEFT: Saguaro National Park.
BELOW: "outlaws" at Old Tucson Studios.

and complained that they spent more time making adobes than in military pur suits. Mexican tenure did little to improve a situation where settlers were at th mercy of Apache raiders. Even after it became American territory, Tucso remained essentially a Mexican town of miners, ranchers and merchants. T Anglo traveler J. Ross Browne, it seemed "a city of mud boxes, dingy and delap idated, cracked and baked into a composite of dust and filth." Only with the com ing of the railroad in the 1880s, linking markets across the country, did Tucso evolve from a rough Wild West outpost to a booming frontier trading center.

The old Presidio

A resident of Pascua, a Yaqui Indian village annexed by Tucson in 1952.

Portions of the original Presidio wall are preserved in downtown's **Presidi Historic District ❸**, a good place to get a feel for Tucson's Spanish, Mexi can and Anglo heritage. Begin your historic walking tour at the **Tucso Museum of Art** (open Mon–Sat 10am–4pm, Sun 12pm–4pm; tel: 520-624 2333; admission fee) on the corner of Alameda and Main Streets. Noted fo its Spanish colonial paintings and furnishings, pre-Columbian artifacts fro Latin America, pleasant courtyard and café (often frequented by downtow office workers), the museum's most interesting feature is the five histori houses incorporated into its layout (all open during museum hours).

La Casa Cordova, built in 1848, is Tucson's oldest home. A classic Mexica adobe with traditional saguaro rib ceiling latillas and dirt floors, it has a centr courtyard and dark interior rooms that have been restored to reflect early life i the Old Pueblo, complete with beds, cribs and furnishings. One room ha exhibits that trace the Presidio's history; an adjoining room contains, fro November to March, the Nacimiento, a traditional Mexican nativity installatio

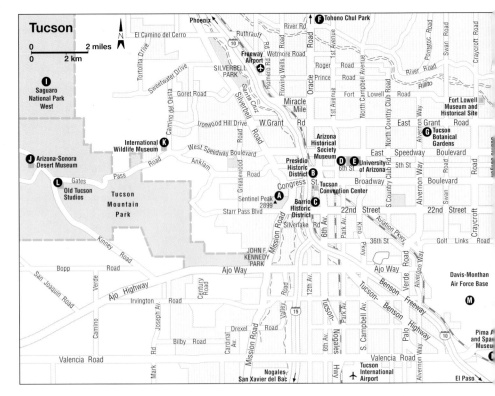

that changes yearly and uses more than 200 hand-painted figurines to create tableaux depicting the life of Christ.

In the museum's southwestern corner, two adjoining houses – the **Stevens House**, started in 1856, and the 1868 **Edward Nye Fish House**, constructed on the site of an old Mexican barracks with 15-foot (4.5-meter) ceilings and adobe walls more than 2 feet (60 cm) thick – were built by wealthy merchants and were the center of social life in Tucson. The Fish House is now home to the **John K. Goodman Pavilion of Western Art**. On the other side of the museum, the 1868 **Romero House**, used by the Tucson Museum of Art School, and the **Corbett House**, a 1906 brick-and-stucco building on Main Street, incorporate the northern boundary walls of the Presidio. Privately owned **Old Town Artisans** carries arts and crafts by more than 150 Western, Indian and Mexican artists and occupies an adobe, parts of which date to between 1862 and 1875.

Distinguished architecture

Stroll along Main and Court Streets to view other houses in **Snob Hollow**, as it was called, including the 1886 American Territorial-style **Julius Kruttschnidt House**, now El Presidio Bed and Breakfast Inn (297 N. Main); the **Owl's Club Mansion** (378 N. Main), a men's club with an ornate façade, and nearby **Steinfeld House** (300 N. Main), both designed by renowned architect Henry Trost in the Spanish Mission style at the turn of the century. **El Charro Restaurant** (311 N. Court), which claims to be the oldest Mexican restaurant in the United States, occupies the 1900 **Jules Flein House**, built of Sentinel Peak basalt by a French stone mason who worked on St. Augustine Cathedral.

To see more of the Presidio, cross Alameda and enter 10-acre (4-hectare)

Map on page 276

LEFT AND BELOW: mural-painting is a longstanding tradition in Tucson.

Artistic details like this painted mailbox add color and whimsy to the Barrio Historic District.

BELOW: *mariachi musicians perform outside St. Augustine Cathedral.*

Presidio Park. **Pima County Courthouse** (115 N. Church), a building tha combines Spanish and Southwestern architectural styles in its columns, arches decorated façade, tiled dome, interior courtyard and fountain, has a portion of th original Presidio wall inside. **St. Augustine Cathedral** (192 S. Stone) was begu in 1896, though by the 1930s it had fallen on hard times and was subsequentl used as a whorehouse, garage, bootlegger warehouse and boxing arena. Com pletely refurbished in 1967, today it is noted for its magnificent 1922 carve sandstone façade, modeled after the Cathedral of Queretaro in Mexico, whic depicts yucca, saguaros and horned toads. The bronze statue of Tucson's patro saint, St. Augustine, above the entry is dramatically floodlit at night.

El Barrio

South of the **Tucson Convention Center** (260 S. Church) is the 13-bloc **Barrio Historic District** **C**, where crumbling adobes with unusual metal flare roof drains, or *canales*, Territorial-style brick homes and skinny row house have been lovingly restored by Bohemians, architects and business people.

The *barrio libre*, "the neighborhood where anything goes," is, according t writer Lawrence Cheek, "a lesson in urban living – courtyards instead of lawns pastel colors that seem to drink the sunlight instead of fighting it." On a forgotte street, you'll come across two entwined cactuses blocking the entry to an ol building or perhaps glimpse a Mexican tin hand of fate over an altar in an artist' compound. A Mexican tortilla factory (corner of Simpson and South Main turns out fresh tortillas daily. Opposite is **El Tiradito**, the **Outcast's Wishin Shrine**, the legendary unconsecrated burial place of a young man killed in a lov triangle and the only national historical landmark dedicated to a sinner. Roun

he corner, the 1880s **Cosa-Carrillo-Fremont House** (151 S. Granada), rented n 1881 to the daughter of fifth territorial governor John C. Frémont, offers uided historic walking tours on Saturday mornings, November to March.

Map
on page
276

Museum row

ast of downtown is a glut of worthwhile museums. The **Arizona Historical ociety Museum ●** (949 E. 2nd; open Mon–Sat 10am–5pm, Sun 12pm–4pm; el: 520-628-5774; donation) is the place to bone up on Arizona's colorful istory, including 1870s Tucson, transportation and mining, with a full replica f an underground copper mine. Other museums can be found across the street n the **University of Arizona ●** campus, founded by the territorial legislature n 1891 (in Old Main, the campus' oldest building) on land donated by a saloon-eeper and two gamblers. The U of A was Tucson's consolation prize after it lost ts bid to host the state capitol and the state insane asylum – both went to 'hoenix – and today most Tucsonans agree they got the better deal.

First stop should be the **Arizona State Museum** (Park and University; open Mon–Sat 10am–5pm, Sun 12pm–5pm; tel: 520-621-6302; free), which occu-ies two buildings inside the west entrance. It was founded in 1893 to collect nd preserve materials related to the native cultures of the Southwest and is he region's oldest anthropological and archaeology museum. An award-win-ing multimedia exhibit, *Paths of Life*, traces the origins, history and con-emporary life of the Seri, Tarahumara, Yaqui, O'odham, Colorado River Yumans, Southern Paiute, Pai, Western Apache, Navajo and Hopi cultures.

Exhibits include a video and full-scale diorama of the Pascua Yaqui Deer Dance, which is performed every Easter by residents of a Yaqui Indian village n the heart of Tucson. Displays on the long-vanished Hohokam, whose major community, Snaketown, was xcavated by the university's Dr. Emil Haury, are ound in the South Building.

No one interested in photography should miss the Center for Creative Photography (open Mon–Sat 11am–5pm, Sun 12pm–5pm; tel: 520-621-7968; free), world-class exhibit and research center with more han 50,000 photographs by leading 20th-century hotographers such as Paul Strand, Edward Weston nd Alfred Stieglitz. It was conceived as a repository or the archive of master landscape photographer Ansel Adams, and one of the best reasons to stop here s to make an appointment to view Adams's soul-stir-ing black-and-white photos of Yosemite and other western parks. Exhibitions of the center's holdings re held year-round.

On the other end of campus, **Flandreau Science Center and Planetarium and Mineral Museum** open Sun–Tue 9am–5pm, Wed–Sat 7am–9pm; tel: 20-621-4515; admission fee) is out-of-this-world fun or kids and adults alike, with hands-on exhibits, ight-sky viewing through a 16-inch telescope, star hows that include an introduction to Arizona skies, Native American skylore, and the demise of the inosaurs, as well as evening laser light shows in the anetarium. Those in town for Tucson's **Rock and Mineral Show** in February (the largest in the world)

BELOW: Pima County Courthouse was built in Spanish Colonial Revival style in 1928 and contains a portion of the original Presidio wall.

BELOW: cactus from both the New and Old World are featured at Tucson Botanical Gardens.

should check out the museum's large mineral collection and exhibit of globa meteorites, one of which, the 1,400-pound (635-kg) Tucson Ring, was used a an anvil in the 1860s.

Urban oases

Escape the dust and artificial hush of the indoors and head north of downtow to **Tohono Chul Park** ❼ (open daily 7am–sunset; tel: 520-575-8468; donation "Desert Corner" in the Tohono O'odham language, the 49-acre (20-hectare park was created to promote conservation of arid lands. It has nature trails an 500 plants from Sonora and the Southwest arranged by genus. Picnic here (have afternoon tea in the popular Tea Room. Closer to downtown, **Tucson Botan ical Gardens** ❼ (open daily 8.30am–4.30pm; tel: 520-326-9255; admissio fee) is in bloom all year. Of particular interest is the Native Seeds/SEARCH Ethno botanical Garden, which cultivates native desert crops in its demonstration ga den and has banked some 1,800 heritage seeds in an effort to preserve nativ foods. (Gardeners can buy these at the garden or by mail order.)

When temperatures top 100°F (38°C) in May and June, before the summe "monsoon" thunderstorms arrive, Tucsonans give up saying "but it's a dry hea and head into the mountains surrounding the city. Trails abound in **Coronad National Forest** atop the rugged **Santa Catalina** and **Rincon Mountain** northeast and east of town, respectively. A 40-mile (64-km) scenic drive into th Santa Catalinas (named by Jesuit missionary Padre Eusebio Francisco Kino i 1697) leads to the summit of 9,157-foot (2,791-meter) **Mount Lemmon** ❼, th highest peak in the area. Motorists pass through five distinct life zones befor reaching the top, where temperatures are about 20 degrees cooler than at th

THE CACTUS LEAGUE

Tolerable desert temperatures and wildflower bloor are two great reasons to travel to southern Arizo in February, March and April. Another is to get an advan preview of the upcoming major league baseball seas during spring training – an annual ritual that offers fans chance to see teams like the Arizona Diamondbacks a Chicago White Sox compete in the Cactus League.

Most teams begin their workouts in mid-February, th play around 15 games in March and the first week April. Games are held at popular venues like Electric Pa in Tucson and Bank One Ballpark in Phoenix, which al offer special events such as fireworks nights, bat a T-shirt giveaways, and visiting sports mascots. T athletes often come over and meet fans after the game an extra thrill for autograph-seeking kids.

Tickets go on sale as early as December and ran from $5 for bleacher seats to $15 for reserved sea Lawn seating is available at most venues, making picn a popular option for those not enamored of hot do barbecue and other stadium fare. Ticket information a game schedules can be obtained by calling the tear Arizona venue or by visiting www.arizonaguide.com www.cactus-league.com.

base. **Mount Lemmon Ski Resort**, the southernmost ski resort in the United States, is a popular winter destination.

Natural treasures

At the base of Mount Lemmon is **Sabino Canyon** (visitor center open Mon–Fri 8am–4.30pm, Sat–Sun 8.30am–4.30pm; tel: 520-749-8700; fee for tram), a lush canyon supporting cottonwood and willow bosque, deer, coyotes, javelinas and numerous birds. One of the most popular day-use areas in Tucson, this historic canyon has seen mammoths, Hohokam irrigation ditches, and pony soldiers from the now ruined Fort Lowell, who used to horseback ride to the "ol' swimming hole." The visitor center has exhibits on the natural and cultural history of the mountains, a butterfly and hummingbird sanctuary, a self-guided nature trail starting behind the building, and daily naturalist-led walks.

From here, you can either hike, horseback ride or take one of the regular narrated shuttle tours (bicycles are allowed on some days) up the 3¾-mile (6.1-km) road that winds through the canyon. Popular trails include 5½-mile (9-km) round-trip **Seven Falls**, which follows the flat floor of **Bear Canyon** (14 stream crossings are necessary during snowmelt periods) to an ephemeral waterfall, a welcome sight in this arid land.

Bike riders will particularly enjoy the two units of 87,000-acre (35,000-hectare) **Saguaro National Park** (open daily 8.30am–5pm; tel: 520-733-5153; admission fee) that bookend the city. **Saguaro National Park East**, off Old Spanish Trail in the 8,400-foot (2,560-meter) Rincons, preserves older stands of the multiarmed cactus. If you choose only one section, though, make it **Saguaro National Park West ❶** (open daily 8.30am–5pm; tel: 520-733-5158; admission

Map on page 276

BELOW: a rock climber scales Windy Point in the Catalina Mountains.

fee), west of the **Tucson Mountains**, which may be entered on the north from the West Ina Road exit off Interstate 19 or from downtown on Speedway via Gates Pass. The graded, 6-mile (10-km) **Bajada Loop Drive** passes through vigorous stands of young saguaro that march across the south-facing bajadas, or slopes, in Jolly Green Giant armies. Surrounding them is typical Sonoran Desert Arizona Upland vegetation of yellow-blossomed paloverde trees, flame-tipped ocotillo, mesquite and ironwood frequented by roadrunners, Harris's hawks, gila woodpeckers and other birds.

Rangers at **Red Hills Visitor Center** on Kinney Road offer orientations and can tell you how to find Hohokam petroglyphs at the **Signal Hill** picnic area.

Desert flora and fauna

Desert animals are largely nocturnal, keeping cool in burrows or beneath rocks or shrubs during the day. Your best chance of seeing and learning about Sonoran Desert flora and fauna is to visit the world-famous **Arizona-Sonora Desert Museum** ❶ (open daily 8.30am–5pm in winter, 7.30am–6pm in summer; tel: 520-883-2702; admission fee) in adjoining **Tucson Mountain Park**. This isn't a museum at all but a large outdoor zoo-botanical garden-nature trail that so effectively re-creates the Sonoran Desert, the 385 species of native animals and 1,400 species of native plants that live here are fooled into thinking they never left home.

You'll need good walking shoes, a hat, sunscreen and at least half a day to see all the exhibits, which include wild cats such as mountain lions, bobcats and jaguarundi; bighorn sheep; Mexican wolves; coyotes; and delightful furballs known as coatis, a relative of the ringtail, which snooze in the trees. Beautifully

Javelinas, indigenous piglike animals, are most active in the early morning and late afternoon.

BELOW: a docent at the Arizona-Sonora Desert Museum introduces visitors to a Harris's hawk.

landscaped paths wander through a wildflower and cactus garden. In the walk-in **Hummingbird Aviary**, hummers divebomb feeders and buzz loudly in the mesquite trees. An engaging **Life Underground** exhibit allows you to observe kit foxes, kangaroo rats, tarantulas and other nocturnal animals asleep in their underground burrows. If you want to understand how elevation affects temperature and moisture for desert plants, check out the **Life Zones** exhibit, which takes you through five life zones – the equivalent of journeying from Mexico to Canada in just a few short steps. After visiting this museum, you'll never look at the desert with the same eyes again.

Two other nearby attractions round out a day in the Tucson Mountains. The **International Wildlife Museum** Ⓚ (4800 W. Gates Pass; open daily 9am–5pm; tel: 520-617-1439; admission fee) features dioramas with more than 400 mammal, bird and insect species from all over the world as well as interactive exhibits, and wildlife films. The displays are quite elaborate and informative, but the museum's conservation message has a distinctly hollow ring considering that the animals on display were hunted and taxidermed; there are no living creatures at this facility at all.

Strike the set

The Wild West takes on a new meaning at **Old Tucson Studios** Ⓛ (open daily 10am–6pm; tel: 520-883-0100; admission fee), one of the most visited attractions in Arizona after the Grand Canyon. Originally constructed in 1939 as a set for the movie *Arizona* (and reconstructed after a major fire in 1995), more than 300 movies and TV shows have been filmed here, including the John Wayne movie *Rio Lobo* and *Tombstone*, starring Kurt Russell. Highlights at this family

Map on page 276

Cactus rustling was a serious problem in the 1970s and 80s as homeowners uprooted saguaros for their own yards.

BELOW: Hohokam petroglyphs are pecked into an outcropping in Saguaro National Park West.

Map
City: 276
Area: 292

theme park include gunfights, saloon shows, musicals, Native American story-telling, games, rides and a Town Hall Museum.

Air and space

Davis-Monthan Air Force Base (open for bus tours Mon–Wed 9am; tel: 520-750-3358 for reservations; free), east of Tucson, was dedicated by Charles Lindbergh in 1927. During World War II, it was a training ground for B-17 bombers and still trains pilots in combat aircraft. One of the base's tenants is the **Aerospace Maintenance and Regeneration Center**, where the U.S. military takes advantage of the dry climate and hard ground surface to mothball an extraordinary 5,000 planes and helicopters before they go to the great Junkyard in the Sky.

Nearby, the **Pima Air and Space Museum** ○ (open daily 9am–5pm; tel: 520-574-0462; admission fee) houses more than 250 planes, one of the largest private aircraft collections in the country. Exhibits include a full-scale replica of the Wright Brothers' *Kitty Hawk* and President John F. Kennedy's *Air Force One*. A Space Gallery offers a look at the history of space exploration. Children will love the **Challenger Learning Center**, housed in the **Aerospace Exploratorium**, which has a mission briefing room, transportation room, mission control area and space station.

Two other museums on the outskirts of Tucson offer entirely different visions of a space-age future. The **Titan Missile Museum** ❷ (open daily 9am–4pm Nov–Apr, Wed–Sun 9am–4pm May–Oct; tel: 520-625-7736), 20 miles (32 km) south of Tucson off Interstate 19, is a sobering reminder of Cold War politics and the only site in the United States with a disarmed US intercontinental ballistic missile (ICBM) still on its underground launch pad. One-hour tours of this declassified subterranean museum allow visitors to hear a tape of an Air Force crew preparing to launch a nuclear missile, then see the missile itself – a 110-foot-tall (34-meter), 170-ton (when fully loaded) monster contained behind 6,000-pound (2,700-kg) blast doors. Not recommended for the squeamish.

A far more positive experience awaits visitors at **Biosphere 2** ❸ (open daily 9.30am–3.30pm; tel: 520-896-6200; admission fee) in the town of **Oracle** 30 miles (48 km) north of Tucson. Basically a 3-acre (1-hectare), glass-enclosed terrarium designed to support the four men and four women who sealed themselves inside the facility for two years in 1991 Biosphere 2 was a grand, private experiment that went awry. Amid accusations of hype, New Age cultism poor science and failed systems that endangered the health of the "bionauts," Biosphere 2 started down the long road to credibility in 1996, when Columbia University's Lamont-Doherty Earth Observatory took over its management. In 2001, the U.S. Energy Department signed a memorandum of understanding that will convert Biosphere 2 into a "national use facility," allowing scientists from across the country to use it for research projects. It's the sort of comeback that, according to some Tucsonans, can happen only in the Southwest – a place, as writer Barbara Kingsolve liked to say, "where mountain lions make bets with rabbits, and rabbits can win."

BELOW: Biosphere 2 is a research facility managed by Columbia University.
RIGHT: a traditional Mexican dancer performs during the Midwinter Fiesta at Tumacacori National Monument.

Fairs and Fiestas

Perhaps it's the Mexican influence, but people in southern Arizona know how to have a good time. The annual calendar is jam-packed with parades, rodeos, fairs and festivals featuring everything from bird-watching to chile tasting.

Fiestas celebrating Arizona's Mexican heritage are among the most popular and are held in every community with a sizeable Mexican-American population. Cinco de Mayo commemorates Mexico's victory over the French at Puebla on May 5, 1862, and is celebrated with spicy Mexican food, music and dance. Mexican Independence Day, September 16, is cause for even more celebration. Phoenix's Civic Plaza holds one of the biggest parties. Booths sell *carne asada*, or flame-broiled beef, and small Mexican flags, while mariachi bands and *ballet folklorico* take the stage, along with speakers reciting the call to arms that started the revolution in 1810.

Mariachi music, a style that traces its roots to 18th-century Spain, has become synonymous with Mexican fiestas. Some of the best bands in America can be heard every April in Tucson at the International Mariachi Conference and at the Christmas Mariachi Concert in Phoenix.

El Día de los Muertos, the Day of the Dead, is commemorated on All Souls Day, November 1–2. Family members decorate the graves of departed loved ones with marigold flowers, candles and sugar skulls bearing the names of the deceased, then picnic at graveside. The historic Sosa-Carillo-Fremont House in downtown Tucson exhibits traditional *nichos*, flowered wreaths and candles.

Christmas is a magical time in southern Arizona. El Centro de Las Americas in Tucson holds a month-long celebration of Mexican Christmas traditions called the Ferías Navideñas and Nacimiento Tour. Events include Las Posadas, a traditional dramatization of Jesus's birth. Tucson and Phoenix Botanical Gardens have elaborate displays of *luminarias* (lit candles in brown paper bags). The Tucson Museum of Art installs an elaborate nativity scene, or *nacimiento*, involving hundreds of figurines, in Casa Cordova, the work of a mother and daughter from a northern Mexican village

Easter has special meaning for the Pascua Yaqui Indians of Tucson, whose Lenten ceremonies include traditional rituals like the Deer Dance. Native festivals occur throughout the year. The normally private Tohono O'odham Nation throws a lively three-day celebration with a powwow and rodeo every February in Sells, southwest of Tucson. The tribe also holds the Wa:k Powwow at Mission San Xavier del Bac in March. The Waila Festival, featuring O'odham "chicken scratch" music, is held at the Arizona Historical Society in Tucson in May.

Cowboys and rodeos are the focal point of the world's longest nonmotorized parade, which takes place at Tucson's La Fiesta de los Vaqueros, a huge outdoor rodeo, in February. Winter also brings the Gem, Mineral, and Fossil Showcase at venues around Tucson. Birders won't want to miss Wings Over Willcox, *the* big birding event in southeastern Arizona. It's held in January at Willcox Playa, winter home of thousands of migratory fowl.❑

Reach for the Stars

The dry air and dark skies of the desert produce what astronomers call "good seeing" and have helped make Arizona a mecca for both professional and amateur skywatchers. Three major observatories are located in southern Arizona, each atop a mountain peak far from the glare of city lights and the dust and moisture that tend to settle at lower elevations. A fourth and much older facility, Lowell Observatory, is in Flagstaff and has been engaged in fundamental research for more than a century.

Kitt Peak, the best known of the state's observatories, stands at an elevation of about 6,900 feet (2,100 meters) in the Quinlan Mountains 56 miles (90 km) southwest of Tucson. The ridge bristles with more than 10 telescopes and radio dishes. The largest is the 4-meter Mayall reflector, which is housed in an 18-story dome. About half a mile away, the white angular housing of the McMath Solar Telescope rises from the mountain's south end, looking more like a modern sculpture than an astronomical instrument. At the top of the structure is a 2-meter mirror that collects the sun's rays and reflects the light down a 530-foot-long (162-meter) diagonal shaft into an underground laboratory.

Given that Kitt Peak is one of the country's most sophisticated astronomical facilities, the observatory is remarkably welcoming to visitors. Tour groups set out from the visitor center daily, though most people choose to follow the self-guided tour. Either way, visitors get an uncommonly close-up look at the workings of the observatory. Nightly viewings give amateurs a chance to probe the heavens with a 16-inch reflector under the guidance of a graduate student. An advanced program limited to two participants per night let's you work side-by-side with professionals. Reservations should be made well in advance; call 520-318-8726 for information.

To the east, in the Pinaleno Mountains outside Safford, tours of the Mount Graham Observatory depart from Discovery Park (Mon–Sat June–mid-Nov; tel: 520-428-6260),

LEFT: swirling lights show the motion of stars around Polaris over several hours. **BELOW:** star trails streak across the sky in a time-lapse photograph of Monument Valley.

a visitor center at the base of the mountain, followed by stargazing through the 20-inch telescope.

Whipple Observatory, in the Santa Rita Mountains about 35 miles (56 km) south of Tucson, offers 6-hour bus tours (Mon, Wed, Fri, mid-Mar–Nov; tel: 520-670-5707). The highlight is a close-up look at the Multiple Mirror Telescope, or MMT, which combines the light from six 1.8-meter mirrors constantly realigned by laser sensors.

Lowell Observatory (open daily; tel: 928-774-3359) is the most visitor-friendly of the four, with a host of interactive exhibits, informative tours, and an array of viewing programs and special workshops. Although best known for Percival Lowell's obsessive search for Martian life, the observatory is also credited with Clyde Tombaugh's discovery of Pluto and observations that led to the discovery of the expanding universe.

Nowadays, a staff of some two dozen astronomers conducts research on the planets, stars, galaxies, comets and asteroids, including a project that locates and tracks objects that could collide with Earth, causing the same ecological catastrophe that wiped out the dinosaurs.

Space junkies can continue the star tour at Tucson's Flandreau Science Center (tel: 520-621-4515), where visitors can see a 200-pound (90-kg) chunk of the Barringer iron that blasted out Meteor Crater, take in a planetarium show, and gaze through a 16-inch telescope in a rooftop observatory. Nearby is the Steward Observatory's Mirror Laboratory, which produces optics for some of the world's biggest telescopes. Tours of the lab must be arranged at least two weeks in advance; call 520-621-1022.

Travelers can rub elbows with stargazers at the annual Grand Canyon Star Party in June, a gathering of amateur astronomers for several days and nights of viewing at the edge of the great abyss. Another option is to check into the Skywatcher's Inn (tel: 520-615-3886), a bed-and-breakfast outside Tucson that caters to astronomers, with an indoor and outdoor observatory, high-end telescopes and all the comforts of a fine inn. ❑

ow: a meter scope at Whipple servatory ects high-rgy gamma s in the osphere.

BORDER COUNTRY

Ghost towns, Spanish missions, Old West history and entrancing desert landscapes lure travelers to "la frontera" – Arizona's colorful borderlands

Map on page 292–293

E dge places: those no-man's lands where foreign entities rub up against each other, boundaries blur, and something entirely new emerges. Arizona's border with the Mexican states of Sonora and Chihuahua is one such frontier, a geographical crossroads that has witnessed cultural confluence and collision for centuries.

The recipe begins geographically with the convergence of both the **Chihuahuan** and **Sonoran Deserts** and the **Rocky Mountains** and **Sierra Madre**. Fold in a huge expanse of volcanic basin-and-range topography rising in elevation from just over 1,000 feet (300 meters) in the west to nearly 10,000 feet (93,000 meters) in the east, and pierce it with one of the last free-flowing rivers in the country, the San Pedro. Then mix in half a dozen Indian cultures, 18th-century Spanish missions, 19th-century American forts and mining towns, modern retirement communities, state-of-the-art astronomical observatories, and twin border towns where cultures constantly meet and merge, and you have a unique salsa – one of the fieriest in the West.

Ecological crossroads

Begin this tour from Interstate 10, just over the New Mexico line. Drop south and west on Highway 80 into the rugged **Chiricahua Mountains** via **Portal**. These high, cool peaks are made of uplifted rhyolite, fused ash from an explosion in nearby Turkey Caldera 25 million years ago.

Erosion by rainfall has created an extraordinary rockscape of spires, pinnacles, pedestals and balanced rocks preserved in 17-square-mile (44 sq km) **Chiricahua National Monument ❶** (visitor center open daily 8am–5pm; tel: 520-824-3560; admission fee). The best way to view the rocks is to follow the 6-mile (10-km) **Bonita Canyon Drive,** which climbs from the visitor center through lush **Bonita Canyon** to **Massai Point** (elevation 6,870 ft/2,094 meters), the starting point for a short nature trail and longer day hikes among the rocks.

Rocky Mountain and Sierra Madrean wildlife mingle in these mountains via a natural corridor running through the Chiricahuas to Mexico. Mexican plants and animals such as rare Apache fox squirrels and Chihuahua and Apache pines live peacefully side by side with species more commonly found north of the border. Of particular interest are the birds that summer in the Cave Creek area. At the top of the list is the elegant trogon, a Mexican native with a long, coppery tail and bright feathers, as well as sulphur-bellied flycatchers, tanagers, chickadees, warblers, and a variety of hummingbirds. Surrounding the monument is **Coronado National Forest** and **Chiricahua**

PRECEDING PAGES: Organ Pipe Cactus National Monument. **LEFT:** an O'odham girl shows her handiwork. **BELOW:** Southern Arizona cowgirl.

Wilderness, which contain 100 miles (160 km) of hiking trails and many delightful camping spots.

On the trail of the Apache

To the Chiricahua Apache Indians, this was the "Land of Standing Up Rocks." Led by Cochise, Victorio and Geronimo, they successfully evaded capture by U.S. Army troops during the 1860s–1880s, when settlers began encroaching on Apache territory. They were eventually forced into surrender by talented army officers who learned how to negotiate with warriors on their own terms.

Massai Point provides a view of **Cochise Head**, said to be the profile of the old Apache warrior, but to learn more about the Apache Wars, visit nearby **Fort Bowie National Historic Site** ➎ (visitor center open daily 8am–5pm; tel: 520-847-2500). This ruined adobe outpost once consisted of barracks, officers' quarters, storehouses, a trader's store, and a hospital. It was built in the 1860s to protect the Butterfield Overland Mail Stage and local residents. A 1½-mile (2.5-km) trail to the ruins leaves from Apache Pass Road.

Highway 80 continues south to the 1902 copper smelting town of **Douglas** ➏ past guest ranches, heart-lifting views of the **Peloncillo Mountains**, and a roadside plaque near **Skeleton Canyon** at the spot where Geronimo surrendered in 1886. The most interesting thing about Douglas is the 1907 five-story **Gadsden Hotel**, a faded beauty that bills itself as "the last of the grand hotels." Once host to Theodore Roosevelt and other dignitaries, its main attraction now is the lobby, which contains massive marble columns decorated with 14-karat gold leaf supporting a vaulted ceiling with stained-glass panels.

About 15 miles (24 km) east of Douglas is 93,000-acre (38,000-hectare) **San**

Geronimo, posing with his wife, at Fort Sill, Oklahoma, where he remained until his death in 1909.

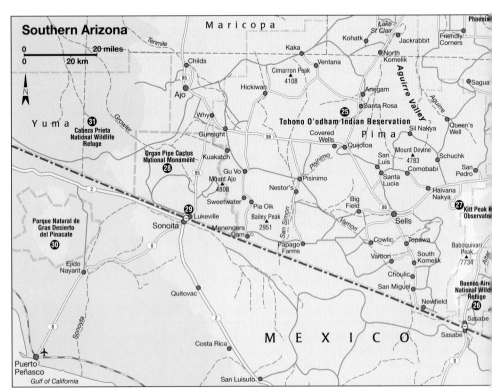

Bernardino National Historical Landmark 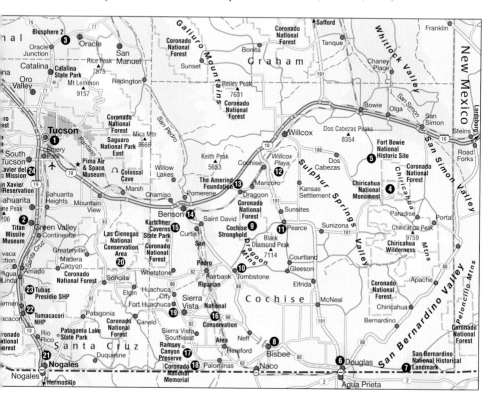, also known as the **Slaughter Ranch** (open Wed–Sun 10am–3pm; tel: 520-558-2474; admission fee), once owned by former Texas Ranger and Cochise County sheriff John Slaughter. His 1890s house, corral, and other buildings have been restored as examples of ranch life during Arizona's territorial years. A 2,330-acre (940-hectare) section is now protected as **San Bernardino National Wildlife Refuge**.

Copper Queen

Douglas served the old copper mining town of **Bisbee**, which spreads for 3 steep miles (5 km) across **Mule Pass Gulch** and **Tombstone Canyon** in the 5,000-foot (1,500-meter) **Mule Mountains**, just west of Douglas. Starting out as a rowdy, cosmopolitan mining camp in 1877, early mining claims were won and lost at the faro table by hard-drinking miners and ex-soldiers. The first major mining operation began when Judge Dewitt Bisbee (who never saw the town named for him) and other San Francisco businessmen bought the **Copper Queen Mine** in 1880. But with underground copper seams running for miles into other claims, cooperation proved the only way for everyone to get rich, and the still-powerful Phelps Dodge corporation was born.

Bisbee's colorful history, including lynchings, murders, a teeming population of miners, working girls, and hopeful immigrants, is showcased in clever, interactive exhibits at the **Bisbee Mining and Historical Museum** (open daily 10am–4pm; tel: 520-432-7071; admission fee), housed in the 1897 **Phelps Dodge General Office Building**. Now a satellite of the Smithsonian Institution, this museum is one of the Southwest's gems – a must for any visitor to Bisbee. A standout is the depiction of the Bisbee Deportation of 1917, when 1,000

Map below

Bisbee – the city of foul odors and sickening smells.
– EDITOR OF THE *TUCSON CITIZEN*, CIRCA 1900

striking miners were loaded at gunpoint into boxcars and expelled from the state for "anti-government" activities.

News from the underground

The other unmissable attraction in Bisbee is the **Queen Mine Tour** (daily tours; call for reservations, tel: 520-432-2071; admission fee). Visitors are equipped with yellow slickers and miner's helmets and lamps, and sit astride an old mine train for the chilly trip down the shaft with a flinty ex-miner – himself a mine of information about drilling, blasting, mining etiquette, and the cushy life of a sanitary engineer, or "shit nipper."

After yielding 8 billion pounds (3.6 billion kg) of copper, Bisbee's 33 mines (and an astonishing 2,500 miles/4,000 km of tunnels) were all closed by 1975, including the yawning abyss of the **Lavender Open Pit Mine**, on the edge of downtown, which long ago swallowed a whole mountain.

Some of the Southwest's funkiest art galleries, museums and offbeat lodgings are housed in historic buildings downtown (including the OK Jail, miner's boarding houses, and a miner's privy museum). Many are on a popular self-guided historic walking tour of downtown's steep hills – you'll soon understand why postal workers in Bisbee refuse to home-deliver mail.

View the 1939 **Phelps Dodge Mercantile**, 1906 **Post Office and Library**, the 1880s **Miners Hotel** in Brewery Gulch, and the 1902 four-story, red-roofed **Copper Queen Hotel,** where you can sleep in the Theodore Roosevelt Suite, John Wayne Room (a straight shot for the Duke after a night in the adjoining saloon bar), or, if you're male, take your chances with the spectral Julia, the "soiled dove" who haunts the Ghost Room on the third floor.

A grave marker in Tombstone's Boothill Cemetery.

BELOW:
the Lavender Open Pit Mine has torn into mountains on the outskirts of downtown Bisbee.

Tough towns

A highway tunnel through the Mule Mountains opens onto the limestone Chihuahuan Desert terrain of creosote, yucca, ocotillo, and sweeping vistas of the alluring **Dragoon Mountains** to the northwest, where you can camp at **Cochise Stronghold ⑨**, the warrior's hideout. Immediately ahead is the "Town too Tough to Die": **Tombstone ⑩**. The old mining town was the setting of the infamous O.K. Corral gunfight in 1881, which pitted U.S. Marshal Wyatt Earp, his brothers Morgan and Virgil, and "Doc" Holliday against the Clanton and McLaury boys, ranchers whose extracurricular activities included cattle rustling and harboring stagecoach robbers. Unless you're in the mood for stage-set Wild West artifice, avoid the costumed cowboys, mock gunfights, and tourist traps, though you may get a kick out of the old **Bird Cage Theater,** where working girls plied their trade in 14 "cages" or "cribs" suspended from the ceiling.

Map on page 292–293

Instead, walk over to the 1882 Victorian red-brick **Tombstone Courthouse State Historic Park** (open daily 8am–5pm; tel: 520-457-3311; admission fee) to view the original courthouse setup and a reconstructed gallows. Diagrammed exhibits offer two theories about what happened during the 30-second OK Corral gunfight, in which Virgil and Morgan Earp were wounded and three members of the Clanton gang killed. The Clantons and other victims of frontier justice are buried in **Boothill Cemetery**, one of the tackiest graveyards you'll ever visit – so kitsch that it's a must – complete with fake-looking headstones, cute epitaphs, and piped-in Willie Nelson music.

Tombstone's eateries also veer toward the hokey, but worth a look is a joint called the **Nellie Cashman Restaurant and Pie Salon**, which was once a hospital run by an Irish mining camp follower known as "the Angel of Tombstone."

Tombstone and Bisbee are resurrected mining towns. To see what happens when boom leads to bust, drive a dirt road east from Tombstone to the ghost mining towns of **Gleeson**, **Courtland** and **Pearce ⑪**. Pearce hosted an 1894 gold rush and is now the only site with sizeable ruins (a two-story corner mercantile store, a post office, and the jail). From Pearce, paved Highway 191 heads north to Interstate 10, past **Willcox Playa ⑫**, which floods in winter to form a wetland that attracts, along with nearby **White Water Draw**, more than 10,000 sandhill cranes, Canada and snow geese, and an array of other waterfowl. Marked side roads lead to viewing areas near the highway.

Located between Willcox and Benson is the **Amerind Foundation ⑬** (open daily 10am–4pm; tel: 520-586-3666; admission fee), one of the Southwest's premier private archaeological and ethnographic collections. The dream of the amateur archaeologist William Fulton, who bought this ranch in 1937 to show off his artifacts, archaeology buffs shouldn't give this one a miss. There are excellent exhibits on the native peoples of the Americas, including beautiful beadwork, and several important archaeological studies copublished with the University of New Mexico.

Some of those books may be found at **The Singing Wind Bookshop** (open daily; tel: 520-586-2425) near

BELOW: gunfights are re-enacted in the streets of Tombstone, the "town too tough to die."

Benson ⓴, known for its wide-ranging selection of books on the Southwest. It is located in the front two rooms of Win Bundy's ranch house.

Subterranean world

From Benson, follow Highway 90 south for 9 miles (14 km) to Arizona's most spectacular new attraction: **Kartchner Caverns State Park** ⓯ (open daily; tel: 520-586-CAVE for reservations, 520-586-4100 for info; admission fee in addition to tour fee). Kartchner is a rare "wet cave," with more than 90 percent of its colorful Escabrosa limestone decorations still growing. It was discovered in 1974 by cavers Randy Tufts and Gary Tenen beneath the **Whetstone Mountains** and Kartchner Ranch. The 2½-mile (4-km) cave was kept secret for 14 years while the cavers, the Kartchner family, and state officials debated how best to develop the caverns without destroying their delicate ecosystem. Using state-of-the-art technology, including misting systems in the caves, double-lock doors to seal in moisture, and specially blasted entrance tunnels, Arizona State Parks spared no expense in doing the job right, eventually opening the caves in November 1999 to widespread acclaim.

Tours leave every 20 minutes from the **Discovery Center**, xeriscaped with interpretive nature trails of varying lengths. Inside, view a 15-minute multimedia film and interactive exhibits that include a simulated cave crawl-through and virtual cave tour. Book ahead; this is currently Arizona's hottest ticket. Or arrive by 7.30am to try for one of 100 tickets released daily on a first-come, first-served basis (hint: stay in the park's large campground to ensure first dibs). Rangers are gung-ho about the caves and offer entertaining and informative talks on the porch before accompanying the tram to the cave entrance. Inside,

BELOW: the weathered ruins of the guardhouse at Fort Bowie, built in 1862 to protect the Apache Pass.

in the **Rotunda** and **Throne Rooms**, the temperature is a steady, steamy 68°F (20°C), with paved, barrier-free walkways leading past deep mud flats and unusual formations, such as colorful shields, streaky "bacon," flowing draperies, wavy helectites, ceiling-hanging stalactites and floor-growing stalagmites. Record-breakers here are the 58-foot-high (18-meter) Kubla Khan column and a 21-foot-long (6-meter) soda straw, the longest in the United States. Both the caves and the strong conservation message being promoted are impressive.

Map on page 292–293

Birding hot spots

Running parallel to Highway 90 is another impressive natural attraction. **San Pedro Riparian National Conservation Area** ⑯ (open Mon–Fri; tel: 520-458-3559) preserves cottonwood-willow *bosque* along the **San Pedro River** for 100 miles (160 km) between St. David and the Mexican border. Named a Globally Important Bird Area by the American Bird Conservancy, this perennial waterway supports more than 80 species of mammals, 45 reptile and amphibian species, 100 species of breeding birds, and 250 species of migrant and wintering birds. An astonishing 4–10 million migratory birds lay over every year.

Bird lovers can help **Southern Arizona Bird Observatory** (based in Bisbee) tag hummingbirds at **San Pedro House** near Sierra Vista in summer, or visit the Nature Conservancy's 300-acre (120-hectare) **Ramsey Canyon Preserve** ⑰ (open daily 8am–5pm, 9am–5pm in winter; tel: 520-378-2785; admission fee). A wonderful little nature center contains exhibits on the San Pedro and Ramsey Canyon ecosystem and a gift store; a staff naturalist leads tours along Ramsey Creek daily. For a real treat, spend the night at the six-room Nature Conservancy-operated **Ramsey Canyon Inn B&B**, which allows 24-hour access to the

TIP

For updates on bird sightings and rare bird alerts, call the Tucson Audubon Society at 520-798-1005.

A Bisbee sculptor shapes a block of local marble.

BELOW:
grasslands flourish
in the high valleys
of desert ranges.

preserve, a boon in August when avian migrants from Mexico, attracted by the warm Sierra Madrean environment of the **Huachuca Mountains**, include painted redstarts, eared and elegant trogons, clouds of butterflies, bats, and 14 hummingbird species, flocking in the huge sycamores and at porch feeders.

Coronado's quest

The Huachucas (highest point, **Miller Peak**, at 9,466 ft/2,885 meters)) are a blessing during the 100°F (38°C) heat of summer, offering breathtaking drives with views into Mexico, camping in **Coronado National Forest**, and hiking on cool mountain trails. The 2,880-acre (1,160-hectare) **Coronado National Memorial** ⑱ (visitor center open daily 8am–5pm; tel: 520-366-5515; admission fee) commemorates the location of what is thought to have been the first Spanish *entrada* into North America by Don Francisco Vásquez de Coronado, in 1540.

Going on information from the advance party of Padre Marcos de Niza and the Moorish slave Esteban in the 1530s, the charismatic 30-year-old Spaniard financed his own expedition from Mexico City, following old Indian trails north across torrid desert and probably passing near 6,844-foot (2,086-meter) **Coronado Peak**. After months of fruitless travel, Coronado's search for gold and glory was deemed a failure, but it set the stage for what would later become a massive colonization effort by Spain.

In 1877, after the Southwest had become American territory, the U.S. Army built **Fort Huachuca** ⑲ as part of its campaign against the Apache. Of the many soldiers who fought during the Apache Wars, none were more respected for their bravery than the fort's black troops, known to the Apache as Buffalo Soldiers. A room in the **Fort Huachuca Museum** (open 9am–4pm Mon–Fri,

pm–4pm Sat–Sun; tel: 520-533-5736; admission free) tells their story through memorabilia, photos, Indian artifacts, and dioramas. It is well worth a stop in the military base town of **Sierra Vista** (you'll pass right by the fort, now a training center for military intelligence).

North of Sierra Vista, turn west on Highway 82. Look for pronghorn as you drive through the tall native grasslands of **Las Cienegas National Conservation Area ㉔** into expansive rolling ranch and wine country. If this area looks familiar, it may be because the 17,500-acre (7,100-hectare) **San Rafael Ranch**, on the Mexican border south of **Patagonia**, doubled as Oklahoma during the shooting of the 1955 film of the Rodgers and Hammerstein musical. By now, it's becoming apparent why southern Arizona was named one of the Top Five Birding Spots in the Nation by *Birding* magazine. Riparian birds like vermilion flycatchers may be glimpsed in these 5,000-foot (1,500-meter) grasslands, and some 300 avian species frequent the Nature Conservancy-run **Patagonia-Sonoita Creek Preserve**, which preserves cottonwood-willow habitat from Patagonia north through **Madera Canyon** in the **Santa Rita Mountains**.

Spanish Missions

Nogales ㉑, which sits astride the U.S.–Mexico border at the junction of Highway 82 with Interstate 19, is where most Arizonans get their border-town fix. Shop 'til you drop, try Sonoran *ranchero* style food, with its emphasis on dishes like the cured meat specialty known as *carne seca,* and, if you're in the mood for dancing, look for a bar playing lively Norteña music. **Northern Sonora** and the stretch of Interstate 19 between Nogales and **Tucson** that follows the beautiful Santa Cruz River Valley contains several 17th-century Indian

Map on page 292–293

BELOW: San José de Tumacacori, a mission church built by O'odham Indians, was abandoned in 1848 due to Apache raids.

TIP

About a dozen vineyards offer tastings in the "wine country" around Sonoita, including Callaghan Vineyards (520-455-5322), Arizona Vineyards (520-287-7972) and Sonoita Vineyards (520-455-5893).

BELOW: San Xavier del Bac, the "White Dove of the Desert," was completed in 1797 and is still an active parish church.

missions founded by Italian Jesuit missionary Padre Eusebio Francisco King during the early Spanish colonial era. **Tumacacori National Historical Park** ㉒ (open daily 8am–5pm; tel: 520-398-2341; admission fee) preserves three mission churches built between 1691 and the early 1800s.

Tumacacori and its sister missions of **Guevavi** (11 miles/18 km south) and **Calabazas** (15 miles/24 km south) were abandoned in 1771, after Spain recalled its Jesuit missionaries and replaced them with Franciscans. The present church began construction in 1800, finishing just before Mexican independence in 1821. Apache raiding grew so bad on the unprotected Mexican northern frontier that, in 1848, the residents moved away and the mission fell into ruin. A peaceful self-guiding trail leads through the church, which remains a remarkable testimony to the skills of Indian craftsmen, with high adobe walls framing a long nave, a white-domed sanctuary, and a distinctive fired brick belltower.

The 5-mile (8-km) **Juan Bautista de Anza National Historic Trail** along the Santa Cruz River connects Tumacacori to **Tubac Presidio State Historic Park** ㉓ (open daily 8am–5pm; tel: 520-398-2252; admission fee) which preserves part of the fort that was erected by the Spanish in 1752 to protect their missions following the 1751 Pima Indian Revolt. Apache raiding and political turmoil caused the site to be abandoned, but the settlement was revived following the 1853 Gadsden Purchase. By 1859, Tubac had become a mining boomtown and home to Arizona's first newspaper, the *Weekly Arizonan*, now on display in the presidio museum. With the founding of an art school in 1948, it morphed into an art colony. Popular with day-trippers, Tubac has about 100 studios and galleries and features an annual Festival of the Arts every February.

When Tumacacori was abandoned in 1848, residents moved north to **San**

Xavier del Bac Mission ㉔, just outside Tucson. Known as the "White Dove of the Desert," San Xavier del Bac is considered the most beautiful of all the Kino church missions, with its classic white plaster exterior and ornate facing. It was founded as a satellite, or *visita*, of Tumacacori in 1700 and built by Tohono O'odham Indians in the late 1700s under the direction of Franciscan priests. It is still the parish church for the San Xavier Reservation today. In the 1990s, the tribe and members of a local friends group worked with an international team (including conservators of the Sistine Chapel in Rome) to restore interior murals that had been damaged by centuries of candle smoke. Restoration of the exterior is now being undertaken, despite recent acts of vandalism.

Map on page 292–293

Desert skies

The 2.8-million-acre (1.1-million-hectare) **Tohono O'odham Reservation ㉕** sprawls west of Tucson across a surprisingly verdant desert landscape of ocotillo, paloverde, mesquite, cholla, and cactus. The signature cactus of this desert, the delightfully anthropomorphic saguaro, can be found on *bajadas,* or mountain slopes, throughout the desert, and seems to wave its many arms in salutes, hugs, handshakes, and finger-pointing disapproval all along the two-lane **Ajo Highway** (Highway 86). Dramatically backlit mountains, huge desert basins, and storms can be seen hundreds of miles away across an almost hallucinogenic landscape.

A distinctive landmark near the U.S.–Mexico border is 7,734-foot (2,357-meter) **Baboquivari Peak** ("narrow about the middle" in the Tohono O'odham language), a brooding volcanic neck believed by the "People of the Desert" to be the home of their creator god, I'itoi. The **Baboquivari Mountains** lie west of the border grasslands of 116,000-acre (47,000-hectare) **Buenos Aires National**

BELOW: restoration of San Xavier del Bac has returned the interior to its original brilliance.

THE DEVIL'S HIGHWAY

El Camino Diablo, the Devil's Highway, is a rough, unpaved route from Carborca, Mexico, to Yuma, Arizona, across one of the most overheated and desolate landscapes in the Southwest. Prehistoric people used the route to transport shells and salt from the Gulf of California. Spanish soldiers led by Melchior Diaz were the first Europeans to travel the route in 1540. More than 150 years later, missionaries Padre Eusebio Kino and Padre Garces, and explorer Juan de Anza also came this way.

After gold was discovered in California in 1849, thousands traveled the Devil's Highway. Between 400 and 2,000 people died of thirst on their way to the gold fields in the 1850s, making this the deadliest immigrant trail in the United States. Many of their graves, marked by heaps of stones and makeshift crosses, are still visible.

The road is best traveled in early spring or fall using a four-wheel-drive vehicle; summer temperatures reach 120°F (49°C), and winter nights can dip below freezing. There are no services or water. Carry one to two gallons (4–8 liters) of water per person per day and pack at least two days' extra water and food, as well as spare tires. Permits are required to enter the Barry Goldwater Range and Cabeza Prieta National Wildlife Refuge.

Map on page 292–293

An inquisitive road sign near the desert town of Why.

BELOW: bird-watcher, Buenos Aires National Wildlife Refuge.
RIGHT: poppies, Sonoran Desert.
FOLLOWING PAGES: Monument Valley

Wildlife Refuge ㉖, which supports pronghorn and numerous bird species, including the endangered masked quail.

Desert skies here are unbelievably clear, making southern Arizona a mecca for stargazers. The **Quinlan Mountains** are home to one of the country's foremost astronomical facilities, **Kitt Peak National Observatory** ㉗ (open daily 9am–4pm and some nights; tel: 520-318-8600; admission fee), which has 22 telescopes of varyious sizes and types, including the huge McGath-Pierce Solar Telescope and the 4-meter Mayall Telescope for dark-sky viewing. A short self-guided tour takes you past the most state-of-the-art telescopes, and a visitor center offers background exhibits that will keep you fascinated for hours.

The big empty

About three hours southwest of Tucson, drop south onto Highway 85 at **Why** (named for the Y in the road), gas up at the quaintly anachronistic **Why Not Café**, and enter 516-square-mile (1,336-sq-km) **Organ Pipe Cactus National Monument** ㉘, which preserves cactus species mainly found south of the border. Remote and lightly visited, this national monument is nestled between the torqued and twisted volcanic **Ajo** and **Puerto Blanco Mountains** and is chock full of coyotes, desert tortoises, rattlers, kit foxes, and other rarely seen desert critters. After a rainfall, brittlebush, desert marigolds, poppies, lupines, and other wildflowers burst into bloom.

Allow enough time to take the 56-mile (90-km) **Pueblo Blanco Scenic Drive** and 21-mile (34-km) **Ajo Scenic Drive** into the backcountry to view organ pipe cactus, rare Mexican elephant trees, limberbush, and senita cactus. Many dirt roads lead to historic ranches, mines, and prehistoric Indian sites.

Highway 85 leads south into **Sonora** and **Baja California,** via the border at **Lukeville** ㉙. If you go into Mexico only once on your travels, this is the best place to do so (armed with Mexican car insurance and proof of citizenship). A few miles south of Lukeville is Mexico's **Parque Natural de Gran Desierto del Pinacate** ㉚, one of the world's truly extraordinary landscapes – an ebony-hued lava land topped incongruously by Sonoran Desert vegetation. Cool off at **Puerto Peñasco** (Rocky Point), 65 miles (105 km) south of Lukeville, where you can swim in the Gulf of California and enjoy endless sandy beaches.

Adjoining Organ Pipe Cactus is 86,000-acre (34,800-hectare) **Cabeza Prieta National Wildlife Refuge** ㉛, a sanctuary for desert bighorn sheep. Though beautiful, travel here is by permit only, due to the presence of the **Barry Goldwater Bombing Range** on the preserve's north side. Fighter jets frequently patrol this area, their engines and explosions rending the profound stillness of what may be one of the last great unpeopled places in the Lower 48.

A campaign to protect Cabeza Prieta and Organ Pipe as **Sonoran Desert National Park** has been proposed by Tucson writer Bill Broyles. Fellow advocate Chuck Bowden has the last word on why Arizona's border country has such magnificent appeal: "I don't have to think much here because everything is stated so plainly. I have found a place that skips the big words." ❏

INSIGHT GUIDES
Travel Tips

✖️ INSIGHT GUIDES Phonecard

One global card to keep travellers in touch. Easy. Convenient. Saves you time and money.

It's a global phonecard

Save up to 70%* on international calls from over 55 countries

Free 24 hour global customer service

Recharge your card at any time via customer service or online

It's a message service

Family and friends can send you voice messages for free.

Listen to these messages using the phone* or online

Free email service - you can even listen to your email over the phone*

It's a travel assistance service

24 hour emergency travel assistance – if and when you need it.

Store important travel documents online in your own secure vault

For more information, call rates, and all Access Numbers in over 55 countries, (check your destination is covered) go to **www.insightguides.ekit.com** or call Customer Service.

JOIN now and receive US$ 5 bonus when you join for US$ 20 or more.

Join today at

www.insightguides.ekit.com

When requested use ref code: **INSAD010**

OR SIMPLY FREE CALL
24 HOUR CUSTOMER SERVICE

UK	0800 376 1705
USA	1800 706 1333
Canada	1800 808 5773
Australia	1800 11 44 78
South Africa	0800 997 285

THEN PRESS **0**

For all other countries please go to "Access Numbers" at **www.insightguides.ekit.com**

* Retrieval rates apply for listening to messages. Savings base on using a hotel or payphone and calling to a landline. Corre at time of printing 01.03

(INS001)

powered by ✦ekit

"The easiest way to make calls and receive messages around the world"

CONTENTS

Getting Acquainted

Time Zones

The continental U.S. is divided into four time zones. From east to west, later to earlier, they are Eastern, Central, Mountain and Pacific, each separated by one hour. Arizona is on Mountain Standard Time (MST), seven hours behind Greenwich Mean Time. One peculiarity to keep in mind: the Navajo Nation observes daylight savings time but the rest of the state (including the Hopi Reservation, which is completely surrounded by the Navajo Nation) does not. On the first Sunday in April, the Navajo Nation sets the clock ahead one hour. On the last Sunday in October, the clock is moved back one hour to return to standard time. Thus, during spring and summer, "Navajo time" is one hour ahead of "Arizona time."

Other states in the region – Colorado, Utah and New Mexico are on Mountain Standard Time and observe daylight savings time.

Public Holidays

On public holidays, post offices, banks, most government offices and a large number of shops and restaurants are closed. Public transport usually runs less frequently.

New Year's Day: January 1
Martin Luther King Day: The third Monday in January
Presidents' Day: The third Monday in February
Good Friday: March/April – date varies
Easter Sunday: March/April – date varies

California is on Pacific Standard Time and observes daylight savings time. Mexico does not observe daylight savings time.

Climate

Arizona spans half a dozen climate and life zones, but by and large you will find sunny skies, low humidity and limited precipitation. Climate varies widely with elevation. Climbing 1,000 feet (300 m) is equivalent to traveling 300 miles (500 km) northwards. In temperature, traveling from the lowest to the highest points of Arizona is like traveling from Mexico to the north of Hudson Bay in Canada. In Tucson, for example, it's possible to sun yourself at poolside in the morning and ski atop nearby Mount Lemmon in the afternoon.

Arizona gets 80 percent of available sunshine annually. Yearly rainfall averages 12½ inches (30 cm); much of it falls in brief, intense thunderstorms during the summer "monsoon" season, when dry washes, arroyos and narrow canyons are prone to flash floods. Wind velocity in the cities is under 8 mph (13 kph), though exposed and high-elevation areas tend to be gusty. The northern region averages around 73 percent sunshine; the southern part of the state averages around 90 percent.

Average temperatures in **Phoenix** and **Tucson** reach 100°F (38°C) in

El Cinco de Mayo: May 5
Memorial Day: Last Monday in May
Independence Day: July 4
Labor Day: First Monday in September
Columbus Day: Second Monday in October
Election Day: The Tuesday in the first full week of November during presidential-election years
Veterans Day: November 11
Thanksgiving Day: Fourth Thursday in November
Christmas Day: December 25

summer and fall but often soar to 110°F (43°C) or higher for long periods. Nights are warm and pleasant, usually ranging from 65°F (18°C) to 75°F (24°C). Winter and early spring are the ideal seasons to visit Phoenix and Tucson, with average daytime temperatures from 65°F (18°C) to 75°F (24°C); nighttime temperatures dip into the 30s°F. Phoenix gets about 7 inches (18 cm) of rain per year, Tucson 11 inches (28 cm).

In **Flagstaff**, 145 miles (230 km) to the north, temperatures range from 75°F to 80°F (24°C to 27°C) in summer and fall to around 15°F (–10°C) in winter. Annual precipitation in Flagstaff averages 84 inches (210 cm), most of it falling in July, August and December. Winter is cold but generally sunny, with occasional snowfall. Average annual snowfall at the Arizona Snowbowl in the nearby San Francisco Peaks is 260 inches (660 cm).

At its hottest, the **South Rim of the Grand Canyon** reaches 90°F. Temperatures run about 20°F (11°C) warmer at **Phantom Ranch** at the bottom of the gorge. Flash thunderstorms are common during the monsoon season.

The weather is more comfortable and the crowds are lighter in spring and fall, with average daytime highs from 65°F (18°C) to 75°F (24°C). Nights are chilly; be sure to bring a sweater or jacket.

Winter is quiet at the South Rim. Temperatures often slip below freezing, and snowstorms are common, though the inner gorge is relatively warm and mild. Expect icy conditions on roads and trails and occasional road closings due to snow.

The **North Rim** is about 1000 feet (300 m) higher than the South Rim and is significantly cooler and breezier, with summer highs around 75°F (24°C). Evening and morning can be nippy; bring long pants and a sweater. The North Rim is blanketed with as much as 200 inches (510 cm) of snow in winter and is closed from mid-October to mid-May.

Planning the Trip

Clothing

Think cool and comfortable. With few exceptions, western dress is informal. A pair of jeans or slacks, a polo or button-down shirt, and boots or shoes are appropriate at all but the fanciest places and events. Shorts and light shirts are suitable for most situations in the warmer months, though it's always a good idea to have a sweater or jacket for evenings, high elevations, or overly air-conditioned shops and restaurants.

If you plan on doing a lot of walking or hiking, it's worth investing in a sturdy pair of hiking shoes or boots. A thin, inner polypropylene sock and a thick, outer sock will help keep your feet dry and comfortable. If blisters or sore spots develop, quickly cover them with moleskin or surgical tape, available at most pharmacies or camping supply stores.

A high-factor sunblock, wide-brimmed hat and sunglasses are advisable too, even if the day starts out cloudy. The sun is merciless, especially in the desert, where shade is scarce.

Electricity

Standard electricity in North America is 110-115 volts, 60 cycles A.C. An adapter is necessary for most appliances from overseas, with the exception of Japan.

Maps

Accurate maps are indispensable in Arizona, especially when leaving primary roads. Highway maps can be found at bookstores,

Film

All consumer formats of photographic films are available in most grocery stores, pharmacies and convenience stores. If you need professional-quality photographic equipment or film (especially transparency or black-and-white films), consult the local telephone directory for the nearest camera shop. If you don't have a camera, consider the relatively inexpensive disposable cameras available at many supermarkets, pharmacies and convenience stores.

convenience stores and gas stations. Free maps may be available by mail from state or regional tourism bureaus. Free city, state and regional maps as well as up-to-date road conditions and other valuable services are also available to members of the Automobile Association of America (AAA). If you are driving any distance, the service is well worth the membership fee.

Maps of national parks, forests and other natural areas are usually offered by the managing governmental agency. Good topographical maps of national parks are available from **Trails Illustrated**, PO Box 3610, Evergreen, CO 80439, tel: 303-670-3457 or toll-free 800-962-1643; these maps are often in bookstores. Extremely detailed topographical maps are available from the **U.S. Geological Survey**, PO Box 25286, Denver Federal Center, Denver, CO 80225, tel: 303-236-7477. Like maps from Trails Illustrated, USGS maps are often available in higher-end bookstores and shops that sell outdoor gear.

Entry Regulations

PASSPORTS & VISAS

A passport, visitor's visa and evidence of intent to leave the U.S. after your visit are required for entry into the U.S. by most foreign nationals. Visitors from the United King-

dom and several other countries staying less than 90 days may not need a visa if entering as tourists. All other nationals must obtain a visa from a U.S. consulate or embassy. An international vaccination certificate may be required depending on your country of origin.

Canadians entering from the Western Hemisphere, Mexicans with border passes and British residents of Bermuda and Canada do not normally need a visa or passport, but it's best to confirm visa requirements before leaving home.

Once in the U.S. foreigners may visit Canada or Mexico for up to 30 days and re-enter the U.S. without a new visa. For additional information, contact a U.S. consulate or embassy or the U.S. State Department, tel: 202-663-1225.

Extensions of Stay

Visas are usually granted for six months. If you wish to remain in the country longer than six months, you must apply for an extension of stay at the **U.S. Immigration and Naturalization Service**, 2401 E St, Washington, DC 20520, tel: 202-514-4330.

CUSTOMS

All people entering the country must go through U.S. Customs, often a time-consuming process. To speed things up, be prepared to open your luggage for inspection and keep the following restrictions in mind.
● You must declare cash in excess of $10,000.
● Anything for personal use may be brought in duty- and tax-free.
● Adults are allowed to bring in one liter of alcohol for personal use.
● You can bring in gifts worth less than $400 duty- and tax-free. Anything over the $400 limit is subject to duty charges and taxes.
● Agricultural products, meat and animals are subject to complex restrictions, especially if entering in California. Leave these items at home if at all possible.

For more details contact a U.S. consulate or write the Department of

Agriculture, or U.S. Customs, 1301 Constitution Avenue NW, Washington, DC 20520, tel: 202-514-4330.

Health

PRECAUTIONS

Insurance: It's vital to have medical insurance when traveling. Though hospitals are obligated to provide emergency treatment to anyone who needs it whether or not they have insurance, you may have to prove you can pay for treatment of anything less than a life-threatening condition. Know what your policy covers and have proof of the policy with you at all times or be prepared to pay at the time service is rendered.

Flash Floods: Sudden downpours – even those falling miles away from your location– can fill canyons and dry river beds with a roaring torrent of water and mud that will sweep away everything in its path. Travelers should be especially careful during the summer monsoon season. Avoid hiking or driving in arroyos or narrow canyons, and never try to wade or drive across a flooded stream. If rain begins to fall or you see rain clouds in the distance, move to higher ground. It's impossible to outrun or even outdrive a flash flood. Take action before water level begins to rise.

Sunburn: Even a couple of hours outdoors can result in sunburn, so protect yourself with a high-SPF sunscreen and polarized sunglasses. The elderly and the ill, small children and people with fair skin should be especially careful. Excessive pain, redness, blistering or numbness mean you need professional medical attention. Minor sunburn can be soothed by taking a cold bath.

Dehydration: Drink plenty of liquids and, if outdoors, carry bottles of water and something to eat. The rule of thumb is a gallon (4 l) of water per person per day. Don't wait to get thirsty – start drinking as soon as you set out. Also avoid the sun at its hottest: 2–4pm.

Drinking water: All water from natural sources must be purified

before drinking. *Giardia* is found throughout the West, even in crystal-clear water, and it can cause severe cramps and diarrhea. The most popular purification methods are tablets or filters (both available from camping supply stores) or by boiling water for at least 15 minutes. Drink only bottled water in Mexico, and avoid ice cubes.

Cactus: To avoid being pricked, stay on trails and wear long pants and sturdy boots. Some people may have allergies to the prickly varieties of these beautiful desert plants.

Hypothermia: This occurs when the core body temperature falls below 95°F (35°C). At altitude, combinations of alcohol, cold and thin air can produce hypothermia. Watch for drowsiness, disorientation and sometimes increased urination. If possible get to a hospital, otherwise blankets and extra clothing should be piled on for warmth. Don't use hot water or electric heaters and don't rub the skin. The elderly should be especially careful in extremely cold weather.

Frostbite: Symptoms of frostbite, which occurs when living tissue freezes, include numbness, pain, blistering and whitening of the skin. The most immediate remedy is to put frostbitten skin against warm skin. Simply holding your hands for several minutes over another person's frostbitten cheeks or nose may suffice. Otherwise, immerse frostbitten skin in warm (not hot!) water. Refreezing will cause even more damage, so get the victim into a warm environment as quickly as possible. If one person is frostbitten, others may be too.

Altitude sickness: This is not a serious consideration in most parts of the state, although people traveling from sea level may feel uncharacteristically winded at elevations as low as 6,000 or 7,000 feet (1,800–2,100 m). The sensation usually passes after a few days. Symptoms, including nausea, headache, vomiting, extreme fatigue, light-headedness and shortness of breath, intensify over 10,000 feet (3,000 m). Although the symptoms may be mild at first,

Abandoned Mines

Exercise caution around old buildings and abandoned mines. Structures may be unstable and the ground may be littered with broken glass, nails and other debris. Mine shafts are particularly dangerous. Never enter a mine shaft or cave unless accompanied by a park ranger or other professional.

they can develop into a serious illness. Move to a lower elevation and try to acclimatize gradually.

INSECTS & ANIMALS

Snakes: Arizona has two venomous snakes – rattlesnakes and coral snakes. Only about 3 percent of people bitten by a rattlesnake die, and these are mainly small children. Walk in the open, proceed with caution among rocks, avoid dark or overgrown places where snakes might lurk, shake out bedding or clothing that has been lying on the ground, and wear sturdy hiking boots. Snakes often lie on roads at night because of the residual heat radiating from the pavement, so use a flashlight if walking on a paved road after dark. Keep your hands and feet where you can see them, and don't let children poke under rocks or logs.

Snakebite kits are good psychological protection but there is controversy over how effective they really are. If bitten, apply a tourniquet lightly above the bite toward the heart. Try to identify the species and go immediately to a doctor.

Gila monsters: North America's only venomous lizard looks menacing but is easily recognized and rarely encountered.

Insects: Bees are abundant, which should concern only those allergic to the sting. The kissing bug is an unusual looking black insect with an unpleasant bite. There are fire ants and some varieties of wasp. Their sting can be painful but isn't dangerous unless you're allergeric to their venom.

The bite of a black widow spider and tarantula and the sting of a scorpion's tail can pack a punch but are rarely a serious health threat to adults. Scorpions are nocturnal, so use flashlights if you walk barefoot in the desert at night. They often hide in recesses, dark corners and old wood piles and like to crawl into protected places, so shake out clothes or sleeping bags that have been on the ground and check your shoes before slipping them on in the morning.

Money Matters

CURRENCY

The basic unit of American currency, the dollar ($1), is equal to 100 cents. There are four coins, each worth less than a dollar: a penny or 1 cent (1¢), a nickel or 5 cents (5¢), a dime or 10 cents (10¢) and a quarter or 25 cents (25¢).

There are several denominations of paper money: $1, $5, $10, $20, $50, $100 and, rarely, $2. Each bill is the same color, size and shape; be sure to check the dollar amount on the face of the bill.

It is advisable to arrive with at least $100 in cash (in small bills) to pay for ground transportation and other incidentals.

AUTOMATIC TELLER MACHINES (ATMS)

ATMs are the most convenient way to access cash and are widely available throughout the state. They are usually found at banks, shopping malls, supermarkets, service stations, convenience stores, and hotels. ATM, or debit, cards may also be used at a growing number of grocery stores and gas stations, much as credit cards are.

TRAVELER'S CHECKS

Foreign visitors are advised to take U.S. dollar traveler's checks since exchanging foreign currency – whether as cash or checks – can be problematic. A growing number of banks offer exchange facilities, but this practice is not universal.

Most shops, restaurants and other establishments accept traveler's checks in U.S. dollars and will give change in cash. Alternatively, checks can be converted into cash at the bank.

CREDIT CARDS

These are very much part of daily life in the U.S. They can be used to pay for pretty much anything, and it is also common for car rental firms and hotels to take an imprint of your card as a deposit. Rental companies may oblige you to pay a large deposit in cash if you do not have a card.

You can also use your credit card to withdraw cash from ATMs (Automatic Teller Machines). Before you leave home, make sure you know your PIN and find out which ATM system will accept your card. The most widely accepted cards are Visa, MasterCard, American Express, Diners Club, and Discovery.

Money may be sent or received by wire at any **Western Union** office (tel: 800-325-6000) or **American Express Money Gram** office (tel: 800-543-4080).

Insurance

Most visitors to the U.S. will have no health problems during their stay. Even so, you should never leave home without travel insurance to cover both yourself and your belongings. Your own insurance company or travel agent can advise you on policies, but shop around since rates vary. Make sure you are covered for accidental death, emergency medical care, trip cancellation and baggage or document loss.

Getting There

BY AIR

The following carriers serve Phoenix Sky Harbor and/or Tucson

International Airports:

Air Canada	888-247-2262
ATA	800-435-9282
America West	800-235-9292
American	800-433-7300
British Airways	800-247-9297
Continental	800-525-0280
Delta	800-221-1212
Northwest	800-225-2525
TWA	800-221-2000
United	800-241-6522
US Airways	800-428-4322

The following commuter airlines offer service within the region, including Phoenix, Tucson, Flagstaff, the Grand Canyon, Las Vegas, Los Angeles, Lake Havasu City, Kingman, Show Low and Yuma:

Air Vegas	800-255-7474
America West	800-235-9292
Mesa	800-637-2247
Scenic	800-446-4584
Southwest	800-435-9792
Sunrise	800-347-3962

BY TRAIN

Amtrak offers more than 500 destinations across the U.S. The trains are comfortable and reliable, with lounges, dining cars, snack bars and, in some cases, movies and live entertainment. Most routes offer sleeper cars with private cabins in addition to regular seating.

Amtrak's **Southwest Chief** runs from Chicago to Los Angeles, with stops in Winslow, Flagstaff (bus service connects to the Grand Canyon) and Kingman, Arizona. The **Sunset Limited** runs from Miami to Los Angeles and stops at Tucson and Phoenix.

Ask about two- or three-stopover discounts, senior citizens' and children's discounts, and Amtrak's package tours. International travelers can buy a USA Railpass, good for 15 to 30 days of unlimited travel on Amtrak throughout the United States.

Call **Amtrak**, tel: 800-872-7245, for detailed scheduling.

BY BUS

One of the least expensive ways to travel in America is by interstate bus. The largest national bus company is **Greyhound**, tel: 800-231-2222. The company routinely offers discounts such as go-anywhere fares. An Ameripass offers unlimited travel for 7, 15, 30 or 60 days. Greyhound generally does not serve remote areas. A rental car or other transport will be necessary from the major hubs.

BY CAR

Driving is by far the most convenient way to travel in Arizona, especially outside the major cities. Major roads are well-maintained, although some backcountry roads may be unpaved. If you plan on driving into remote areas or in heavy snow, mud or severe weather, it's a good idea to use a four-wheel-drive vehicle with high clearance.

Maps & Information

Your greatest assets as a driver are good road maps. They can be obtained from state tourism offices, filling stations, supermarkets and convenience stores. Although roads are maintained even in remote areas, it is advisable to listen to local radio stations and to check with highway officials or police officers for the latest information on weather and road conditions, especially in winter or if planning to leave paved roads.

Driving in Remote Areas

If you plan to drive in uninhabited areas, carry a spare tire and extra water – at least 1 gallon (4 l) per person per day. A cell phone is a good idea, too, though some areas will be out of range of the nearest communications tower.

Service stations can be few and far between in remote areas. Not every town will have one, and many close early. It's always better to have more fuel than you think you will need.

Hitchhiking

Hitchhiking is illegal in many places and ill-advised everywhere. It's an inefficient and dangerous method of travel. Don't do it!

A word of caution: If your car breaks down on a back road, do not attempt to strike out on foot, even with water. A car is easier to spot than a person and provides shelter from the elements. If you don't have a cell phone or your phone doesn't work, sit tight and wait to be found.

Vehicle Rental

CAR RENTALS

Auto rental agencies are located at all airports, in cities and many large towns. In most places, you must be at least 21 years old (25 at some locations) to rent a car and you must have a valid driver's license and at least one major credit card. Drivers under 25 may have to pay an extra fee, as will additional drivers. Foreign drivers must have an international driver's license. Be sure that you are properly insured for both collision and personal liability. Insurance won't be included in the base rental fee. Additional cost varies depending on the car and the type of coverage, but it is usually $15–25 per day. You may already

AAA

If you intend to do a lot of driving, consider joining the American Automobile Association (AAA). Fees are reasonable and benefits many: emergency road service, maps, insurance, travelers' checks, bail bond protection and other services. AAA has reciprocity agreements with many foreign automobile associations.

AAA, 4100 E. Arkansas Drive, Denver CO 80222, tel: 800-222-4357; www.aaa.com

be covered by your own auto insurance or credit-card company, so check with them first.

Most companies offer unlimited mileage. If not, you may be charged an extra 10–25¢ or more per mile over a given maximum. Rental fees vary depending on the time of year, location, how far in advance you book your rental, and if you travel on weekdays or weekends. Inquire about discounts or benefits for which you may be eligible, including corporate, credit-card or frequent-flyer programs.

Alamo	800-327-9633
Avis	800-331-1212
Budget	800-527-0700
Dollar	800-800-4000
Enterprise	800-325-8007
Hertz	800-654-3131
National	800-227-7368
Thrifty	800-367-2277

RV RENTALS

No special license is necessary to operate a motor home (or recreational vehicle – RV for short), but they aren't cheap. When you add up the cost of rental fees, insurance, gas and campsites, renting a car and staying in motels or camping may be less expensive.

Keep in mind, too, that RVs are large and slow and may be difficult to handle on narrow mountain roads. If parking space is tight, driving an RV may be extremely inconvenient. Still, RVs are extremely popular, and some travelers swear by them. For additional information about RV rentals, call the **Recreational Vehicle Rental Association**, tel: 800-336-0355; www.rvra.org.

Practical Tips

Newspapers

Every city and most large towns have a local newspaper. For national and international news, along with local and regional events, check the following papers. Also available are *The New York Times, Los Angeles Times, Washington Post, USA Today* and *The Wall Street Journal*. Forget about finding overseas newspapers, except in a few hotels and specialty bookstores.

Arizona Daily Star
4850 S. Park Avenue,Tucson, AZ 85714; tel: 520-573-4220.
Arizona Daily Sun
1751 S. Thompson, Flagstaff, AZ 86001; tel: 928-774-5454.
Arizona Republic
200 E. Van Buren, Phoenix, AZ 85004; tel: 602-444-8000.
Lake Powell Chronicle
3 Elm Street Mall, Page, AZ 86040; tel: 928-645-8888.
Navajo-Hopi Observer
417 W. Santa Fe Avenue, Flagstaff, AZ 86001; tel: 928-226-9696.
Navajo Times
Highway 264 & Route 12, Window Rock, AZ 86515; tel: 928-871-6642.
Tucson Citizen
4850 S. Park Avenue, Tucson, AZ 85714; tel: 520-573-4561.
Yuma Daily Sun
2055 Arizona Avenue, Yuma 85364; tel: 928-783-3333.

The following magazines feature profiles of interesting destinations and local people as well as restaurant listings and a calendar of events.
Arizona Highways
2039 W. Lewis Avenue, Phoenix, AZ 85009; tel: 800-543-5432; www.arizonahighways.com

Phoenix
4041 N. Central Avenue, Suite 530, Phoenix, AZ 85012; tel: 602-234-0840.
Tucson Lifestyle
7000 E. Tanque Verde Road, Suite 11, Tucson, AZ 85715; tel: 520-721-2929.

Postal Services

Even the most remote towns are served by the U.S. Postal Service. Smaller post offices tend to be limited to business hours (Monday–Friday 9am–5pm), although central, big-city branches may have extended weekday and weekend hours.

Stamps are sold at all post offices. They are also sold at some convenience stores, filling stations, hotels and transportation terminals, usually from vending machines.

For reasonably quick delivery within the U.S. at a modest price, ask for priority mail, which usually reaches its destination within two or three day.

For overnight deliveries, try U.S. **Express Mail** or one of several domestic and international courier services:
Fedex, tel: 800-238-5355
DHL, tel: 800-345-2727
United Parcel Service, tel: 800-742-5877

Poste Restante
Visitors can receive mail at post offices if it is addressed to them, care of "General Delivery", followed by the city name and (very important) the zip code. You must pick up this mail in person within a

Business Hours

Standard hours for business offices are Monday–Friday 9am–5pm. Many banks open a little earlier, usually 8.30am. A few open on Saturday morning. Post offices are usually open Monday–Friday 8am–5pm and Saturday 8am–noon. Most stores and shopping centers are open weekends and evenings.

week or two of its arrival and will be asked to show a valid driver's license, passport or some other form of picture identification.

Telephone, Telegram, and Internet Access

Public telephones are located at many highway rest areas, service stations, convenience stores, bars, motels and restaurants.

To call from **one area to another**, dial 1 before the three-digit area code, then the local seven-digit number. If you want to pay for the call with coins, a recorded voice will tell you how many to insert. Unless you have a calling card, your only other option is to call your party "collect" (reversing the charges) by dialing 0 before the number. Rates vary for long-distance calls, though you can often take advantage of lower long-distance rates on weekends and after 5pm on weekdays.

Many businesses have **toll-free** (no charge) telephone numbers; these are always prefaced with 800, 888 or 887 rather than an area code. Note that if you dial a toll-free number from abroad, you will be charged the normal international rate for the call.

The quickest way to get information is to dial 0 for the operator. Directory Assistance calls from pay telephones are free. However, to be connected to some of them you must first insert a coin, but as soon as you are connected with the operator it will be returned to you. To get the **information operator** dial 411, but to get an information operator in another city, dial 1-(area code of the city)-555-1212.

Dialing Abroad
To dial abroad (Canada follows the U.S. system), first dial the international access code 011, then the country code. If using a U.S. phone credit card, dial the company's access number below, then 01, then the country code.
Sprint, tel: 10333
AT&T, tel: 10288.

Country codes:

Australia	61
Austria	43
Belgium	32
Brazil	55
Denmark	45
France	33
Germany	49
Greece	30
Hong Kong	852
Israel	972
Italy	39
Japan	81
Korea	82
Netherlands	31
New Zealand	64
Norway	47
Singapore	65
South Africa	27
Spain	34
Sweden	46
Switzerland	41
United Kingdom	44

Western Union (tel: 800-325-6000) can arrange money transfers and telegrams. Check the Web (www.westernunion.com) or phone directory or call information for local offices.

Fax machines are available at most hotels and motels. Printers, copy shops, stationers and office-supply shops may also have them, as well as some convenience stores.

Dataports for laptop computers and Palm Pilots are available at most business hotels. **E-mail and Internet access** is also available at public libraries, Internet cafes and copy shops like Kinkos.

Weights & Measures

Despite efforts to convert to metric, the U.S. still uses the Imperial System of weights and measures.

1 inch	=	2.54 cm
1 foot	=	30.48 cm
1 yard	=	0.9144 meter
1 mile	=	1.609 km
1 pint	=	0.473 liter
1 quart	=	0.946 liter
1 ounce	=	28.4 grams
1 pound	=	0.453 kg
1 acre	=	0.405 hectare
1 sq mile	=	259 hectares
1 centimeter	=	0.394 inch
1 meter	=	39.37 inches

1 kilometer	=	0.621 mile
1 liter	=	1.057 quarts
1 gram	=	0.035 ounce
1 kilogram	=	2.205 pounds
1 hectare	=	2.471 acres
1 sq km	=	0.386 sq. mile

Useful Addresses

ARIZONA TOURISM OFFICES

Arizona Office of Tourism
2702 N. Third Street
Suite 4015
Phoenix, AZ 85004
Tel: 602-230-7733 or toll free 888-520-3433.
www.arizonaguide.com

Bisbee Chamber of Commerce
P.O. Box BA
Bisbee, AZ 85603
Tel: 520-432-5421.
www.bisbeearizona.com

Flagstaff Convention and Visitors Bureau
211 W. Aspen Avenue
Flagstaff, AZ 86001
Tel: 928-779-7611.
www.flagstaffarizona.org

Grand Canyon Chamber of Commerce
P.O. Box 3007
Grand Canyon, AZ 86023
Tel: 928-638-2901.
www.thecanyon.com/chamber

Lake Havasu Tourism Bureau
Tel: 800-242-8278.
golakehavasu.com

Mesa Convention and Visitors Bureau
P.O. Box 5529
Mesa, AZ 85201

Tipping

Service workers in restaurants and hotels depend on tips for a significant portion of their income. With few exceptions, tipping is left to your discretion and gratuities are not automatically added to the bill. In most cases, 15–20 percent is typical for tipping waiters, taxi drivers, bartenders, barbers and hairdressers. Porters and bellmen usually get $1 per bag.

Tel: 480-827-4700.
www.mesacvb.com

Navajo Nation Tourism Office
P.O. Box 663
Window Rock, AZ 86515
Tel: 928-871-6436.
www.navajo.org

Nogales–Santa Cruz County Chamber of Commerce
123 W. Kino Park Way
Nogales, AZ 85621
Tel: 520-287-3685.
www.nogaleschamber.com

Page–Lake Powell Visitors Bureau
644 N. Navajo Drive, Dam Plaza
Page, AZ 86040
Tel: 928-645-2741 or toll free 888-261-7243.
www.pagelakepowellchamber.org

Parker Area Chamber of Commerce
1217 California Avenue
Parker, AZ 85344
Tel: 928-669-2174.

Phoenix Convention and Visitors Bureau
400 E. Van Buren #600
Phoenix, AZ 85004
Tel: 602-254-6500.
www.phoenixcvb.com

Pinetop–Lakeside Chamber of Commerce
102-C W. White Mountain Boulevard
Lakeside, AZ 85929
Tel: 928-367-4290 or toll free 800-573-4031.
www.pinetoplakesidechamber.com

Prescott Chamber of Commerce
117 W. Goodwin Street
Prescott, AZ 86303
Tel: 928-445-2000.
www.prescott.org

Rim Country Chamber of Commerce
100 W. Main Street
Payson, AZ 85547
Tel: 928-474-4515 or toll free 800-672-9766
www.rimcountrychamber.com

Scottsdale Chamber of Commerce
7343 Scottsdale Mall
Scottsdale, AZ 85251
Tel: 602-945-8481.
www.scottsdalechamber.com

Sedona Chamber of Commerce
P.O. Box 478
Sedona, AZ 86336
Tel: 928-282-7722 or toll free 800-288-7336.
www.sedonachamber.com

Foreign Embassies in the United States

Australia: 1601 Massachusetts Ave NW, Washington, DC 20036, tel: 202-797-3000.

Belgium: 3330 Garfield St NW, Washington, DC 20008, tel: 202-333-6900.

Canada: 501 Pennsylvania Ave NW, Washington, DC 20001, tel: 202-682-1740.

Denmark: 3200 Whitehaven St NW, Washington, DC 20008, tel: 202-234-4300.

France: 4101 Reservoir Road NW, Washington, DC 20007, tel: 202-944-6000.

Germany: 4645 Reservoir Road NW, Washington, DC 20007, tel: 202-298-4000.

Great Britain: 3100 Massachusetts Ave NW, Washington, DC 20008, tel: 202-462-1340.

Greece: 2221 Massachusetts Ave NW, Washington, DC 20008, tel: 202-667-3168.

India: 2536 Massachusetts Ave NW, Washington, DC 20008, tel: 202-939-7000.

Israel: 3514 International Drive NW, Washington, DC 20008, tel: 202-364-5500.

Italy: 1601 Fuller St NW, Washington, DC 20009, tel: 202-328-5500.

Japan: 2520 Massachusetts Ave NW, Washington, DC 20008, tel: 202-939-6700.

Mexico: 1911 Pennsylvania Ave NW, Washington, DC 20006, tel: 202-728-1600.

Netherlands: 4200 Wisconsin Ave NW, Washington, DC 20016, tel: 202-244-5300.

New Zealand: 37 Observatory Circle NW, Washington, DC 20008, tel: 202-328-4800.

Norway: 2720 34th Street NW, Washington, DC 20008, tel: 202-333-6000.

Portugal: 2125 Kalorama Road NW, Washington, DC 20008, tel: 202-328-8610.

Singapore: 3501 International Place NW, Washington, DC 20008, tel: 202-537-3100.

South Korea: 2600 Virginia Ave NW, Washington, DC 20037, tel: 202-939-5600.

Spain: 2375 Pennsylvania Ave NW, Washington, DC 20037, tel: 202-452-0100.

Taiwan: 4201 Wisconsin Ave NW, Washington, DC 20016, tel: 202-895-1800.

NATIONAL PARKS & WILDERNESS AREAS

Arizona State Parks Office
1300 W. Washington
Phoenix, AZ 85007
Tel: 602-542-4174.
www.pr.state.az.us

Arizona Public Lands Information Center
Bureau of Land Management
222 N. Central Avenue
Phoenix, AZ 85004
Tel: 602-417-9200.
azwww.az.blm.gov/azso.htm

National Forest Service
Southwest Regional Office
517 Gold Avenue SW
Albuquerque, NM 87102
Tel: 505-842-3292.
www.fs.fed.us

National Park Service
3115 N. 3rd Avenue, Suite 101
Phoenix, AZ 85013
Tel: 602-640-5250.
www.nps.gov

Security & Crime

Emergency (police/fire): **911**

A few common-sense precautions will help keep you safe while traveling in Arizona. For starters, know where you are and where you're going. Whether traveling on foot or by car, bring a map and plan your route in advance. Don't be shy about asking for directions. Most people are happy to help.

Don't carry large sums of cash or wear flashy or expensive jewelry. Lock unattended cars and keep your belongings in the trunk. If possible, travel with a companion, especially after dark.

If involved in a traffic accident, remain at the scene. It is illegal to leave the scene of an accident. Find a nearby telephone or ask a passing motorist to call the police, then wait for emergency vehicles to arrive.

Driving under the influence of alcohol carries stiff penalities, including fines and jail. Wearing seatbelts is required. Children under four must be in a child's safety seat.

Sierra Vista Convention and Visitors Bureau
21 E. Wilcox Drive
Sierra Vista, AZ 85635
Tel: 520-417-6960.

Sonoita Chamber of Commerce
P.O. Box 607
Sonoita, AZ 85637
Tel: 520-455-5498.

Tempe Convention and Visitors Bureau
51 W. 3rd Street, Suite 105
Tempe, AZ 85281
Tel: 480-894-8158.

Tombstone Office of Tourism
P.O. Box 917
Tombstone, AZ 85638
Tel: 520-457-3929.

Tonto Basin Chamber of Commerce
P.O. Box 687
Tonto Basin, AZ 85553
Tel: 800-404-8923.

Tubac Chamber of Commerce
P.O. Box 1866
Tubac, AZ 85646
Tel: 520-398-2704.

Tucson Convention and Visitors Bureau
110 S. Church Ave. #7199
Tucson, AZ 85701
Tel: 520-624-1817 or toll free 800-638-8350.
www.visittucson.org

Williams–Grand Canyon Chamber of Commerce
200 W. Railroad Avenue
Williams, AZ 86046
Tel: 928-635-4061.
www.williamschamber.com

Yuma Chamber of Commerce
377 S. Main Street, Suite 101
Yuma, AZ 85364
Tel: 928-782-2567
www.yumachamber.org

Where to Stay

Arizona offers a great variety of accommodations, ranging from rustic cabins with little in the way of amenities to some of the most extravagant resorts in the country. Some places – inexpensive chain motels, for example – are suitable for a single night on the road. Others such as golf resorts and dude ranches are destinations in and of themselves and offer enough diversions to keep guests busy for a lengthy visit. It's always advisable to make reservations well in advance for the high season – winter in the southern deserts and summer in the high country. Travelers in search of a bargain will find hefty off-season discounts.

Chain motels. Chains are reliable and convenient but tend to lack unique character. You can usually depend on a clean, comfortable room for a reasonable cost. In general, prices range from $50 to $150 depending on location and additional amenities such as a pool, exercise room and restaurant.

Moderate to Expensive

Best Western	800-528-1234
Hilton	800-HILTONS
Holiday Inn	800-HOLIDAY
Hyatt	800-228-9000
Sheraton	800-325-3535
La Quinta	800-531-5900
Marriott	800-228-9290
Radisson	800-333-3333
Ramada	800-2-RAMADA
Westin	800-228-3000

Budget

Comfort Inn	800-228-5150
Days Inn	800-325-2525
Econo Lodge	800-553-2666
Howard Johnsons	800-654-2000
Motel 6	800-466-8356

Quality Inn	800-228-5151
Red Lion Inn	800-733-5466
Super 8	800-800-8000
Travelodge	800-578-7878

Hotels. Larger and generally more comfortable than motels, hotels are designed for upscale business travelers and tourists, and are usually situated in a central area with easy access to attractions and public transportation. Nearly all have at least one restaurant and bar and such amenities as a pool, a fitness center, meeting facilities, room service, a gift shop and an extensive lobby. Some such as Embassy Suites or Summerfield Suites offer one- or two-bedroom suites (some with kitchenettes) that are suited for long stays or families. Always look for new or newly renovated properties as these will be in the best condition and have the most up-to-date facilities.

Resorts. Arizona is justifiably renowned for its fine resorts. Luxury, relaxation and recreation are emphasized at these properties, most of which have large, sumptuous rooms, suites or casitas (Southwestern-style cottages), fine dining, extensive grounds with manicured desert landscaping, and such recreational facilities as golf courses, tennis courts and elaborate pools as well as health and beauty spas. A minimum stay of two or three nights is sometimes required.

Bed and breakfasts. B&Bs tend to be more homey and personal than hotels. In many cases, you're a guest at the innkeeper's home. Some are historic houses or inns decorated with antiques, quilts, art and various period furnishings; others offer simple but comfortable accommodations. Before booking, ask if rooms have telephones or televisions and whether bathrooms are private. Ask about breakfast, too. The meal is included in the price but may be anything from a few muffins to a multicourse feast. Guests may be served at a common table, a private table or in

their rooms. For more information contact:

Arizona Association of Bed and Breakfast Inns
P.O. Box 22086
Flagstaff, AZ 86002-2086
Tel: 800-284-2589
www.arizona-bed-breakfast.com

Guest ranches. Guest, or dude, ranches range from working cattle operations with basic lodging to full-fledged "resorts with horses" that have swimming pools, tennis courts and other amenities. Most ranches offer horseback riding lessons, guided pack trips, entertainment like rodeos, square dances and storytellers, and plenty of hearty food. If traveling with a family, be sure to ask about a children's program. For more information and an extensive list of dude ranches contact:
The Arizona Dude Ranch Association
P. O. Box 603
Cortaro, AZ 85652
www.azdra.com
Dude Ranchers Association
P.O. Box 471
LaPorte, CO 80535
Tel: 970-223-8440
www.duderanch.org
Guest Ranches of North America
www.guestranches.com

Lodging by Area

Hotels are listed in alphabetical order by region.

GRAND CANYON

Best Western Grand Canyon Squire Inn
Highway 64
Grand Canyon, AZ 86023
Tel: 928-638-2681 or toll free 800-622-6966
www.grandcanyonsquire.com
Larger and better appointed than most properties in the Best Western chain, this hotel – on a commercial strip just outside the national park – offers large rooms and a plethora of distractions, including a bowling alley, a game room and tennis courts. Amenities:

pool, restaurant, coffee shop, bar, exercise room, sauna, air conditioning, television. **$$–$$$**

Bright Angel Lodge & Cabins
W. Rim Drive
Grand Canyon, AZ 86023
Tel: 928-638-2631 or 303-297-2757 (reservations)
www.amfac.com
This rustic lodge, designed by Mary Colter in 1935, offers a variety of accommodations, ranging from dormitory-style rooms with shared baths to private cabins with canyon views. Creature comforts are simple, but the location and price make the lodge a good value. Reservations for the rim cabins should be made at least a year in advance. Amenities: restaurant, coffee shop, ice cream parlor. **$$**

El Tovar Hotel
Grand Canyon, AZ 86023
Tel: 928-638-2631 or 303-297-2757 (reservations)
www.amfac.com
This rustic lodge, built in 1905 of stone and Oregon pine, offers a level of luxury not found elsewhere on the South Rim. Standard rooms tend to be small, though deluxe rooms and suites (which have terraces with spectacular views) are quite commodious. The dining room serves the best food on the South Rim. The lobby, with mission-style furnishings, cathedral ceilings, a fireplace and assorted moose and antelope heads hanging from dark log walls, is worth seeing even if you're not spending the night. Amenities: restaurant, bar, gift shop, air conditioning, television. **$$$$**

Grand Canyon Lodge
Bright Angel Point, AZ 86052
Tel: 928-638-2611 or 303-297-2757 (reservations)
www.amfac.com
A log-and-limestone lodge with 50-foot (15-m) cathedral ceilings and a glass-walled sunroom overlooking the canyon is the centerpiece of this complex – the only lodging at the North Rim. A few motel-style rooms are available but lack the rustic charm of the small log cabins clustered around the main building. Cabins are available in four sizes,

Price Guide

Price categories are based on the average cost of a double room per night.

$	$50 or less
$$	$50–150
$$$	$150–250
$$$$	$250 or more

some better appointed than others. A few have canyon views but are usually booked a year or more in advance. The dining room is wrapped in windows, but the cuisine generally falls short of the setting. No matter. The views can't be beat. Be sure to make dinner reservations several weeks before your arrival. Amenities: restaurant, cafeteria, bar, gift shop. **$$**

Grand Hotel
P.O. Box 3319
Grand Canyon, AZ 86023
Tel: 928-638-3333 or toll free 888-634-7263
Large, comfortable rooms, an airy lobby with Western styling, and live entertainment are among the attractions of this new hotel on Highway 180/64 in Tusayan just outside the national park. Amenities: restaurant, bar, indoor pool, fitness room, air conditioning, television. **$$**

Maswik Lodge
Grand Canyon, AZ 86023
Tel: 303-297-2757 (reservations)
www.amfac.com
About 300 guest rooms and cabins are offered at this lodge, a 15-minute walk to the South Rim. The cabins tend to be a little rough around the edges. Ask for a room in Maswick North if you're concerned about comfort. Amenities: restaurant, bar, gift shop, phone, television. **$$**

Phantom Ranch
Tel: 928-638-2631 or 303-297-2757 (reservations)
www.amfac.com
The only lodging at the bottom of the Grand Canyon offers basic log-and-stone cabins and single-sex dormitories. Make reservations as early as possible (Amfac accepts bookings up to 23 months in

advance). Meals at the dining hall are served family-style and should be reserved ahead of time. Check the Bright Angel transportation desk (928-638-2631) for last-minute openings. Postcards mailed from here are carried out of the canyon by mule. Amenities: restaurant. **$–$$**

Quality Inn & Suites Grand Canyon
P.O. Box 520
Grand Canyon, AZ 86023
Tel: 928-638-2673 or toll free 800-221-2222
Next to the IMAX Theater in Tusayan, a short drive from the park entrance, this property is a cut above most chain hotels. The rooms are large and comfortably furnished, the public spaces are airy and well-maintained, and the suites are roomy enough for families. Amenities: restaurant, bar, outdoor pool, whirlpool, air conditioning, television. **$$–$$$**

Yavapai Lodge
Grand Canyon, AZ 86023
Tel: 303-297-2757 (reservations)
www.amfac.com
Situated back from the canyon near the South Rim visitor center, this lodge, built in the early 1970s, offers more than 350 motel-style rooms. Though the facility has little in the way of charm, accommodations are often available on fairly short notice. Rooms in Yavapai East are somewhat more expensive but have more space and better views. Amenities: cafeteria, gift shop. **$$**

PAGE AND THE ARIZONA STRIP

Best Western Arizona Inn
716 Rimview Drive
Page, AZ 86040
Tel: 520-645-2466 or toll free 800-826-2718
This modern motel about a mile from downtown Page has large rooms with queen-size beds and sweeping views of the desert. Amenities: outdoor pool, restaurant, bar, fitness room, air conditioning, television. **$$**

Canyon Colors Bed and Breakfast
225 South Navajo
Page, AZ 86040
Tel: 520-645-5979 or toll free 800-536-2530
canyon-country.com/colors
Guests enjoy cheery, contemporary bedrooms at this house in a quiet residential area of Page. All rooms have a queen bed, futon, private bath, fireplace, television, VCR and access to an extensive video library. A full breakfast is included in the rate. Amenities: pool, television, air conditioning. **$$**

Courtyard by Marriott
600 Clubhouse Drive
Page, AZ 86040
Tel: 928-645-5000 or toll free 800-851-3855
www.courtyard.com
This pleasant, Pueblo-style hotel offers comfortable, commodious lodging adjacent to the Lake Powell National Golf Course, one of the most scenic in the state. Amenities: restaurant, bar, laundry facilities, gift shop, outdoor pool, exercise room, air conditioning, television. **$$**

Jacob Lake Inn
Highway 67 and 89A
Jacob Lake, AZ 86022
Tel: 928-643-7232
www.jacoblake.com
The inn is a welcome hub of activity in this sprawling, lonely country. Basic cabins and motel units have seen better days, but the coffee shop is lively, the food is simple and filling, and the milkshakes are decadent. Amenities: restaurant, gift shop, gas station. **$$**

Kaibab Lodge
HC 64, Box 64
Fredonia, AZ 86022
Tel: 928-638-2389 or toll free 800-525-0924
Rooms at this mountain lodge, located on Highway 67 about 18 miles (29 km) from the North Rim of the Grand Canyon, are tucked away in rustic cabins at the edge of a meadow. The main lodge, built in the 1920s, has an airy lobby with log beams, a big fireplace, Adirondack-style furniture, and television room (there are no televisions in the guest rooms). Amenities: restaurant, gift shop. **$$**

Wahweap Lodge and Marina
100 Lakeshore Drive
Page, AZ 86040
Tel: 928-645-2433
www.visitlakepowell.com
This large, busy hotel is a hub for tourists exploring Lake Powell. All rooms have balconies or patios, but only about half overlook the lake. The Rainbow Room serves good American and Southwestern fare and has panoramic views of the lake. Rentals of powerboats, houseboats, and other watercraft are available. Amenities: two pools, snack bar, lounge, air conditioning, television. **$$–$$$**

NAVAJO AND HOPI RESERVATIONS

Cameron Trading Post Motel
U.S. 89
P.O. Box 339
Cameron, AZ 86020
Tel: 520-679-2231 or toll free 800-338-7385
www.camerontradingpost.com
The motel adjoins a busy trading post built in the early 20th century and still serving the Navajo Nation. Rooms are comfortable and attractive, but it's the trading post itself – and the treasures it contains – that are the real attraction. Amenities: restaurant, television, air conditioning. **$$**

Coyote Pass Hospitality
Route 12, Box 91B
Tsaile, AZ 86556
Tel: 520-724-3383 or toll free 800-258-3929
A genuine Navajo experience is had at Coyote Pass near Canyon de Chelly. Anywhere from one to 15 guests sleep in a dirt-floor hogan and are served a traditional Navajo

Price Guide

Price categories are based on the average cost of a double room per night.

$	$50 or less
$$	$50–150
$$$	$150–250
$$$$	$250 or more

breakfast. Guided hikes, nature programs and tours of Navajo sites are also available. **$$**

Goulding's Lodge
P.O. Box 360001
Monument Valley, UT 84536
Tel: 435-727-3231
www.gouldings.com
This former trading post – the only accommodations in Monument Valley – has more than 60 motel-style rooms with Southwestern decor and balconies. The restaurant serves solid American dishes and has spectacular views. The hotel can arrange horseback riding and backcountry tours with Navajo guides. Amenities: restaurant, gift shop, indoor pool, tour desk, air conditioning, television (with VCR and collection of films shot in Monument Valley). **$$**

Holiday Inn Kayenta
P.O. Box 307
Kayenta, AZ 86033
Tel: 928-697-3221 or toll free 800-465-4329
A busy place with large and well-kept, if predictable, lodging. The hotel is at the intersection of US 160 and 163 about 24 miles from Monument Valley Navajo Tribal Park. The restaurant serves American and Navajo fare. Amenities: restaurant, gift shop, outdoor pool, tour desk, air conditioning, television. **$$**

Hopi Cultural Center Inn
P.O. Box 67
Second Mesa, AZ 86043
Tel: 928-734-2401
The motel is nothing special, but it's the only lodging in the area. The restaurant serves a few Hopi specialties, including blue-corn pancakes and paper-thin piki bread. Amenities: restaurant, television. **$$**

Navajo Nation Inn
48 Highway 264
Window Rock, AZ 86515
Tel: 520-871-4108 or toll free 800-662-6189
Simple, comfortable motel located in the capital of the Navajo Nation. Indian tacos and other local fare are served in the dining room. Amenities: restaurant, air conditioning, television. **$$**

Thunderbird Lodge
P.O. Box 548
Chinle, AZ 86503
Tel: 928-674-5841 or toll free 800-679-2473
Fax: 928-674-5844
www.tbirdlodge.com
Well-maintained accommodations set on shady grounds near the visitor center at Canyon de Chelly National Monument. Amenities: cafeteria, Jeep tours, gift shop, air conditioning, television. **$$**

FLAGSTAFF AND ENVIRONS

Fray Marcos Hotel
235 N. Grand Canyon Boulevard
Williams, AZ 86046
Tel: 928-635-4010 or toll free 800-843-8724
A reconstruction of the original 1908 Fray Marcos, this new 89-room hotel at the historic depot mixes turn-of-the-century ambiance with convenience. The Western-style lobby celebrates the art of Frederic Remington; a saloon features a player piano and a beautifully carved bar from a London pub. Amenities: restaurant, bar, air conditioning, television. **$$**
Hilton Garden Inn Flagstaff
350 W. Forest Meadows Street
Flagstaff, AZ 86001
Tel: 928-226-8888
Set along a busy commercial strip a few minutes from downtown Flagstaff, this property – one of the newer hotels in town – delivers what one expects of the Hilton chain: efficient, contemporary lodging with few surprises. Amenities: pool, fitness room, whirlpool, air conditioning, television. **$$**
Hotel Monte Vista
100 N. San Francisco Street
Flagstaff, AZ 86001
Tel: 928-779-6971 or toll free 800-545-3068
Dark and a bit threadbare, this downtown landmark, opened in 1927, was once a favorite of celebrity guests such as John Wayne, Clark Gable and Spencer Tracy. You can still find some old-time charm here, but the hotel is best suited for students, backpackers and other budget travelers. Some rooms have shared baths. Amenities: restaurant, bar, television. **$**

The Inn at 410
410 N. Leroux Street
Flagstaff, AZ 86001
Tel: 928-774-0088 or toll free 800-774-2008
www.inn410.com
This handsome woodframe bed and breakfast set on a quiet downtown lot offers nine rooms and suites beautifully decorated in styles ranging from Old West and Victorian to French Country, some with fireplace and Jacuzzi. An inviting living and dining room, big front porch and backyard garden give guests plenty of room to roam. Breakfasts are bountiful and expertly prepared. **$$–$$$**
La Posada
303 E. 2nd Street (Route 66)
Winslow, AZ 86047
Tel: 928-289-4366
Designed in the late 1920s by Mary Colter, who considered it her masterpiece, this rambling Hacienda-style hotel was only open for 27 years before it was closed and later gutted. Restoration began in 1997, and the hotel now offers more than 20 guest rooms furnished in the spare but elegant style of the period and named after such famous guests as Bob Hope, Carol Lombard and Howard Hughes. The hotel's grand public spaces, with their heavy beams and vaulted ceilings, have been faithfully restored using Colter's original plans. This is a fascinating historic site and a good value. Amenities: restaurant, bar, television. **$$**
Radisson Woodlands Hotel Flagstaff
1175 W. Route 66
Flagstaff, AZ 86001
Tel: 928-773-8888 or toll free 800-333-3333
www.radisson.com
A lobby with Italian marble floors, granite architectural details, and plush European-style furnishings set the tone of this hotel, among the most sumptuous in town. Accommodations are roomy and tasteful. A Japanese restaurant and sushi bar are a pleasant surprise. Amenities: two restaurants, outdoor pool, fitness center, air conditioning, television. **$$**

ARIZONA'S WEST COAST

Havasu Springs Resort
2581 Highway 95
Parker, AZ 85344
Tel: 928-667-3361
The resort encompasses three motels about 20 miles south of Lake Havasu City, but the real attraction is houseboat rentals. The vessels sleep up to 12 people and have various features, but all are equipped with bathrooms and complete galleys. **$$$–$$$$**
London Bridge Resort
1477 Queens Bay
Lake Havasu City, AZ 86403
Tel: 888-587-0846
Part Tudor mansion, part Southwestern oasis and part tropical getaway, the resort is popular with the party crowd who come more for the pools, water sports and open-air nightclub than the large condominium-style guest quarters. Tennis courts and a golf course are on the premises, and the London Bridge is in the backyard. Expect a glut of revelers during spring break. Amenities: restaurant, nightclub, three pools, tennis courts, golf course, marina, boat rentals, air conditioning, television. **$$–$$$$**
Shiloh Inn
1550 S. Castle Dome Avenue
Yuma, AZ 85365
Tel: 928-782-9511 or toll free 800-222-2244
Spacious rooms with couches, microwaves, refrigerators and patios or balconies are among the most comfortable in Yuma, and the well-maintained lawn is a welcome patch of green in an otherwise stark landscape. Suites with kitchenettes are also available. Amenities: pool, restaurant, bar, exercise room, television, air conditioning. **$$–$$$**
Temple Bar Resort
Temple Bar, AZ 86643
Tel: 928-767-3211 or toll free 800-752-9669

This 18-unit motel is set on the shore of Lake Mead surrounded by miles of open desert. A variety of watercraft, including ski boats, patio boats, fishing boats and jet skis, are available to rent at a fully equipped marina. Amenities: restaurant, marina, RV facilities, television, air conditioning. **$$**

SEDONA AND THE VERDE VALLEY

Briar Patch Inn
3190 N. Highway 89A
Sedona, AZ 86336
Tel: 928-282-2342 or toll free 888-809-3030
www.briarpatchinn.com
Set on the shady banks of Oak Creek a few miles north of Sedona, the inn offers cozy cabins with stone and wood-panel walls, rustic Western-style furnishings, and Indian rugs; some cabins have decks and fireplaces. Breakfast is served on a terrace overlooking the creek, often to the strains of live classical musicians. Massages and a variety of New Age programs are also available. Amenities: complimentary breakfast, swimming in the creek. **$$$–$$$$**
Cathedral Rock Lodge & Retreat Center
61 Los Amigos Lane
Sedona, AZ 86336
Tel: 928-282-7608 or toll free 800-352-9149
www.cathedralrocklodge.com
The lodge has three separate areas ideal for large groups or families: a suite, a cottage, and a 2-bedroom house, with views of gardens or Sedona's red-rock scenery. Amenities: television, VCR. **$$**
Enchantment Resort
525 Boynton Canyon Road
Sedona, AZ 86336
Tel: 928-282-2900 or toll free 800-826-4180
www.enchantmentresort.com
A glorious Boynton Canyon location with luxurious accommodations. Pueblo-style casitas have single rooms as well as one- and two-bedroom suites, many with living rooms, fireplaces and patios. All are

decorated in a contemporary Southwestern style, and the views are universally smashing. The Yavapai Dining Room specializes in fine Southwestern and Continental cuisine and has panoramic views of the canyon. A second restaurant, Tii Gavo, offers a more casual atmosphere. A spa with a wide range of facilities and services is also on the grounds. Amenities: four pools, two restaurants, full-service spa, fitness center, pitch and putt golf course, nature walks, mountain bike rentals, tennis courts, meeting facilities, children's program, air conditioning, television. **$$$–$$$$**
Horseshoe Ranch
HCR 34, Box 5005
Mayer, AZ 86333
Tel: 928-632-8813
www.cowboys.com/horseshoeranch
One of Arizona's oldest and most hospitable working ranches, the 100-square-mile (260,00-sq-km) Horseshoe is located at an elevation of 3,200 feet (975 m) on the Agua Fria River, 42 miles (68 km) from Prescott. Guests rise early to help hired hands with the ranch's 1,700 cattle. The Horseshoe has eight large, tastefully decorated rooms. A three-day minimum stay is required. **$$$**

MOGOLLON RIM AND TONTO BASIN

Grey Hackle Lodge
HC 2, Box 145
Payson, AZ 85541
Tel: 928-478-4392
www.greyhacklelodge.com
Eleven log cabins are set on 4 acres (1.6 hectares) just east of Payson. Some are one-room cabins with kitchenettes; others are two-story cabins with full kitchens and fireplaces. Furnishings are simple, but the cabins are clean and well-maintained. Amenities: private bath, television. **$$**
Majestic Mountain Inn
602 E. Highway 260
Payson, AZ 85541
Tel: 928-474-0185 or toll free 800-408-2442
www.majesticmountaininn.com

Regular rooms at this attractive stone-and-timber lodge in Payson have the style and comfort of a standard motel unit. If you're looking for something more comfortable, the luxury rooms are larger and have a Jacuzzi and gas fireplace. Amenities: pool, meeting facilities, television, air conditioning. **$$**
Kohl's Ranch Lodge
Highway 260
Payson, AZ 85541
Tel: 928-478-4211 or toll free 800-521-3131
www.ilxresorts.com
The lodge is set on Tonto Creek in the ponderosa forest east of Payson. Cabins are quite roomy, with dining areas, kitchenettes, patios and fireplaces. Rooms in the main lodge are somewhat more modest, though several also have fireplaces. All are furnished in contemporary Western style. Amenities: restaurant, cowboy bar, outdoor pool, horseback riding, mountain bike rentals, exercise room, putting green, playground, television, air conditioning. **$$–$$$**
Mountain Meadows Cabins
HC 2, Box 162E
Payson, AZ 85541
Tel: 928-478-4415
www.mountainmeadowscabins.com
Six cabins are situated east of Payson under the Mogollon Rim at an elevation of 6,400 feet (1,950 m). Each has a private bath, kitchen and fireplace. Most of the land surrounding the cabins is part of a national forest. Amenities: kitchen, television, VCR, barbecue grill. **$$**

WHITE MOUNTAINS

White Mountain Lodge
140 Main Street
P.O. Box 143
Greer, AZ 85927
Tel: 928-735-7568 or toll free 888-493-7568
www.wmlodge.com
Set in an 1892 log home overlooking Greer Meadow and the Little Colorado River, this welcoming

high-country bed and breakfast has seven rooms with rustic Mission-style furnishings as well as cabins with kitchens and fireplaces or wood-burning stoves; some cabins also have whirlpool tubs. A large family-style breakfast is served; there's a two-night minimum stay. **$$–$$$**

Molly Butler Lodge
P.O. Box 134
Greer, AZ 85927
Tel: 928-735-7226
The first lodging in Greer (1910) – run by Mormon pioneers Molly and John Butler – is rather run-down now but still a lively place for a fish fry, steak and beer on a Friday night. Guest rooms are furnished in a simple country style. **$**

Spanish Trails Bed and Breakfast
1111 Spanish Trails
P.O. Box 1922
Eagar, AZ 85925
Tel: 928-333-4034
www.wmonline.com/spanishtrails
Ornate furnishings in a variety of styles characterize the decor in the guest rooms and public spaces of this bed and breakfast, set in a modern residence on five acres (2 hectares) near Eagar. Even if you don't stay here, it's worth eating at the Bistro, which specializes in French cuisine (try the tarts and cheesecakes) served in the entry courtyard. **$$**

PHOENIX

Arizona Biltmore Resort & Spa
24th Street and Missouri Avenue
Phoenix, AZ 85016
Tel: 602-955-6600 or toll free 800-950-0086
Fax: 602-954-2571
www.arizonabiltmore.com
This elegant grand hotel inspired by Frank Lloyd Wright (who acted as consultant on the project) is the last word in grace, dignity and architectural distinction and a favorite among celebrities and other high-profile guests. Amenities: Two 18-hole golf courses, full-service spa, fine dining in two restaurants, bars, five swimming pools, fitness center, biking, shops, business

center, air conditioning, television, valet parking. **$$$$**

Desert Rose
3424 E. Van Buren Street
Phoenix, AZ 8500
Tel: 602-275-4421
A modest but comfortable small hotel a short drive from downtown. Amenities: pool, restaurant, air conditioning, television. **$**

Doubletree La Posada Resort
4949 E. Lincoln Drive
Scottsdale, AZ 85253
Tel: 480-952-0420 or toll free 800-222-8733
Large, plush rooms, two golf courses, a full-service spa, tennis courts and many other amenities delight vacationers at this resort. But the real attraction is the pool, a million-gallon fantasia with artificial boulders, a swim-through grotto, a cascading waterfall and great views of Camelback Mountain. Dining options range from fine American cuisine and healthy nouvelle dishes to a snack bar and café. Amenities: three pools, two golf courses, tennis courts, sand volleyball court, two restaurants, bar, café, full-service spa, room service, children's program, air conditioning, television. **$$–$$$$**

Embassy Suites Phoenix Airport
1515 N. 44th Street
Phoenix, AZ 85008
Tel: 602-244-8800 or toll free 800-447-8483
Just minutes from Sky Harbor Airport, this all-suites hotel offers spacious accommodations with separate bedrooms and living rooms and substantial contemporary furnishings. The high-rise surrounds a central courtyard with an outdoor pool. A good choice for business travelers who need extra room or families with small

children. Amenities: restaurant, bar, pool, exercise room, meeting facilities, airport shuttle, air conditioning, television. **$$–$$$**

Fairmont Scottsdale Princess
7575 E. Princess Drive
Scottsdale, AZ 85255
Tel: 480-585-4848
Fax: 480-585-0086
www.fairmont.com
This luxurious resort sprawls over 450 acres (180 hectares) at the base of the McDowell Mountains north of Scottsdale. Spanish Colonial architecture, antique furnishings, fountains, generous patios and immaculate landscaping create a rich and exotic ambiance. Spacious rooms and casitas are decorated in muted desert tones, with fine Southwestern furnishings, large bathrooms and terraces. Restaurants serve splendid Spanish and Mexican cuisine. Amenities: Restaurants, bars, two golf courses, tennis courses, three pools, fitness center, spa services, shops, business center, meeting facilities, television, air conditioning. **$$$$**

Holiday Inn SunSpree Resort
7601 E. Indian Bend Road
Scottsdale, AZ 85250
Tel: 480-9912400 or toll free 800-852-5205
Recently renovated, this 200-unit hotel offers many of the attractions of a resort at a price that families will find attractive. Set on 16 acres (7 hectares) of landscaped grounds in the heart of Scottsdale, the property encompasses an 18-hole golf course, tennis courts and heated pool. The restaurant has a view of the lake; special deals for kids ease pressure on your budget. Amenities: restaurant, bar, golf course, pool, fitness center, tennis courts, meeting facilities, children's program, television, air conditioning. **$$–$$$**

Maricopa Manor
15 W. Pasadena Avenue
Phoenix, AZ 85013
Tel: 602-274-6302 or toll free 800-292-6403
www.maricopamanor.com
When it was built in 1928, this Hacienda-style manor was in the

countryside outside town. Now it's in the heart of the city, a block from the busy Camelback Corridor. An acre of landscaped grounds shelter the property from the surrounding bustle. All rooms are suites with plush, mostly contemporary furnishings. Four luxury suites have fireplaces and whirlpool tubs. Amenities: pool, air conditioning, television, gardens, complimentary breakfast. **$$–$$$**

The Phoenician
600 E. Camelback Road
Scottsdale, AZ 85251
Tel: 480-941-8200 or toll free 800-888-8234
www.thephoenician.com
No extravagance is overlooked at this landmark resort at the base of Camelback Mountain. Guest rooms, suites and casitas are lavishly furnished, with marble bathrooms, patios, Italian linens and original art; some have travertine fireplaces. The grounds and public spaces are equally elaborate. The resort's 250 acres (100 hectares) encompass a world-class 27-hole golf course, nine pools (including a 165-foot/50-m water slide), manicured gardens, 11 tennis courts, a full-service spa, and an extensive art collection. The 11 restaurants and lounges range from Mary Elaine's, perhaps the finest French cuisine in the state, and the Praying Monk, set in a wine cellar with barrel-vaulted ceilings, brick archways and European antiques, to casual outdoor dining and an ice-cream parlor. All this luxury doesn't come cheap, though you may be surprised at just how affordable a standard room can be during the sweltering off-season. Amenities: several restaurants and bars, nine pools, tennis courts, 27-hole golf course, full-service spa, bike rentals, gift shops, children's program, meeting facilities, air conditioning, television. **$$$–$$$$**

Pointe Hilton Squaw Peak Resort
7677 N. 16th Street
Phoenix, AZ 85020
Tel: 602-997-2626 or toll free 800-876-4683
With an elaborate water park and extensive children's program, this

Price Guide

Price categories are based on the average cost of a double room per night.

$	$50 or less
$$	$50–150
$$$	$150–250
$$$$	$250 or more

luxury resort is a hit with kids. Guest quarters are mostly two-room suites furnished in contemporary style with a few Spanish Colonial touches. Adults may prefer to avail themselves of the 18-hole golf course, full-service spa or four other pools. Jogging trails meander through immaculate grounds. Eight restaurants range from quick, casual eats to haute cuisine. Amenities: water park, pools, 18-hole golf course, tennis courts, full-service spa, shopping, restaurants, children's program, air conditioning, television. **$$$–$$$$**

Ritz-Carlton Phoenix
2401 E. Camelback Road
Phoenix, AZ 85016
Tel: 602-468-0700 or toll free 800-241-3333
Fax: 602-468-9883
www.ritzcarlton.com
This grand hotel across from the Biltmore Fashion Park shopping center offers impeccable service and elegant accommodations. Antique furnishings and paintings in public spaces lend an air of Old-World sophistication. Guest quarters are furnished with reproductions and have marble bathrooms. Amenities: pool, fitness center, restaurants, bar, air conditioning, television. **$$$–$$$$**

Royal Palms Hotel and Casitas
5200 E. Camelback Road
Phoenix, AZ 85018
Tel: 602-840-3610 or toll free 800-672-6011
Fax: 602-840-6927
www.royalpalmshotel.com
You'll feel as if you've wandered into a Mediterranean villa at this newly renovated hotel, built in the 1940s by Cunard Steamship executive Delos T. Cooke. Walled

courtyards with antique fountains, hidden gardens, antique European furnishings and beautifully restored architectural details create an atmosphere of romance and opulence. Each deluxe casita is designed in a distinctive style, ranging from Spanish Colonial to contemporary. Other rooms aren't quite so lavishly appointed. The restaurant, T. Cook's, is considered one of the finest in the city. Amenities: restaurant, bar, pool, tennis court, fitness room, air conditioning, television. **$$$$**

TUCSON

Adobe Rose Inn
940 N. Olsen Avenue
Tucson AZ 85719
Tel: 520-318-4644 or toll free 800-328-4122
Built in 1933 and enclosed by one-foot-thick pink adobe walls, this snug bed and breakfast is in a quiet residential neighborhood near the University of Arizona. Rooms and cottages are furnished in a rustic Southwestern style; one room has a beehive fireplace. A full breakfast is included. Amenities: pool, television, air conditioning. **$$**

Arizona Inn
2200 E. Elm Street
Tucson, AZ 85719
Tel: 520-325-1541 or toll free 800-933-1093
Fax: 520-325-1541
www.arizonainn.com
Guest rooms and suites with patios and fireplaces are set on 14 acres (6 hectares) of manicured grounds and gardens. Understated, elegant lodging only five minutes from the University of Arizona. Amenities: outdoor pool, tennis courts, massage, exercise room, fine dining, bar, air conditioning, television. **$$$**

Clarion Hotel Randolph Park
102 N. Alvernon Way
Tucson, AZ 85711
Tel: 520-795-0330
This comfortable chain hotel is within walking distance of shopping malls, theaters and restaurants. The room rate includes a breakfast

buffet. Amenities: whirlpool, in-room microwave, laundry service, air conditioning, television. **$$–$$$**

El Presidio Bed and Breakfast
297 N. Main Avenue
Tucson, AZ 85701
Tel: 520-623-6151
Since 1985, innkeeper Patti Toci has run an elegant bed and breakfast in the 1886 Julius Kruttschnitt House, part of downtown's El Presidio Historic District. Four comfortable suites (two with private entrances) are furnished with antiques. All have telephones, televisions, complimentary beverages, fruit and snacks. Guests enjoy a full gourmet breakfast around a single table in the sunny veranda room, which looks out onto a restful flowered courtyard with fountain. Awarded Best B&B in Southern Arizona in 1998; two-night minimum. **$$–$$$**

Elysian Grove Market
400 W. Simpson
Tucson, AZ 85701
Tel: 520-628-1522
www.bbonline.com/az/elysiangrove
Connoisseurs of the unusual will be delighted by this adobe bed and breakfast, set in a converted grocery store in the Historic Barrio district. The four guest rooms are furnished with Mexican antiques and folk art. Two bedrooms are in the old wine cellar, the other two open to the garden. The meat locker now serves as a kitchen. **$$**

Hotel Congress
311 E. Congress
Tucson, AZ 85701
Tel: 520-622-8848 or toll free 800-722-8848
www.hotcong.com
John Dillinger and his gang stayed at this quirky 1919 hotel near the Amtrak station, though the clienetele nowadays is mostly young backpackers and budget travelers. Rooms offer basic comforts, but the place has some interesting touches such as old-fashioned radios and telephones and an Internet café and a lively saloon. Idiosyncratic and inexpensive. Private and shared hostel rooms are available. Amenities: café, bar, nightclub. **$**

Lazy K Bar Guest Ranch
8401 N. Scenic Drive
Tucson, AZ 85743
Tel: 520-744-3050 or toll free 800-321-7018
The ranch's nine adobe cabins are set in the Tucson Mountains overlooking the Santa Cruz Valley, about 16 miles (26 km) northwest of Tucson. Recreational opportunities abound, with an extensive riding program, heated pool, spa, tennis courts, square-dancing lessons, live entertainment and cookouts. A three-night minimum stay is required. Amenities: meals, pool, hot tub, tennis, volleyball and basketball courts, ranch store, meeting facilities, air conditioning. **$$$–$$$$**

Lodge on the Desert
306 N. Alvernon Way
Tucson, AZ 85711
Tel: 520-325-3366 or toll free 800-456-5634
www.lodgeonthedesert.com
Built in 1936 and thoroughly renovated, this in-town resort consists of a compound of casitas amid well-tended gardens, cacti and shady palms, with views of the Santa Catalina Mountains. Most rooms have red tiled patios and fireplaces; some have tile floors and exposed beams. A restaurant, Cielos, is highly regarded. Amenities: pool, restaurant, air conditioning, television. **$$–$$$**

Loews Ventana Canyon Resort
7000 N. Resort Drive
Tucson, AZ 85750
Tel: 520-299-2020 or toll free 800-234-5117
www.loewshotels
Tucson's premier resort is an island of luxury and comfort in the desert outside the city. Rooms are large and beautifully furnished, each with a private balcony overlooking the city or Santa Catalina Mountains. The design of public spaces, including terraces, meeting rooms, restaurants and the lobby, feature an understated elegance in keeping with the desert setting. Diversions range from two world-class 18-hole golf course, a complete spa, and one of the best restaurants in

Tucson. Amenities: two pools, 8 tennis courts, golf courses, spa services, fitness center, meeting facilities, restaurants and lounges, shops, bike rentals, air conditioning, television. **$$$$**

Omni Tucson National Golf Resort and Spa
2727 W. Club Drive
Tucson, AZ 85742
Tel: 520-297-2271 or toll free 800-528-4856
www.omnihotels.com
Golfers will think they have died and gone to heaven at this luxury resort in the foothills of the Santa Catalina Mountains, home of the annual PGA Tucson Open golf tournament. Rooms and suites are very large and furnished in contemporary style, some with fireplaces and/or kitchenettes, many with patios or balconies. The real attraction, however, is the 27-hole golf course, one of the most beautiful and challenging in the region. Non-golfers can have themselves pampered at the full-service spa or lounge by one of two pools. Two restaurants serve American and Southwestern cuisine. Amenities: golf course, two pools, tennis courts, basketball courts, full-service spa, fitness center, nature trails, lounges, air conditioning, television. **$$$–$$$$**

Sunstone Guest Ranch
2545 N. Woodland Road
Tucson, AZ 85749
Tel: 520-749-1928
Expansive lawns and shady mesquite trees surround adobe casitas at this bed and breakfast, a short drive from downtown Tucson. Guest rooms are large and furnished in Southwestern style; all have private baths. Although it's not a real ranch in the sense that it offers horseback riding, the property has a secluded country feeling without being too far from city attractions. Amenities: pool, tennis court, meeting facilities, air conditioning, complimentary breakfast. **$$**

Tanque Verde Guest Ranch,
14301 E. Speedway Boulevard
Tucson, AZ 85748
Tel: 520-296-6275 or toll free 800-234-3833
www.tanqueverderanch.com

More of a resort than a ranch, Tanque Verde is sandwiched between Saguaro National Park and Coronado National Forest at the base of the Rincon Mountains. More than 70 rooms and suites are simple and comfortable; many have fireplaces and/or patios. Casitas are large and sumptuous. The ranch is a destination in itself, and there's never a dull moment. Activities include trail rides, complimentary tennis lessons, nature hikes, lectures, live entertainment and bountiful meals and cookouts. Amenities: indoor and outdoor pools, horseback riding and lessons, tennis courts, fitness room, basketball and volleyball courts, children's program, airport shuttle, air conditioning, all meals included. **$$$$**

Westward Look Resort
245 E. Ina Road
Tucson, AZ 85704
Tel: 520-297-1151 or toll free 800-722-2500
www.westwardlook.com
This elegant ranch resort was built around a 1912 hacienda on 80 acres (32 hectares) in the Santa Catalina foothills. More than 200 guest rooms are all suite-sized, furnished in luxurious Southwestern style, and grouped in graceful casitas that ensure complete privacy. Opportunities for recreation and relaxation are numerous; facilities include three pools and whirlpools, a fitness center, spa, Celestron 2000 telescope for stargazing, hiking on the resort's own nature trails, horseback riding, mountain biking, and strolls through a variety of gardens. A fine restaurant, the Gold Room, overlooks the city and features innovative Western cuisine by an award-winning chef using produce grown on the property. Amenities: pools, fitness center, full-service spa, tennis courts, hiking trails, meeting facilities, air conditioning, television. **$$$–$$$$**

White Stallion Ranch
9251 W. Twin Peaks Road
Tucson, AZ 85743
Tel: 520-297-0252 or toll free 888-977-2624
www.wsranch.com

Guests get an authentic taste of the Old West at this working cattle ranch on 3,000 acres (1,200 hectares) bordering Saguaro National Park. Accommodations range from snug, stripped-down single rooms to larger and more comfortable two-bedroom suites with living rooms. The emphasis is on horseback riding, but a variety of other activities, including nature hikes, tennis, swimming, hayrides, cookouts, and a weekly rodeo, provide plenty of other diversions. Kids enjoy the petting zoo. Meals are served family style in the dining room. Amenities: horse stables and riding lessons, children's program, outdoor pool, tennis courts, petting zoo, nature trails, hayrides, cookouts. All meals included. **$$$$**

BORDER COUNTRY

Beatty's Miller Guest Ranch and Orchard
2173 E. Miller Canyon Road
Hereford, AZ 85615
Tel: 520-378-2728
personal.riverusers.com/~beattybb
This retreat occupies an apple orchard adjacent to the Miller Peak Wilderness Area. Accommodations include two apartments and one cabin, each with a bedroom, sitting room and full kitchen. Visitors have access to the hummingbird and butterfly gardens. This is a great place for serious birders. **$$**

Bisbee Grand Hotel
61 Main Street
Bisbee, AZ 85603
Tel: 520-432-5900
An elegantly restored Victorian bed and breakfast with period decor. A saloon on the first floor evokes an Old West atmosphere, and the

theme is carried through 13 guest rooms upstairs. In some cases, private bathrooms are located down the hall. Amenities: saloon, billiard room, free breakfast. No in-room telephones or televisions. **$$**

Circle Z Ranch
P.O. Box 194
Patagonia, AZ 85624
Tel: 520-394-2525 or toll free 888-854-2525
www.circlez.com
Accommodations range from individual rooms to suites or private cottages in several adobe buildings at the foot of the Santa Rita Mountains about 60 miles (100 km) south of Tucson. The main activities are horseback riding, pack trips and birding at the adjoining Nature Conservancy preserve. There is a three-day minimum stay. **$$**

Cochise Hotel
P.O. Box 27
Cochise, AZ 85606
Tel: 520-384-3156 or 384-3414
The one-story Cochise, built in 1882 to serve railroad workers, is still going strong, though it's a bit faded. The hotel has five guest rooms with private baths and period furniture, and maintains a studied austerity. Reservations must be made at least one week in advance. **$–$$**

Copper Queen Hotel
11 Howell Avenue
Bisbee, AZ 85603
Tel: 520-432-2216
This turn-of-the-century landmark built during the heyday of the Copper Queen Mine drips with Old West atmosphere; guests have included John Wayne and Teddy Roosevelt. Rooms vary in size, are furnished with antiques, and most but not all have been recently renovated. Amenities: restaurant, saloon, pool, television, air conditioning. **$$**

Inn at Castle Rock Bed and Breakfast
112 Tombstone Canyon Road
P.O. Box 1161
Bisbee, AZ 85603
Tel: 520-432-4449
www.theinn.org
This old two-story Victorian boardinghouse is a down-home,

granny's-attic kind of place. Rooms are small but very authentic, and the location is advantageous for exploring Old Bisbee. Overall the place is a bit funky, but where else will you find a flooded mineshaft in the center of the breakfast room? **$$–$$$**

Portal Peak Lodge
P.O. Box 364
Portal, AZ 85632
Tel: 520-558-2223
Just south of Chiricahua National Monument, the lodge's 16 rooms are attractively furnished in Southwestern style. Rooms open to a long deck, with magnificent views of the mountains. A restaurant, grocery store and gift shop are on the premises. **$$**

Ramsey Canyon Inn Bed and Breakfast
27 Ramsey Canyon Road
Hereford, AZ 85615
Tel: 520-378-3010
This stone inn, managed by the Nature Conservancy, is adjacent to the Conservancy's 380-acre (155-hectare) Ramsey Canyon Preserve. The bed and breakfast has six guest rooms, each with a private bath; two apartments have kitchens. A gourmet breakfast is included in the rate. Naturalists lead walks along Ramsey Creek into the Huachuca Mountains for some of the West's best bird-watching. Guests have after-hours access to the preserve and are welcome to enjoy the library, great room and fireplace. There is a three-night minimum stay in the apartments and a two-night minimum in the inn. **$$**

San Pedro Bed and Breakfast
3123 Thistle Road
Sierra Vista, AZ 85636
Tel: 520-458-6412
This bed and breakfast is set on 5 acres (2 hectares) in the San Pedro Riparian National Conservation Area. A suite in the ranch house has a sitting room, refrigerator and balcony. A separate guest house offers a room with refrigerator. Guests are treated to a full Southwestern-style breakfast. **$$**

San Pedro River Inn
8326 S. Hereford Road
Hereford, AZ 85615

Tel: 520-366-5532
www.sanpedroriverinn.com
Four adobe guest houses are spread out on the inn's 20 acres (8 hectares), where cottonwood trees attract a variety of birds. Each adobe has a living room, kitchen and private bath; two- and three-bedroom units are also available. A continental breakfast is served. The San Pedro Riparian National Conservation Area is a five-minute walk away. **$$**

Schoolhouse Inn
818 Tombstone Canyon
Bisbee, AZ 85603
Tel: 520-432-2996 or toll free 800-537-4333
www.bestinns.net/usa/az/school
Guests stay in a 1918 brick schoolhouse at the west end of Tombstone Canyon. Themed suites, which have 12-foot (4-m) ceilings, include the Principal's Office and Art, Reading and Writing rooms. Three-room suites are available. Amenities: full breakfast included in rate, cable television in common room. **$$**

Tombstone Boarding House Bed and Breakfast
108 N. 4th Street, Box 906
Tombstone, AZ 85638
Tel: 520-457-3716
Built in the 1880s and remodeled in the 1930s, this cluster of adobes occupies a quiet spot one block from town. Seven guest rooms, each with private bath, are furnished with antiques and collectibles associated with Tombstone's Old West history. A small, two-room miner's cabin has a private bath. **$$**

Vineyard Bed and Breakfast
92 S. Los Encinos Road
Sonoita, AZ 85637
Tel: 520-455-4749
Situated in the rolling wine country around Sonoita, the pink adobe Hacienda Los Encinos ("House of the Oaks), built in 1910, has been updated to include three suites in the main house and a charming Southwestern-style guest house. Amenities: full breakfast included in rate, stone fireplace in the living room, patio. **$$**

Camping

Most tent and RV sites in national and state parks and in national forests are available on a first-come, first-served basis, although increasingly campground space in popular parks is on a reservation basis. Campgrounds fill early during the summer season in the high country and winter in the southern deserts. Contact the parks for information on availability. Fees are usually charged for campsites. Backcountry permits may be required for wilderness hiking and camping.

There are hundreds of private campgrounds, too, some with swimming pools, RV hookups, showers and other facilities. The largest network is:

Kampgrounds of America (KOA)
P.O. Box 30558
Billings, MT 59114
Tel: 406-248-7444
www.koakampgrounds.com

Where to Eat

What to Eat

Southwestern cuisine is as varied and interesting as the land itself. A single dish may include a savory mix of red and green chile, yellow and blue cornmeal, a dark brown mound of beans with snowy sour cream, a pile of shredded lettuce, an improbably neon-green whip called guacamole with salty fried tortilla chips stuck in like banners, and a brightly colored salsa of red tomatoes, green chile, cilantro and white onions.

A couple of local customs to keep in mind: you may be asked by your waiter if you prefer red or green chile (green tends to be milder but it depends on the crop); and some traditional meals are served with sopapillas, a puffy fried dough eaten with honey. Southern Arizona is deeply influenced by the Sonoran tradition, which is known for ranch-style beef dishes such as *carne seca* – sun-dried beef simmered with onions and peppers.

In addition to the native dishes, large towns like Phoenix, Tucson and Flagstaff offer everything from pasta parlors to sushi bars. Many of

Price Guide

Price categories indicate the rough cost of dinner for one, excluding beverages, tax and tip. The standard tip is 15 percent, more for exceptional service or a large party. In some cases, the gratuity may be included in the bill.

$	$20 or less
$$	$20–40
$$$	$40–60
$$$$	$60 and up

the most interesting restaurants have built their reputations on blending Southwestern flavors with a variety of international cuisines. Still, it's hard to go wrong with the traditional repertoire: enchiladas, tacos, burritos, flautas, chile rellenos, posole, guacamole and lots of red-hot chile.

Restaurants by Area

GRAND CANYON

Arizona Steakhouse
Bright Angel Lodge
Grand Canyon, AZ
Tel: 928-638-2631
The service is generally slow and the chefs rarely distinguish themselves, but views from the lodge are stunning and on the South Rim, where options are few, this isn't a bad choice. The menu concentrates on steak and grilled chicken and fish. The simpler dishes are the best. Reservations are not accepted so arrive early. **$–$$**

Bright Angel Restaurant
Bright Angel Lodge
Grand Canyon, AZ
Tel: 928-638-2631
Diner food – indifferently prepared and served – is offered at this coffee shop. Expect familiar choices – burgers, steaks, patty melts, spaghetti, and chile. As always, simpler is usually better. Stick with burger and fries. **$**

El Tovar Restaurant
El Tovar Lodge
Grand Canyon, AZ
Tel: 928-638-2631
As good as it gets on the South Rim, which is to say not fantastic but not bad. The rustic dining room is fetching, with pine walls and Indian murals, but the food, which leans toward Continental dishes laced with Southwestern accents, falls short. Views are wonderful from the few tables near the windows. Otherwise, you'll have to be content studying the lodge interior, which really is quite remarkable. Make dinner reservations weeks in advance. **$$–$$$**

Maswick and Yavapai Cafeterias
Maswick and Yavapai Lodges
Grand Canyon, AZ
Tel: 520-638-2631
You'll find no frills here, just cheap, fast, filling food. If you're famished after a day of hiking, these may be better choices than one of the fancier restaurants. **$**

Grand Canyon Lodge Dining Room
Grand Canyon Lodge
Bright Angel Point, AZ
Tel: 928-638-2611
The only full-fledged restaurant on the North Rim is set in a grand, window-wrapped room on the edge of the canyon. The menu is dominated by American and Continental dishes – prime rib, rosemary chicken, pasta in pesto sauce with asparagus, and the like. The food is not particularly memorable, and the service is inconsistent, but considering the remote and magnificent setting, there's little cause to complain. If possible, make dinner reservations many weeks in advance. **$$**

Grand Snack Shop
Grand Canyon Lodge
Bright Angel Point, AZ
Tel: 928-638-2611
A small cafeteria good for a quick, cheap bite when a meal at the dining room is just too daunting. **$**

PAGE AND THE ARIZONA STRIP

Butterfield Stage Co.
704 Rimview Drive
Page, AZ
Tel: 928-645-2467
Set on a bluff overlooking Lake Powell, the restaurant serves satisfying portions of straightforward American and Southwestern fare. No surprises, few disappointments. **$–$$**

Dos Amigos
608D Elm Street
Page, AZ
Tel: 928-645-3036
There's nothing fancy here, just simple, belly-filling Mexican and American meals offered in an inviting, family-friendly setting. **$**

Jacob Lake Inn
Highway 67 and 89A
Jacob Lake, AZ 86022
Tel: 928-643-7232
The inn's chummy coffee shop
is a welcome break during a long,
lonesome traverse of the
Arizona Strip. There's a dining
room with regular table service,
but the old-fashioned counter is
more fun. The menu features
family recipes such as Southwest
baked chicken, *jagerschnitzel*
and baked trout. Of course,
you can't go wrong with a
burger and fries. Leave room for
dessert. The baked goods are
scrumptious, and the milkshakes
(ask for extra thick) are a meal in
themselves. **$**

Lees Ferry Lodge
U.S. 89A
Marble Canyon, AZ
Tel: 928-355-2231
Simple, hearty American fare
served in a rustic wood-paneled
dining room makes this Western-
style lodge popular with river guides
and rafters who are preparing to
take on "the Grand." An extensive
selection of beers is available, and
the wine list is an unexpected
pleasure. **$–$$**

Rainbow Room
Wahweap Lodge
100 Lakeshore Drive
Page, AZ
Tel: 928-645-1162
Dine on American and Continental
cuisine while enjoying sweeping
views of Lake Powell at this popular
hotel restaurant, often crowded with
bus tours. **$$**

Zapata's
614 N. Navajo Drive
Page, AZ
Tel: 928-645-9006
Burritos, enchiladas and other
Mexican staples are specialties at
this casual eatery. Wash your meal
down with a Margarita. **$**

NAVAJO AND HOPI RESERVATIONS

Garcia's Restaurant
Holiday Inn–Canyon de Chelly
Indian Route 7

Chinle, AZ
Tel: 520-674-5000
Predictable Southwestern and
American food and a few Navajo
specialties fill the menu at this
well-maintained restaurant near
the entrance of Canyon de Chelly
National Monument. **$**

Goulding's Lodge
Monument Valley, UT
Tel: 435-727-3231
The lodge's Stagecoach Dining
Room has gorgeous views of
Monument Valley and an
entertaining collection of movie
memorabilia. The chefs turn out
solid American fare, Navajo tacos
and a few other local specialties. **$**

Wagonwheel Restaurant
Holiday Inn–Kayenta
Kayenta, AZ 86033
Tel: 928-697-3221
This is a fairly standard motel
restaurant with a slight difference.
Part of the decor is modeled on an
Ancient Pueblo ruin. The menu
offers solid but unimaginative
American food with a few local
specialties like Navajo tacos. Bus
tours often stop here, so don't be
surprised to find a crowd. **$**

Hopi Cultural Center Restaurant
Second Mesa, AZ
Tel: 928-734-2401
A basic diner with predictable
American and Southwestern fare as
well as a few local specialties such
as paper-thin *piki* bread, lamb stew
and blue-corn pancakes. **$**

Navajo Nation Inn
48 Highway 264
Window Rock, AZ 86515
Tel: 928-871-4108
A favorite meeting place for locals
and people visiting on business,
the restaurant serves Navajo tacos
and a few other local specialties as
well as standard American diner
food. **$**

Thunderbird Lodge
Chinle, AZ 86503
Tel: 928-674-5841
Set at the mouth of Canyon
de Chelly, the old stone
trading post now serves as a
cafeteria. The food is cheap
and simple, but the walls are
hung with beautifully crafted
Navajo rugs. **$**

FLAGSTAFF AND ENVIRONS

Beaver Street Brewery
11 S. Beaver Street, #1
Flagstaff, AZ
Tel: 928-779-0079
Flagstaff's only brewpub pairs
delicious woodstove pizza, hefty
salads, gooey fondue, and an
assortment of bar food with an
interesting selection of specialty
suds, from a robust stout to a light
berry ale. Expect a spirited college
crowd. **$**

**Black Bean Burrito Bar and
Salsa Company**
12 E. Route 66
Flagstaff, AZ
Tel: 928-779-9905
A tasty variety of rib-sticking burritos
are the specialty here, served in foil
and plastic and eaten at the
counter. Just the thing for a quick,
cheap face-stuffing. **$**

Café Espress
16 N. San Francisco Street
Flagstaff, AZ
Tel: 928-774-0541
A favorite with the mountain-biking
crowd, this arty, laid-back café
offers fresh, healthy, somewhat
eccentric food ranging from
huevos rancheros and other
filling Mexican specialties to
vegetarian dishes such as
spanakopita, tofu mushroom
stroganoff and artichoke scampi.
The baked goods and desserts
are yummy. **$**

Chez Marc Bistro
503 Humphreys Street
Flagstaff, AZ
Tel: 928-774-1343
This unpretentious little cottage
houses an oasis of fine French
cuisine in the heart of downtown
Flagstaff. Both cuisine and
atmosphere are refined but not
stuffy. **$$–$$$**

Cottage Place Inn
126 W. Cottage Avenue
Flagstaff, AZ
Tel: 928-774-8431
This unassuming 1909 bungalow
harbors an elegant little dining room
where customers feast on rich
Continental dishes such as
chateaubriand, dijon crusted

salmon, veal chops and seafood fettuccine. **$$**

Macy's European Coffee House and Bakery
14 S. Beaver Street
Flagstaff, AZ
Tel: 928-774-2243
The coffee is rich, pastries fresh and conversations earnest at this classic college-town hangout. Sandwiches, pasta, and a variety of vegetarian specialties round out the menu. **$**

Pasto
19 E. Aspen Street
Flagstaff, AZ
Tel: 928-779-1937
From the people who brought you Café Espress, another restaurant for the hip and hip-at-heart. This one specializes in creative Italian fare, with a few local twists, like the Southwestern black-bean ravioli. The atmosphere is casual, the decor imaginative. **$**

ARIZONA'S WEST COAST

California Bakery Company
284 S. Main Street
Yuma, AZ
Tel: 928-782-7335
An airy contemporary interior sets the scene for a selection of well-prepared entrées as well as a bakery and cappuccino bar. The menu runs the gamut from beef, poultry, lamb and seafood to lighter pastas, soups and salads. A good choice if you've had enough of cookie-cutter family restaurants. **$–$$**

Chretin's Mexican Food
485 S. 15th Avenue
Yuma, AZ
Tel: 928-782-1291
Filling, homemade Mexican specialties are the attraction at this no-frills restaurant, a favorite with locals for more than five decades. **$**

City of London Arms Pub & Restaurant
422 English Village
Lake Havasu City, AZ
Tel: 928-855-8782
Often crowded with tourists, this kitschy pub-style restaurant at the London Bridge offers such British imports as fish-and-chips, bangers and Guinness stout as well as a selection of more familiar American fare. An on-site brewery turns out several specialty beers. **$–$$**

Garden Café
250 Madison Avenue
Yuma, AZ
Tel: 928-783-1491
Birdsong and the scent of lemon trees delight customers at this leafy oasis, which serves a delectable assortment of pancakes, eggs, sandwiches, quiches, salads and tempting desserts. Breakfast and lunch only. **$**

Lutes Casino
221 S. Main Street
Yuma, AZ
Tel: 928-782-2192
Not a real casino but a domino parlor and pool hall, this local standby looks scruffy but is a popular family stop for burgers and brew. **$**

Mr. D'z Route 66 Diner
105 E. Andy Devine Avenue
Kingman, AZ
Tel: 928-718-0066
Flamboyant colors, doo-wop tunes, and lots of formica, vinyl and chrome give this modern diner lots of kitsch-appeal. The atmosphere is strictly cornball, but it's a good place for root beer, burgers and fries. **$**

Shugrue's
1425 McCulloch Boulevard
Lake Havasu City, AZ
Tel: 928-4531400
Diners enjoy a view of the London Bridge as they chow down on pasta, seafood, steak, and sandwiches. Food and service are consistently satisfying; families appreciate the kid's menu. **$$**

SEDONA AND THE VERDE VALLEY

Cowboy Club
241 Highway 89A
Sedona, AZ
Tel: 928-282-4200
Cowboy cuisine takes a Sedona twist at this stylish eatery adorned with spurs, boots, lariats and other buckaroo gear. Ribs, meatloaf, and juicy slabs of beef are given gourmet treatment with novel but savory pairings of spices, sauces, and creative side dishes. Don't pass up the chance to try such Western oddities as fried cactus, snake and buffalo meatloaf. **$$**

Dahl & DiLuca
2321 Highway 89A
Sedona, AZ
Tel: 928-282-5219
Flavorful Italian dishes are the specialty at this cheerful ristorante. The emphasis is on pasta – there are at least a half dozen choices, including a tangy linguine with prawns in a lemon-garlic sauce and a hearty rigatoni and sausage – as well as veal, chicken and pork. **$$**

Heartline Café
1610 Highway 89A
Sedona, AZ
Tel: 928-282-0785
An eclectic mix of flavors pours from the kitchen at this snappy restaurant, where diners enjoy such creatively prepared and presented entrées as smoked mozzarella ravioli, pecan-crusted trout and chicken breast with prickly-pear sauce. If weather permits, ask for a table in the courtyard. **$$**

Pietro's
2445 Highway 89A
Sedona, AZ
Tel: 928-282-2525
Consistently praised as one of the finest Italian restaurants in the state, Pietro's brings style and imagination to even its most traditional offerings. A few recent options include grilled eggplant rolled with goat cheese and sweet pepper sauce, red-pepper ravioli filled with smoked mozzarella, and filet mignon grilled in a wine-shiitake mushroom sauce, not to mention a delectable array of desserts and an impressive wine list. **$$**

The Palace
120 South Montezuma
Prescott, AZ
Tel: 928-541-1996
Wyatt Earp and Doc Holliday probably knocked a few back at this historic saloon on Prescott's infamous Whiskey Row. Splendidly restored, it now serves up ribs,

steaks, chops and a memorable corn chowder as well as plenty of Old West atmosphere. **$$**

Prescott Brewing Company
130 W. Gurlet Street
Prescott, AZ
Tel: 928-771-2795
The beer is good, the crowd is spirited, and the food is cheap and filling at this popular brewpub, housed in an old mercantile building in downtown Prescott. The menu is quite eclectic, ranging from bangers and mash, pot pies and burgers to fajitas, enchiladas and portabello linguine. Wash it all down with a few home brews: seasonal specialties fill out the regular lineup of ales and porters. **$**

Sasaki
65 Bell Rock Road
Oak Creek, AZ
Tel: 928-284-1757
Sushi lovers congregate at this low-key restaurant, though the menu features a wide variety of Japanese specialties. **$$**

Sedona Coffee Roasters
2155 Highway 89A
Sedona, AZ
Tel: 928-282-0282
The aroma of freshly roasted coffee beans lures the caffeine-deprived masses to this inviting café, where you can nosh on pastries and sandwiches while sipping your joe of choice. **$**

MOGOLLON RIM AND TONTO BASIN

Kohl's Ranch Lodge
Highway 260
Payson, AZ 85541
Tel: 928-478-4211
Hearty Western fare is offered at this mountain lodge. Choices range from a buttery filet mignon, rib-eye steak and baby-back ribs to rainbow trout with a pinyon-nut crust. You'll find an assortment of good pastas and salads, too, as well as such recent specials as Cajun-style catfish and hush puppies. **$$**

The Oaks Restaurant
302 W. Main Street
Payson, AZ
Tel: 928-474-1929

You'll find no fancy footwork here and nothing even remotely nouvelle. Steaks and seafood are the mainstay, simply prepared and efficiently presented. The patio is a delightful place to spend a warm summer evening enjoying a meal and nursing a glass of wine. **$$**

Swiss Village Bakery
800 N. Beeline Highway
Payson, AZ
Tel: 928-474-0891
Salads, homemade soups and sandwiches on freshly baked breads are served for lunch. While you're here, pick up a bag of fresh pastries. **$**

Price Guide

Price categories indicate the rough cost of dinner for one, excluding beverages, tax and tip.

$	$20 or less
$$	$20–40
$$$	$40–60
$$$$	$60 and up

WHITE MOUNTAINS

Booga Reds
521 E. Main Street
Springerville, AZ
Tel: 928-333-2640
Travelers stop here for comfort food – roast beef, mashed potatoes and gravy, pancakes, homemade pie – as well as a selection of Mexican dishes. **$**

Christmas Tree
453 N. Woodland Road
Pinetop, AZ
Tel: 928-367-3107
Who could resist a steaming bowl of chicken and dumplings "just like Grandma used to make"? That's the specialty at this out-of-the-way country restaurant, which also offers such satisfying entrées as beef Stroganoff, lamb chops, roasted honey duck, New York steak and barbecued ribs. **$$**

Hannagan Meadow Lodge
HC 61, P.O. Box 335
Alpine, AZ
Tel: 928-339-4370
Diners can watch deer and elk browse in the meadow around this

rustic lodge's restaurant, a lovely room with wood beams and linen-covered tables. The menu offers a choice of hearty steaks, burgers and chops as well as pan-fried trout, grilled salmon, jumbo fried shrimp. and baked chicken breast with lime-butter sauce. Breakfast and lunch are also served. **$–$$**

Molly Butler Lodge
109 Main Street
Greer, AZ
Tel: 928-735-7226
Rustic surroundings and lovely forest views complement a menu of seafood, chile, and tender, aged steaks at this venerable mountain lodge. **$–$$**

Paint Pony Rustic Steakhouse
571 W. Deuce of Clubs
Show Low, AZ
Tel: 928-537-8220
Generous portions of steak, seafood, pasta and salad are the formula at this Western-style restaurant adjacent to a Best Western motel. **$**

Pasta House
2188 E. White Mountain Boulevard
Pinetop, AZ
Tel: 928-367-2782
As the name suggests, homemade pasta and sauces are the cornerstone of the menu, though you will also find savory veal, chicken and seafood. **$–$$**

PHOENIX AND THE VALLEY OF THE SUN

Blue Burrito Grille
Biltmore Plaza
118 E. Camelback Road
Phoenix, AZ
Tel: 602-955-9596
This snazzy contemporary eatery in a shopping center on the busy Camelback corridor puts a healthful spin (no lard or MSG) on Mexican cuisine. The fish taco, *carne asada*, and fajitas are good choices. If you're really hungry, ask for the Big Blue Burrito, a double-size burrito with steak or chicken. There are six other locations in the Phoenix area, each with a full bar. A good choice for vegetarians. **$–$$**

Café Terra Cotta
6166 N. Scottsdale Road
Scottsdale, AZ
Tel: 480-948-8100
Foodies praise the novel flavor combinations and creative presentations at this snazzy Southwestern restaurant, an offshoot of the Tucson original. Try these dishes: chile-roasted Muscovy duck with chipolte sauce on a potato-horseradish pancake; grilled scallops with a three-pepper sauce over angel hair pasta tossed with smoked bacon and hot basil slaw; or Angus filet wrapped in bacon with a gorgonzola-sage sauce. Those who want to sample a variety of food can order a selection of "small dishes," pasta and wood-fired pizza. **$$**

Christopher's Fermier Brasserie
Biltmore Fashion Park
2584 E. Camelback Road
Phoenix, AZ
Tel: 602-522-2344
Contemporary French-inspired cuisine is beautifully presented at this lively four-in-one location – a restaurant, wine bar, brewery and cigar lounge. Highlights include the wild mushroom and foie gras soup, risotto, and wood-roasted seafood. Leave room for such gloriously indulgent desserts as chocolate bread pudding. **$$–$$$**

Cowboy Ciao
7133 E. Stetson Drive
Scottsdale, AZ
Tel: 480-946-3111
This quirky contemporary eatery brings new meaning to the term "spaghetti Western," with playful culinary pairings such as porcini-crusted ribeye steak, pesto-crusted elk loin, and smoked pork in chipolte balsamic barbecue sauce atop soft polenta. Sounds odd, perhaps, but the chefs pull it off with an infectious sense of fun and daring. **$$–$$$**

Ed Debevic's Short Orders Deluxe
2102 E. Highland Avenue
Phoenix, AZ
Tel: 602-956-2760
This frenetic old-fashioned diner has a mini-jukebox in every booth, loads of retro charm (harassed waitresses notwithstanding), and a choice of familiar, almost-like-mom's fare – burgers, fries, meatloaf, malteds and more. **$**

Hap's Real Pit BBQ
101 S. 24th Street
Phoenix, AZ
Tel: 602-267-0181
Forget the low-rent atmosphere and dig into some of the best barbecued spareribs in the city. **$**

House of Tricks
114 E. Seventh Street
Tempe, AZ
Tel: 480-968-1114
Ask for a table on the leafy covered patio, order a round from the open-air bar, then prepare to enjoy such tasty and creative dishes as pork rack with jalapeño-orange marmalade; grilled Middle Eastern spiced salmon; and grilled Angus sirloin with mashed potatoes and shiitake mushroom sauce. A fireplace keeps patrons toasty on chilly nights. A winning marriage of cuisine and atmosphere. **$$**

La Hacienda
7575 E. Princess Drive
Scottsdale, AZ
Tel: 480-585-4848
You'll find gourmet Mexican at this low-key but elegant restaurant at the Scottsdale Princess Resort. Order a heavenly Margarita, then treat yourself to the chef's signature dish – *cochinillo asado*, a barbecued suckling pig marinated in bitter orange, pepper and tamarind. Other specialties include *costillas de Cordero*, a charbroiled rack of lamb with pumpkin seed crust and chile plum sauce; *mezcla de carnes y mariscos*, grilled beef tenderloin, shrimp and chicken; and *atún a la plancha*, seared tuna, crusted with wheat flour. Don't dare leave without sampling at least one of the mouth-watering desserts. **$$–$$$**

Pho Dinh Restaurant
2025 N. Dobson Road
Chandler, AZ
Tel: 480-812-1877
Set in a corner of a large Asian marketplace known as Lee Lee is this casual Vietnamese restaurant, where the food is authentic and the prices reasonable. Come with an appetite and sample such specialties as barbecued pork with charbroiled ground shrimp; spicy salt-and-pepper squid; rice noodles tossed with shrimp, beef, pork and chicken; and sizzling clay hot pots loaded with meat, shrimp and veggies heaped atop crunchy rice. **$**

RoxSand
Biltmore Fashion Park
2594 E. Camelback Road
Phoenix, AZ
Tel: 602-381-0444
The owner of this slick contemporary restaurant is a proponent of "fusion cuisine," a cross-cultural approach to combining flavors and ingredients. It's not unusual to open the meal with a Middle Eastern braised curried chicken, rice tamale with Thai peanut sauce, or short ribs with Korean soy and honey marinade, then move to air-dried duck with buckwheat crepes and pistachio-onion marmalade, or chicken breast with Louisiana etouffe sauce. Leave the jeans at home. **$$–$$$**

The Stockyards
5001 E. Washington Street
Phoenix, AZ
Tel: 602-273-7378
Steakhouse with 19th-century decor and Old West specialties like Rocky Mountain oysters (the bits you remove to make a bull into a steer) and hand-cut beef. **$–$$**

T. Cook's
5200 E. Camelback Road
Phoenix, AZ 85018
Tel: 602-808-0766
Set amid the manicured gardens of the Royal Palms Resort, this Mediterranean-style restaurant drips romance. It's hard to go wrong here. Wood-fired poultry, beef and pork are favorites, though other dishes such as

Price Guide

Price categories indicate the rough cost of dinner for one, excluding beverages, tax and tip.

$	$20 or less
$$	$20–40
$$$	$40–60
$$$$	$60 and up

paella and sauteed lobster are equally tempting. Chocoholics may want to skip dinner and move directly to the heavenly chocolate sampler. **$$–$$$**

San Carlos Bay Seafood Restaurant
1901 E. McDowell Road
Phoenix, AZ
Tel: 602-340-0892
Mexican seafood is the bill of fare here. Highlights include a surprisingly tender octopus cocktail; fiery shrimp endiablados; a rich seven seas stew stocked with crab, cockles, shrimp and squid; shrimp with tangy green-chile sauce; and *pescado à la Veracruzana* (grilled snapper with olives, tomatoes, onions and peppers). **$**

TUCSON

Beyond Bread
Campbell Village
3055 N. Campbell Street
Tucson, AZ
Tel: 520-322-9965
What could be simpler or more delicious than a loaf of bread still warm from the oven and a steaming cup of coffee? You'll find more than 20 varieties of bread as well as thick sandwiches, salads, pastries and cakes at this gloriously aromatic bakery/café. **$**

Café Poca Cosa
88 E. Adway Boulevard
Tucson, AZ
Tel: 520-622-6400
Chef and owner Susana Davila serves innovative Sonoran cuisine that is the talk of Tucson, including tamales with unusual nouveau Mexican fillings and sauces. Her daughter runs a second, smaller restaurant nearby. **$**

Café Terra Cotta
3500 Sunrise Drive
Tucson, AZ
Tel: 520-577-8100
Now at a new location, this Tucson favorite produces crowd-pleasing dishes on the creative edge of Southwestern cuisine. Don't pass up the garlic custard or one of a half-dozen wood-fired pizzas as a starter for the table. A few notable entrées

include rack of lamb with chile bread pudding; duck carnitas spring roll; prawns stuffed with herbed goat cheese; and salmon crusted with sunflower seeds served on masa corncakes. There's a second restaurant in Phoenix. **$–$$**

Dakota Café
6541 E. Tanque Verde Road
Tucson, AZ
Tel: 520-298-7188
Set in a complex of faux Old West buildings known as Trail Dust Town, the restaurant has been winning kudos for its healthful and imaginative cooking. The menu ranges from meatloaf sandwiches, burgers and several vegetarian dishes to specials like chicken enchiladas, tempura shrimp and lavosh pizza. Patio dining is available.**$–$$**

El Charro Mexican Café
311 N. Court Avenue
Tucson, AZ
Tel: 520-622-1922.
A venerable stone building in the Presidio Historic District houses what claims to be the oldest family-operated Mexican restaurant in the United States. Tasty Sonoran-style food is the bill of fare, including spinach enchiladas, chimichangas, tamales, and carne seca (dried beef), a house specialty. Satellite restaurants are located at El Mercado (Broadway and Wilmot) and Tucson International Airport. **$**

Elle: A Wine Country Restaurant
3048 E. Broadway Boulevard
Tucson, AZ
Tel: 520-327-0500
Pasta, risotto and other Italian-inspired dishes are refreshing in their simplicity yet intriguingly creative. Clear, natural flavors add nuance to entrées such as risotto with butternut squash, balsamic roasted onion and sage or a simple capellini with tomatoes, basil and garlic. True to its name, the restaurant offers more than 40 wines by the glass. **$–$$**

El Minuto
354 S. Main Avenue
Tucson, AZ
Tel: 520-882-4145
Spicy and filling Mexican food are served at this stripped-down cantina

near El Tiradito shrine. The place is popular with both locals and tourists, so expect a lively crowd. **$**

Firecracker
2990 N. Swan Road
Tucson, AZ
Tel: 520-318-1118
The flamboyant decor is your first indication of the no-holds-barred approach to Asian-American food at this fun and popular bistro. A few winners include the wok-charred salmon with cilantro pesto, grilled spicy duck breast served over a bed of spinach, and chicken breast stuffed with wasabi cream. There's almost always a crowd here, so arrive early to avoid a long wait. **$$**

Janos
3770 E. Sunrise Drive
Tucson, AZ
Tel: 520-615-6100
Now ensconced in elegant new digs at the Westin La Paloma hotel, Janos continues its tradition of blending French and Southwestern influences to produce one of Tucson's most rewarding gastronomic experiences. The menu changes often, but a recent sampler menu (a series of small courses each accompanied by a different wine) included lobster and brie relleno, cognac-scented beef tenderloin, and lamb sirloin marinated in lemon, basil, garlic and olive oil. The desserts are equally entrancing, and a wine cellar with 700 selections (20 are offered each night) will keep oenophiles happy on return visits. The more casual J Bar next door is a less expensive alternative to pricey Janos. **$$$**

Native Café
3073 N. Campbell Avenue
Tucson, AZ
Tel: 520-881-8881
Come to this friendly little place for bountiful salads, overstuffed sandwiches and an arty, laid-back vibe. All ingredients are organically grown and extremely fresh. A few more substantial eats include the Maya burger (a grain patty with cheese), pad Thai, and pesto chicken. Vegetarians will have plenty of options. **$**

Tack Room
7300 E. Vactor Ranch Trail
Tucson, AZ
Tel: 520-722-2800
Trying to impress your in-laws with your taste and maturity? Take them to this old hacienda, a bastion of old-fashioned elegance and service (the waiters wear tuxedos) in this otherwise casual town. The menu is filled with substantial entrées prepared and served with unimpeachable care – filet mignon, chateaubriand, lobster Thermidor, grilled Norwegian salmon. Jackets and ties are recommended but not required. **$$$**

Tohono Chul
7366 N. Paseo del Norte
Tucson, AZ
Tel: 520-797-1222
It's difficult to imagine a more peaceful spot than the patio at this restaurant in Tohono Chul Park. Watch hummingbirds sip nectar in the garden as you enjoy a breakfast of English scones, buttermilk pancakes or *huevos rancheros*. The lunch menu offers raspberry chipolte chicken, spinach fettuccine alfredo, grilled salmon, and large salads, among quite a few other choices. You can browse the gift shop after your meal, or burn off a few calories by strolling through the desert park. **$**

Wildflower
7037 N. Oracle Road
Tucson, AZ
Tel: 520-219-4230
This classy, contemporary bistro has a knack for pleasing patrons with a worldly mix of American, Asian and European cuisines. Clear, earthy flavors are artfully assembled in such dishes as roasted rack of lamb with Dijon crust, Tuscan white-bean ravioli with wood-grilled chicken, and meatloaf with whipped potatoes. **$$**

BORDER COUNTRY

Café Roka
35 Main Street
Bisbee, AZ
Tel: 520-432-5153

Price Guide

Price categories indicate the rough cost of dinner for one, excluding beverages, tax and tip.

$	$20 or less
$$	$20–40
$$$	$40–60
$$$$	$60 and up

Chef Rod Kass has created an upscale, arty environment in which to present his creative brand of northern Italian cuisine. Four-course meals might include artichoke and portabello mushroom lasagne, scallops with spinach pasta, rack of lamb, roasted duck, or grilled salmon. The menu is not extensive but changes frequently. You're unlikely to find exactly the same choices on any two visits. **$$**

Café Sonoita
3280 Highway 82
Sonoita, AZ
Tel: 520-455-5278
Maybe it's a sort of culinary Napoleon complex. Anyway, the menu here is quite ambitious for such a tiny place, covering imaginative Southwestern dishes as well as carefully prepared international fare. There are only a few tables, so be sure to make reservations. **$–$$**

Cantina Romantica
Rex Ranch
off Amado exit 48 on I-19
Tubac, AZ
Tel: 520-398-2914
The menu is not extensive at this rustic hacienda on the 4,000-acre (1,620-hectare) Rex Ranch north of Tubac, but, in this case, small is beautiful. Grilled meats are the specialty, although you'll find a tasty selection of vegetarian dishes as well, including bountiful salads. Several varieties of chile are used to great advantage, as are tequila, citrus and prickly pear. A few recent highlights include pecan-crusted pork roulade with chile sauce; grilled double-cut lamb chops with a port wine cherry jalapeño jus; grilled citrus chicken and shrimp with tequila

prickly pear sauce; and wild mushroom and basil lasagna. Be forewarned: there's no bridge across the Santa Cruz River to the ranch. You have to drive through the water. **$$–$$$**

Cose Buone
436 Naugle Avenue
Patagonia, AZ
Tel: 520-394-2366
Convincing northern Italian cuisine is served at this cozy ristorante. The menu changes often, but diners can expect a medley of Italian favorites with a few unexpected riffs. The wine list has some interesting and reasonably priced Italian labels. Spill some *vino rosso* on your new white shirt? No problem. There's a laundromat next door to the restaurant. **$$**

High Desert Inn Restaurant
8 Naco Road
Bisbee, AZ
Tel: 520-432-1442
The old Cochise County Jail has been transformed into a classy eatery where gastronomes savor such varied offerings as three-cheese eggplant torta, Pacific salmon baked with a coating of stone-ground mustard and pepper, Southwest chicken with three salsas, and New Zealand mussels poached in a white wine and saffron cream sauce. **$$**

Karen's Wine Country Café
3266 Highway 82
Sonoita, AZ
Tel: 520-455-0075
This European-style café in the heart of Patagonia's Wine Country offers fresh soups, salads and other light fare in a cheery dining room with views of the surrounding grasslands. A good lunch stop between Ramsey Canyon and Tucson. **$**

Marie's European Cuisine
340 Naugle Avenue
Patagonia, AZ
Tel: 520-394-2812
Set in a 1918 adobe cottage, this snug restaurant serves a tempting variety of dishes inspired by the cuisine of central and southern Europe. **$–$$**

Melio's Trattoria
12 Plaza Road
Tubac, AZ
Tel: 520-398-8494
This trattoria offers familiar but
well-done Italian food in a cozy,
unpretentious setting. **$–$$**
Velvet Elvis
292 Highway 82
Patagonia, AZ
Tel: 520-394-2102
This eccentric little place has thin-
crusted, stone-fired pizza piled
high with a variety of toppings.
Wash down a few slices with a
choice of freshly pressed juices,
organic wines, or micro brews.
Soups and salads are also quite
good. **$**
Wagon Wheel Saloon
400 W. Naugle Avenue
Patagonia, AZ
Tel: 520-394-2433
This authentic cowboy bar and
restaurant has been catering to
local buckaroos for more than 60
years and offers exactly what you
would expect from a cowboy joint –
barbecued ribs, steaks, burgers,
and plenty of ice cold beer. **$**

Culture

Performing Arts

PHOENIX

Actors Theatre of Phoenix
P.O. Box 1924
Phoenix, AZ
Tel: 602-253-6701
Lesser-known, off-Broadway
dramas, comedies and musicals as
well as a few old favorites like *A
Christmas Carol*, with a new spin.
Arizona Theatre Company
502 W. Roosevelt Street
Phoenix, AZ
Tel: 602-256-6995
Dramas, comedies and musicals
presented in both Phoenix and
Tucson.
Ballet Arizona
3645 E. Indian School Road
Phoenix, AZ
Tel: 602-381-0184
Nutcracker, Swan Lake and other
classics as well as lesser-known
and contemporary works.
Blockbuster Desert Sky Pavilion
2121 N. 83rd Avenue (83rd Avenue
and Encanto Boulevard)
Phoenix, AZ
Tel: 602-254-7200
Rock concerts and other big shows
at a 20,000-seat outdoor venue.
Center Dance Ensemble
231 W. Frier Drive
Phoenix, AZ
Tel: 602-997-9027

Tickets

Tickets for most sport and
cultural events can be
purchased by phone from ETM
Ticketing/Dillard's (800-638-
4253), Ticketmaster (480-784-
4444) or directly from the box
offices (see individual listings).

Modern dance at the Herberger
Theater Center and other venues.
**Grady Gammage Memorial
Auditorium**
Mill Avenue and Apache Boulevard
Tempe, AZ
Tel: 480-965-3434
One of Frank Lloyd Wright's last
major works, this 3,000-seat venue
on the ASU campus presents a
variety of productions, from
classical music to contemporary
drama.
Herberger Theater Center
222 E. Monroe Street
Phoenix, AZ
Tel: 602-252-8497
This downtown venue houses two
theaters and is home to the Arizona
Theatre Company, Ballet Arizona
and Actors Theatre of Phoenix and
presents a variety of visiting dance
troupes, orchestras and plays.
Mesa Amphitheater
University Drive and Center Street
Mesa, AZ
Tel: 480-644-2178
A wide range of music, dance and
theater, including a series of free
shows, at an outdoor amphitheater.
Orpheum Theatre
203 W. Adams Street
Phoenix, AZ
Tel: 602-262-7272
A gorgeous 1929 movie palace,
now fully restored to its original
glory, presents a variety of touring
shows.
Phoenix Symphony
3707 N. 7th Street
Phoenix, AZ
Tel: 602-264-6363
The region's best symphony
presents classical, pops and
chamber music series at Phoenix
Symphony Hall and is host to a
variety of distinguished guest
performers.
Phoenix Symphony Hall
225 E. Adams Street
Phoenix, AZ
Tel: 602-262-6225
This 2,590-seat hall is the home of
the Phoenix Symphony Orchestra
and Arizona Opera, as well as the
site for Broadway touring
companies, Ballet Arizona and
appearances by popular
entertainers.

Scottsdale Center for the Arts
7380 E. 2nd Street
Scottsdale, AZ
Tel: 480-994-2787
Theaters and an outdoor venue for a variety of live performances and film festivals.

Scottsdale Symphony Orchestra
P.O. Box 460
Scottsdale, AZ
Tel: 480-945-8071
The symphony offers a regular season of 15 concerts, plus community concerts at schools, parks and local festivals.

TUCSON

Arizona Opera Company
501 N. Mountain Avenue
Tucson, AZ
Tel: 520-293-4336
Mostly classics – Rigoletto, Don Giovanni, Madame Butterfly and the like – performed in Phoenix and Tucson.

Centennial Hall
1020 E. University Boulevard
Tucson, AZ
Tel: 520-621-3341
This theater on the University of Arizona campus presents touring theater, music and dance companies.

The Gaslight Theatre
7010 East Broadway
Tucson, AZ
Tel: 520-886-9428
Over-the-top melodrama in the tradition of the Old West.

Invisible Theatre
1400 N. First Avenue
Tucson, AZ
Tel: 520-882-9721
Experimental and off-Broadway theater.

Orts Theatre of Dance
P.O. Box 85211
Tucson, AZ
Tel: 520-624-3799
A modern dance company that incorporates trapeze-style aerial work.

Temple of Music and Art
330 S. Scott Avenue
Tucson, AZ
Tel: 520-622-2823
This refurbished 1927 stage and movie theater is the home of the

Arizona Theatre Company and other arts groups.

Tenth Street Danceworks
3400 E. Speedway, Suite 118
Tucson, AZ
Tel: 520-622-1793
Contemporary dance.

Tucson Symphony
2175 N. 6th Avenue
Tucson, AZ
Tel: 520-882-8585
The symphony performs a combination of classical and pop at the Tucson Convention Center Music Hall.

Tucson Center for the Performing Arts
408 S. Sixth Avenue
Tel: 520-792-8480
The center is used for an assortment of small theatrical performances and concerts.

SEDONA AND FLAGSTAFF

Flagstaff Symphony Orchestra
P. 0. Box 122
Flagstaff, AZ
Tel: 928-774-5107
Pops, classics and guest performers.

Sedona Arts Center
Highway 89A and Art Barn Road
Sedona, AZ
Tel: 928-282-3809
Music and plays, including the work of local theater companies.

Sedona Cultural Park
Tel: 800-780-2787
A new outdoor venue for a variety of events and productions, including Shakespeare Sedona, Sedona International Film Festival and Jazz on the Rocks.

Theatrikos Theatre Company
11 West Cherry Avenue
Flagstaff, AZ
Tel: 928-774-1662
This community theater group performs at the Flagstaff Playhouse.

Native American Cultures

Cultural sensitivity is vital in Indian Country. Because some Indian people may feel uncomfortable or ambivalent about the presence of

outsiders, it is very important to be on your best behavior. Below are a few "dos" and "don'ts" to keep in mind.

● Don't use racist terms. Referring to an Indian as chief, redskin, squaw, buck, Pocahontas, Hiawatha or other off-color terms is highly offensive.

● Abide by all rules and regulations while on Indian land and at Indian events. These may include prohibitions on photography, sketching, taking notes, video and audio recording. In some cases a photography fee may be required. If you wish to take an individual's picture, you must ask permission first (a gratuity may be requested).

● Respect all restricted areas. These are usually posted, but ask permission before hiking into wilderness or archaeological areas, driving on back roads, wandering around villages, entering ceremonial structures, or attending events.

● Try to be unobtrusive. Remember that you are a guest at Indian communities and events. Be polite and accommodating. In general, it is better to be too formal than too casual.

● Don't ask intrusive questions or interrupt during Indian ceremonies or dances. Even if an Indian event is not explicitly religious (such as a powwow), it may have a spiritual component. Show the same respect at Indian ceremonies that you would at any other religious service. At all events, try to maintain a low profile. Do not talk loudly, push to the front of a crowd, block other people's view, or sit in chairs that do not belong to you.

● Keep in mind that many Indian people have a looser sense of time than non-Indians. You may hear jokes about "Indian time." Prepare for long delays before ceremonies, powwows and other events.

Ak Chin Indian Community, Route 2, Box 27, Maricopa, AZ 85239, tel: 520-568-2227.
Cocopah Tribe, P.O. Bin G, Somerton, AZ 85250, tel: 602-627-2102.

Colorado River Indian Tribes, Route 1, Box 23B, Parker, AZ 85344, tel: 928-669-9211.
Gila River Pima-Maricopa Indian Community, P.O. Box 97, Sacaton, AZ 85247, tel: 520-562-3311.
Havasupai Tribe, P.O. Box 10, Supai, AZ 86435, tel: 928-448-2961.
Hopi Tribe, P.O. Box 123, Kykotsmovi, AZ 86039, tel: 928-734-2445.
Hualapai Tribe, P.O. Box 179, Peach Springs, AZ 86434, tel: 928-769-2216.
Kaibab Band of Paiute Indians, Tribal Affairs Building, HC 65, Box 2, Fredonia, AZ 86022, tel: 928-643-7245.
Navajo Nation, P.O. Box 308, Window Rock, AZ 86515, tel: 928-871-6352.
Pascua Yaqui Tribe, 7474 S. Camino de Oeste, Tucson, AZ 85746, tel: 520-883-5000.
Quechan Tribe, P.O. Box 11352, Yuma, AZ 85364, tel: 928-572-0213.
Salt River Pima-Maricopa Indian Community, Route 1, Box 216, Scottsdale, AZ 85256, tel: 602-941-7277.
San Carlos Apache Tribe, P.O. Box 0, San Carlos, AZ 85550, tel: 928-475-2361.
Tohono O'odham Nation, PO Box 837, Sells, AZ 85634, tel: 520-383-2221.
Tonto Apache Tribe, Tonto Reservation No. 30, Payson, AZ 85541, tel: 928-474-5000.
White Mountain Apache Tribe, P.O. Box 700, White River, AZ 85941, tel: 928-338-4346.
Yavapai-Apache Tribe, P.O. Box 1188, Camp Verde, AZ 86322, tel: 928-567-3649.

Indian Casinos

A compact signed by the governor in 1993 allows the state's Indian tribes to establish casinos with slot machines on their reservations. The compact doesn't allow for any table games but some casinos offer video versions of blackjack, craps and roulette.

Apache Gold Casino Resort
P.O. Box 1210
San Carlos, AZ 85550
Tel: 520-475-7800
Blue Water Casino
119 W. Riverside Drive
Parker, AZ 85344
Tel: 928-669-7777
www.bluewaterfun.com
Bucky's Casino & Resort
530 E. Merritt
Prescott, AZ 86301
Tel: 928-776-1666
www.buckyscasino.com
Casino Arizona–Salt River
524 N. 92nd Street
Scottsdale, AZ 85256
Tel: 480-850-7777
www.casinoaz.com
Casino Arizona–Indian Bend
9700 E. Indian Bend
Scottsdale, AZ 85256
Tel: 480-850-7777
www.casinoaz.com
Casino of the Sun
7406 S. Camino De Oeste
Tucson, AZ 85746
Tel: 520-883-1700
www.casinosun.com
Cliff Castle Casino & Hotel Lodge
353 Middle Verde Road
Camp Verde, AZ 86322
Tel: 928-567-9031
www.cliffcastle.com
Cocopah Casino & Bingo
15136 S. Avenue B
Somerton, AZ 85350
Tel: 520-726-8066
Desert Diamond Casino
7350 S. Old Nogales Highway
Tucson, AZ 85734
Tel: 520-294-7777
Fort McDowell Casino
P.O. Box 18359
Fountain Hills, AZ 85269
Tel: 602-837-1424
www.fortmcdowellcasino.com
Gila River Casino–Vee Quiva
6443 N. Komatke Lane
Laveen, AZ 85339
Tel: 520-796-7777
Gila River Casino–Wild Horse
5512 W. Wild Horse Pass
Chandler, AZ 85226
Tel: 520-796-7727
Golden Hasan Casino
P.O. Box 10
Ajo, AZ 85321
Tel: 520-362-2746

Harrah's Ak Chin Casino
15406 Maricopa Road
Maricopa, AZ 85239
Tel: 602-802-5000
www.harrahs.com
Hon-Dah Casino
P.O. Box 3250
Pinetop, AZ 85935
Tel: 928-369-0299
www.hon-dah.com
Mazatzal Casino
P.O. Box 1820
Highway 87, Milemarker 251
Payson, AZ 85547
Tel: 928-474-6044
www.777play.com
Paradise Casino
450 Quechan Drive
Yuma, AZ 85364
Tel: 760-572-7777
www.paradisecasinoyuma.com
Spirit Mountain Casino
8555 South Highway 95
Mohave Valley, AZ 86440
Tel: 520-346-2000
Yavapai Casino
1501 E. Highway 69
Prescott, AZ 86301
Tel: 928-445-5767
www.buckyscasino.com

Calendar of Events

January
Arizona Livestock Show and Rodeo
Phoenix
Tel: 602-258-8568
Fiesta Bowl Football Classic
Tempe
Tel: 480-350-0911
First People's World's Fair and Powwow
Tucson
Tel: 520-622-4900
Parada del Sol and Rodeo
Scottsdale
Tel: 480-990-3179
Phoenix Open Golf Tournament,
Scottsdale
Tel: 480-870-4431
Wings Over Willcox
Willcox
Tel: 520-384-2272

February
All-Arabian Horse Show
Scottsdale
Tel: 480-515-1500

Arizona Renaissance Festival
Apache Junction
Tel: 480-982-3141
Festival of the Arts
Tubac
Tel: 520-398-2704
Gold Rush Days
Wickenburg
Tel: 928-684-5479
Matsuri Japanese Festival
Phoenix
Tel: 602-262-5071
O'odham Tash Indian Celebration
Casa Grande
Tel: 520-836-4723
**Quartzite Powwow Gem and
Mineral Show**
Quartzite
Tel: 928-927-6325
Scottish Highland Games
Mesa
Tel: 602-431-0095
Silver Spur Rodeo
Yuma
Tel: 928-344-5451
Tucson Gem and Mineral Show
Tucson
Tel: 520-322-5773
Tucson Open Golf Tournament
Tucson
Tel: 520-571-0400
**Tucson Rodeo–La Fiesta
de los Vaqueros**
Tucson
Tel: 520-741-2233
Winterfest
Flagstaff
Tel: 928-774-4505
Winterfest Jamboree
Lake Havasu City
Tel: 928-855-4115

March
Balloon Fest
Parker
Tel: 928-669-9265
Festival of the West
Scottsdale
Tel: 602-996-4387
**Franklin Templeton Tennis
Classic**
Scottsdale
Tel: 480-922-0222
**Heard Museum Indian Fair and
Market**
Phoenix
Tel: 602-252-8848
**Lost Dutchman Gold Mine
Superstition Mountain Trek**

Apache Junction
Tel: 480-258-6016
**Native American Festival and
Art Market**
Scottsdale
Tel: 480-502-5600
Ostrich Festival
Chandler
Tel: 480-963-4571
Sedona International Film Festival
Sedona
Tel: 928-203-4849
Scottsdale Arts Festival
Scottsdale
Tel: 480-994-2787
Territorial Days
Tombstone
Tel: 520-457-9317
**The Tradition–Senior PGA
Tournament**
Scottsdale
Tel: 480-595-4070
Waik Powwow
Tucson
Tel: 520-294-5727

April
Celebrity Golf & Tennis Tournament
Tucson
Tel: 520-884-9920
Culinary Festival
Scottsdale
Tel: 480-945-7193
El Tour de Phoenix Bicycle Race
Mesa
Tel: 480-745-2033
Glendale Jazz & Blues Festival
Glendale
Tel: 623-930-2299
International Mariachi Conference
Tucson
Tel: 520-884-9920
La Vuelta de Bisbee Bicycle Race
Bisbee
Tel: 520-432-5421
Maricopa County Fair
Phoenix
Tel: 602-252-0717
Route 66 Fun Run Weekend
Seligman to Topock
Tel: 928-753-5001
Yaqui Easter
Tucson
Tel: 520-791-4609

May
Chamber Music Festival
Sedona
Tel: 928-204-2415

Cinco de Mayo
Phoenix and Tucson
Tel: 602-262-5025 (Phoenix) 520-292-9326 (Tucson)
Mountain Man Rendezvous
Williams
Tel: 928-635-4061
**Pine–Strawberry Arts & Crafts
Festival**
Pine
Tel: 928-476-4647
**Spring Festival of Food, Music and
Folklore**
Tucson
Tel: 520-888-8816
Wyatt Earp Days
Tombstone
Tel: 520-457-3291

June
Bluegrass Festival
Prescott
Tel: 928-445-2000
Folk Arts Fair
Prescott
Tel: 928-445-3122
Grand Canyon State Summer Games
Phoenix
Tel: 480-517-9700
Juneteenth Festival
Tucson
Tel: 520-791-4355
Old Miners Day
Chloride
Tel: 928-565-2204
Old West Days
Holbrook
Tel: 928-524-6558
Pine Country Pro Rodeo
Flagstaff
Tel: 800-842-7293

July
Cowpunchers Reunion Rodeo
Williams
Tel: 928-635-4061
Frontier Days
Prescott
Tel: 800-266-7534
Hopi/Navajo Marketplace
Flagstaff
Tel: 928-774-5213
**Native American Arts & Crafts
Festival**
Pinetop–Lakeside
Tel: 928-367-4290
Pioneer Day Celebration
Snowflake
Tel: 928-536-4331

Prescott Indian Market
Prescott
Tel: 928-445-3122
Territorial Days and Rodeo
Prescott
Tel: 928-445-2000

August
Arizona Cowboy Poets Gathering
Prescott
Tel: 928-445-3122
Fiesta de San Agustin
Tucson
Tel: 520-624-1817
Flagstaff Festival in the Pines
Flagstaff
Tel: 928-779-7611
Hon-Dah Powwow in the Pines
Whiteriver
Tel: 520-369-0299
Norteño Music Festival
Tucson
Tel: 520-622-2801
Southwest Wings Birding Festival
Sierra Vista
Tel: 520-459-3868
Vigilante Days
Tombstone
Tel: 520-457-3197
World's Oldest Continuous Rodeo
Payson
Tel: 928-474-4515

September
Festival of Science
Flagstaff
Tel: 800-842-7293
Fiesta del Tlaquepaque
Sedona
Tel: 928-282-4838
Gold Camp Days
Oatman
Tel: 928-768-6222
Grand Canyon Music Festival
Grand Canyon
Tel: 800-997-8285
Jazz on the Rocks
Sedona
Tel: 928-282-1985
Navajo Nation Fair
Window Rock
Tel: 928-871-6436
White Mountain Apache Tribal Fair
& Rodeo
Whiteriver
Tel: 928-338-4346

October
Arizona State Fair

Phoenix
Tel: 602-254-6500
La Fiesta de los Chiles
Tucson
Tel: 520-326-9686
Helldorado Days
Tombstone
Tel: 520-457-9317
London Bridge Days
Lake Havasu City
Tel: 928-453-3444
Prescott Folk Music Festival
Prescott
Tel: 928-445-3122
Rex Allen Days
Willcox
Tel: 520-384-2272
Sedona Arts Festival
Sedona
Tel: 800-288-7336
Tucson Heritage Experience Festival
Tucson
Tel: 520-624-1817

November
Thunderbird Balloon Classic
Scottsdale
Tel: 480-254-6500
El Tour de Tucson Bicycle Race
Tucson
Tel: 520-745-2033
Western Music Festival
Tucson
Tel: 520-743-9794
WorldFest Flagstaff International
Film Festival
Flagstaff
Tel: 928-913-0444

December
Christmas Mariachi Festival
Phoenix
Tel: 602-379-7800
Cowboy Christmas & Cowboy
Poets Gathering
Wickenburg
Tel: 928-684-5479
Festival of the Arts
Tempe
Tel: 480-967-4877
La Fiesta de Tumacacori
Tumacacori
Tel: 520-398-2341
Indian Market
Phoenix
Tel: 602-254-6500
Pueblo Grande Indian Market
Phoenix
Tel: 602-495-0901

The Great Outdoors

Parks & Historic Sites

NORTHERN ARIZONA

Canyon de Chelly National
Monument
P.O. Box 588, Chinle, AZ 86503.
Tel: 928-674-5500.
Coconino National Forest
Supervisor's Office, 2323 E.
Greenlaw Lane, Flagstaff,
AZ 86004. Tel: 928-527-3600.
Glen Canyon National
Recreation Area
P.O. Box 1507, Page, AZ 86040.
Tel: 928-608-6404.
Grand Canyon National Park
P.O. Box 129, Grand Canyon
AZ 86023. Tel: 928-638-7888.
Grand Canyon–Parashant
National Monument
Bureau of Land Management, 222
N. Central Avenue, Phoenix,
AZ 85004. Tel: 602-417-9200
Hubbell Trading Post National
Historic Site
P.O. Box 150, Ganado, AZ 86505.
Tel: 928-755-3475.
Kaibab National Forest
800 S. 6th Street, Williams,
AZ 86046. Tel: 928-635-8200.
Monument Valley Navajo Tribal Park
Box 93, Monument Valley,
UT 84536. Tel: 801-727-3287.
Navajo National Monument
HC 71, Box 3, Tonalea, AZ 86044-
9704. Tel: 928-672-2366.
Pipe Spring National Monument
HC 65, Box 5, Fredonia, AZ 86022.
Tel: 928-643-7105.
Riordan State Historic Park
1300 S. Riordan Ranch St, Flagstaff,
AZ 86001. Tel: 928-779-4395.
Sunset Crater National Monument,
Route 3, Box 149, Flagstaff,
AZ 86004. Tel: 928-556-7042.

Canyon Mule Rides

Reservations for one-, two- or three-day mule trips into the Grand Canyon should be made months in advance by contacting **Amfac Parks and Resorts**, 14001 E. Iliff, Suite 600, Aurora, CO 80014, 303-297-2757. The trips aren't for the faint of heart or tender of bottom. Trails are narrow and precipitous, the inner canyon can be blisteringly hot, and riders are expected to spend as much as six hours in the saddle.

Walnut Canyon National Monument
Walnut Canyon Road, Flagstaff, AZ 86004-9705. Tel: 928-526-3367.
Wupatki National Monument
HC 33, Box 444A, Flagstaff, AZ 86004. Tel: 928-556-7040.

CENTRAL ARIZONA

Apache–Sitgreaves National Forest
P.O. Box 640, Springerville, AZ 85938. Tel: 928-333-4301.
Dead Horse Ranch State Park
675 Deadhorse Ranch Road, Cottonwood, AZ 86326.
Tel: 928-634-5283.
Fool Hollow Lake Recreation Area
off Highway 260, Show Low, AZ.
Tel: 928-537-3680.
Fort Verde State Historic Park
P.O. Box 397, Camp Verde, AZ 86322. Tel: 928-567-3275.
Jerome State Historic Park
P.O. Box D, Jerome, AZ 86331.
Tel: 928-634-5381.
Lake Havasu State Park
1801 Highway 95, Lake Havasu, AZ 86406. Tel: 928-855-2784.
Lyman Lake State Park
U.S. 191, Springerville, AZ.
Tel: 520-337-4441.
Montezuma Castle National Monument
P.O. Box 219, Camp Verde, AZ 86322. Tel: 928-567-3322.
Petrified Forest National Park
P.O. Box 2217, Petrified Forest, AZ 86028. Tel: 928-524-6228.
Prescott National Forest
344 S. Cortez, Prescott, AZ 86302.
Tel: 928-771-4700.

Red Rock State Park
Lower Red Rock Loop Road, Sedona, AZ. Tel: 928-282-6907.
Slide Rock State Park
off State Route 89A, Sedona, AZ.
Tel: 928-282-3034.
Tonto Natural Bridge State Park
off State Route 87, Payson, AZ.
Tel: 928-476-4202.
Tuzigoot National Monument
P.O. Box 68, Clarkdale, AZ 86324
Tel: 928-634-5564.

SOUTHERN ARIZONA

Alamo Lake State Park
P.O. Box 38, Wenden, AZ 85356.
Tel: 928-669-2088
Boyce Thompson Arboretum State Park
37615 U.S. 60, Superior, AZ.
Tel: 520-689-2723.
Buenos Aires National Wildlife Refuge
P.O. Box 109, Sasabe, AZ 85633.
Tel: 520-823-4251.
Cabeza Prieta National Wildlife Refuge
1611 N. Second Avenue, Ajo, AZ 85321. Tel: 520-387-6483.
Casa Grande National Monument
1100 Ruins Drive, Coolidge, AZ 85228. Tel: 602-723-3172.
Chiricahua National Monument
Dos Cabezas Route, Box 6500 Willcox, AZ 85643.
Tel: 520-824-3560.
Coronado National Forest
Federal Building, 300 W. Congress, Tucson, AZ 85701.
Tel: 520-670-5798.
Coronado National Memorial
4101 E. Montezuma Canyon Road, Hereford, AZ 85615.
Tel: 520-366-5515.
Fort Bowie National Historic Site
P.O. Box 158, Bowie, AZ 85605.
Tel: 520-847-2500.
Kofa National Wildlife Refuge
356 W. First Street, Yuma, AZ 85366. Tel: 520-783-7861.
Lost Dutchman State Park
Apache Junction, AZ.
Tel: 480-982-4485.
Organ Pipe Cactus National Monument
Route 1, Box 100, Ajo, AZ 85321.
Tel: 520-387-6849.

Patagonia Lake State Park
P.O. Box 274, Patagonia, AZ 85624. Tel: 520-287-6965.
Picacho Peak State Park
P.O. Box 275, Picacho, AZ 85241.
Tel: 520-466-3183.
Saguaro National Park
3693 S. Old Spanish Trail, Tucson, AZ 85730. Tel: 520-733-5153.
San Xavier del Bac Mission
1950 W. San Xavier, Tucson AZ 85706. Tel: 520-294-2624.
Tombstone Courthouse State Historic Park
219 Toughnut Street, Tombstone, AZ 85638. Tel: 520-457-3311.
Tonto National Forest
2324 E. McDowell Road, Phoenix, AZ 85545. Tel: 602-225-5200.
Tonto National Monument
HC 02, Box 4602, Roosevelt, AZ 85545. Tel: 520-467-2241.
Tumacacori National Historical Park
P.O. Box 67, Tumacacori, AZ 85640. Tel: 520-398-2341.
Yuma Territorial Prison State Historic Park
P.O. Box 10792, Yuma, AZ 85366.
Tel: 928-783-4771.

National Park Passes

If you plan to visit several parks on your vacation, consider buying a 12-month **National Park Pass**. The pass costs $50 and covers entrance fees to all National Park Service areas, but does not cover camping fees or other use fees, such as cave tours.

The **Golden Age Passport** is available to U.S. citizens who are age 62 or older. There is a one-time charge of $10, but the pass is good for life. It provides free entrance to most federal recreation areas and provides a 50 percent discount on use fees, such as camping fees.

The **Golden Access Passport** is available to U.S. citizens who have a permanent disability. The pass is free and is good for life. It provides free entrance to most federal recreation areas and provides a 50 percent discount on use fees.

Passes are available at parks that charge an entrance fee.

Tours and Outfitters

Air Adventures

Air Grand Canyon
6000 Janine Drive, Prescott,
AZ 86301. Tel: 928-776-6000.
AirStar Helicopters
P.O. Box 3379, Grand Canyon,
AZ 86023. Tel: 800-962-3869.
Arizona Air
13236 N. 7th Street, Phoenix,
AZ 85022. Tel: 877-436-5508.
Blue Yonder
P.O. Box 1291, Benson, AZ 85602.
Tel: 520-586-7651. Ultralight
aircraft tours.
Grand Canyon Airlines
Highway 64, P.O. Box 3038, Grand
Canyon National Park Airport, Grand
Canyon, AZ 86023. Tel: 928-638-
2407.
Kenai Helicopters
Grand Canyon, AZ
Tel: 800-541-4537.
Turf Soaring School
8700 W. Carefree Highway
Peoria, AZ 85382. Tel: 623-439-
3621. Glider rides.
Unicorn Balloon Company
15001 N. 74th Street, Suite F,
Scottsdale, AZ 85260. Tel: 480-
991-3666. Hot-air ballooning.

Ecotours

Arizona Ed-Venture Tours
P.O. Box 4137, Prescott, AZ 86302.
Tel: 928-541-0734.
Espiritu Ecotours
1805 N. 10th Street, Phoenix,
AZ 85006. Tel: 602-258-6330.
Flagstaff Mountain Guides
P.O. Box 2383, Flagstaff,
AZ 86003. Tel: 928-635-8414.
Fossil Creek Llamas
10379 W. Fossil Creek Road,
Strawberry, AZ 85544.
Tel: 928-476-5178.

Grand Canyon Field Institute
P.O. Box 399, Grand Canyon,
AZ 86023. Tel: 928-638-2485.
High Lonesome EcoTours
570 South Little Bear Trail, Sierra
Vista, AZ 85635. Tel: 520-458-9446.
K5 High Country Adventures
P.O. Box 240, Springerville,
AZ 85938. Tel: 800-814-6451.
La Ruta de Sonora
P.O. Box 699, Ajo, AZ 85321.
Tel: 520-387-3499.
Marv's Private Tours
P.O. Box 544, Williams, AZ 86046.
Tel: 928-635-4948.
Payson Adventures
408A S. Beeline Highway, Payson,
AZ 85541. Tel: 928-474-8808.
Sacred Play Nature Tours
P.O. Box 1192, Patagonia,
AZ 85624. www.sacredplay.com.
Sierra Club
Grand Canyon Chapter, 812 N. 3rd
Street, Phoenix, AZ 85004.
Tel: 602-253-8633.
Southern Arizona Adventures
P.O. Box 1032, Bisbee, AZ 85603.
Tel: 520-432-9058.
**Southeastern Arizona Bird
Observatory**
P.O. Box 5521, Bisbee, AZ 85603.
Tel: 520-432-1388.
Tucson Audubon Society
300 E. University Boulevard, Suite
120, Tucson, AZ 85705. Tel: 520-
578-1330.
Upper San Pedro Ecosystem Program
Ramsey Canyon Preserve, 27
Ramsey Canyon Road, Hereford,
AZ 85615. Tel: 520-378-2640.

Wilderness Adventures
4211 East Elwood Street,
Suite 1, Phoenix, AZ 85040.
Tel: 602-438-1800.
Women's World Adventures
215 Disney Lane, Sedona,
AZ 86336. Tel: 520-282-0916.

Historic Railways

Grand Canyon Railway
123 N. San Francisco Street, Suite
210, Flagstaff, AZ 86001.
Tel: 928-773-1976.
**Verde River Canyon Excursion
Train**
300 N. Broadway, Clarkdale,
AZ 86324. Tel: 800-293-7245.
Yuma Valley Railway
2nd Avenue and 1st Street, Yuma,
AZ. Tel: 928-783-3456.

Horseback Riding

Anderson Riding Academy
1415 N. Houghton Road, Tucson,
AZ 85749. Tel: 520-885-6779.
Big Sky Rides
6501 W. Ina Road, Tucson, AZ.
Tel: 520-744-3789.
Cave Creek Park Riding Stables
2502 W. New River Road, Phoenix,
AZ 85027. Tel: 623-465-9559.
Cocoraque Ranch
6255 N. Diamond Hills Lane,
Tucson, AZ. Tel: 520-682-8594.
Don Donelly Stables
6010 S. Kings Ranch Road,
Gold Canyon, AZ 85219.
Tel: 480-982-7822.

Environmental Ethics

Remember the old saying: "Take
nothing but pictures, leave nothing
but footprints." The goal of low-
impact/no-impact backpacking is
to leave the area in the same
condition as you found it, if not
better. If you're camping in the
backcountry, don't break
branches, level the ground or alter
the landscape in any way. Make
fires in designated places only.
Otherwise, use a portable
camping stove. When nature calls,
answer with a trowel: dig a hole 6
inches (15 cm) deep and at least

100 feet (30 m) from water, campsites and trails. Take away all
trash, including toilet paper.

Wildlife
Never approach wild animals. Use
binoculars, a spotting scope or a
camera with telephoto lens to get
a good look. Don't try to feed or
touch wildlife, not even the "cute"
ones like chipmunks, squirrels
and prairie dogs (they may carry
diseases). Don't try to move
animals into a better position by
calling or herding them.

Hiking Safety

Avoid solitary hiking. The best situation is to hike with at least two other partners. That way, if one person is injured, another member of the party can seek help while two remain behind. If you must hike alone, be sure to tell someone your intended route and time of return. Backcountry hiking may require a permit. Ask a ranger before setting out.

Use common sense on the trail. Don't attempt routes that are too strenuous for your level of fitness. Concentrate on what you're doing and where you're going. Even well-trodden and well-marked trails can be dangerous. Be careful near cliffs, rocky slopes, ravines and rivers. Don't attempt anything you're not comfortable with or that's beyond your level of skill.

Ironhorse Ranch
P.O. Box 536, Tombstone, AZ 85638. Tel: 520-457-9361.
MacDonald's Ranch
26540 N. Scottsdale Road, Scottsdale, AZ. Tel: 480-585-0239.
Monument Valley Navajo Tribal Park
Box 93, Monument Valley, UT 84536. Tel: 801-727-3287.
Pioneer Stables
4354 W. Watson Lane, Safford, AZ 85546. Tel: 520-428-7441.
Ponderosa Stables
10215 S. Central Avenue, Phoenix, AZ. Tel: 602-268-1261.
Pusch Ridge Stables
13700 N. Oracle Road, Tucson, AZ. Tel: 520-825-1664.
Rancho de la Osa Guest Ranch
P. O. Box 1, Sasabe, AZ 85633. Tel: 520-823-4257.
Red Buck Ranch
30212 N. 154th Street, Scottsdale, AZ 85262.
Tel: 480-471-0011.
Rex Ranch
P.O. Box 636, Amado, AZ 85645. Tel: 520-398-2914.
South Mountain Stables
10005 S. Central Avenue, Phoenix, AZ. Tel: 602-276-8131.
Trail Horse Adventures
85 Five J Lane, Sedona, AZ 86336. Tel: 800-723-3538.
Walking Wind Stables
10811 N. Oracle Road, Tucson, AZ. Tel: 520-742-4422.
White Stallion Ranch
9251 W. Twin Peaks Road, Tucson, AZ 85743.
Tel: 520-297-0252.
Windwalker Expeditions
Cave Creek, AZ. Tel: 480-585-3382.

Jeep Tours

A Day in the West
P.O. Box 10867, Sedona, AZ 86339. Tel: 928-282-4320.
Apache Trail Tours
P.O. Box 6146, Apache Junction, AZ 85278. Tel: 480-982-7661.
Arizona Desert Mountain Jeep Tours
6303 E. Cochise Street, Scottsdale, AZ 85253. Tel: 480-860-1777.
Arizona Unique Buggy Adventures
13221 N. 19th Place, Phoenix, AZ 85022. Tel: 602-971-2469.
Arrowhead Desert Jeep Tours
841 E. Paradise Lane, Phoenix AZ 85022. Tel: 602-942-3361.
Canyon de Chelly Tours
Chinle, AZ. Tel: 520-674-5433.
Earth Wisdom Jeep Tours
293 Highway 89A, Sedona, AZ. Tel: 520-282-4714.
Grand Canyon Outback Jeep Tours
Tel: 800-320-5337.
Outback Off-Road Adventures
P.O. Box 1969, Lake Havasu City, AZ 86405. Tel: 928-680-6151.

Backcountry Permits

Backcountry travel on public lands may require a permit, and there may be quotas on the number of visitors. To find out if permits are necessary, inquire at state or national parks well in advance of your arrival. For trips on National Forest or BLM land, contact the Arizona Public Lands Information Center, 222 N. Central Avenue, Phoenix, AZ 85004, tel: 602-417-9200; azwww.az.blm.gov/azso.htm.

Pink Jeep Tours
P.O. Box, 1447, Sedona, AZ 86339. Tel: 928-282-9000.
Sedona Red Rock Jeep Tours
P.O. Box 10305, Sedona, AZ 86339. Tel: 928-282-1851.
Sunshine Jeep Tours
9040 North Oracle Road, Suite D, Tucson, AZ 85737. Tel: 520-742-1943.

River Running

Aramark-Wilderness River Adventures
P.O. Box 717, Page, AZ 86040. Tel: 800-992-8022.
Arizona Raft Adventures
4050F E. Huntington Drive, Flagstaff, AZ 86004. Tel: 928-526-8200.
Arizona River Runners
P.O. Box, 47788, Phoenix, AZ 85068. Tel: 602-867-4866.
Arizona Salt River Tubing
P.O. Box 6568, Mesa, AZ 85216. Tel: 480-380-9792.
Back Bay Canoes and Kayaks
1450 Newberry Drive, Bullhead City, AZ 86442. Tel: 520-758-6242.
Canyon Explorations
P.O. Box 310, Flagstaff, AZ 86002. Tel: 928-774-4559.
Canyoneers
P.O. Box 2997, Flagstaff, AZ 86003. Tel: 928-526-0924.
Cimarron River Company
7902 E. Pierce, Scottsdale, AZ 85257. Tel: 480-994-1199.
Colorado River & Trail Expeditions
P.O. Box 57575, Salt Lake City, UT 84157. Tel: 801-261-1789.
Diamond River Adventures
916 Vista, P.O. Box 1300, Page, AZ 86040. Tel: 928-645-8866.
Desert River Outfitters
2649 Highway 95, Suite 23, Bullhead City, AZ 86442. Tel: 888-529-2533.
Far Flung Adventures
P.O. Box 2804, Globe, AZ 85502. Tel: 800-231-7238.
Grand Canyon Dories
P.O. Box 216, Altaville, CA 95221. Tel: 209-736-0805.
Grand Canyon Expeditions
P.O. Box O, Kanab, UT 84741. Tel: 435-644-2691.

Hatch River Expeditions
P.O. Box 1200, Vernal, UT 84078.
Tel: 435-789-3813.
High Desert Adventures
P.O. Box 40, St. George, UT 84771.
Tel: 435-673-1733.
High Sonoran Adventures
10628 N. 97th Street, Scottsdale,
AZ 85620. Tel: 602-614-3331.
Hualapai River Runners
P.O. Box 246, Peach Springs,
AZ 86434. Tel: 928-769-2210.
Jerkwater Canoe & Kayak
P.O. Box 800, Topock, AZ 86436.
Tel: 800-421-7803.
Lake Powell Resorts & Marinas
P.O. Box 56909, Phoenix,
AZ 85079. Tel: 602-331-5200.
Mild to Wild
11 Rio Vista Circle, Durango, CO
81301. Tel: 970-247-4789.
Moki Mac River Expeditions
P.O. Box 21242, Salt Lake City, UT
84121. Tel: 801-268-6667.
OARS
P.O. Box 67, Angels Camp, CA
95222. Tel: 209-736-2924.
Outdoors Unlimited
6900 Townsend Winona Road,
Flagstaff, AZ 86004.
Tel: 928-526-4546.
Permagrin River Adventures
107-B E. Broadway Road, Tempe,
AZ 85283. Tel: 480-755-1924.
Tours West
P.O. Box 333, Orem, UT 84059.
Tel: 801-225-0755.
Western Arizona Canoe & Kayak
2505 Cielo Drive, Lake Havasu City,
AZ 86403. Tel: 520-855-6414.
Western River Expeditions
7258 Racket Club Drive, Salt Lake
City, UT 84121. Tel: 801-942-6669
or 800-453-7450.
Wilderness River Adventures
P.O. Box 717, Page, AZ 86040.
Tel: 928-645-3279.

Wilderness Guides

Ascend Guide Service
6648 E. Corrine Drive, Scottsdale,
AZ 85254. Tel: 480-596-9126.
Barnes Guide Service
P.O. Box 801, Safford, AZ 85548.
Tel: 520-428-3197.
Chaparral Guides and Outfitters
P.O. Box 1332, Payson, AZ 85547.
Tel: 928-474-9693.

Sport

Spectator Sports

Arizona sports news and
schedules are available at
www.azcentral.com.

BASEBALL

The major league **Arizona
Diamondbacks** (602-514-8400)
play in downtown Phoenix at the
Bank One Ballpark (401 E.
Jefferson Street, Phoenix;
tel: 602-462-6000). Several
pro teams come to Arizona for
spring training as well.
The **Chicago Cubs** play at Tucson
Electric Park (520-434-1111);
the **Oakland A's** at Phoenix
Municipal Stadium (602-392-
0217); the **San Francisco
Giants** at Scottsdale Stadium
(602-990-7972), the **Anaheim
Angels** at Diablo Stadium
(602-350-5205) in Tempe;
the **Seattle Mariners** and **San
Diego Padres** at Peoria Stadium
(602-878-4337); the **Milwaukee
Brewers** at Compadre Stadium
(602-895-1200) in Chandler;
and the **Colorado Rockies** at
Hi Corbett Field (520-327-9467)
in Tucson.

Check www.cactus-league.com or
the stadiums for schedules.

BASKETBALL

The NBA **Phoenix Suns**
(602-379-7867) and the
WNBA (women's league)
Phoenix Mercury play at the
America West Arena (201 E.
Jefferson Street, Phoenix; tel: 602-
379-2000).

FOOTBALL

The NFL **Arizona Cardinals** (602-
379-0102) and the Arizona State
University **Sun Devils** (480-965-
2381) play at Sun Devil Stadium in
Tempe. The **University of Arizona
Wildcats** (520-621-2287) play at
Arizona Stadium on the University of
Arizona campus in Tucson. The
Arizona Rattlers, an arena football
team, play indoors at the America
West Arena.

GOLF

The **Phoenix Open Golf Tournament**
(602-870-0163) is held in January
at the Tournament Players Club in
Scottsdale. The **Tucson Open** (800-
882-7660) is held at the Omni
Tucson National Golf Resort in
February. In March, women golfers
compete at the **Standard Register
PING LPGA Tournament** (602-495-
4653) at a course in the Phoenix
area and the **Welch's/Circle K
LPGA Championship** (520-791-
5742) in Tucson. The Senior PGA
Tour comes to the Desert Mountain
Golf Course for **The Tradition** (480-
595-4070) in April. The **Phoenix
Amateur Golf Championship** (877-
988-4653) is held in August.

HOCKEY

The NHL **Phoenix Coyotes** (480-
563-7825) play at the America
West Arena.

AUTO RACING

NASCAR, USAC, Indy and Grand Am
cars race at **Phoenix International
Raceway** (7602 S. 115th Avenue,
Avondale; tel: 602-252-2227)
outside Phoenix.

HORSE AND
DOG RACING

Horse racing is held at **Turf
Paradise** (1501 W. Bell Road,
Phoenix; tel: 602-942-1101) and

Rillito Park (4502 N. First Avenue, Tucson; tel: 520-293-5011). Greyhound racing is at Phoenix Greyhound Park (3801 E. Washington Street, Phoenix; tel: 602-273-7181) and Tucson Greyhound Park (2601 S. 3rd Avenue, Tucson: tel: 520-884-7576).

TENNIS

The Franklin Templeton Tennis Classic (480-922-0222), a men's pro tennis tournament, is played at the Scottsdale Princess Resort (7575 E. Princess Drive, Scottsdale). The Tucson Classic Celebrity Tennis Tournament (520-623-6165) is held in May at the Sheraton El Conquistador (10000 N. Oracle Road, Tucson)

Participant Sports

BICYCLING

Opportunities abound for mountain and road biking in Arizona. Several organizations provide information on trails, races, group tours and other events. The Greater Arizona Bicycling Association (www.sportsfun.com/gaba/index.html) and the Arizona Bicycle Club (www.oneandzero.com/abccazb) have chapters throughout the state.

FISHING

Fishing licenses are required and can be obtained from the Arizona Game and Fish Department (2222 W. Greenway Road, Phoenix, AZ 85023; tel: 602-942-3000). Fishing on the White Mountain Apache Indian Reservation (Wildlife & Outdoor Recreation Division, P.O. Box 220, Whiteriver, AZ 85941; tel: 928-338-4385) and San Carlos Apache Indian Reservation (P.O. Box 0, San Carlos, AZ 85550; tel: 520-475-2361) require a tribal fishing license.

GOLF

There are scores of public and private golf courses as well as full-fledged golf resorts throughout the state. For a complete list, contact the Arizona Golf Association (7226 N. 16th Street, Suite 200, Phoenix, AZ 85020; tel: 602-944-3035; www.azgolf.org) or pick up a copy of Golf Arizona (16446 Tombstone Drive, Fountain Hills, AZ 85268; tel: 800-942-5444).

TENNIS

Public tennis courts are available in just about every city and large town in Arizona, although avid players may find it more convenient to stay at a hotel with courts. Contact the city or county Parks and Recreation Department for locations and hours. For information on tournaments, lessons and leagues, contact the Arizona Tennis Association (7335 E. Indian Plaza, #124, Scottsdale, AZ 85251; tel: 480-970-0599).

KAYAKING, CANOEING AND RAFTING

Arizona offers an abundance of both whitewater and flatwater paddling. For information on routes and conditions, consult the agency that manages the river or lake. Other sources of information are paddling clubs and outdoor-gear retailers. For more information, call the Central Arizona Paddlers Club (602-271-4012), Prescott Paddle America Club (928-445-5480) or Southern Arizona Paddlers Club (520-602-327-5717). For stream-flow conditions, check the USGS Web site (wwwdaztcn.wr.usgs.gov).

SKIING

Arizona has four downhill skiing areas but none with snow-making capabilities.

Arizona Snowbowl
P.O. Box 40, Flagstaff, AZ 86002. Tel: 928-779-1951.
Sunrise Ski Resort
P.O. Box 217, McNary, AZ 85930. Tel: 928-735-7669.
Mount Lemmon Ski Valley
10300 Ski Run Road, Mount Lemmon, AZ 85715. Tel: 520-576-1321.
Williams Ski Area
P.O. Box 953, Williams, AZ 86046. Tel: 520-635-9330.

Arizona Snowbowl also runs the Flagstaff Nordic Center (928-779-1951), which has 25 miles (40 km) of groomed cross-country trails, instruction and equipment rentals.

Further Reading

Nonfiction

Adventuring in Arizona, by John Annerino. San Francisco: Sierra Club Books, 1996.

Ancient Ruins of the Southwest: An Archaeological Guide, by David Grant Noble. Flagstaff: Northland Publishing, 2000.

And Die in the West: The Story of the O.K. Corral Gunfight, by Paula Mitchell Marks. Norman: University of Oklahoma Press, 1996.

Answered Prayers: Miracles and Milagros along the Border, by Eileen Oktavec. Tucson: University of Arizona Press, 1995.

The Architecture of the Southwest, by Trent Elwood Sanford. Tucson: University of Arizona Press, 1997.

Arizona: A Cavalcade of History, by Marshall Trimble. Tucson: Treasure Chest Publications, 1989.

Arizona: A History, by Thomas E. Sheridan. Tucson: University of Arizona Press, 1995.

Arizona Myths, Fallacies and Misconceptions, by John D. Neuner. Phoenix: First Leaf Publishing, 2001.

The Arizona Rangers, by Bill O'Neal. Austin, TX: Eakin Press, 1986.

Arizona-Sonora Desert Museum Book of Answers, by David Wentworth Lazaroff. Tucson: Arizona–Sonora Desert Museum Press, 1998.

Arizona's Ghost Towns and Mining Camps: A Travel Guide to History, by Philip Varney. Phoenix: Arizona Highways, 1998.

Arizona's Greatest Golf Courses, by Bill Huffman. Flagstaff: Northland Publishing, 2000.

Arizona's Wilderness Areas, by Tom Dollar. Englewood, CO: Westcliffe Publishers, 1998.

Art of the Golden West, by Alan Axelrod. New York, Abbeville Press, 1990.

Best of the West: An Anthology of Classic Writing from the American West, edited by Tony Hillerman. New York, Harper Collins, 1991.

Beyond the Hundredth Meridian, by Wallace Stegner. New York: Penguin, 1953.

Book of the Hopi, by Frank Waters. New York: Penguin, 1963.

Book of the Navajo, by Raymond Locke. Los Angeles: Mankind Publishing, 1976.

Buckaroo, edited by Hal Cannon and Thomas West. New York, Callaway, 1993.

Burntwater, by Scott Thybony. Tucson: University of Arizona, 1997.

Cinema Southwest: An Illustrated Guide to the Movies and Their Locations, by John A. Murray. Flagstaff: Northland Publishing, 2000.

Dancing Gods, by Erna Ferguson. Albuquerque: University of New Mexico, 1931.

The Desert, by John C. Van Dyke. Scribner, 1901, reprinted by Peregrine Smith Books, 1980.

Desert Notes: Reflections in the Eye of a Raven, by Barry Holstun Lopez. New York: Avon, 1981.

The Desert Year, by Joseph W. Krutch. Tucson: University of Arizona, 1990.

The Exploration of the Colorado River and its Canyons, by John Wesley Powell. New York: Penguin, 1987.

Exploring Arizona's Wild Areas, by Scott S. Warren. Seattle: The Mountaineers, 1999.

A Field Guide to the Plants of Arizona, by Anne Orth Epple. Helena: Falcon Publishing Company, 1997.

Geronimo: The Man, His Time, His Place, by Angie Debo. Norman: University of Oklahoma, 1976.

Getting Over the Color Green: Contemporary Environmental Literature of the Southwest, Scott Slovic, ed. Tucson: University of Arizona Press, 2001.

Ghost Towns of the American West, by Bill O'Neal. Lincolnwood, IL: Publications International, 1995.

Going Back to Bisbee, by Richard Shelton. Tucson: University of Arizona Press, 1992.

Grand Canyon: An Anthology, by Bruce Babbitt. Flagstaff: Northland Press, 1978.

Grand Canyon: A Traveler's Guide, by Jeremy Schmidt. Jackson Hole: Free Wheeling Travel Guides, 1991.

Grand Canyon National Park: A Natural History Guide, by Jeremy Schmidt. Boston: Houghton Mifflin Company, 1993.

Grand Canyon: Today and All Its Yesterdays, by Joseph Wood Krutch. Tucson: University of Arizona, 1989.

Greater Phoenix: The Desert in Bloom, by Hugh Downs. Towery Publications, 1999.

The Guide to National Parks of the Southwest, by Nicky Leach. Tucson: Southwest Parks & Monuments Association, 1992.

Hopi, by Susanne and Jake Page. New York: Abradale Press, 1994.

Hopi Kachinas: The Complete Guide to Collecting Kachina Dolls, by Barton Wright. Flagstaff: Northland Publishing, 1985.

In the House of Stone and Light: A Human History of the Grand Canyon, by Donald J. Hughes. Grand Canyon: Grand Canyon Natural History Association, 1978.

The Man Who Walked Through Time, by Colin Fletcher. New York: Random House, 1989.

Masked Gods, by Frank Waters. Athens: Swallow Press, 1950.

The Mysterious Lands: A Naturalist Explores the Four Great Deserts of the Southwest, by Ann H. Zwinger. Tucson: University of Arizona, 1989.

Mythmakers of the West: Shaping America's Imagination, by John A. Murray. Flagstaff: Northland Publishing, 2001.

A Natural History of the Sonoran Desert, by Steven J. Phillips. Berkeley: University of California Press, 1999.

The Peaks: Flagstaff, Williams, and Northern Arizona's High Country, by Rose Houk. Phoenix: Arizona Highways, 1995.

The People: Indians of the American Southwest, by Stephen Trimble. Santa Fe: School of American Research Press, 1993.

Quest for the Dutchman's Gold: The 100-Year Mystery, by Robert Sikorsky. Golden West, 1991.

Reopening the American West, by Hal K. Rothman, ed. Tucson: University of Arizona, 1998.

Roadside Geology of Arizona, by Halka Chronic. Missoula: Mountain Press, 1983.
A Sense of Mission: Historic Churches of the Southwest, by David Wakely and Thomas A. Drain. San Francisco: Chronicle Books, 1994.
Vacant Eden : Roadside Treasures of the Sonoran Desert, by Abigail Gumbiner. Balcony Press, 1999.
Warriors: Navajo Code Talkers, by Kenji Kawano. New York: Abradale Press, 1990.
The West: A Treasury of Art and Literature, edited by T.H. Watkins and Joan Watkins. New York, Hugh Lauter Levin Associates, 1994.
Wyatt Earp: The Life Behind the Legend, by Casey Tefer. New York: John Wiley & Sons, 1999.

Fiction & Poetry

The Bean Trees, by Barbara Kingsolver. New York: Harper, 1998.
Bisbee '17, by Robert Houston. Tucson: University of Arizona Press, 1999.
The Dance Hall of the Dead, by Tony Hillerman. New York: Harper & Row, 1973.
Days of Plenty, Days of Want, by Patricia Preciado Martin. Tucson: University of Arizona, 1999.
The Dark Wind, by Tony Hillerman. New York: Harper & Row, 1982.
In Search of Snow, by Luis Alberto Urrea. Tucson: University of Arizona, 1999.
Riders of the Purple Sage, by Zane Grey. New York: Penguin, 1990.
Skinwalkers, by Tony Hillerman. New York: Harper & Row, 1987.
To the Last Man, by Zane Grey. New York: Forge, 2000.
Waiting to Exhale, by Terry McMillan. New York: Pocket Books, 1996.

Movies/Videos

Arizona, 1940. The movie set at Old Tucson Studios was built for this film, the story of a feisty, Tucson woman (Jean Arthur) and the tough-as-nails drifter (William Holden) who wins her heart.

The Dark Wind, 1991. This adaptation of a Tony Hillerman mystery takes place on the Navajo and Hopi Reservations.
Gunfight at the OK Corral, 1957, and **High Chaparral** (television series). Just two of the many Westerns filmed at Old Tucson Studios.
Geronimo, 1994. Yet another telling of Geronimo's story, much of it shot in southern Arizona.
My Darling Clementine, 1946. John Ford's version of the infamous gunfight at the O.K. Corral with Henry Fonda as Wyatt Earp and Victor Mature as Doc Holliday.
The Quick and the Dead, 1994. A stylish homage to the spaghetti Western filmed at Old Tucson Studios, starring Gene Hackman as a sadistic sheriff who stages a quick-draw contest and Sharon Stone as the flinty shooter who bests him.
Red River, 1948. Although the story is set in Texas, much of the film was shot in Arizona. The movie is largely a Western retelling of **Mutiny on the Bounty**, with John Wayne and Montgomery Clift.
Rio Bravo, 1959. Shot at Old Tucson Studios but set in Texas, the story hinges on the efforts of a sheriff, played by John Wayne, to keep a murderer in jail with the help of a drunken ex-deputy (Dean Martin), a cocky young gunfighter (Ricky Nelson), and lame old man (Walter Brennan).
Stagecoach, 1939, and **Fort Apache**, 1948. The stunning landscape of Monument Valley is featured in countless Westerns, most notably in these two John Ford classics.
Tombstone, 1993. Kurt Russell and Val Kilmer, as Wyatt Earp and Doc Holliday, do an admirable job interpreting the OK Corral gunfight and its aftermath.
Wyatt Earp, 1995. Kevin Costner takes a shot at the classic gunfighter with lackluster results.

Other Insight Guides

Nearly 200 companion titles to this volume cover every continent. More than 40 of the titles are devoted to the US and include:

Insight Guide: American Southwest highlights the best of this visually dramatic region, ranging from Albuquerque to Tucson, from Santa Fe to Las Vegas, from Zion National Park to the ancient Pueblos.

Insight Guide: US National Parks West, written by park rangers and other experts, ranges from Texas to North Dakota, from California to Colorado, and then on to the national parks of Alaska and Hawaii. It includes top nature photography.

Insight FlexiMap: USA Southwest includes Arizona and the Grand Canyon and extends its clear and up-to-date cartographic coverage to the west coast. The map's laminated finish makes it easy to fold and extremely durable.

ART & PHOTO CREDITS

Index

Numbers in italics refer to photographs